SOCIAL SECURITY PERSPECTIVES

SOCIAL SECURITY

PERSPECTIVES

Essays by EDWIN E. WITTE

EDITED BY ROBERT J. LAMPMAN

MADISON · 1962 · THE UNIVERSITY OF WISCONSIN PRESS

Frontispiece photo by Herb Kratovil
courtesy of Business Week

Published by the University of Wisconsin Press
430 Sterling Court, Madison 6, Wisconsin
Copyright © 1962 by the
Regents of the University of Wisconsin
Printed in the United States of America by
Vail-Ballou Press, Inc., Binghamton, New York
Library of Congress Catalog Card Number 62-17401

Editor's Note

Many of the essays in this book have been modified for the purpose of reducing repetition or selecting sections which are of particular interest on certain topics. Deletion of a paragraph or more of the original text is indicated by a short line of angle marks at the point of deletion. Deletion of a significant portion at the beginning or ending of a speech or article is indicated by the phrase "Excerpts from" at the beginning of the bibliographical description of the paper.

We are pleased to acknowledge the permission to reprint articles which have appeared in books or journals, which was graciously granted to us in every case. The photographs used on the jacket and for the frontispiece, together with that taken in front of Sterling Hall, were taken by Herb Kratovil and are reproduced here by courtesy of *Business Week*, whose issue of November 26, 1955, carried a feature article on Witte.

The original stimulus for the preparation of this volume came from the Honorable Wilbur J. Cohen, Assistant Secretary of Health, Education, and Welfare. Further encouragement and advice came to the editor from a number of Witte's colleagues, most notably from Dean H. Edwin Young and Professor Elizabeth Brandeis. The bibliography was prepared by Mrs. Edwin E. Witte and Mrs. Jack Barbash. The editor claims responsibility for errors of commission as well as omission.

R. J. L.

Contents

Illustrations

Edwin E. Witte, 1955, *frontispiece*

Following page 138

The Social Security Advisory Council, 1937

Witte on the Wisconsin campus, 1955

Introduction

THIS VOLUME, intended as a kind of intellectual autobiography, brings together a selected set of papers which show one man's scholarly encounters with a particular range of economic problems over a period of several decades. The problems are those arising out of old age, premature loss of family bread-winner, unemployment, and illness and disability.

The author's career spanned a period in which there was significant evolution of the institutions which are designed to prevent and alleviate these problems. As a graduate student he was a participant-observer in the passage of the first workmen's compensation law and shortly thereafter played a part in a leading experiment in governmental form, namely, the Wisconsin Industrial Commission. Subsequently he was at the forefront of a number of other important departures in the broad field of social security. He sought to place social security issues in a broad historical and comparative perspective and to advocate a positive role for government wherever it could, in his view, "promote the general welfare."

Edwin Emil Witte was born on a farm in Jefferson County, Wisconsin in 1887. After graduating from Watertown High School, he entered the University of Wisconsin, earning a B.A. degree in 1909 with a major in history. His graduate work, under John R. Commons, was in economics and led to a Ph.D. in 1927. His first job was as Secretary to Congressman John M. Nelson in 1912–1914. In 1914–1915 he was a special agent for the U.S. Commission on Industrial Relations. This was followed by service as statistician and later as secretary of the Wisconsin Industrial Commission, and as chief of the Wisconsin Legislative Reference Library from 1922 to 1933. Concurrently with his work in the Legislative Reference Library, he served first as lecturer and later as professor in the Department of Economics of the University of Wisconsin and in 1933 he left the State Capitol for a full-time university career. This attachment to the university was maintained until his retirement in 1957, and as professor emeritus until his death, at the age of 73, in 1960. For twelve years he served as chairman of the Department of Economics.

Witte combined an academic career with governmental service. He held more than thirty governmental positions during his exceedingly active life, nine of them full time. In addition to those mentioned above, some of the more important of his public responsibilities included the following: Member, Wisconsin Labor Relations Board; Executive Director, President's Committee on Economic Security (which drafted the Social Security Act of 1935); Chairman of the Detroit Regional War Labor Board; Public Member, National War Labor Board; and Member, U.S. Atomic Energy Labor Relations Panel.

Witte's career exemplifies the Wisconsin school of "institutional economics" by its attention to problems in the area of practical affairs. This is illustrated by his best-known publication, *Government in Labor Disputes,* and by his readiness to step into the role of expert on the drafting of the Social Security Act. He made important contributions in several fields of "political economy," namely, labor economics (and within this to governmental regulation of labor, collective bargaining, and arbitration), governmental regulation of business, and social security. The breadth of his interest is suggested by the fact that his courses were commonly cross-listed with some department other than economics, such as law, political science, commerce, or social work. Throughout his teaching career he objected to restrictive or confining definitions of academic disciplines and urged his colleagues and students to study "real problems" with little regard as to whether such study would take them away from "pure economics." This particular approach is also reflected in the list of journals in which he published and in the groups with which he associated. In addition to economics journals, he published in law reviews, business journals, professional publications of physicians, social workers, educators, and governmental administrators. In addition to this, he welcomed the opportunity to communicate via mass media with the general public. His work brought him into close association with representatives of a wide range of professions.

Witte's role in the field of economics was one of action and of teaching the need for action. He observed in a reflective statement in 1956 that "the most significant work on practical economic problems has been done by people who have been inspired by a desire to change and improve what exists." He cited one of his heroes, Senator Robert M. La Follette, as saying that "service for country" is a "glorious service," and that "each one should count it a patriotic duty to build at least a part of his life into the life of his country." Perhaps Witte tells us a good deal about himself in his quotation of Theodore Roosevelt: "It is not the critic who counts; not the man who points out how the strong man stumbled.... The credit belongs to the man who is actually in the arena...who knows the great enthusiasms, the great devotions, and spends himself in a worthy cause...so that his place shall never be with those cold and timid souls who know neither defeat nor victory."

Witte's involvement in the great events of his time was referred to in a 1957 letter to him from his long-time friend, Sumner Slichter:

You have seen great changes and great progress since the days when you debated the principle of the British Industrial Disputes Act in old Music Hall in 1909, and since we worked together for the Industrial Relations Commission in Chicago and roomed together on the North Side and got fired together because Frank P. Walsh did not wish to spend too much of the Commission's money on research.

Your life epitomizes America and its democracy at its best—study at a great state university, work as secretary for a Congressman in Washington, research for a government commission, administration of state labor laws, running a library to help legislators draft laws, teaching at many universities, directing the research for the drafting of a comprehensive social security law, helping keep labor peace during time of war. A good history of our times could be written in terms of the activities in which you participated.

Witte's interest in public affairs seems to have been well fixed by the time he enrolled as a freshman at the University of Wisconsin in 1905. His family background may have contributed to this. His grandparents, both the Wittes and the Jaeckes, were devout Moravians who emigrated from Bavaria in the 1850's and settled in the German-speaking farming area near Watertown, Wisconsin, a community which was home to numerous leaders, including Carl Schurz, the editor and political figure, and Joseph E. Davies, attorney and ambassador to Russia.

In Edwin Witte's sixteenth year his father died. In spite of this and even though there were four other children in the family, his mother encouraged him to go to Madison and become the first member of the family to graduate from college. During his undergraduate and graduate years, 1905–1912, he kept a detailed diary which provides a unique history of university affairs during this period. Witte's diary recounts the economic hardship involved in his attending the university, but it also records the excitement and inspiration he found there.

He expressed much of his undergraduate enthusiasm in debate and discussion. In a diary entry dated October 22, 1906, Witte wrote:

I spent the afternoon in getting some little knowledge upon the question "Resolved that in times of depression the municipalities should give work to the unemployed" which I have to close on the affirmative against Fischer a week from Friday. Fischer I know is one of the toughest nuts in all our sophomore class, and as I seem to have the rotten side of this socialistic measure I will have to work to prevent being whipped.

He later wrote in his diary that his team won this first debate and that he "set them up" for his group at a cost of thirty cents, "which I could hardly afford." The debate topics of those years included the income tax, workmen's compensation, and various propositions in the field of social legislation, many of which were to occupy him professionally in later years. In the debating society he met many of his lifelong friends, including Selig Perlman and David Saposs. The latter two, like Witte, went on to make distinguished contributions in the field of labor economics. In the 1920's Witte spent some time as a volunteer debate coach, giving guidance to Philip F. La Follette, among others.

Witte's diary evidences a lively interest in many topics in the field of social security. A February 17, 1909, entry reads as follows:

Paid up my fees for next semester. This semester the incidental fee is $12 as against $11 previously. The increase is due to the fact that the University has employed a physician who will give medical advice to students gratis. The physician employed, pre-medic students tell me, is a very excellent one. Wisconsin is the first university to adopt such a principle, although it has long been a feature in German universities. Physicians of the state are objecting, because they regard this as the entering wedge for the contract system of practising medicine.

In October of that same year he wrote, "Today I made an extended report on poor vagabond laws under James I in my English history seminary."

Witte's undergraduate activities in debate and student politics and his eager listening to such political greats as William Jennings Bryan, Robert M. La Follette, and William F. Vilas were set against a stern discipline. His diary sets forth his resolution for daily Bible reading, for regularly writing a letter in German to his mother, and for the thorough study which led to election by Phi Beta Kappa in his junior year.

Witte's talent for scholarship took him into graduate study in history under the tutelage of Dana Munroe, Carl Russell Fish, and Frederick Jackson Turner. When Turner left Wisconsin in 1911 he said, according to Witte, that "the best historian, among many good historians on our campus, was John R. Commons, although he was attached to the economics department." By that time Witte was no stranger to Commons. His diary records that Commons had tried to recruit him for economics on February 5, 1910. On that date he wrote, "Was asked by Commons today to help him correct exam papers in Public Utilities and Labor Problems.... Commons suggested that next year I work for him upon the labor history he is preparing for the Carnegie Foundation.... If I should fall in with this proposition, I would transfer to economics from history...." "Whether I ought to stay in history or go over into economics I cannot decide," he confided to his diary on February 17. By October of that year Commons was making an economics career quite irresistible to Witte. "He also assured me that La Follette means to tackle the reform of labor law aggressively in the Senate during the next years and infers that he would rely mainly upon him [Commons] for arguments if not for bills." So it was that Witte came to make his career in economics, and so it was that all his work reflected appreciation for the study of American history. His relationship with Commons was close and remained so over many years.

When Commons retired from the university in 1933, Witte accepted a full-time appointment as professor to replace him. In 1956, when Witte was elected president of the American Economic Association, he was still following in the footsteps of his teacher, who had held that office in 1917. (Interestingly, there was a close student-teacher relationship between Commons and Richard T. Ely, who was president of this association in 1899–1901; Ely, Commons, and Witte are the only Wisconsin faculty members to have been so honored.)

In his half-century of work in government and in academic life Witte influenced the course of events in many direct and indirect ways. He impressed people by his energy and industry and by his extraordinary command of detailed information. In several newspaper accounts of his work he was referred to as a "walking encyclopedia." He also impressed people by his sense of purpose. John M. Gaus has called him "the perfect measure of what a public servant should be, beginning with such fundamental qualities as integrity, industry, and dedication to justice and the public interest." A 1957 Joint Resolution of the Wisconsin Legislature characterized him as "a retiring, kindly gentleman with prodigious capacity for work, a vast fund of information, and an unrestrained desire to serve." The capacity for work was accompanied by an even greater capacity for friendship. Witte was attractive to many people because he emphasized the positive and hopeful aspects of human behavior. He respected and enjoyed other people and gave unselfishly to them.

Witte was unusually effective as a teacher partly because he demonstrated a fruitful mingling of the science of society with the art of government. One of his students wrote to him: "Not by preachment but by simple example of your daily life your students saw and learned of the satisfactions and values of work, of thoroughness, of integrity, of moderation, of dedication to public interest, of affection for your fellow man." He made an effort to know his students. He had the practice of opening a seminar by asking students to tell about their home towns and on such occasions was often able to supplement a student's account with salient facts about the history of the community and its citizenry. He managed to keep in close touch with large numbers of former students and colleagues across time and distance. At Wisconsin breakfasts during American Economic Association meetings he frequently introduced, without reference to notes, over a hundred alumni by name and affiliation.

Many of his students will recall that Witte's office door was characteristically open and that his home, with the enthusiastic help of his "lady" (as he called his wife, Florence Witte), was often the scene for gatherings of students mixed in with family friends and notables from near and far. The close-knit Witte family figured in many of Professor Witte's activities and interests. Family outings were combined with trips to lectures and teaching assignments. Summer and visiting appointments took them to ten university campuses. On eight different occasions the family drove to the West Coast. Witte shared his enthusiasms for gardening, sports, the out-of-doors, for travel, for dogs, with a wide circle of family and friends and made them all feel richer for having known him.

His outgoing quality is, perhaps, best illustrated by his willingness to accept speaking engagements. He was always challenged by a new audience and, after 1933, never seemed to let a month go by without a half-dozen or more scheduled talks. Mrs. Witte reports that he thoroughly enjoyed lecturing and was willing to talk "to everyone everywhere." In one year he talked to groups as diverse as members of Parliament in London; high school students in Ramallah, Jordan; nurses in Beloit, Wisconsin; and personnel managers in Detroit. Bert Seidman recalls that in the busy war year of 1944 Witte was willing to journey from Washington to the eastern shore of Maryland to talk to fifty conscientious objectors on the subject of industrial relations. In 1956 the editor of this volume asked him why he took time out of a particularly strenuous week to talk to a handful of farm co-op members. His answer was, "They asked me."

Since he was a professor who professed to a wide audience, we believe Witte would have rejoiced with us in the opportunity this volume affords both old and new friends to become acquainted with ideas and issues in one of his favorite fields for discussion.

While Witte wrote extensively in several fields, we have elected to limit this volume to selected works within the one field of social security. The bibliography included herein lists over 300 titles, from which we have selected 40, some of which have been reduced in length. The bases for selection among the many articles and speeches should be explained.

On the one hand it was felt that the selections should emphasize topics of continuing interest in the several broad areas of social security. On the other hand, there is legitimate interest in showing how matters in this field have changed over a rather long period, so some articles are included because they illuminate the distance between one generation and another insofar as social security questions are concerned. Finally, selections were made to include representative statements of Witte's unique philosophy or position on controversial matters. It is regrettable that these bases did not allow the inclusion of some of Witte's best scholarly contributions which tended to be historical in character (e.g., "The Development of Unemployment Compensation," *Yale Law Review,* December, 1945).

The reader is urged to view this volume as part of a trilogy (this being the most "popular" of the three) which all taken together will give him a good insight into Witte's role in the field of social security. The first volume in this trilogy is Social Security Board Publication No. 20, *Social Security in America: The Factual Background of the Social Security Act as Summarized from Staff Reports to the Committee on Economic Security* (Washington: GPO, 1937). This publication is 592 pages in length, carries a preface by Witte, and includes a complete list of the staff reports, a good number of which were written by him or under his direction.

The second volume of the trilogy is his *Development of the Social Security Act,* which is a detailed and intimate history of the work of the Committee on Economic Security and the subsequent consideration and passage of the Act by Congress. This volume, written in 1936, was first published in 1962 by the University of Wisconsin Press.

This, then, should be thought of as a third part of a series of publications; it complements and rounds out the picture presented by the other two.

Witte's changing role in this field is highlighted by the articles here presented. In the years 1921–1935 his work was primarily analytical and often confined to very specific questions. Thus, the earliest title in the bibliography, "Increased Compensation to Minors Illegally Employed under The Wisconsin Workmen's Compensation Statute," illustrates his concern as a technical expert. From 1935 to 1939 his writings took on a protagonistic quality. He was "in the arena" and pamphleteering in support of a particular set of programs to which he was committed. From 1939 forward we can observe that he was gradually writing in a more detached manner and assuming the role of philosopher and critic. A good example of his philosophic writing is presented in the article herein entitled, "Social Security—1948."

The table on the following page, which was prepared by Professor Witte in 1954, will help the reader orient himself to the field under discussion.

TYPES OF SOCIAL SECURITY AND RELATED INSTITUTIONS IN THE UNITED STATES, 1954

Social Security Institutions			Private Institutions Related to Social Security	Social Security Institutions Existent in Other Countries but not in the United States
Social Insurance	*Public Assistance*	*Public Social Services Related to Social Security*		
1. Old Age and Survivors' Insurance	1. Old Age Assistance	1. Veterans' Services and Pensions	1. Industrial Pensions	1. Compulsory Health Insurance
2. Unemployment Insurance	2. Aid to Dependent Children	2. Public Health and Medical Care Services	2. (Company, Union, and Joint) Health and Welfare Plans	2. Invalidity (Disability) Insurance
3. Workmen's Compensation	3. Aid to the Blind	3. Child Health and Welfare Services	3. Other Private Pension, Health, and Welfare Plans	3. Family (Children's) Allowances
4. Disability (Cash Sickness) Compensation	4. Aid to the Permanently and Totally Disabled	4. Vocational Rehabilitation	4. Voluntary Health Insurance	4. Maternity Benefits and Mothers' Pensions
5. Social Security Programs for Special Groups (Public Employees, Veterans, Railroad Workers)	5. General Assistance	5. Other Services for the Disabled and Handicapped	5. Industrial and Union Medical Services	
	6. Soldiers' Aid	6. Public Employment Services	6. Life Insurance	
		7. Public Welfare (Charitable) Institutions	7. Savings Plans and Institutions	
			8. Guaranteed Wage and Employment Plans	
			9. Private Charitable Institutions	
			10. Private Social Work	

I

GENERAL
CONSIDERATIONS
OF
SOCIAL SECURITY

WITH THESE PAPERS Witte takes the reader through many of the leading issues of the field, most of which persist in the 1960's. Among questions raised and discussed are the following: What is social security? What are its goals, methods, and limitations? What is the principled basis for governmental intervention in family economic security matters? How should public and private approaches to economic security be related? Do we outgrow the need for social security with economic progress? How can corruption of well-intentioned programs be avoided? Is the "welfare state" desirable? How do the basic concepts of social security apply to non-Western or "developing" economies?

The papers seem to invite the reader to engage in retrospective dialogue with the author. To what extent did he shift his position or emphasis over the years? Does there seem to be internal consistency among the several discussions? Did he have a developed philosophy and master plan for an ultimate social security system in his mind? There is more than historical interest in participating in such a dialogue.

In asking these questions of one of the leading men in American social security, the reader, be he a novice or a veteran in the field, will synthesize his own position on leading issues that persist into the present.

Social Security:
A Wild Dream or
a Practical Plan?

Address to the
Wisconsin Alumni Institute
on June 17, 1938

A LOGICAL BEGINNING in a discussion of "social security" is a consideration of what is meant by the term. Unfortunately, however, this is a new term that still lacks precise definition. As now applied, it is used only in the United States and in this country was unheard of before 1935.

As the term developed during the consideration of the bill that became the Social Security Act, it is generally thought of as including everything that is dealt with in this act: old-age assistance, old-age insurance, unemployment insurance, aid to dependent children, blind pensions, maternity and infancy health services, crippled children's services, rural children welfare service, vocational rehabilitation, and certain aspects of preventive state and public health services. Since all advocates of social security believe that the present legislation is only the beginning, they are already talking about its extension to other fields; health insurance, invalidity insurance, widows' and orphans' pensions, and workmen's compensation must also be included within the present meaning of the term "social security." So must the entire relief program, both direct and work relief in all of its many forms, be included.

3

So great are the differences among these institutions associated with the term social security that I doubt whether it is possible to define this term sufficiently broadly to include them all. It will suffice to note that all of them are concerned with the relief and prevention of dependency—with "the major hazards and vicissitudes of life which cannot be wholly eliminated in this manmade world of ours" (quoting from President Roosevelt's social security message of June 8, 1934).

While many of its manifestations are of recent origin, the fundamental ideas in social security are old. From time immemorial, religion has made it a duty to feed the hungry and clothe the naked. As far back as the Elizabethan poor law, it has been an obligation of the local governments in every Anglo-Saxon country to support the poor who have a legal settlement in the community and no other means of support.

For long years this obligation was discharged by indiscriminately treating all of the poor alike—the young and the old, the sick and the well, the able bodied and the unemployables. All were provided at public expense with either maintenance in a poor house or with enough outdoor relief to keep body and soul together, but were branded as paupers and ne'er-do-wells and treated as such.

Not until the nineteenth century was there any differentiation of treatment in accordance with the particular needs of distinguishable groups among the poor. Such differentiated treatment was first provided with regard to institutional care, but after the opening of the present century also was extended to noninstitutional types of public assistance. In order of their development emerged blind pensions, workmen's compensation, aid to dependent children, and old-age assistance, all of which operated to take out of the undifferentiated mass of the poor the distinguishable groups requiring special treatment.

European countries had already made great progress in this direction. Particularly noteworthy was their development of social insurance as a method of coping with the hazards which result in poverty and dependency for many millions: accidents, sickness, invalidity, old age, and unemployment.

The explanation for our slower progress was that in our newer country it was far less evident than in Europe that poverty is not solely, nor even principally, a matter of individual fault. With a continent thrown open to exploitation in two generations, it appeared that everyone who made a real effort could have a sufficiency. With a rapidly expanding economy, the unemployment problem seemed to be one involving only the lazy and the misfit. A young nation, the percentage of the old people was small; even the children deprived of family support by the death of their father were generally provided for by their relatives.

Actually, there was considerable unemployment even then that was nobody's fault. Throughout the prosperous 'twenties, the costs of relief were rapidly growing; and, quite unknown to the public, the percentage of old people in our population had been increasing each decade.

When the depression came, the floodgates gave way. Until 1931 poor relief was regarded in each state as exclusively a local responsibility; not one dollar was ever contributed for unemployment or any other form of relief by either the federal or the state governments. (With the enormous increase in relief burdens which came with the depression, the local governments were unable to meet their responsibility for support of all the poor, resident within their respective jurisdictions.)In Wisconsin the costs of relief increased from a little more than one million dollars, in the last years preceding the depression, to 20 million dollars in 1932 and to 40 million dollars in 1935. In 1936 and 1937 relief and welfare activities combined cost considerably in excess of 100 million dollars each year—an amount exceeding the total property tax levies of these years. Relief in all its forms has cost more than one-half billion dollars in Wisconsin since 1932—double the amount collected from our income tax in all the years since the beginning of the state income tax in 1911.

In this emergency, the state and federal governments had to help the localities, and the national government had to assume the major part of the relief costs. Nearly three-quarters of the total relief expenditures, both in Wisconsin and throughout the nation, have been borne by the federal government and more than 10 billion dollars has been expended for this purpose.

At the peak, in midwinter 1935, 22 million people throughout the United States subsisted from relief. And even this figure, approximating 19 per cent of our entire population, gives only an inadequate picture of the seriousness of the situation, as is suggested in the statistics from the relief agency of Milwaukee County. In that county in 1930 there were 177,000 families. When the relief load was largest, 38,000 of these families were dependent upon the public for support; but in excess of 90,000 different families—more than one-half the total number—have been on relief at one time or another since 1932.

It was out of this frightful situation that the present social security movement developed. As early as 1932 the Democratic national platform committed the party which won the election of that year to both old-age pensions and unemployment insurance. Before the President sent the social security message of June 8, 1934, to Congress, the Republican national committee put this great party also behind both of these major social insurance institutions. The Social Security Act was passed by Congress in August 1935 with but 6 senators and 33 members of the House casting their votes in opposition, the great majority of the adherents of all parties voting for the measure.

The Social Security Act, while basically only a modern expression of the age-old principle of public concern with dependency, included some important innovations. It was the first act in which the federal government recognized a permanent responsibility in this field. It did so, moreover, in such a manner as to commit the state governments to recognition of a like responsibility. In a very real sense, it provided for a coöperative effort by all governments in this country in coping with the problem of dependency, which has become so very serious.

Among the many different aspects of this problem, the Social Security Act dealt mainly with three: (1) security for children; (2) old-age security; and (3) unemployment compensation. It provided for federal aid to improve the provisions made by the states for aid to dependent children. It also granted aid for child and maternal health services, crippled children services, and rural child welfare services.* In furtherance of old-age security it provided for aid to the states for old-age assistance, by which is meant public assistance to aged dependents given on the basis of need. It also provided for old-age insurance on a quasi-contractual basis, to be operated by the federal government (this is the only part of the Social Security Act which

---

* The last refers to protection and care of homeless, dependent, and neglected children in predominantly rural areas.—EDITOR.

is federally administered) and applying compulsorily to practically the entire industrial population of the country. In the field of unemployment compensation it did not set up a federal system of unemployment insurance, but afforded a stimulus to the enactment of state unemployment insurance laws through the device of a uniform tax on employers throughout the country, against which an offset of up to 90 per cent of the federal tax is allowed for contributions by the employers to state unemployment insurance funds.

Although this act passed Congress nearly unanimously, it is, nevertheless, true that it was launched under most inauspicious omens. When the bill was introduced in Congress with the President's recommendation, it was popularly expected that it would be passed within less than two months. Not until after seven months' consideration in Congress, however, did the Act become law and then only after many changes that materially narrowed its scope and otherwise weakened the measure. When the Act was finally passed, Congress failed to make an appropriation to put it into operation. It was not until February, 1936, that any funds were available to carry out any part of the Social Security Act. Thereafter, the Act was subjected to attacks in court, with committees of the American Bar Association and the Liberty League asserting that it was clearly unconstitutional.

Since the first appropriation became available, only a little more than two years have elapsed. The progress made has belied the early ill-fated omens. When the Supreme Court reviewed the legislation, it held all major provisions of the Act to be constitutional. The administration of the Act has proven far less difficult than was expected and the progress made can best be described as phenomenal. When the social security bill was introduced in Congress, only the state of Wisconsin had an unemployment insurance law. Today all the 48 states, the two territories, and the District of Columbia have such laws. In 23 states unemployment insurance benefits have been paid since January 1, 1938, and in the rest of the states, benefits will become payable within a year. Where there were 28 states with old-age assistance laws and 235,000 old-age pensioners, such laws are now in operation in every state and there are in excess of 1,700,000 old-age pensioners. The number of dependent children aided has more than doubled. Whereas 18 states had crippled children's services when the Social Security Act was passed, 44 states now have such services; and every state has taken advantage of the federal aids for maternal and child health services, rural child welfare services, and state and local public health services. Perhaps most surprising has been the ease with which the federal old-age insurance system has been put into operation. More than 39 million Americans now have social security account numbers and are developing credits convertible into retirement allowances when they reach old age, or into lump sum benefits to their dependents should they die before they attain the retirement age.

By this I do not intend to convey the impression that everything is perfect and that no difficulties have arisen. Large numbers of the recipients of old-age pensions are dissatisfied with the meagerness of the grants; on the other hand, taxpayers in many states are becoming aroused about the alarming increase in the cost of the pensions. Because unemployment insurance payments came into operation in 1938 during the sharpest downswing of the business cycle since the great depression started, inevitably there was much confusion and delay within many of the states which began payments on January 1, 1938. In nearly every state there has been great improvement in this respect within the last few months and nowhere is there the slightest danger that the unemployment insurance laws will be repealed. In Wisconsin we have been particularly fortunate in having a very fine administration and above all in having the whole-hearted coöperation of both employers and employees through the Advisory Committee.... But problems remain in this state, as elsewhere, and it will be a long time, if ever, before all of them will be solved.

Of the present social security program, old-age insurance remains the part that is most criticized. The criticisms come from both the Left and the Right and, strangely, both the Left and the Right are making substantially the same arguments. The criticisms of both center around the alleged large reserve in the old-age insurance system. Both the radicals and conservatives are saying that if the attempt to build up any reserve is abandoned and a "pay-as-you-go" system of financing is substituted, it will be possible at one and the same time to increase benefits and to reduce taxes.

The term "pay-as-you-go" has a great popular appeal and thus far the public has not grasped the idea that the so-called pay-as-you-go method of financing old-age insurance is a complete misnomer. As used by both its radical and conservative advocates, it means raising enough money only to meet current cash outlays, without paying any attention to accruing liabilities. In old-age insurance, the accruing liabilities are necessarily the major part of the costs in the early years of the system. The benefits provided in the Social Security Act were estimated by the actuaries to cost forty-three times as much in 1980 as in 1942. Under the so-called pay-as-you-go method of financing, however, no provision would be made to meet the rapidly accruing liabilities. It is even proposed by some that no record be kept of these accruing liabilities, so were this plan adopted, the United States government would have a vast hidden debt, in addition to the acknowledged federal debt.

Conservative groups, by hammering away at the reserves in the old-age insurance system, hope to get a reduction in social security taxes. Were the old-age insurance system financed as are commercial annuities sold by private insurance companies, taxes equal to 5.5 per cent of payrolls would be necessary from the beginning. Actually, the present combined rates on employers and employees total only 2 per cent, and 5.5 per cent will not be collected until 1949, beginning in which year, however, 6 per cent will be collected to make up for the insufficient collections in the early years. But while the present taxes are far less than those which would have to be charged were the old-age insurance system financed on private insurance company principles, the advocates of pay-as-you-go financing urge that these taxes be lowered, because even the present inadequate rates yield more money than is necessary to meet the cash disbursements of the early years of the old-age insurance system.

Radicals of all stripes want the benefits increased. Concern is expressed by them over the inadequate benefits which will be paid to the wage-earners who will reach retirement age in 1942 or soon thereafter. While the people retired in 1942 will, on the average, receive sixty times as much in benefits as they paid in taxes, it is nevertheless urged that their benefits be further increased, so they can live in comfort on their retirement annuities without income from any other source. There are also proposals for supplementing old-age insurance with invalidity insurance and with widows' and orphans' pensions, which alone would cost fully as much as do the old-age insurance benefits now provided. At the extreme are the advocates of the General Welfare Bill, the 1938 version of the Townsend Plan. While the $200 per month has been dropped out of the formal statement of the plan, the poor old people who are contributing to the many organizations that support this measure still hope for $200 per month for everybody over sixty.

As I see the situation, either the conservatives or the radicals are bound to be disappointed should they be able to continue to work together until the Social Security Act is amended. While, for a few years, it is possible both to keep taxes down and to increase benefits, if no account is taken of accruing liabilities, this possibility will not long endure. The present taxes will probably prove to be inadequate to fully finance the old-age benefits now contemplated, without subsidies, in distant future years, from the general treasury. Any increase in these benefits will necessitate additional taxes.

It is my conviction that the conservative groups who have assailed the old-age insurance system are playing with fire and are likely to produce a blaze that will cause tremendous losses to American business ere long. If the people who are attacking the reserves succeed in convincing the American public that it is not necessary to pay any attention to accruing liabilities, we will have such a large increase in benefits that they cannot possibly be financed without a very great increase in taxes.

As I see it, the underlying principles of the federal old-age insurance system are fundamentally sound. This country faces a very serious old-age problem in the years lying ahead. That problem can be most wisely met through a contributory insurance system, in which the principles are observed that accruing liabilities shall, as far as practicable, be met currently and that the prospective beneficiaries must pay one-half of the costs. Abandon the contributory feature, or substitute for the principle of meeting all accruing costs currently an assessment system of financing, to which is given the misleading designation of a "pay-as-you-go" plan, and you will find it impossible to keep the old-age security costs within any reasonable limits.

But whether I am right or wrong in the views I hold regarding the soundness of the present legislation, I think there can be little dispute over its fundamental objectives. These objectives represent not a new departure, out of line with our past traditions, but merely a development and expansion of old American ideals adapted to present-day conditions. Social security does not assert, as some have said, that the government owes every man a living. In relation to the relief of want and suffering, it goes beyond the long-established principles of the poor law only to the extent that it insists that each clearly distinguishable group among the poor shall be dealt with in accordance with its peculiar characteristics and needs. The objective in thus dealing with the dependents in our population is not merely to sustain life, but to preserve self-respect and, as far as possible, to restore the dependents to self-support. Going beyond relief on such a modernized basis, social security emphasizes the importance of the prevention of dependency. In doing so it makes extensive use of the principles of insurance which have been accepted by the American people to such a degree that there is more insurance in the United States than in all other countries combined. The only innovation in this respect lies in the extension of what is known as group insurance to the entire mass of the wage-earners and salaried employees, and in the conduct of such social insurance directly by the government on a nonprofit basis.

Social security is not a remedy for all economic ills. It does not even attempt to deal with the most serious difficulties in our economic system, which are associated with its violent fluctuations and the apparently increasing severity of depressions. Only to a very minor degree does it modify the distribution of wealth and it does not alter at all the fundamentals of our capitalistic and individualistic economy. Nor does it relieve the individual of primary responsibility for his own support and that of his dependents; nor is any change contemplated in family responsibility; on the contrary many parts of the social security program treat the family as the basic unit in our social structure and seek to strengthen its foundations by repairing the underpinning of family support. Social security does not dampen initiative or render thrift outmoded. Private saving will be quite as necessary as ever, and social security will prove a failure unless investment is revived and enterprise prospers. Social security is clearly secondary to economic security and is less important than economic recovery and business stability. In determining how far and how fast we shall move in the direction of social security, consideration must be given to costs and business conditions. It would be killing the goose that laid the golden egg if in seeking to establish social security we burdened enterprise so that it cannot function.

It is my belief that what has been done to date does not constitute an unfair or impossible burden on industry. The combined total of 4 per cent of their payrolls which employers throughout the country

are now paying for unemployment compensation and old-age insurance for their employees represents, on the average, an increase
in labor costs of less than 1 per cent (assuming that none of this
cost is shifted to the employees in the form of lower wages); and
even when allowance is made for indirect labor costs reflected in the
prices of materials purchased, the increased cost is, on the average,
less than 3 per cent. On the other side of the ledger must be put
a resulting saving in reduction in present and future costs of relief
and old-age support. Relief has cost more in the United States since
the depression began in 1929 than all other countries in the world
combined have spent for social insurance in all the years since Bismarck put through the first compulsory social insurance law in 1881.
The social security program we now have will not obviate the necessity for relief, but it should lighten the burden and with comparatively minor changes can be made to operate more effectively to this
end than now.

It is my conviction, further, that, while social security is not the
most important thing we need to attain the economic security everyone is seeking, it is very essential in this day and age. Social security
has been described as a socialized attack upon the problems of economic insecurity from an essentially individualistic point of view.
It is concerned not with the fundamental causes of insecurity, but
with their manifestation as they affect the individual. It deals with
the immediate causes of poverty and dependency as they appear to
the individual—the "major hazards and vicissitudes of life which
cannot be wholly eliminated in this man-made world of ours."

Granting that such an approach is not fundamental and less important than, for instance, the elimination of the violent fluctuations of
the business cycle, it is, nevertheless, very necessary, whatever we
may be able to do with the more fundamental problems; we cannot
afford to neglect the immediate manifestations of maladjustments.
People who are in need must have assistance if our social order is to
endure, and they should get assistance in such a form that their working capacity and morale will be preserved. It will not do to place all
our reliance in the possibilities of solving the problems of the business cycle, while we do nothing for the victims of our failure to solve
these problems earlier.

Moreover, if the millennium should ever come when our economies function with entire smoothness, there will still be need for measures for social security. Sir William Beveridge, the English economist who knows more about the unemployment problem than anyone else, has shown beyond all question that employment and unemployment exist side by side in modern society and often grow simultaneously. In the periods of greatest prosperity, there are still many people who do not have steady employment through no fault of their own. The economic hazards of old age are largely independent of the business cycle. People grow old whether we have prosperity or depression, and the period of old age, when earnings are decreased or stop entirely, is on the average one-third as long as the period of productive employment. One-third of all wage-earners die before they reach retirement age and almost invariably when the breadwinner in the family dies young, his dependents are left without adequate means.

These and other hazards lead to poverty and dependency for millions of Americans, even in times of prosperity. In accord with dictates of common humanity, we cannot neglect these problems of dependency, even though we direct our major attention to economic recovery and business stabilization. In this age of urbanization and economic interdependence, a socialized approach to the problems of dependency is clearly necessary. (Industry and thrift are still very important and are in many respects the best security that any individual can ever have. In this day and age, however, even the value of private savings is dependent upon social factors. If we are to deal with such problems as accidents, sickness, unemployment, old age, and the early death of the wage-earner, we must provide social safeguards to supplement the efforts which the individual may make in his own behalf. That is all that the social security program aims to do.)

So, I conclude that social security is not a wild dream, but a practical plan. Insofar as it is a dream, it is the dream of American democracy throughout our history; it is a dream of a secure existence in all contingencies of life, or at least of a minimum sufficient for the decent existence for all who make an honest effort. The methods by which the social security program hopes to give reality to this dream represent a natural development from principles long recognized in this country. The recent expansion of these methods follows policies which have been in successful operation for a considerable period of time in nearly every other civilized country. Other countries have made a success of social insurance; the United States can do as well and better. Social security, as now conceived is, I believe, a practical plan. Present defects are minor and can and will be remedied by the American people; the fundamentals are sound and practical in all essential respects.

Postwar Social Security

Chapter XV in *Postwar
Economic Problems,* edited by
Seymour E. Harris, copyright,
1943, New York: McGraw-Hill
Book Company, 1943, pages
263–277, used by permission

HE TERM *social security,* in the connotation it now has, is of
American origin and less than 10 years old. It did not gain wide
currency until the House Ways and Means Committee in 1935, looking about for a title distinguishing the substitute bill it reported for
the Administration's "Economic Security Bill," hit upon the "Social
Security Act," for no particular reason. Ever since, the term has been
applied to everything included in this important federal law and to
other similar institutions.

Today *social security* is an immensely popular term, not only in
the United States, but throughout the British Dominions and in other
lands as well. In Article V of the Atlantic Charter, President Roosevelt and Prime Minister Churchill proclaimed "improved labor
standards, economic advancement and social security for all" to be one
of the major postwar objectives of the two great English-speaking nations. In the United States, both major political parties are pledged
to the "extension of social security." In England, Ernest Bevin recently said: "I suggest that at the end of this war we accept social
security as the main motive of our national life"; and the same view
has been expressed by Anthony Eden and Lord Halifax. Elsewhere

15

the term is not so well established, but it is gaining acceptance in Latin America and is at least understood by informed people throughout the world.

Yet this term lacks precise meaning even in the United States. The most widely prevalent usage is that adopted by the International Labour Office,[1] which includes within the term both *social assistance* and *social insurance* and also *social security systems.* Social insurance systems "represent an integration of social insurance and assistance." Social assistance stems from the old institution of poor relief and "expresses the obligation of the community toward its needy members." It includes noncontributory pensions for the aged and for invalids (the American *old-age assistance* and *aid to the blind*), mothers' pensions (in statutes called *aid to dependent children* in this country), unemployment assistance, medical assistance, and rehabilitation of the disabled. Social insurance, in contrast, "is situated between social assistance and commercial insurance." It is established by law and serves social purposes but utilizes insurance principles. It first made its appearance in Europe in the 1880's. Its foundations were not poor relief, but the employer's liability principle, voluntary sickness funds, and pension funds for small groups in the population, such as civil servants, miners, and seamen. Today it includes workmen's compensation (or industrial accident insurance), sickness (or health) insurance, old-age, invalidity, and survivors' insurance (called *pensions* in Europe), and unemployment insurance.

As thus defined, *social security* is broader than social insurance, although the latter term is often loosely used to include social assistance and integrated social security systems. It is narrower than the English *social services* and the Scandinavian *social policy,* which include, besides social security institutions, such other governmental services as public education, public health and medical services, public housing developments, and still other publicly financed and directed programs for the benefit of people in low-income groups. It is also narrower than *economic security* or *security,* as economists use these terms. The social security approach is basically that of individual and family welfare. Its concern is with the immediate hazards that spell want and dependency to many individuals and families, not with ultimate causes or basic reforms.

[1] International Labour Office, *Approaches to Social Security: An International Survey* (Montreal, 1942), pp. i, ii.

As thus conceived, social security has but limited values. It is not a panacea, nor a cure for any of the conditions it seeks to relieve. Yet it serves vital needs of society. Without maintenance of individuals and families in all contingencies of life, the hope of fundamental remedies for economic ills is but illusory.

For this reason, relief is as old as is civilization. In this day and age, it is predominantly a responsibility of the state. Social assistance is specialized relief, adapted to the needs of clearly distinguishable groups among the people without adequate means for individual or family maintenance (not mere subsistence, but a level of maintenance compatible with prevailing concepts regarding the needs of the beneficiaries of the several programs). Increasingly, social assistance has come to include not merely cash grants for maintenance, but health and other services designed to reduce the need for assistance in the future.

Social insurance serves, basically, the same purposes. Through social insurance, the costs of meeting the economic hazards whose consequences are want and dependency are reduced from the maximum costs which the individual must be prepared to meet if he does so on an individual basis to the average costs of affording protection. Like private insurance, social insurance serves as a method of distributing the costs of meeting economic risks over large numbers of people and over periods of time appropriate to the particular hazard. In addition, it has some distinctive advantages that private insurance does not have. It is generally compulsory, which ensures normal distribution and reduces costs. In social insurance, also, only part of the costs fall on the insured, the balance being met through contributions from the employers or the government or both. These characteristics make social insurance peculiarly valuable to people with small but fairly stable incomes. From society's point of view, moreover, its values do not lie solely in the fact that it affords insurance protection to many people who otherwise would have little or no insurance. It has important repercussions on the economic system and can be utilized for socially desirable ends beyond those of providing insurance protection for the masses. In theory, the large reserves, which are no less necessary in social than in private insurance, can be so managed as to increase the stability of the economic system. At least some forms of social insurance can be set up in such a way that they will operate as a strong stimulus to preventive efforts, thereby lessening the seriousness of the hazards against whose economic consequences they are designed to provide protection.

Yet the great extension of social security in recent years and its present immense popularity are not due solely to its intrinsic values. In large part, this is but one manifestation of the broader quest for security which, in all industrially mature countries, has become the economic objective of the great majority of the people. The factors which have led so many people to value security above opportunity cannot here be discussed. Suffice it to repeat that this is the age in which people in all walks of life are searching for security. Seniority rights in jobs, guaranteed employment, restrictive union rules, parity prices for farm products, the open-price practices of trade associations, the "live and let live" policy pursued by businessmen toward competitors, the growing number of licensed occupations, and the great concern of economists over economic fluctuations, are only a few of the many illustrations of the ever-growing present-day interest in security. Social security is but another manifestation of the same phenomenon. It is the quest for security on the personalized level of the common man and the everyday family. Some people may see in it far more of danger than of promise, but it is a natural, if not inevitable, development in the day and age in which we are living.

Poor relief is as old as is civilized society. In this country it dates back to the earliest days of settlement. The institutions out of which social insurance developed in Europe antedated the nineteenth century. Social insurance itself and specialized forms of relief now known as *social assistance* first developed in the last decades of that century. In the United States, aid to the blind, aid to dependent children, and workmen's compensation, our first form of social insurance, all were started before the First World War. Out of that war we got vocational rehabilitation and public medical care for veterans, and in the 'twenties old-age assistance. In Europe, the decade following the war was that of the most rapid progress in social insurance. In this country, the great spurt did not come until the 'thirties, when want and dependency became the lot of many millions of American families. In the depression we passed the Social Security Act, and in the space of a few years registered the greatest growth in social security institutions ever recorded in any country. When World War II began in 1939, we had all forms of social security known in Europe except health insurance and dis-

ability insurance. Our social assistance payments were the most liberal in the world. In a decade, our expenditures for social security
purposes increased more than twentyfold. Yet we had by no means
satisfied the popular demand.

In the present war, social security has been pretty much at a stand-
still in the United States. In his message recommending passage of
a selective service law, the President urged Congress to include provisions for the protection of the social security rights of workers
called to the colors, but no concrete plan for doing so has ever been
presented. At the present writing (late in 1942), this country is the
only major belligerent which has failed to protect its servicemen
in this respect. In January of this year, the President, in his budget
message, recommended increase of the rates of the social security
taxes, the extension of coverage of the old-age insurance system, the
establishment of a national system of disability and hospital insurance, and the liberalization of unemployment insurance under standards to be established by the national government. But the promised
detailed Administration proposals to give effect to these recommendations have not yet made their appearance. A plan for war-displace-
ment benefits to supplement unemployment insurance was brought
forward soon after the President's message, but did not even get out
of committee, because it aroused fears that it was designed to federalize unemployment compensation. Less than a month before Hitler
started the shooting war and in face of warnings that this nation
would soon need all the revenues it could get, Congress reduced the
social security taxes. Since Pearl Harbor, Administration leaders
have repeatedly urged that the social security taxes be increased, but
Congress has been deaf to these recommendations. Numerous bills
to extend and strengthen our provisions for social security are pending in Congress, but none of them have been even accorded a hearing,
except the Downy bill for a flat pension of $30 per month to every-
body over sixty-five (a modified Townsend plan), which was favorably reported by a special committee but which the Senate refused
to swallow.

A very different story is to be told for other countries.[2] Beginning
with England, it is to be noted, first, that the rights of men called to

---

[2] The information in this and succeeding paragraphs about developments in the
social security field during the war comes mainly from the *International Labour Review,* published monthly by the International Labour Office, whose headquarters are
now at Montreal.

the colors have been preserved, as to both old-age and health insurance. To meet the costs of providing this protection a small deduction is made from the soldiers' pay, but the Treasury defrays most of the expense. Similarly, the government has assumed responsibility for medical and hospital care for civilian war victims and, in connection with this service, has given financial assistance for hospital improvements and extensions. It also has undertaken large social service programs to meet needs peculiar to the war, such as the feeding of school children, communal food kitchens, and subsidies to the producers of essential foods, to make certain that people in low-income groups will be able to get these foods at prices they can afford to pay.

In addition to these wartime innovations, quite extensive changes have been made in the old social security institutions. In all the social insurance systems—health insurance, old-age and survivors' insurance, unemployment insurance, and workmen's compensation —coverage has been extended and benefits and contributions increased. Since the war started, the unemployment insurance fund has finished paying off its debt to the Exchequer and is now trying to build up a large reserve for meeting the situation of mass unemployment with which it is again likely to be confronted after the war. In the social assistance programs, benefits have been increased to keep pace with increases in the costs of living and a long-standing grievance of the working people has been corrected through the abolition of the household means test and the substitution therefor of a family and individual basis for determining need. Unemployment assistance, through which, since 1935, the national government has assumed responsibility for all relief necessary to workers normally employed regularly in industry, has been extended to include all pensioners and has been renamed "public assistance." Finally, the government has recently organized an Interdepartmental Committee on Social Insurance and Allied Services to consider how a unified social security system may be developed after the war.[3]

For other parts of the British Empire, similar developments are to be recorded. Canada established a national unemployment insurance system which came into operation on July 1, 1941. It has also

---

[3] This committee has issued the Beveridge Report, which provides for a comprehensive program of social security. This report has been published by Macmillan here and is having a significant influence in the United States.—Editor.

adopted a comprehensive plan for the restoration of discharged soldiers to civilian life, which includes payments by the government to the unemployment insurance fund to give all servicemen the same rights under the unemployment insurance system as if they were in private employment, and special grants if, during the first 18 months after their discharge, they become unemployed and exhaust their unemployment compensation benefits. New Zealand, likewise, gives its servicemen the same credits in its social insurance system for time spent with the military forces as they would get in private employment, with the government paying the entire costs, and it has organized a National Rehabilitation Council to make plans for the restoration of the servicemen to civilian life when the war ends. In Australia, the Commonwealth in July, 1941, set up a Joint Parliamentary Committee on the Improvement of Social Legislation and Social Conditions, charged with the duty of developing a coördinated plan for social services. In an interim report made by a committee late in 1941, it took the position that in view of the federal system of government which exists in Australia as in the United States the best results could be secured "if future services are to be administered on the basis of Commonwealth-State coöperation," with grants-in-aid to the states by the Commonwealth for social services "to be administered by the States on lines laid down in Commonwealth legislation." It also announced that it expected at a later date to make recommendations for a Commonwealth Social Security Act. More recently, the Commonwealth government has asked the committee to make a special study of the feasibility of unemployment insurance, and it has been giving a great deal of attention to a national plan for public medical services.

Very notable also has been the progress of social insurance in the last few years in the Latin-American countries. Costa Rica and Peru in 1941 enacted comprehensive social insurance laws, which include all forms except unemployment insurance. Brazil has extended its previously very limited pension insurance system to substantially all employees except agricultural workers, and, under it, affords combined old-age, invalidity, and survivors' insurance protection. In both Argentina and Mexico, governmental commissions are at this writing engaged in studies looking toward the establishment of comprehensive social security systems. There has also been organized, at the instance of the International Labour Organization, a Social In-

surance Commission of the American Countries to assist the participating countries in developing social security systems on a coördinated and sound basis.

In enemy countries, particularly in Germany, there also have been
important developments affecting social security. Not only has Germany provided that men called to the colors retain all social security
rights without cost to them, but their dependents are automatically
included in health insurance. Additionally, health insurance has
been extended to war widows and orphans and to all pensioners, and
its benefits have been liberalized, particularly by the medical care
services. There also has occurred some extension of coverage and
liberalization of benefits in accident insurance and in old-age, invalidity, and survivors' insurance.

These developments do not differ fundamentally from those in
the free countries, but something radically different is foreshadowed
in the announcement made by the government, early in 1942, that
it is working on a plan for a universal pension system, which will
include all the German people and which will be based on National
Socialist principles, not on the social insurance concepts of the
"plutocratic-democratic countries." What appears to be contemplated is to make old-age, invalidity, and survivors' insurance a direct
government obligation, but with all payments based on need, rather
than right. In unemployment insurance such a transition has already
been effected. Since the beginning of the war, no one in Germany
has gotten unemployment insurance as a right, but payments have
been made only to unemployed workers on a basis of their actual
needs. The old contributions from employers and employees, averaging a combined 6.5 per cent of payrolls, have been retained but are
now commingled with other government funds. Thus, while Germany has been extending its social insurance institutions, it has also
been remaking them in accordance with the Nazi philosophy and
what they are developing is something very different from social
security as known elsewhere in the world.

In the countries overrun by the Nazis, the established social security institutions have been nominally continued. From such scattered
information as is available about the actual situation, however, it
would appear that for most of the conquered people, at least, loss of
freedom has also meant loss of all social security protection.

These wartime developments forecast what is likely to be the future of social security. Should the Axis powers win the war, there will be no social security worth discussing in any of the defeated nations. For the white and yellow "Aryans," also, social security will not be a right, but a payment which the government may withhold at any time.

Assuming the victory we still have to win, great advances in social security are to be anticipated. Precisely what will be done in each country to give reality to the pledges made by the political leaders of social security for all, it is, of course, impossible to say. But something of the probable lines of development can be forecast, if past trends, current needs, and popular demands are correctly appraised.

Dealing in this forecast only with the United States, it is of but slight significance that we have been laggard in the adaptation of social security to war conditions. It is unthinkable that this country will not protect the social security rights of the men it calls to the colors. Before the war ends national legislation to accomplish this purpose will be passed. The fact that this has not been done to date may create injustices in a few cases, involving men discharged during the war, but for the great majority of the servicemen it will be timely if such legislation is passed before the war ends. And we may hope that this country will deal with the men who are risking their lives in its service as generously as have other belligerents, allowing them the same credits as if they had been in private employment, without requiring any contributions from them.

Very probable also is legislation before the war ends to facilitate the return of the demobilized servicemen to civilian employment. The provision which is included in the Selective Service Act that the drafted men are to get their jobs back if they still exist will not alone prove sufficient. We shall have need for expanded vocational training services and educational bonuses and, probably, also for cash payments to men who cannot find jobs or hold them, which should be conditioned upon participation in training programs designed to make them more valuable to industry.

The problem of demobilization after the war, of course, will involve much more than merely the return of the servicemen to civilian life. It includes also the problem of transferring many millions of workers from war production to production for peacetime needs. This is likely to be accompanied by much unemployment and clearly will necessitate widespread movements of workers and shifts of occupations. This is much more than a problem of social security, but one of its most important aspects is that in the transition period millions of Americans will have low or no earnings and many of them and their families are likely to be in want.

Various proposals have been put forward for meeting this situation. Among these is the establishment of a dismissal wage, to be paid on discharge to the workers no longer needed in war production, either from a social insurance fund or directly by the employers. This proposal has recently been endorsed by the National Association of Manufacturers, but it is not clear whether this organization favors legislation on the subject or merely voluntary action on the part of the employers. To be more than a salving of the conscience of employers who dismiss workers after they have helped them earn large profits, dismissal compensation must be compulsory and a fund should be built up on a contributory basis, while profits and earnings are good, to ensure payments when needed. The early establishment of such a system of dismissal compensation is much to be desired, but politically it as yet commands little support.

Within Administration circles and also on the part of organized labor, the most highly favored proposal for meeting the social security problems of postwar readjustment is "the federalization of unemployment insurance." By this is meant the replacement of the existing federal-state system of unemployment insurance (which is really a system of 51 separate state funds, but with a large measure of control over administration vested in the national government) by a unified system, exclusively administered and controlled by the national government. There are many arguments to be made for federalization, as well as arguments against it, but the most popular at this time is that such action is necessary to meet the problem of the expected large volume of postwar unemployment. At the moment, federalization of unemployment insurance has little support in Congress, but it is a distinct possibility that as the war approaches its end and fears develop about the mass unemployment which is expected to accompany postwar readjustments we shall "federalize" our system of unemployment compensation. This cannot be regarded as a certainty, however, because federalization has aroused bitter opposition. Regardless of whether we should federalize unemployment compensation, other measures will clearly be necessary if we are to make the transition from war to civilian production without a large and dangerous increase in want and dependency. There will be need for a planned and controlled transition, assisted migration, extensive retraining, and expanded public works programs, as well as for both unemployment insurance and dismissal compensation. But there is danger that, in the bitterness of the controversy over the federalization of unemployment compensation, little or nothing will be done in preparation for meeting what might be called the human or family aspects of civilian demobilization.

Beyond the period of demobilization lies that of recovery from the ravages of war and of the establishment of a world in which the four basic freedoms will prevail. The basic economic problem will doubtless be that of maintaining full employment, but their will also be many social security problems requiring attention.

Of these it is quite likely that major attention will again be given to old-age security. For the moment, even the Townsendites are more interested in the war and its outcome than in old-age pensions. Yet the politicians continue to make vague promises of support to the Townsendites. This situation is indicative of the fact that there is much dissatisfaction with the present provisions for old-age security, although as a group the old people are being treated much more generously than any other large element among the poor in our population.

Beyond question the present provisions for old-age security are far from being completely satisfactory. Old-age assistance, which is now and for many years will remain by far the larger part of our total program for old-age security as measured by benefits currently paid, varies greatly in actual operation from state to state and often within the same state. Grants in many areas are miserably small and the conditions under which they are made are deemed humiliating by many of the old people. The greatest defect in the present provisions is that the Federal aid for old-age assistance goes mainly and very disproportionately to the wealthier states. This could be corrected through a system of variable grants, but Congress has refused to accept this recommendation of the Social Security Board. The old-age insurance part of the program also has many defects. It is not financed on an actuarially sound basis. The so-called *dependents' benefits* which it provides are illogically set up and the survivors' benefits are very limited. Most serious of all, large groups in the population are excluded from coverage, and under the present law at least one-third, and probably more, of the people who are covered for tax purposes will never be able to qualify for benefits.

In trying to forecast what is likely to happen after the war, account needs also to be taken of popular feeling in relation to old-age security. Most important in this connection are the widespread sentiment that all Americans should enjoy old-age protection and the belief that excessive reserves are being collected and that much larger benefits might be paid without any increase in contributions. Out of these popular beliefs arises the danger that after the war we may replace our present contributory old-age insurance system with a "baby Townsend plan"—a flat pension payable to all old people regardless of need. Such a program would either prove financially impossible ere long or become something closely akin to the German *Volksversicherung*, under which everybody would be taxed for old-age insurance purposes but only the people in need would get benefits. Yet it is quite likely that we shall experiment with a baby Townsend plan, unless very soon we extend the present contributory system to include all our people and correct the injustices and anomalies which now exist in both old-age assistance and old-age insurance.

But urgent as is the need for betterment of the present provisions for old-age security, there is equal, if not greater, need for more adequate protection against other social security risks. Of these, health and disability are among the most important.

Besides China and India, the United States is the only major country in the world which does not have a national health insurance law. There have been two periods of great interest in compulsory health insurance in this country, 1915–1920 and 1932–1939, but neither resulted in the passage of such a law in any state. Very considerable progress has been made in recent years in voluntary medical care and, particularly, in voluntary hospital insurance. But compulsory health insurance seems remote. While endorsed by organized labor, farmers' organizations, and women's clubs, there are but few people who are very much interested in it, while organized medicine fights it relentlessly as "socialized medicine."

In the meantime, actual socialized medicine—medical care at public expense—has increased at a rapid pace. Medical care, in the United States as elsewhere, has long been furnished under a mixed system of private and public care. During the Depression and still more in wartime, the public part of this mixed system has become increasingly important. It is probable that this trend will continue. One reason for expecting this is that the veterans of the present war will doubtless get medical care very largely at public expense for the rest of their lives, as did veterans of the last war. There is also reason to expect that the American people will in the near future manifest much more concern than they have done to date over the large number of rejections for physical reasons in the draft, which, while not indicating lack of progress since the last war, nevertheless reveals that many Americans suffer from curable and preventable diseases, largely because they lack sufficient income for adequate medical care.

Equally clear, if not more so, is the need for social insurance institutions to provide income in replacement of lost wages, in cases of illness and permanent disability. In most countries the former is provided through compulsory health insurance, the latter in connection with old-age insurance.[4] In this country, because compulsory health insurance has met with such violent opposition from the doctors, the Social Security Board has proposed that compensation for both temporary and permanent disability be administered along with old-age and survivors' insurance. It was hoped that such a program would be acceptable to the doctors, but organized medicine, while not unqualifiedly opposed, seems fearful that anything of this sort will serve as an entering wedge for compulsory health insurance.

The final form of social insurance, workmen's compensation, is seldom mentioned in discussions of social security in this country, but in benefits paid it ranks among the most important of our social security institutions. By and large, workmen's compensation has been a success and is exceedingly popular. But there is need for extension of coverage, liberalization of benefits, and inclusion within its scope in all states of all occupational diseases, along with industrial accidents.

Finally, in relation to social insurance, note needs to be taken of the fact that after the war—possibly even before its close—we are likely to have proposals for a unified social insurance for all contingencies of life. Anything along this line is difficult to work out and is likely to become snarled up in a federal-state controversy, but it merits attention.

In any reasonably satisfactory social security program, social assist-

[4] In England, as a part of health insurance.

ance will have almost as large a part as social insurance. There is need for the improvement of our social assistance institutions in many respects. Particularly if it should prove impossible to get disability insurance, we shall need to consider assistance to the disabled as a new form of specialized assistance. And we clearly need to improve our measures for security for children. With children becoming more valuable in our society as they become scarcer, and with two-thirds or more of all children born in the homes of the poor, it is to be hoped that the American people will ere long come to realize that security for children merits quite as much attention as does old-age security.

In addition to all specialized programs, we shall need to give thought to the leftover group provided for under general relief. In the depression period we spent many times as much for direct and work relief as we spent for all other types of social security put together. Millions of Americans had personal experience with relief, and to but few of them was this experience one that they care to repeat. Almost unanimously, our relief institutions were regarded as most unsatisfactory. Yet at the end of the Depression these institutions were pretty much what they have always been, and we lacked a national program for handling relief. A committee working under the National Resources Planning Board, appointed at the suggestion of the President, studied the problem for nearly two years, but its long-overdue report has still not been made public. In the meantime the Civilian Conservation Corps has been liquidated, and the Works Progress Administration is gradually being liquidated. But relief is still a very sizable problem and, almost certainly, will be much larger after the war ends. While we cannot be optimistic about what will be done, the development of something like a permanent relief policy is one of our most urgent social security needs.

The program that has been suggested for social security after the war is a large order. Many people will think that it is not financially possible, while others will take the position that it is futile to talk about social security apart from attaining full employment. Both points of view have some merit but are false in their extreme form of statement. Under present conditions, adequate social security can be financed only on a contributory basis, and there are limits to the benefits that can be provided. But social security costs are largely in the nature of a better distribution of costs which society must meet in any event. Our economy, moreover, cannot survive at all unless it satisfies the mass of the people, and social security is their rightful demand. How far we can go toward satisfying this demand will depend upon our total volume of production, but full employment will not eliminate the need for social security. Even when we have what may be technically termed *full employment,* there is much unemployment, and most other hazards leading to poverty and dependency have little or no relation to employment. In the postwar world we must provide reasonably adequate social security protection for all our people in all contingencies of life or we will have dictatorship and chaos.

What forms social security will take in future years is uncertain. In this chapter a conservative program of development has been discussed, but more radical measures are well within the range of possibility. Social security has no meaning apart from the government and the economic and social systems which prevail in a given nation at a given time. Its content and underlying purposes, even its meaning, will change with changes in the government and the economic system. Social security appropriate to our old Federal system of government, in which there were sharp lines of distinction between the authority of the national and the state governments, is different from that which suits a coöperative or a unitary government, either of which we may be developing in this country. Similarly, social security consistent with an economy of free enterprise differs from social security in a planned economy. The future of social security is unseverably tied up with the future of our government and of our economy and will reflect changes which may occur in those basic institutions. But social security has become an important part of the American way of life and in the years which lie ahead will become increasingly important.

Social Security—1948

Chapter 26 in *Saving
American Capitalism: A
Liberal Economic Program,*
edited by Seymour E. Harris,
New York: Alfred A. Knopf,
1948, pages 309–317

SOCIAL SECURITY is not something that can ever be devised once
and for all. What is a sound program for social security depends
upon the conditions prevailing in a given nation at a given time. To
be taken into account are both economic and political considerations.
What is practical and attainable is at least as important as a guide
to policy as is what is theoretically most desirable.

It is probable that the Congress within the next few years will
materially revise the social security program of the United States.
Extensive changes in their social security programs to fit postwar
conditions have been made in all other English-speaking nations as
well as in many other countries. In the United States, hearings on
several proposals for far-reaching changes were conducted in both
houses in the 1946 and 1947 sessions. As this is written (December,
1947), a Citizens' Advisory Committee, named pursuant to Senate
action and headed by former Secretary of State Stettinius and
Sumner H. Slichter of Harvard, is holding meetings to consider the
recommendations it should make for thoroughgoing revision of the
Social Security Act. It is the author's opinion that such a revision,
while possible, is not likely in a presidential election year. But the

present program is so out of line with conditions now existing or likely to develop in the not distant future that extensive changes seem inevitable ere long.

Theoretically most desirable is a unified social security program which would assure a minimum income to all American families and self-supporting individuals in all contingencies of life. Such a program would provide "cradle-to-grave" security, but in amounts not so large as to discourage industry and initiative, providing only a floor below which Americans would not fall whatever catastrophe might strike them. Such an ideal program, while recognizing that social security institutions are necessary even under conditions of full employment, would integrate them with other economic policies designed to insure full employment and itself contribute to this major objective. To that end, the contributions (earmarked taxes) to support the program would be varied with the level of employment, while benefits would be increased, regardless of the state of social security funds, when necessary to sustain purchasing power. Such a program would, at least, have to be federally controlled, if not federally administered.

Such an ideal program has never been worked out by anyone and in its entirety exists nowhere in the world. Bills approximating cradle-to-grave security for all Americans, without the feature of contributions and benefits varying with over-all business conditions, have been before Congress and have received considerable support. These bills, popularly known as "the Wagner–Murray–Dingell bill," however, have never won even a favorable committee report. At present, they have no prospects of passage. Their advocacy, to the neglect of less comprehensive changes, may well result in letting people who have little use for social security "write the ticket" when Congress in the near future revises the Social Security Act.

This danger arises not only because there are large conservative majorities in both houses of Congress, but because the groups interested in extending social security are disorganized and at this time much more concerned about other matters. On the other hand, the opponents from the right, for the first time, have developed comprehensive counter-proposals, which have considerable popular appeal. It is unlikely that even a conservative Congress will go so far as to adopt the proposal of Lewis Meriam in his Brookings Institution study, *Relief and Social Security* (1946). This is a proposal that social security be made over into nothing more than a relief program, with benefits being paid only to people in need but with all workers required to meet a major part of the costs through a tax on wages and salaries, levied without exemptions. But the program of the Chamber of Commerce of the United States must be taken much more seriously, if for no other reason than that the people who wrote that program are strongly represented on the Citizens' Advisory Committee. This is a program which, while proposing some desirable changes, also includes others, the net effect of which would be to weaken what we now have and to block progress for quite a few years to come.

Opinions will differ as to what people who believe in cradle-to-grave security should do in this situation. To the author, it seems sound to recognize that this country is not ready for any Beveridge Plan. We must take account of our stage of development and must build upon what we have rather than to imitate what any other country may have done. The United States has a federal, not a unitary, government, and any social security program which fails to take account of this basic fact is doomed. While near full employment continues, or until some crisis develops, the most that can be hoped for is piecemeal progress. It is from such premises that the rest of this chapter is devoted to practical suggestions for improving the social security protection of the American people, although combined they fall far short of an ideal program and of what other countries have accomplished.

Old-Age and Survivors' Insurance

In such a practical approach, major attention at this time needs to be given to old-age and survivors' insurance. This need arises because this is the part of the Social Security Act most likely to be materially changed ere long and also because it is at present the least adequate of all existing social security programs. Benefits to workers receiving retirement benefits under the present system average only a little more than $25 per month, contrasted with averages over $36 per month to the recipients of old-age assistance, over $40 to the general relief recipients, and $78 per month to workers receiving unemployment insurance under state laws, and $85 to unemployed veterans. Even a more serious weakness is the fact that less than 10 per cent of the people over 65 years of age are receiving any benefits under the system. This fortunate minority, moreover, does not include any large percentage of those who have the greatest need for retirement allowances.

This situation results in part from the newness of the system. In large part, however, it is due to changes in the conditions of eligibility for benefits made in the Social Security Act Amendments of 1939. Under the original Social Security Act of 1935, nearly all those who paid old-age insurance taxes could look forward to becoming eligible for retirement benefits on retirement at age 65 or later. In 1939 the conditions of eligibility were changed to deny benefits to all who are not "fully insured" at the time of retirement. This is a term applied only to those who have paid taxes on at least $50 of earnings in covered employment in half of the quarters which have elapsed since January 1, 1937, or since they became 21, if later, or in 40 quarters altogether. The effect of this provision is to deny benefits to most who shift between covered and uncovered employment and also to most of the women workers. Of nearly 80,000,000 living Americans who have paid old-age insurance taxes, less than one half are now fully insured. It is optimistically estimated that in course of time, if employment conditions continue good, 60 per cent of the workers who will have to pay taxes will also acquire eligibility to benefits by the time they get to be 65 years of age. Broadening the coverage for tax purposes would operate to increase this percentage, but would still leave ineligible most of the women workers who leave employment to become married.

There are many other needed changes in the old-age and survivors' insurance system. Coverage should be extended, as the Social Security Administration recommends, to include nearly all employed and self-employed persons. Persons permanently and totally disabled should be entitled to benefits even if not yet 65. For women employees also, a younger retirement age than 65 is in line with actual conditions, and both the minimum and maximum benefits should be increased to correspond with the lessened value of the dollar. Clearly, also, the veterans of World War I should be credited in the old-age and survivors' insurance system with at least the average earnings of stay-at-homes for the period of their service, instead of having the time they spent with the colors count against them as it does under the present law. With these changes go a fairer method of computing average earnings for purpose of determining benefits than the 1939 plan of dividing the lifetime taxable earnings by the total number of quarters since 1937, including all those in which the worker was not in covered private employment.

In a sound old-age and survivors' insurance system, the author believes, the costs should be more nearly met by current taxes than they are under the present system. The slogan "pay as you go," which carried the 1939 Amendments, was spurious, as it amounts to disregarding all accruing liabilities. It is a very bad practice not only to fail to meet current liabilities but to keep from the public the fact of an ever-growing debt additional to the acknowledged debt of the United States. It was most unfortunate that the social security taxes were reduced just as World War II was beginning and remained frozen throughout the war boom and the present inflationary period. But there is no prospect that Congress will now increase the tax rates, and probably not even that it will require disclosure of the accruing liabilities. So the author believes that it is wisest to concentrate upon the extension of coverage and the improvement of the benefit provisions, with special emphasis upon the elimination of the extremely restrictive eligibility conditions and the accompanying unfair method of computing average earnings.

Unemployment Insurance

Organized labor is strongly in favor of the federalization of unemployment insurance, which is now largely under state control as well as administered by the states. But it is clear that Congress and the country in its present mood do not want such a basic change. Accordingly, if progress toward more adequate unemployment insurance is to continue, it must at this time be made on the state level.

Unemployment compensation benefits are not nearly as low as those of the old-age and survivors' insurance system. The benefit scales, however, were established before the great postwar price increases. Increases in these benefits to at least the extent of the increases in the cost of living are imperative.

The coverage of the unemployment insurance laws is much less broad than that of the old-age and survivors' insurance system. That system is a demonstration that it is administratively feasible to eliminate the exemption of small employers which still prevails in unemployment insurance.

Cash sickness insurance is now a supplement to unemployment insurance in Rhode Island and California, as well as in the federal railroad unemployment insurance law. This represents one of the most promising present opportunities for the improvement of the social security protection enjoyed by American workers.

A final suggestion of a negative character is appropriate. Supporters of unemployment insurance should resist all efforts further to reduce unemployment insurance taxes, whether this be done through experience rating or across-the-board tax reductions. While present tax collections greatly exceed the benefit payments, it needs to be remembered that the federal government has been meeting the costs of unemployment among the veterans from the United States Treasury but will not continue to do so much longer. In 1946, the total of the benefit payments under state laws and the unemployment allowances paid veterans was twice as great as the total unemployment insurance tax collections. And 1946 was not a year of depression; in fact, ever since unemployment compensation payments first began, business has either been on the upgrade or at a very high level.

Workmen's Compensation

The third social insurance institution, workmen's compensation, is entirely state-controlled. It has generally been neglected by academic advocates of social security, but is our oldest form of social insurance and, probably, also the most popular.

The greatest need in workmen's compensation is an increase in benefits to bring them in line with the existing price levels. Even before the price increases, workmen's compensation, on the average, compensated only 50 per cent of the wage loss of the workers suffering industrial accidents. Today, that percentage is much less. Great also is the need for the extension of the coverage of the workmen's compensation laws.

Social Assistance and Social Services

Social assistance, a term applied to noncontributory types of public aid to people in need and in varying amounts measured by their needs, is very important in this country. Total payments under the social assistance programs exceed those under any type of social insurance other than unemployment insurance.

Under the Social Security Act, federal aid is extended to the states for three of the social assistance programs, old-age assistance, aid to dependent children, and aid to the blind. The administration of these programs, however, is within control of the states, as are all major conditions governing the aid to be given except that it may be granted only on the basis of need. The fourth major program, general public assistance, or relief as it is more commonly known, is not only under exclusive state and local control but also is financed without any federal aid.

The organized social workers have long proposed that federal aid be given to the states for general public assistance. This is logical and desirable. While making such a forward-looking proposal, attention needs also to be given to the counter proposal of the Chamber of Commerce of the United States, which is that the federal aid for the three federally recognized programs of social assistance be gradually tapered off and ultimately totally discontinued. In the present drive for federal tax reduction, this proposal seems more likely to be adopted than any extension of federal aid. Cutting off or reducing the federal aid, however, will not solve the problem but only shift the part of the costs of supporting the needy now falling upon federal corporation and individual income taxes to the property and sales taxes, which are the main sources of state and local revenues.

In addition to social assistance, there is great need for the development of many types of social services designed to prevent dependency or to provide better care for dependents than is afforded through cash grants. A good illustration of such services is vocational rehabilitation, which is restoring many seriously injured and handicapped people to self-support. Foremost among additionally needed social services are medical and hospital services for people unable to pay the total costs of needed care. There is much need also for recognition that many of the old people require care in addition to financial support. This calls for improved homes for the aged and public nursing homes or closely supervised private homes, partially publicly supported.

Health Insurance and Public Medical Services

Left for discussion are health insurance and public medical services. It is here that the frontier in social security now lies in the United States, with new fertile territory within near reach, which should be developed for the benefit of the American people.

Health insurance is the oldest form of social insurance and, except for old-age insurance, now the most widely prevalent the world over. In the United States, it has been discussed for more than 30 years, but so far not even a single state has enacted a compulsory health insurance law. The proposal, however, has shown remarkable vitality and probably has more support today than ever before. This is attributable primarily to the fact that a large percentage of all Americans are not getting adequate medical care because they are unable to pay for it. Until fairly recently this fact was disputed by organized medicine, but it is today conceded even by the American Medical Association. This great medical organization has now reversed its earlier position and is supporting voluntary forms of health insurance. Some progress has been made with voluntary medical care insurance and voluntary hospital insurance has attained large proportions, now covering approximately one-fifth of all Americans. There is little prospect, however, that voluntary health insurance will ever reach anywhere near all Americans who do not get adequate medical care for economic reasons. Even compulsory health insurance will not alone meet this need. It will have to be supplemented by expanded public health services, particularly preventive services and medical care at public expense for the more expensive diseases, which require long-continued treatment.

The alternatives before the American people are pretty well illustrated by the position on this issue taken by leading candidates for the Presidency. Senator Taft is the author of a bill in Congress to give aid to the states, in the amount of $200,000,000 per year, for medical and hospital care for indigents or for payments by the states to voluntary health insurance plans on behalf of such indigents. Governor Stassen has come out for compulsory health insurance, limited to the payment of medical bills in excess of $250. Governor Warren put before the California Legislature, both in 1945 and 1947, a complete compulsory health insurance program. President Truman has recommended a national health program, which includes compulsory health insurance and expanded public health services.

If any legislation in this field is passed by the present Congress, it probably will be some version of the Taft bill. This would be in line with the trend toward more medical care at public expense, which has been very pronounced in this country in recent years. While this is socialized medicine, it is much less opposed by organized medicine than is compulsory health insurance, which at least to some extent, is a substitute for state-financed medical care. Passage of the Taft bill would represent progress toward more adequate medical care for all Americans. A more complete program which seems within possibility of attainment in the not distant future includes both compulsory health insurance and expanded public health services of the types previously mentioned.

The "Bug-a-Boo"
of the Welfare State

Address at the Town Hall of
Los Angeles, July 25, 1949.
Inserted by Senator Wayne
Morse in the *Congressional
Record,* October 19, 1949,
pages 15381–15383

W HEN [I WAS asked] to talk to you on the subject of "The
Bug-a-Boo of the Welfare State," I accepted because I was intrigued
by the "Bug-a-Boo." I believed "bug-a-boo" to be accurately de-
scriptive, not only because people who talk about the "welfare
state" picture it in most alarming terms, but also because I believed
that this term was being misused by many of these alarmists. Examination of as many of these alarmist statements as I have been able
to find, which I have made since then, has convinced me that my
impressions were correct. At least most of those who talk so much
about the welfare state in such alarming terms are using this term
as a propaganda slogan to oppose pending legislative measures. In
doing so they display shocking lack of knowledge of our American
Constitution and of our history and traditions.

I believe in the "welfare state," but only in the meaning in which
"welfare" is used in the Constitution of the United States and in
which our American government has always been a welfare state. I
am opposed as are the alarmists to the sort of welfare state they picture. I regard the American government as the best on earth and our
most precious heritage. I look upon the Constitution as the finest

39

political instrument ever conceived by man. In making this statement, I have in mind, particularly, the remarkable adaptability of the Constitution to changing conditions. This characteristic has enabled the United States to grow from a small, almost exclusively rural and agricultural state to the greatest nation on earth, with predominant industrial strength, without fundamental changes in the basic principles which were incorporated in the Constitution and the first ten Amendments, the Bill of Rights, which were adopted so early that they must be regarded as a part of the original Constitution. It is only through the three Amendments resulting from the Civil War and the adoption of the Twentieth Amendment in 1920 that any major changes were made in the basic principles in which our government was grounded, and these were to extend to all Americans regardless of race or color and to women rights previously enjoyed only by whites and males. Yet with such a paucity of basic changes, our nation, operating under the Constitution, has always been able to alter its laws and institutions in accordance with changing conditions and the needs of the times. It is the kind of a welfare state conceived by the Founding Fathers—one which ever serves the welfare of the people, in accordance with the varying needs of the times, which I staunchly support.

There are concepts of the welfare state which are foreign to American principles, traditions, and ideals. Totalitarian government, whether of the left or the right, is un-American. So is an all-powerful government . . . which dominates the lives of its citizens in all respects. Advocates of foreign ideologies like to describe their systems of government as those of a welfare state, but their welfare state is not the sort of a welfare state grounded in the Constitution and the American traditions which I favor. I am equally opposed to those who denounce the welfare state to foster reaction completely at variance with the American concepts of continuous progress. I recognize that the legislative measures which these politicians seek to defeat by their outcry against the welfare state are debatable and I do not condemn them because they oppose these measures. But I do not want them, in their political endeavors, to play directly into the hands of our foreign enemies, by giving the impression that it is only a socialistic or communistic government which is concerned with the welfare of its citizens.

Such propaganda is not only against the best interests of our country, but is completely false and contrary to concepts of the Founding Fathers and all of American history. These propagandists would make "welfare" a suspect word and talk as if a government which seeks to promote or protect the welfare of its citizens were un-American. But the Founding Fathers in the Preamble to the Constitution of the United States recited as one of the six reasons for the adoption of the Constitution, "to promote the general welfare." In Article I, Section 8, they specifically gave the Congress the power "to lay and collect taxes . . . for the general welfare of the United States," which the Supreme Court has held includes also the power to spend money for this purpose.

The American concept has never been that of a government removed from the people which oppresses them. Rather the American theory of government has always been that expressed by Abraham Lincoln in the closing line of the Gettysburg Address, "a government of the people, by the people, and for the people." It is the concept of a government which is the servant of the people, not their master, which they control, which aids them, and which serves their purposes. Again quoting Lincoln, from his "Fragment on Government," written in 1854, when he first identified himself with the Kansas-Nebraska Movement out of which grew the Republican Party: "The purpose of government is to do for the people what they cannot do for themselves or cannot do so well for themselves."

An examination of what our government has done in the past establishes that from the very outset it was concerned with and sought to promote the economic and social welfare of its citizens. All the powers under which the government now regulates our economy were incorporated in the Constitution adopted in 1789 and soon thereafter were given broad construction by the Supreme Court under John Marshall, a Federalist and a conservative in politics. The first Congress of the United States, on the basis of Alexander Hamilton's famous report on "manufactures"—the first of many instances of economic planning in the history of the United States—adopted a protective tariff for the express purpose of aiding manufactures and promoting the development of industry in the United States. Later Henry Clay championed protection and internal improvements as "the American system," urging most eloquently, with help from Daniel Webster, that governmental aid to industry was in the general public interest.

Tariff duties were repeatedly increased with this objective in mind, and supplemented in many instances by direct subsidies to industry. To supply capital for their development, the railroads were given public lands equal in area to the entire state of Texas. More recently, the government has subsidized the airlines and merchant shipping. Even more important are vast public expenditures for improved highways upon which the development of our great automobile, oil, trucking, and numerous other industries is dependent. Directly beneficial to industry, also, are the rapidly increasing expenditures for research, which, particularly in the atomic energy field, afford hope for putting American industry even much farther ahead of the rest of the world than it is today. When industry in the 1930's faced universal bankruptcy, the government came to its rescue through the Reconstruction Finance Corporation—established while Herbert Hoover was in the White House and with his approval—and through numerous other agencies. Again at the end of World War II, aid was given to industry in effecting reconversion to civilian production, by the refund of wartime taxes where losses resulted during the two years following the war. These are only a few of many instances in which government in the United States has aided either industry generally or particular industries. Numerous instances of such aid continue to this day and have become a definite part of the American way of life.

But it is false, as the critics of our way of life are saying, that government in the United States has been concerned only with the welfare of industry. To the contrary, the American concept that government shall "promote the general welfare" has extended to all citizens, the poor and the weak, no less than the rich and successful. Every American state almost as soon as it was organized wrote into its statutes the obligation that the public must foot the bill for the support and care of those of its numbers who are without other means of support. The national government began its activities in the relief field at least as early as 1798 when Congress established a hospital service for indigent seamen. Early in the nineteenth century, it adopted the policy of disposing of the public domain in such a way as to give aid to the actual cultivators, rather than to land speculators. This culminated, when Lincoln was President and the Republicans for the first time controlled the government, in the enactment of the Homestead Act, under which most of the tillable lands of this country were given free to bona fide settlers. As was noted recently by Nelson Cruikshank and earlier by President Roosevelt, this policy was in effect a social security program suited to the then-prevailing conditions. It enabled the unemployed and the poor of the East to make a new start on the wild lands of the West, which the government made available to them.

Beyond that, when the frontiersman found that there were no schools on the frontier and he lacked the means to pay for private schools, he demanded that his government provide the schools at general expense. It was on the frontier that our free public school system first developed, which, as an educator, I believe, had a lot to do with the great progress which has since been made by American industry. The frontiersman also called on government to provide roads, canals, and later, railroads, because they were needed to enable him to make a living on the land which the government gave him for settlement. Ever jealous, as nearly all Americans have been, to guard their individual rights from encroachment by government, the frontiersman yet expected the government to help him when he needed help with his economic and social problems. And it was a frontiersman, Abraham Lincoln, who most truly expressed the basic American principle regarding how far the government should go in promoting the general welfare—"to do for the people what they cannot do for themselves or cannot do so well for themselves."

I could go on much longer with this recital of what the American government has done in the past in aiding its people with their economic problems, but what I have brought to your attention should suffice to establish that it is thoroughly American for the government to concern itself with the welfare of its citizens. And what it should do at a given time depends upon the conditions and the needs of the time.

But I must come back to the current alarm regarding the welfare state. Nearly all the propaganda along this line seems to arise from opposition to legislative measures now before the Congress of the United States which have been recommended by the President. Specifically these appear to be the proposals against which the propaganda about the welfare state is directed: legislation to abolish the poll tax in the South and to make lynching a federal offense; the Brannan program for a new form of aid to agriculture, which will at the same time benefit many urban dwellers (but not the continuance of the existing program for aid to agriculture); the proposed increase in the minimum rate for workers employed in industries engaged in interstate commerce to 75 cents per hour; federal aid for housing, including a modest program of public housing for veterans; federal aid for education; compulsory health insurance (but not the counter-proposal of Senator Taft and other Republicans for greatly increased federal aid for public medical services); and the Administration program for extension and improvement of the Social Security Act. All these, as I have indicated, are debatable proposals, about which something is to be said on both sides.

In the time remaining, I shall deal only with the last of these measures, in part because it appears to be the one which is most frequently referred to when the alarmists about the welfare state come down to particulars.

I was the executive director of the President's Committee on Economic Security which sponsored the Social Security Act in 1935. That Act was the result of an extensive study by a staff which embraced most of the specialists in this field, including some of the country's ablest actuaries. It also was gone over by an advisory council which had on it some of the leading industrialists of the country, among them Mr. Swope, president of General Electric; Mr. Teagle, president of the Standard Oil Company of New Jersey; Mr. Folsom of Eastman-Kodak; and Mr. Raymond Moley, then one of the closest advisors of the President. The Administration bill, prepared by our Committee, was given extended hearings by the House Ways and Means Committee and the Senate Finance Committee, and was altered quite extensively by these committees. The bill was brought before both Houses under an open rule. It was long debated and numerous amendments were offered and some of them adopted. But when it came to passage, the great majority of both the Democrats and the Republicans voted for it, with only 6 votes against the measure in the Senate and 23 in the House.

The assistance programs included in the Social Security Act became operative early in 1936 when Congress passed the first appropriation for this purpose. The social insurance parts of the program came into operation January 1, 1937. That was after something like a referendum on the Act had been held in the presidential election of 1936, when the Republican National Committee distributed millions of copies of attacks upon the Act, which were put into the last payroll envelopes before the election by thousands of companies, only to have its candidate defeated in the most one-sided contested election we have ever had. Since then no major political party or its candidates have ever attacked any of the basic provisions of the Social Security Act.

In many respects the old-age insurance system has worked remarkably well. It is the world's largest insurance institution, with 80,000,000 living Americans having credits in the system. Before the Act came into operation, it was feared by many that the American workers would resent having to contribute to the costs of their old-age benefits. But the workers never complained nor have they ever objected to increases in contribution rates to provide better benefits. From an efficiency standpoint, also, the old-age insurance system has had an unusually fine record. Today, its costs of administration are only 2.5 per cent of the contributions or 4.5 per cent of the total benefit payments.

But it is far from an adequate system. Since the Social Security Act was passed fourteen years ago, it has been extensively amended only once—in 1939. The amendments then adopted were of a very mixed character. Retirement benefits were increased in the early years of the system and small dependents' and survivors' benefits were added. At the same time, the percentage of all those who would have been entitled to benefits on attainment of age 65 was reduced. Contribution rates were frozen immediately preceding the outbreak of World War II, during which it would have been no hardship upon either employers or employees to have paid the full costs of the system, which has been accumulating large actuarial deficits year after year.

Since 1939, the old-age and survivors' insurance system has not been involved in any major respect and has been definitely weakened in some respects. In the meantime, the real value of the benefits in the contributory old-age and survivors' insurance has been reduced by the increase in prices. On the other hand, noncontributory old-age assistance payments, made under state laws but with federal financial aid, have been greatly increased. Where originally they were less than the benefits in the contributory insurance system—as they should be—these noncontributory old-age assistance payments are now nearly twice as large on the average throughout the country and in California three times as large.

The consequences of the failure of Congress to change the old-age and survivors' insurance system as required by changed conditions have been well nigh tragic. The present law fails to cover two out of every five jobs in this country. Among the people excluded, moreover, are many who need old-age protection most: to mention only a few of the excluded groups—the domestics, the farm workers, the employees of educational, religious and charitable organizations, and all the self-employed. At least equally serious are the tricky eligibility provisions introduced in 1939 to keep down costs, under which close to half of all those who pay contributions can never hope to get benefits. The retirement benefits paid under the Act average only $25 per month and all benefits only $20 per month, in contrast with average old-age assistance payments in May in this state of $71 per month.

Amendments to correct these obvious inadequacies have been repeatedly recommended by the Social Security Administration and the Presidents in their messages to the Congress. In the 80th Congress, the Republican Senate Finance Committee organized the Social Security Advisory Council, many of whose members were leading industrialists who also served on the Social Security Committee of the Chamber of Commerce of the United States. This Social Security Advisory Council in a unanimous report presented to the Congress in April, 1948, urged prompt extension of the coverage of the old-age and survivors' insurance system to include practically the entire adult population of the United States, liberalization of benefits, and an increase in contribution rates. Congress instead narrowed the coverage and otherwise did nothing about the recommendations of the Advisory Council. In the present Congress, the Administration has come forward with a bill for amendment of the federal old-age and survivors' insurance system, which follows very closely the recommendations of the Social Security Advisory Council of the 80th Congress. Extensive hearings were held on this bill by the Ways and Means Committee and it then considered the measure for several weeks in executive sessions. Very recently it has been reported to have reached agreement upon a bill which does not go nearly as far as did the Administration bill or the Social Security Advisory Council.

This bill would extend the coverage of the old-age and survivors' insurance system by somewhere around 8,000,000 people, principally the urban self-employed and the domestics, but still leaving outside the Act the farmers and farm laborers. It would change the benefit provisions to increase the average payments throughout the nation to slightly more than the present average payments in old-age assistance, but this is still a third less than California's present old-age assistance grants. And it proposes to increase the tax rates from the present 1 per cent each on employers and employees to 1.5 per cent, to be further increased to 2 per cent in 1952, to 2.5 per cent in 1960, and 3 per cent in 1965.

It is this prospect of an increase in social security taxes, more than anything else, which has led to the alarms about the welfare state. Combined with the costs of other parts of President Truman's Fair Deal, the increase in social security taxes is represented as being certain to destroy our economy of free enterprise. The entire program, it is claimed, is one under which government responsibility for support is substituted for self-support with results which will be ruinous to thrift, initiative, and enterprise. The final consequence will be the regimentation of everybody by government, with complete loss of individual freedom.

These results are ascribed to a program for a more inclusive and liberal system of old-age insurance, financed by equal contributions of employers and employees. The Social Security Advisory Council of the 80th Congress and the Administration's bill in the present Congress proposed ultimate triparty financing of old-age and survivors' insurance, with the costs equally shared among employers, employees, and the government. The Ways and Means Committee has again rejected all commitments even for ultimate government contributions and is proposing tax rates which it believes will be sufficient for financing the program from employer and employee contributions alone for at least a generation. This is possible only because the Committee's program calls for retirement benfits which will be only slightly better than the present average noncontributory old-age assistance payments—approximately $50 per month to the fully insured, retired workers, with lesser payments to some of their dependents and survivors, with an absolute maximum of $150 per month to any family, regardless of the number of primary beneficiaries or dependents.

The merits of this proposal must be appraised in the light of possible alternatives. A civilized society cannot do what Hitler did, condemn the dependent aged to the gas chambers. As we have done in this country from the beginning of settlement, the public must support the aged dependents and all the rest of the people who have no other means of support.

There are only three possible methods for dealing with this problem of the people who in old age, when they can no longer work, lack means of support, ruling out Hitler's gas chamber and the equally barbarous method of letting them starve. The first of these is a universal pension system in which payments of a flat amount are made to everybody who attains specific age, say 60 or 65, regardless of his financial situation, which are financed from taxes levied upon everyone. The second is old-age assistance, in which payments are made to old people in need and in varying amounts depending upon their needs, again financed from general tax sources. The third is a contributory old-age insurance system, in which the benefits are paid to persons qualifying by reason of the contributions which they have consciously made to the costs of the system and which vary, at least to some degree, with the total or average contributions by the individual prior to retirement. The last two of these possible programs are now in operation in this country: old-age assistance, a state-determined and state-administered program, but with more than half of the financing provided by the national government; and old-age and survivors' insurance, nationally controlled and administered and financed exclusively from payroll taxes on employers and employees. Universal old-age pensions have not been adopted in this or any country, except for veterans.

Of these alternatives, I rule out universal old-age pensions because of their costs and uncontrollability. With 11,000,000 old people now in the United States, even a modest universal pension of $50 per month would cost $6,600,000,000 per year, contrasted with a total of $2,000,000,000 to be raised by employer and employee payroll taxes under the plan for an improved old-age insurance system recommended by the Ways and Means Committee. The number of the aged is increasing nearly 3 per cent per year and the costs of universal pensions will, at the minimum, increase correspondingly. With many millions of people who make no direct contributions to the costs on the rolls as beneficiaries, it is, also, completely unrealistic to assume that universal old-age pensions can be kept down to $50 per month or any similar figure.

Old-age assistance appeals to many people as a potentially less costly method of dealing with the problem of old-age support, because only old people in need are to receive benefits and only in amounts measured by their needs. As experience with old-age assistance has demonstrated, however, these expectations are illusory. "Need" is a flexible concept and already half the old people are qualifying for old-age assistance in some states, with the percentage still increasing. As your Referendum Proposition No. 4 illustrates, the amounts of the old-age assistance payments tend to become uncontrollable, where prospective beneficiaries do not consciously contribute to the costs.

There is some danger also that benefits may be increased unreasonably in a contributory old-age insurance system. But that has not occurred in any country which, unlike the United States, places reliance for the support of the aged dependents principally upon contributory old-age insurance. The fact that prospective beneficiaries know that increased benefits will also require increased contributions serves as a powerful deterrent against unreasonable increases.

A contributory old-age insurance system is not inconsistent with an economy of free enterprise; rather, it is a bulwark to such an economy. A proper system of social security is not a featherbed, but a net to catch those that fall, or rather it is a floor of protection assuring all Americans the minimum income needed for a decent existence in all contingencies of life. Above such a minimum, individual and family responsibility must be retained. For the luxuries and even the conveniences of life, reliance must be placed upon individual savings and insurance and supplemental private pension, health, and welfare plans. Social security, thus conceived, is clearly essential to private enterprise, as it is the only basis on which it can survive.

In presenting this viewpoint, I recognize that the social security movement, like everything else, is fraught with dangers. As John Maurice Clark has observed, there is far less danger of a "police state" in this country than of a "Santa Claus state to which the people in general look for handouts, with no thought of reciprocal obligations." It is precisely because I want a welfare state, in the sense contemplated by the Constitution, and not a Santa Claus state, that I am so strongly urging extension and improvement of our old-age and survivors' insurance. As I see it, unless this is done very promptly, Referendum No. 4 is only the beginning of what we will have to face, and the contributory principle in relation to old-age support will be entirely lost.

But I may be wrong and those who favor universal pensions or exclusive reliance upon old-age assistance and private pension programs may be right. Similarly, there is much to be said against all the other parts of President Truman's Fair Deal program, just as there is a case to be made for each of these proposals.

But I submit, it is regrettable that so many of the opponents have substituted the outcry about the welfare state for solid arguments against the Truman proposals. This outcry is contrary to American concept of a "government of the people, by the people, and for the people," one of whose purposes is "to promote the general welfare." In conveying the impression, at home and abroad, that the American government is not interested in welfare, it undermines the foundation of our democracy, our economy, and our security. Let us continue to debate, as we have always done, what will best promote the general welfare, but let us not play Stalin's game by proclaiming that our government is not interested in the welfare of the common man.

Address to the Panel Session
on Social Security, Tenth
Biennial General Assembly of
States, Chicago, Illinois,
December 7, 1950

SOCIAL SECURITY is an appropriate subject for discussion at this
General Assembly of the States because Public Law 734, enacted by
the Congress late in the summer, will require the attention of all
state legislatures meeting in 1951.

The tragic developments in Korea have made consideration of
social security even more appropriate than it was when this program was planned. In the situation our nation faces, every public
policy, institution, or proposal needs to be tested on the basis of
whether it does or will contribute to the victory of the forces of
freedom in their struggle for survival with the ruthless hordes of
communism.

It is natural that in the present situation a good many people in
their thinking about social security should jump to the conclusion
that the perils we face call for curtailment of all social security programs. This I believe to be an erroneous view. This is the time for
expanding and liberalizing social security programs, particularly
social insurance and services designed to preserve and improve the
health of all our people, and to rehabilitate as many as we can of
those who have become well-nigh useless.

《《《《《《《《《O》》》》》》》

What can be done by way of social security obviously depends upon production. Soundly devised social security systems should operate to increase production. While its objective is the protection of the individual and the family, it also serves the interests of the nation.

In a democracy like ours, the government exists to protect and promote the welfare of the citizen . . . the citizen does not exist for the benefit of the state, as is the creed of our totalitarian enemies. It is our belief that in protecting and promoting the welfare of its citizens, our nation attains maximum strength and stability. Social security is premised upon this fundamental democratic principle. We cannot afford to abandon this principle in this time of national peril. We need to preserve and strengthen social security because it is helpful in enabling us to obtain the maximum national strength.

《《《《《《《《O》》》》》》》

Now is the time for making our old-age and survivors' system truly all-inclusive. It is also the time for increasing contributions to cover the accruing costs, not only of the relatively few benefits we are now paying, but of the much larger number of benefits we have promised to our younger workers. Again, increased contributions would not be burdensome, but would be helpful in checking the inflation now threatening and, in part, already upon us.

As I see it, this is, also, the time for including benefits for permanent and total disability in our system, as all other countries with old-age insurance systems are doing. Further, we should make provisions for genuine dependents' allowances rather than the benefits we now provide to wives in their own rights upon attaining age 65—something radically different and far less desirable than real dependents' allowances.

The case for preserving and strengthening our social assistance programs may be less clear. We do not want to support, by assistance grants, people who could be self-supporting at a time when we need to utilize all available labor. In World War II, aid to dependent children decreased greatly, as did general assistance, because the mothers with children—and also the people on general assistance—

found it possible to get employment. The increase in the old-age assistance rolls was temporarily checked, and many oldsters in receipt of old-age insurance benefits gave them up for the time being to take jobs. This should occur again, and in increased volume. I have no doubt, also, that it will occur again, if the jobs are available, as there is every reason to believe that they will be.

The fact remains, however, that there are many people who cannot support themselves even when jobs are abundant. Young children cannot do so, and in a war which promises to be of long duration and, in part, a battle of nerves, we cannot afford to use up our oncoming manpower prematurely. The old and the disabled also cannot all work, although we can find employment for many people in these groups who are now unemployed. In the unutilized manpower among our older people and those who are handicapped, we have probably the largest source for the needed increase in our labor force. But some people are so badly disabled or handicapped, mentally and physically, that they cannot be employed, at least steadily or full time.

Also, despite all the progress we have made in combating the diseases and disabling conditions of old age, the advanced years are still periods of increased sickness, and ultimate invalidity if people live long enough. People who cannot work still require support. Sometimes, indeed, costs are increased by reason of sickness and invalidity. We cannot abandon people thus afflicted without giving up an essential part of the American way of life for the preservation of which we are fighting. To do so would be to surrender to the ideals and concepts of our enemies, and would operate to sap our strength as a nation, which rests above all else on what the nation does for its citizens, and finds response in their loyalty and willingness to make sacrifices that may be necessary for the maintenance of their freedom and the nation's preservation.

Beyond this we must preserve and improve social security here at home, to give hope to the masses of the oppressed and underprivileged people everywhere, in countries which may be potential allies, as well as in countries under the heel of the Communist dictators. . . .

We cannot survive in a world in which we and the democratic peoples are a minority if we are distrusted. Repeatedly we have declared that our aim is not imperialism but a peaceful world, in which all peoples can live and improve their standards of living. Woodrow

Wilson's "Fourteen Points" in World War I and the "Four Freedoms" of the Atlantic Charter in World War II not only truly reflected the peace-loving objectives of this country, but served to gain
us the support we needed to bring these wars to a victorious conclusion, probably earlier than we would have been able to do otherwise.

Among the Four Freedoms of the Atlantic Charter, "freedom from
want" and "social security for all peoples" are cardinal principles.
We cannot expect people anywhere to believe that we are seeking
merely peace and freedom—as, indeed, we are—if we do not carry
out at home what we profess abroad.

I do not argue for assistance grants or other social security provisions which will maintain in idleness people who should be working, or operate to discourage savings, which we also urgently need
at this time. Chiselers and loafers should be eliminated at this time
from the assistance rolls. And it is complete nonsense now, as ever,
that we can create real wealth by revolving pensions or similar
schemes for large governmental spending.

There is need, however, for sane, well-administered social assistance programs in times of war, no less than at other times. There
are still millions of people in need, for whom the government must
provide the minimum required for a decent existence, if they cannot
get it otherwise. Because the cost of living has been rising and seems
certain to increase further, under the impetus of full employment
and immense military expenditures, assistance grants and also social
insurance payments will have to be increased in terms of the cash
money payments. The greater the inflation, the greater the necessary
increase in money payments to maintain something like the same
real income.

Important as are the maintenance of social assistance programs
and the improvement of our social insurance institutions (and I
have particularly in mind the federal old-age and survivors' system,
which is least liberal of all social security programs) the most urgent
need along social security lines in a time like the present, I believe,
is the extension of social services of a remedial, restorative, and preventive character.

The sort of services to which I have reference are such services
as vocational rehabilitation, training programs, the most efficient
possible public employment service, crippled children's services,

maternal and child health services, child welfare services, nursery schools, school lunches, and many types of public health services. Services of these types are especially important because they help to increase our effective labor supply and its efficiency.

As Governor Stevenson emphasized in his recent address here in Chicago to the American Public Welfare Association, particular attention needs to be given to rehabilitating those who, in their present condition, are of little use to themselves or society. We need to preserve our population in the best state of health we can, and to train people for the jobs that have to be done, and for which they are not trained.

It goes without saying that we need a stronger employment service, at a time when manpower shortages seem certain to develop on a large scale. In this connection, I remind you that in the present situation the states have been left in control of the public employment offices, unlike the situation that prevailed in World War II.

Services of the types I have mentioned have been growing apace, much more rapidly than either social insurance or social assistance. On the various types of public health services we are expending more today than on all social assistance programs. Services of a restorative, remedial, and preventive character should not be curtailed however much we may have to spend for military purposes. Rather, we need to expand such services, as we appear to be in for a long struggle with the Communist oppressors.

In advocating the maintenance—and, in some instances, the improvement—of our social security institutions as being vitally necessary and very valuable in the present time of great peril, I do not overlook the importance of nongovernmental agencies and efforts. Existing social agencies, employers, and labor organizations all need to contribute their part to the attainment of the objectives I have discussed. Private citizens, too, will have to help, both financially and through personal services, more than ever. But in a time like the present, the government cannot shirk its responsibility without disastrous consequences. The governments closest to the people—those that administer all of these programs other than old-age and survivors' insurance—are the state governments and their political subdivisions. They, hence, have very great responsibilities in this respect.

I now come to the Social Security Act Amendments of 1950. I

shall discuss these amendments only briefly, because other members of the panel are more acquainted with the details than I am.

The most important changes made by this law are perhaps those affecting the federal old-age and survivors' insurance system. While this is a program exclusively controlled and administered by the national government, the changes made are of interest to the states. This is true because these amendments should operate to lighten the burden of old-age assistance—to some extent immediately and still more in the future. They have also made it possible for the states, or at least many of them, to bring some of their own employees or those of their local governments under the protection of the old-age and survivor's insurance system.

The most important changes from the prior old-age insurance law which should benefit the states through reduction in old-age assistance rolls and costs are those relating to coverage, eligibility for benefits, amount of benefits, and financing.

I will not discuss the details of the extension of coverage. The most important extension lies in making the law applicable to the urban self-employed, with the exception of those in certain professions, who saw fit to get themselves excluded. There is further extension in the inclusion of a considerable number of domestic workers and a small number of agricultural workers, although the amendment to include certain agricultural workers is so worded that commercialized agriculture, again, escapes pretty much all responsibility for contributions, while the small farmers who employ even one person regularly are covered. Coverage may, also, at the option of the employers, be extended to the employees of religious, charitable and educational institutions. Similarly, states may bring under the Act such state and local government employees for whom no other retirement provision has been made.

More important as a potential source of savings to the states are the changes in eligibility for benefits. Until now we have had a system in which more than eighty million living Americans have paid taxes, but certainly less than half that number have had any prospect of ever getting benefits. Thanks to the ingenious device of a new starting date, that situation has now been greatly improved. Many more people who pay old-age and survivors' insurance taxes will hereafter also be able to get benefits. The benefit provisions still are not completely satisfactory to my thinking, but we have made considerable progress. The new law increases the amount of the benefits, from an average primary benefit—the retirement benefit—to a man retiring at age 65 or later of $26 a month to $46 a month. Even $46 per month will not provide a life of luxury and ease, but it comes closer to providing the minimum old-age and survivors' insurance protection which we need for all our people.

Regarding the financing, even under the new law we will not immediately be financing the costs of old-age and survivors' insurance currently. We will continue to operate, in large part, on the method of financing misnamed "pay as you go," which really means "pay no attention to your liabilities." We are not meeting our accruing costs. But Congress has made provision in the Social Security Act Amendments of 1950 for the levy, at specified future dates, of rates which will be sufficient to meet all costs of the system, without government contributions.

Provisions making it possible for some states to bring a part of their employees and those of their political subdivisions under the protection of old-age and survivors' insurance systems are very restrictive, illogical, and not at all to my liking. But they have value to at least some states, and, I believe, should be taken advantage of in the coming sessions of the legislatures to the fullest extent possible.

[States and political subdivisions] cannot include any person covered by any [state or local] retirement system that already is in force. Private employers may have all their employees covered, although they may also have their own pension systems. Since public employees are excluded from the protection of the law when their employers have brought them under a retirement system, this is a discrimination against public employees, and against the states and local governments, which is completely illogcal and unnecessary.

《《《《《《《《O》》》》》》》

However, the new law at least makes a beginning in the coverage of state and local government employees, who have heretofore been completely excluded.

Other changes of major importance to the states which are made in the Social Security Act Amendments of 1950 concern increases in the federal aid for the three types of social services for which aid has heretofore been given. The authorized appropriation for federal aid to the states for maternal and child health services is increased from $11,000,000 per year to $15,000,000 this year and $16,500,000 next year and thereafter; the aid for crippled children's services is increased from $7,500,000 to $12,000,000 this year, and $15,000,000 thereafter; that for child welfare services from $3,500,000 to $10,-000,000 per year. In the last-mentioned type of aid there is also an important change in the basis of distribution: federal aid is now to be distributed not on the old basis of rural population in a given state as compared with the total rural population, but on the basis of number of rural children under 18 years of age. This benefits particularly the states with high birth rates, which also tend to be the states with low per capita income.

In the social assistance field, an entirely new form of federal aid is provided for the first time . . . . This is aid to the permanently and totally disabled. Laws for this special type of assistance have heretofore been in effect in only two states. Federal aid in a total amount of $50,000,000 per year is now authorized. To get this aid some states will have to pass new legislation. In some states the general assistance legislation now in effect may enable individuals to take advantage of this new federal aid, without any change in laws.

Because of time limitations, I will leave entirely to others the discussion of the details of the changes in the three assistance programs for which aid has heretofore been given by the federal government— old-age assistance, aid to the dependent children, and aid to the blind. These, too, afford opportunities for improvement in your programs, without additional state appropriations, and perhaps for some savings.

The changes made by the Congress in the Social Security Act Amendments of 1950 will have the immediate effect of somewhat reducing their assistance rolls. Reductions in numbers on the rolls will to some degree be offset by the necessity of increasing the grants because of the rising costs of living. With the rapidly changing costs of living and the prospects of much greater rises ere long, it is probable that grants will have to be increased . . . to keep body and soul together for the people on the assistance rolls who cannot work or help themselves.

The changes made in the old-age insurance system doubtless will make it possible to take some people off old-age assistance immediately. In future years this contributory system—particularly if it is further improved, as it should be—will have a much more pronounced effect in reducing the costs of old-age assistance. The main opportunity that this legislation affords, however, is to do a better job, . . . to make freedom in this country more meaningful than it has been for many of the less privileged of our fellow citizens, and to make more vivid to the peoples of other lands, whose friendship we must win, that our freedom includes, in concrete terms, minimum necessary security for all people in all the hazards of life. In this, I feel sure, the States will not fail.

A World View
of Social Security

Excerpts from a lecture at
a convocation at the
American University of
Beirut, in the Lebanese
Republic, March 4, 1954

I HAVE BEEN ASKED to talk to you on "social security"—a term of considerable popularity throughout the world in this day and age. "Freedom from want and social security" for all peoples was one of the Four Freedoms set forth in the Atlantic Charter of World War II as the major objectives of the two most powerful Western Allies, the United States and Great Britain. The same thought was expressed in Article 25 of the Universal Declaration of Human Rights adopted and proclaimed by the United Nations in 1948.

《《《《《《《《《〇》》》》》》》》

In the Draft Covenant on Economic, Social, and Cultural Rights, promulgated by the United Nations in 1952, when Dr. Charles Malik of Lebanon was the Chairman of its Human Rights Commission, Article 8 provides: "The States Parties to the Covenant recognize the right of everyone to social security."

Every nation now has at least some social security institutions. Yet only one tenth of all the people of the world are actually covered by these institutions. In many nations, expenditures for social security hold first place among all governmental expenditures for civilian purposes. In several Western European countries more than 10 per cent of the national income is devoted to social security. While begun earlier, the greatest progress in social security has been made since World War II. No nation other than the Soviet Union ever abandoned any program for social security it has once adopted—the Soviet Union has the unenviable distinction of having abandoned unemployment insurance in the late 1920's on the special plea that it no longer had any unemployment. Today, at least in all free countries, the demand is for better and broader social security.

Meaning and Objectives of Social Security

Despite its great popularity in all countries, the term "social security" has no universally accepted definition. It is a term which originated in the United States and came into general use in our country only after the enactment of the Social Security Act of 1935. It was first used by the International Labour Office in 1941 in a report by the late Dr. Emanuel Stein on *Approaches to Social Security*. It is now used widely in all countries, with somewhat the same meaning everywhere. But ... it is a developing concept whose specific meaning changes as conditions and institutions change.

The general meaning of the term is pretty well indicated in the Article on the subject from the Declaration of Human Rights of the United Nations in 1948. This Article speaks of "the right to security in the event of unemployment, sickness, disability, widowhood, old age or other lack of livelihood in circumstances beyond his (the individual's) control," also of "a standard of living adequate for the health and well-being of himself and his family, including food, clothing, housing, medical care, and necessary social services." Social security is concerned with a minimum income adequate for a decent living for the individual and his family on the occurrence of the great personal contingencies of life, the most important of which are those enumerated in the Declaration of Human Rights, "unemployment, sickness, disability, widowhood, and old age." Implicit is the assumption that it is the duty of the government of a nation to see to it that all its people have a minimum income adequate for a decent living in all circumstances beyond their control.

《《《《《《《《〇》》》》》》》》

What is required for an adequate standard of living varies with the place and time. In the language of the Declaration of Human Rights, the standard of living to be provided through social security should be "adequate" with respect to "food, clothing, housing, medical care, and necessary social services." In its recommendations on social security of 1952 the International Labour Organisation, however, has recognized that for many countries of low incomes this standard of adequacy can be attained only gradually. In the poorest countries, nothing more may be possible than a bare subsistence standard—enough to keep body and soul together. As national income increases, the standard of living which it is deemed that all people must have, will also increase. In the wealthiest countries even higher standards of social security are possible and essential. In a progressive and reasonably prosperous society, the standard of living of all inhabitants should ever be improving. The benefits of prosperity and progress should be shared by the poor and unfortunate, as well as the rich and the fortunate. But the benefits provided through social security should never be as high as the income which workers can earn by working.

Limitations of Social Security

Social security, as thus conceived, clearly is not an all-sufficient objective. Its major purpose is not the creation of wealth. It is directly concerned not with the production of income, but with its distribution. What a nation can do by way of social security, in a very real sense, depends upon its national income.

This fact has been recognized by every authority on social security. Lord Beveridge of England, the world's greatest authority on social security, named as the four horsemen leading to economic ruin: disease, idleness, want, and ignorance. Social security is directly concerned with only one of these, want, and is by no means a complete protection against even this one horseman of the apocalypse of the modern economic world. Similarly, Article 8 of the Draft Covenant on Economic, Social, and Cultural Rights is only one of eight articles dealing with the economic rights which the contracting nations agree to take steps to establish "individually and through international coöperation, to the maximum of available resources." Enumerated with the right of everyone to social security, are these rights: the right to work, to just and favorable conditions of work, to adequate food, clothing, and housing, to an adequate standard of living and the continuous improvement of living conditions, to the attainment of the highest attainable standard of health, and special [protective] measures for maternity, . . . children, and the family. Beyond these are intellectual, religious, cultural, civil, and political rights, which . . . are of even greater importance to individual and social welfare than is economic security.

It is important to have ever in mind that for true economic security all the rights and conditions which have been enumerated are essential. There must be a high level of employment and production and high standards of living and of health. Without all of these, social security cannot be even reasonably adequate.

It needs to be noted also, however, that the United Nations and the International Labour Organisation recognize that a truly satisfactory social security system cannot be attained through a single legislative enactment. Before World War II, all conventions and resolutions of the International Labour Organisation relating to aspects of social security—of which there were no less than 42— called for the same standards for all countries of the world. This was also a characteristic of the great forward-looking social security program promulgated by the Philadelphia Conference of 1944, at which the International Labour Organisation was reorganized. Following this occurred the greatest expansion of social security legislation to new countries in all history. Many of the less industrialized countries adopted social security legislation ranking in excellence, on paper, with the laws of the most advanced countries, only to find it completely impossible to put their legislation into practical operation.

In the social security recommendations adopted by the International Labor Organisation in 1952, after several years' consideration, it was recognized that it is necessary to take account of the stage of economic development reached by a given nation in planning for social security legislation. In these 1952 recommendations, two different sets of standards are presented. One of these is designated "Minimum Standards," which are recommended for less industrialized countries, the other "Advanced Standards" for the industrially more advanced countries. The 1952 social security recommendations also recognize that many countries will not be able immediately to put into operation even the minimum standards in all branches of social security. In the language of Article 1 of the Draft Convention on Economic, Social, and Cultural Rights, each covenanting nation is merely asked to take measures "individually and through international coöperation, to the maximum of its available resources, with a view to achieving progressively the full realization of the rights recognized in this Covenant by legislative as well as other means."

Even in the industrially advanced United States, President Roosevelt in his recommendations in 1939 to the Congress for broadening and improving the Social Security Act said: "We will make the greatest progress if we regard social security not as a finished project but as an objective to which we are committed and toward which we should progress." In every country, social security has been an historical and piecemeal development. Lord Beveridge has expressed the same idea in his statement that what is suitable for a given nation at a given time depends upon many factors peculiar to that nation, including its history, its institutions, its national income, and prevailing economic conditions.

Value of Social Security

Recognizing these limitations upon what can be accomplished through social security, the fact remains that social security is very much needed in our present-day society and in all civilized countries. This need exists because "unemployment, sickness, disability, widowhood, old age or other lack of livelihood in circumstances beyond his (the individual's) control" are very common and most serious hazards everywhere, even in the most progressive societies. Some of these hazards, indeed, are somewhat less serious in industrially advanced countries—for example, sickness and unemployment. Some of these hazards actually increase with industrialization. A larger percentage of all people will be exposed to the economic hazards of old age in countries with high per capita incomes and low death rates than in underdeveloped areas. Similarly, industrialization and mechanized agriculture almost inevitably result in an increase in industrial accidents. While the incidence of the several personal hazards of life differs, there is need for social security institutions in all countries. But what institutions should be established first or at a given time will vary with conditions and circumstances.

The economic consequences of the personal hazards of life everywhere present are poverty, want, and dependency for a larger or smaller percentage of the people in all nations, also disease and suffering, and, in extreme cases, death itself. No progressive, civilized society can tolerate such conditions without doing something about them. Every religion worthy of being called a religion—I almost said, except communism—has stressed the sanctity of the individual human being and has made his welfare a prime concern. While stressing the life hereafter, at least most religions have concerned themselves also with human welfare "in this vale of tears."

At an earlier date, the prevention of the extremes of suffering resulting from the personal hazards of life was in most countries a function of religion, rather than of the employer or the government. Religious organizations and places of worship still carry a part of this responsibility; through legislation, most modern nations have also placed some of this responsibility on the employer. At all times, individual private charity has been practical, and in western nations there are now many private charitable organizations. Overshadowing all other agencies in this domain in modern times, however, is the government.

With the secularization of government has come the shift in the major responsibility for the support of the poor, the needy, and the infirm from religion to the government. This has occurred most completely in democratic countries. A government "of the people, by the people, and for the people" must concern itself with the welfare of all the people. Democratic governments, in the language of the Preamble to the Draft Covenant on Human Rights, must safeguard "the equal and inalienable rights of all members of the human family . . . without distinction of any kind, such as race, color, sex, language, religion, political or other opinion, national or other social origin, property, birth, or other status."

No material need is greater or right more basic than that of social security—a minimum income adequate for individual and family support even on the occurrence of contingencies beyond the control of the individual. Not only is such a minimum adequate income an absolute necessity for the survival of the individual and his family, but it is also an essential for the continuance of government and, in a sense, of society itself. People in the present day and age do not starve peaceably. Lack of at least minimum income necessary for an acceptable standard of living breeds riots, wars, and revolutions and is a fertile field for absolutism and communism. Social security is not all that is needed for economic, social, and political security, but is one important element for security in all these respects. It is oriented toward the welfare of the individual and his family, but is also very necessary to a sound foundation for national welfare and for world peace and freedom.

Types of Social Security

In a new country, such as is the Lebanese Republic, modern forms of social security, inevitably, are of recent origin and are still only partially developed. The objectives of social security, however, are age-old. In western European countries and also in the United States, moreover, some of the present-day social security institutions had their beginnings long ago.

In the important study of the International Labour Office, *Approaches to Social Security,* already referred to, two major types of social security institutions are distinguished. Both have the same objective, but differ in their history and methods. One of these is public (or social) assistance; the other, social insurance.

Public assistance is the older of these two. It is a term applied to a group of institutions operated and financed by governments for the relief of people in extreme economic distress. It takes the form of payments, in cash or in kind, made to people in dire need. It is usually financed from general tax funds, without contributions by the direct beneficiaries or prospective beneficiaries. No one is eligible for public assistance who is not in need and generally the benefits vary with the extent of the need.

《《《《《《《《《O》》》》》》》

Social insurance has developed in a considerable variety of forms. Of these most widely prevalent, as far as the number of countries in which it exists is concerned, is industrial accident insurance, or workmen's compensation as it is known in the United States. This institution provides social security protection against the hazard of industrial accidents and occupational diseases. Under it two types of benefits are provided to the injured workers: necessary medical, surgical, and related care and cash compensation to cover part of the wage loss. The financing in nearly all countries comes exclusively from the employers, but the institution is established by the government and the right to benefits in individual cases is determined by governmental authority.

To be found in a somewhat smaller number of countries but applying to even more people is health insurance. This was literally the first type of social insurance established on a national basis in any country. The first national social insurance law was the health insurance act of Germany in 1881. Today health insurance exists on a compulsory basis in all European countries, and also in many non-European countries, excluding the United States and Canada. Voluntary health insurance has spread widely in the United States, often being provided at the initiative of the employers or under agreements between employers and unions. But legally established health insurance, while long proposed in my country, has never been adopted. But all other major countries either now have compulsory health insurance or are contemplating its early adoption.

Health insurance, like other forms of social insurance, at first applied only to employed workers. In many countries it has now been extended not only to the dependents of the workers but also to many other groups in the population and in some countries it has become truly nationwide. In most countries it provides two types of benefits: medical and related care in kind and cash compensation covering a part of the wage loss. In Great Britain since 1948, social insurance includes only this last feature—cash compensation for part of the wage loss resulting from sickness, while medical care is provided for the entire population as a public service from general tax funds.

Covering even more people than health insurance is old-age, invalidity, and survivors' insurance. This is the largest social insurance institution in the United States, although in our country we do not as yet provide benefits for the contingency of invalidity, as is usual in European systems. Old-age, invalidity, and survivors' insurance is everywhere operated on insurance principles, with regular advance contributions from employers and employees, and generally also, but not in the United States, from the government. It provides benefits to old people on their retirement from their usual employment and also to the dependent survivors of insured workers in the event of their death. Where invalidity insurance is included in the system, benefits are also provided for persons who become permanently and totally incapacitated before attaining old age. Old-age, survivors, and invalidity insurance is of increasing importance nearly everywhere, because of the growing numbers and percentages of old people. Old age is a long period of life and a period in which income from earnings is reduced or ceases altogether. Of all forms of social insurance, it is probably the most expensive, but is clearly necessary for a complete program of social insurance. In many countries, however, it clearly should not be the first social insurance program attempted.

The fourth major social insurance program is unemployment insurance. This form of social insurance is very important in the United States, Great Britain, and other highly industrialized countries. It is difficult and very costly, however, in nations which suffer from underemployment even more than from unemployment. It is not at all applicable to self-employed people and presents peculiar, although not insurmountable, difficulties in its application to agricultural workers. So, while in the United States unemployment insurance is regarded by many people as the most necessary part of social security, it is not recommended for immediate adoption in the less fortunate nations of the world, particularly in countries which are mainly agricultural and badly overpopulated.

Other Social Security Institutions

The other forms of social insurance now in existence are really parts of the four main institutions that have been discussed. They include maternity insurance, disability insurance, cash sickness compensation, dismissal wages, and still others. Note should also be taken of another institution that has had great growth in recent years and generally is classified as social security, although it is neither social insurance nor public assistance. This is the institution known as family allowances and in Great Britain as children's allowances. This institution has not developed in the United States but exists in nearly all European countries, in most Latin-American countries, in our neighbor Canada, and in some other non-European nations, including Lebanon. Lord Beveridge has said that children's allowances are the foundation for a satisfactory system of social security. A governmental guarantee of minimum support for all children is socially very important, because children hold the future of the society and in all countries many of the children are born in the homes of the poor. Because there are so many children, a family allowance system is necessarily very expensive; moreover, the direct beneficiaries, the children, cannot pay the costs and the parents often are too poor to make substantial contributions. So the costs of family allowances, necessarily, must be borne either by the employers or by the government from general taxes, with the latter being by far the most common source of financing. Wherever family allowances financed by the government exist, they are a large item in total governmental expenditures and, hence, are not too well suited to the poorer nations of the world.

Finally, there are many direct governmental services to the victims of the personal hazards of life, which are classifiable either as social security institutions or as being closely related to social security. Among such services we have in the United States many types of veterans' services, civilian vocational rehabilitation, maternal and child health services, crippled children's services, child welfare services, and many forms of public health services. Other countries have still other services of the same general character. They are essentially preventive of disaster or curative for the victims of disaster. Invariably, they are financed from general tax funds, without contributions from the beneficiaries. Benefits may be extended only on a needs basis, but more commonly are rendered independent of any showing of economic distress.

Of these services, the most important and costly are public health services. These have grown apace in nearly all countries. In Great Britain, as has been noted, they have developed to the point where the government now provides medical and related care at public expense to practically the entire population. Developments in this direction have not gone as far in other European countries except in the countries controlled by the Soviet Union, in which there are public health services for all nationals, but the financing is from contributory social security, not from general tax funds. But public medical care is also developed very extensively in the Scandinavian countries and in Latin America. It bulks large even in the United States, despite the strong opposition of our medical profession to "socialized medicine." More is spent for public medical care in the United States today than for all types of public assistance combined and half as much as for all forms of social insurance. There is some warrant for believing that more extensive public medical care services are an alternative to compulsory health insurance. Countries that do not want the latter are developing a vast amount of public medical care for many groups in the population, provided at the expense of the general taxpayers.

Concluding Observations

.... The greatest spread of social security followed World War II. Many countries not far industrialized enacted quite comprehensive social security laws. There was implicit confidence on the part of many people in these nations that want would disappear once comprehensive social security laws were placed on the statute books.

Much of the enthusiasm for social security has disappeared in at least some of the countries which were ill-prepared for the legislation they adopted. Some social security laws have remained dead-letter legislation. Elsewhere it has been realized that social security alone will not abolish want.

But despite such disappointments, the demand for social security continues very strong among the common people of all nations. This is a result of the great need for assurance of a minimum income adequate for support in all contingencies of life for all people. No modern nation can long fail to do something to satisfy this demand.

Fortunately, there is now a realization that complete economic security cannot be attained overnight; many things are needed for economic security besides social security, above all increased production and a just and an equitable distribution of national production. Social security itself must be established on a piecemeal basis and needs to take account of the entire environment in a given country in which it is instituted.

Clearly, it is sound to proceed first with those forms of social security which fit in best with the needs and conditions in the given country. In this connection it is highly desirable, particularly in countries with presently low per capita incomes, that preference be given to measures of social security which will tend to increase production. It is for this reason that many countries are giving high preference to the improvement of the health of the population and to measures for the benefit of children. In all forms of social security it is possible to include provisions which will tend to increase rather than retard production. This is clearly an essential in sound planning for social security.

The Changing Role of
Labor, Management, and
Government in the Quest
for Security

Excerpt from address at the
Conference on the Quest for
Security—1955 Version,
November 16, 1955, published
by the Institute of Industrial
Relations, Wayne State
University, Detroit, Michigan

ONE MAJOR 1955 development affecting unemployment compensation was the appearance of supplemental unemployment insurance in the Ford–UAW contract early in June and its spread since then with modifications to other companies employing, together with Ford Motor, more than 1,000,000 workers. At this stage most of these companies are accumulating reserves—most of them at the rate of 5 cents per hour per worker employed. Supplemental unemployment compensation benefits are not payable for approximately another year.

There is still uncertainty as to how many of these plans will actually come into full effect. This is because nearly all include provisions making effectiveness conditional upon the states being willing to pay the regular unemployment compensation, regardless of any payments of supplemental unemployment insurance to a stated percentage—most commonly 65 per cent. This turns upon whether supplemental unemployment insurance is compensation for work to an unemployed worker receiving such a payment. Six states—Michigan, New York, Massachusetts, Connecticut, Delaware, and most recently New Jersey—have held that supplemental unemployment insurance is not a wage payment for work performed. A proposal to amend the Ohio law to spell out that supplementary unemployment insurance is not a wage payment—which was initiated before any of the recent labor-management agreements were concluded and which, also, included material increases in state unemployment compensation benefits—was rejected by a thumping 5 to 3 majority in a referendum vote in the elections of last week.

At this moment, the National Association of Manufacturers and some other business organizations are exerting all the pressure they can to get state authorities to hold supplemental unemployment compensation to be a wage payment. They are threatening court tests in states where the administrative rulings have gone against them.

There is every evidence that the companies which have entered into the supplemental unemployment compensation agreements in good faith want them to go into effect. But with major business organizations fighting stubbornly both improvements in state unemployment insurance and supplemental unemployment compensation, there is grave danger that industry will be charged with double dealing. What the final outcome will be is still not entirely certain, but this can be stated very positively: should the NAM succeed in blocking the supplementary unemployment compensation agreements from going into effect—which I do not expect—increased industrial unrest and serious political repercussions in an election year lie ahead.

The growth of private institutions for collective economic security has, indeed, been phenomenal. By the close of 1954, 26,573 pension and profit-sharing funds had been approved for tax deduction purposes by the Internal Revenue Service. In 1951, the total income tax deductions for contributions to such industrial pension funds exceeded $2.3 billion. Since then the number of approved plans has increased more than 50 per cent. Business sources "conservatively" estimate that at least $3 billion per year is being contributed by employers under industrial pension plans at the present time; and other estimates put this figure as high as $3.5 billion. Either figure is considerably greater than the total of the employers' payments under the national OASI program.

Around 13,000,000 persons are employed by companies with industrial pension or profit-sharing plans for retirement. Only an unknown percentage of these 13,000,000 employees have any real prospects of ever getting retirement benefits under these plans, as the majority require present and long prior service with the employer at the time of attainment of the retirement age. Relatively few vest accrued benefits in the employee when he leaves the employment.

An estimated maximum of 750,000 persons now are receiving benefits under industrial pension plans, contrasted with more than 7,500,000 beneficiaries in the OASI system. Because a majority of the industrial pension plans are only a few years old, the number of beneficiaries under these plans will increase rapidly. Unless vesting provisions become practically universal, however, it remains probable that the majority of all workers now covered by the private plans will never get benefits.

There are also other respects in which the rapid growth of industrial pension plans is likely to produce serious problems for industry. As has been noted, employers are now expending for industrial pensions more than the total of their contributions to OASI. These expenditures are certain to increase in the years ahead. This is primarily because most of the people who get on the pension rolls in any year remain on them for many years to come, so that costs under all types of retirement systems increase cumulatively for 35 years or more. Plus this the work force is aging and there is certain to be continued pressure for upping pensions. Many employers—I am glad to note, not the largest employing corporation, General Motors—are financing their industrial pension programs on what is incorrectly referred to as "a pay-as-you-go" plan, but which is really "hand-to-mouth" financing, taking no account of accruing liabilities. Under such financing it is certain that the impression of many employers that industrial pensions cost less than they feared will be rudely reversed ere long. Should some of the plans later have to be abandoned, the repercussions are likely to prove very serious for our system of free enterprise.

Health and welfare plans established either unilaterally by employers or under collective bargaining agreements are at least as common as industrial pension plans and probably include as many employees and dependents. More frequently than industrial pension systems, they are jointly financed and their cost to employers is considerably less. As sickness is a hazard from which the costs do not inevitably increase from year to year, the problems of financing are less serious than in industrial pensions. But other difficulties have arisen.

One of these is corruption in the administration of union health and welfare plans, kickbacks from insurance agents, downright theft of funds by administrators, and racketeering of many types. So far, practically the entire blame has fallen on union officials, most commonly of local unions. Although until now principally union-managed funds have been investigated, there is abundant evidence that the guilty persons are not all union men. Insurance agents and even some insurance companies have bribed fund administrators and trustees. Frauds have been disclosed not only in the administration of union funds, but also in the handling of some joint employer-union funds, where the employer trustees failed completely to discharge their responsibilities. The Senate subcommittee investigating these frauds has announced that it now wants to take a further look at joint health and welfare funds and at exclusively employer-controlled funds. Quite possibly the full story of the abuses in health and welfare plans has not yet come to light, although when the complete picture has been revealed, I am satisfied that, whatever else may be their weaknesses, most of these plans will be found to have been honestly managed.

The stated purpose of all the investigations is to determine what legislation is needed not only to insure honest management but the fulfillment of the objectives for which health and welfare plans were established. That the existing legislation is very weak is clear. Health and welfare funds are in essence insurance funds; however, they are subject to but few of the controls long applied in all other forms of insurance. I do not look for much legislation on the subject next year, but it seems to me a safe guess that further controls will be imposed ere long, through state or federal action and possibly both. How rigid government controls will become is likely to depend upon whether employer trustees and top union officials can be made to recognize their responsibilities and the dangers which mismanaged or inadequate funds constitute for both industry and labor.

Brief mention is warranted at this point of the slow progress in the last few years with what has come to be known in this country as "disability insurance," but what is most aptly described by its earlier designation, "cash sickness compensation"—provision for protection against wage loss by reason of sickness. In the early years after World

War II, income-loss insurance grew rapidly, along with other forms of voluntary health insurance. Four states, and the national government, for railroad employees, enacted laws making it compulsory for employers to provide cash sickness compensation for their employees. No state has enacted such a law since 1949. Today fewer people have loss-of-income insurance under individual insurance policies than in 1947. Group insurance has continued to grow, but only one-half or less of all American workers have protection for any part of the wage loss resulting from sickness. Nearly 40 per cent of all those who have such protection are in the three states of California, New Jersey, and New York, all of which have compulsory disability insurance laws.

Significant progress is still being made in other forms of voluntary health insurance; but voluntary health insurance is encountering many problems. One of these is the great and continuing increase in medical care costs. Hospital care bills per day have increased more than fourfold in ten years; other forms of medical care costs have increased less but still considerably more than the total cost of living. This increase in costs has necessitated frequent and very considerable raises in the rates charged by the Blue Cross plans, which have service-type contracts. In consequence, Blue Cross is growing much more slowly than hospital insurance written by commercial insurance companies on the basis of stated cash payments. There is no necessity for increasing rates under contracts guaranteeing only payments of stated amounts of money, but as medical care charges increase, the insurance covers only an ever-decreasing part of the bills of the insured.

Another great problem in voluntary health insurance is its failure to cover a large percentage of the Americans who most need insurance protection. Even the most prevalent form of voluntary health insurance, hospital insurance, covers only 60 per cent of our population. The noncovered 40 per cent are the people who need protection most. These are the retired workers, the old people generally, the people with low or no incomes, the farm population, and so on. Our country is committed to voluntary action, in preference to compulsion. But the faith we have in voluntary health insurance is apt to be badly shaken before long unless its coverage and protection are greatly improved. What seems most likely is continued expansion of tax-supported medical care, which has been developing most rapidly in the United States in recent years.

At this point in my address it is appropriate to come to the broader implications of the recent developments. These center around the place of the individual, labor, industry, and government in providing economic protection against the many personal hazards of life.

With all the increase in government, industry, and labor and management programs, it is a fundamental part of the American way of life that primary responsibility in preparations for meeting the economic consequences of the many great personal hazards of life rests upon the individual and his family. Social security and private institutions for economic security have not rendered unnecessary or valueless individual initiative, enterprise, and thrift. This is clearly demonstrated by the fact that the number and percentage of Americans working, their production, and their savings have all greatly increased since social security has become popular and governmental and private economic security institutions have multiplied. Social security not only is consistent with free enterprise, but is a bulwark for its continuance.

What should be labor's role may be debatable, but what that role actually is bound to be seems to me quite clear. It was an absurd proposal for some people to suggest that, if workers want more unemployment insurance, the unions should pay for supplemental insurance from their union dues. Not only was this like expecting the workers to pay their own wages, but it implied that unions are very different organizations than they really are or can be. Unions on many occasions have tried to provide security services for their members at their expense, but with indifferent success. At this time, union health services are increasing and seem to be fairly successful, but limited. Some further developments along that line may be expected. But the principal function of the unions in the economic security field is to prod government and management to provide more and improved economic security programs.

On what should be expected from industry, two widely differing views have strong support. At the one extreme are a good many informed and thoughtful observers who see in the development of industrial security programs a lot of trouble in the future for industry, labor, and the nation. Among these is numbered the academic economist with the greatest repute with industry, my very good friend, Sumner H. Slichter of Harvard. Slichter is not worried about supplemental unemployment insurance, except that he holds that the increase of benefits under the state unemployment insurance laws would help much larger numbers of workers. He expects a lot of trouble for employers under the industrial pension plans—greatly increased costs and a serious threat to good relations between employers and workers in the years to come. He staunchly supports the view that instead of expanding the private economic security institutions, the governmental programs should be strengthened.

At the other extreme are many industrialists who believe that the government should be kept out of the picture as much as possible, who want no new governmental programs and little, if any, extension or liberalization of the existing systems. Their creed is that private industry can do everything, including making provision for protection against the economic consequences of the personal hazards of life, cheaper and much better than can government.

My own position is one between these extremes. I believe that government has important responsibilities in this field. Government should and alone can provide minimum necessary security assuring protection to all Americans and their families in all personal contingencies of life. It can and should attempt no more than necessary minimum protection, in accordance with American standards and concepts, on the occurrence of all the personal hazards of life. This is not a mere subsistence income, but a reasonable minimum, such as this great and wealthy nation can afford, taking into account that progress is a fundamental part of our American way of life, and that the poor and the unfortunate must have improving standards as well as all the rest of our population.

It is at this point at which I believe private and industrial programs must come in. Governmental programs cannot provide more than a reasonable minimum of security; to date, we fall far short of that. Social security as I conceive it, is not a featherbed, nor a concrete floor, but a net to catch those who fall. For the luxuries and even some of the comforts of life, under the American philosophy of social security, dependence is placed upon the individual and the family with assistance from the employer.

Private social security programs, such as industrial pensions, health and welfare plans, and supplemental unemployment insurance, are often referred to as "fringe benefits" and discussed principally in terms of costs. The costs of private social security programs are important and cannot be ignored. But costs are not the only or the most important aspect of these plans. They are an expression of the vital interest of industry in the welfare, including the economic security, of its employees. This is not paternalism, but a recognition of the fundamental truth expressed by the late Msgr. John A. Ryan: "Industry exists for man—not man for industry; and industry exists for every man who is connected with it or dependent upon it." Leading industrialists have often declared that industry serves not merely the interests of the stockholders and of management, but of its employees and of the entire nation. I, for one, believe these professions to be sincere and genuine. This is part of the American way of life, no less than the quest for profits.

Industry's responsibility to its employees does not end with the payment of the daily wage. The development of at least a large core of regular employees has been a characteristic of American industry in recent decades. With this has come a recognition that industry owes employees help in developing economic security in all contingencies of life.

With management, the industrial workers are the greatest contributors to our marvelous production. This, of course, determines what economic security we can have in this country. As active contributors to production, the industrial employees are entitled to something better than the minimum for a decent existence, even when personal hazards strike. The minimum, of course, is all that the government can provide. Such a reasonable minimum of economic security is very important. No civilized country can permit starvation in its midst. How a nation provides for its poor and unfortunate is a mark of its civilization, as well as of its humanity. But those who contribute actively to production have a strong claim for additional security, beyond the reasonable minimum to which all Americans are entitled. American industry can, should, and increasingly does provide such additional economic security through what have come to be known as private social security institutions.

Appreciation of the necessary and proper roles of the individual, government, labor, and industry in the quest for security is one of the major directions in which we are advancing in this country. While we still have a long way to go, we are making gratifying progress and, on the whole, in the right direction!

Social Welfare Legislation
of the 1930's

Address at Rosary College,
Riverside, Illinois,
February 16, 1956

T HE TERM "social welfare legislation," which I have selected for my talk this afternoon, is of vague and debatable meaning. The second part of my title, "the 1930's" is definite and, I trust, more politically neutral than "New Deal" or the "New Deal Period." It is also more accurate, as some of the legislation I shall discuss was enacted while Hoover was President of the United States and nearly all of it was passed by large bipartisan majorities in both Houses of Congress. "Social welfare legislation," while not a precise term, relates to legislation concerned with the needs and particularly the economic well-being of the individual citizen and his family.

As I use the term, the social welfare legislation of the 1930's includes the many "relief" programs of this period—programs designed to provide the necessities of life to people who were without them, principally because they lacked employment; the social security program, embodied in the Social Security Act of 1935 and supplemental state legislation; the governmental protection accorded to the right of workers to form labor unions and to bargain collectively; protective labor legislation, according protection to children against exploitation in industry, establishing minimum wage rates for many

79

groups of workers, membership by the United States in the International Labour Organisation and a considerable volume of other legislation protective of the workers of this country; also, public housing legislation, which had its beginnings in the 1930's. There was still other social welfare legislation in this decade, nearly all of which has remained in effect to this day. But the enumerated legislation is so extensive that I can deal only most inadequately with the measures I listed, without going further afield to develop or even mention other legislation of this disturbed but fruitful decade.

《《《《《《《《◊》》》》》》》》》

The 1930's were notable for their advances in social welfare legislation. It was in this decade that, viewed as a whole, we made the greatest advances in social welfare. Legislation in this field took pretty much the form it now has. Most important of all was a broader recognition of human rights and human welfare, and of the government's duties in these respects.

This progress was, in large part, a consequence of the Great Depression, although enlightened leadership, also, deserves such credit, as do the people who in this troubled decade preached the doctrine of human brotherhood and gave effective support to the forward-looking leaders of that day.

The Great Depression, which set in during the second half of 1929 and did not end until after we were in World War II, was the worst in all American history. I shall not dwell on the shrinkage of the total national income by more than one half, the complete "wiping out" of many businessmen and farmers through bankruptcy, the collapse of our banking system, the destruction of more than half of all property values, and many other aspects of the worst depression the world seems ever to have known. . . . The first recognition of the national government's responsibility came in the Hoover Administration, in the form of legislation allowing states to borrow from the national government to meet relief costs. Under Roosevelt came outright grants to the states for relief to needy people [and the setting up of] such agencies as the CWA, the WPA, the FSA, and the NYA. To summarize the significance on the relief legislation of this period let me cite a view expressed by the late Miss Grace Abbott of Chicago, long the head of the United States Children's Bureau.

Miss Abbott said that when the story of the Great Depression is written in future years, without bias or emotion, relief will appear as the brightest spot among all the things that happened in the Depression. Despite the taxpayers' complaints and the many manifestations of lack of preparedness, inefficiency, and wastefulness, the entire expenditures for this purpose totaled less than 16 billion dollars—less than a sixth of the annual expenditures of our government in the war years. As was demonstrated when war came, we got through the prolonged depression without impairment of the health of the nation and its citizens or of their willingness to work and without damage to industrial morale—not an inconsiderable accomplishment that paid dividends when we were subject to the firing test of the greatest war of all history.

Since then, in the war and postwar years, relief needs have not been nearly so great. Although the relief payments to individuals and families now average considerably higher than in the 'thirties, it seems clear that in many respects we have gone backward in the treatment of our needy poor who are not covered by special assistance programs. The federal government again has nothing to do with general assistance and a large majority of the states also do not participate financially. Poor relief, or as now known, "general assistance," is nearly everywhere locally administered, and often very politically. A matter of law existent everywhere, there are many communities where it is not in operation.

More lastingly important was the Social Security Act of 1935 and the related state legislation of this period. The Social Security Act represented for this country a new approach to the age-old problems of want and relief from its worst consequences. This Act included three major types of provisions: social insurance, federal aid under specialized forms of public assistance, and social services, mainly preventive in character. These had their origins in Europe, but developed distinct American features, and were combined in the only broad program we have ever had for coping with the problems of need arising from the immediate personal hazards of life, so disastrous to millions of families and unattached individuals.

Social insurance is a planned program for meeting the problems of need resulting from the personal hazards of life, which involves advance budgeted methods of meeting the costs and provides for the payment of benefits on the occurrence of the hazards without any individual needs test. One form of social insurance was in operation almost everywhere in the United States before the Social Security Act, although not then recognized to be social insurance by many people. This was workmen's compensation, to provide necessary medical care and partial compensation for wage loss to the victims of industrial accidents and occupational diseases and their dependents. Workmen's compensation, then and now, was established under state laws and was state administered.

To this earliest form of social insurance, the Social Security Act added two other forms concerned with even greater hazards than is workmen's compensation: old-age insurance and unemployment insurance. The first of these, broadened in 1939 to become old-age and survivors' insurance, is today the world's largest insurance program, in which 100,000,000 Americans have credits and more than 8,000,-000 are now receiving benefits, with the number of beneficiaries increasing at a rate of 100,000 per month. It is the only general social security program exclusively controlled and administered by the national government. Unemployment insurance, in contrast, is mainly state controlled and exclusively state administered. Like all other American social insurance programs it is self-financed, without one cent of contributions from general tax funds.

The national government's role in unemployment insurance under the Social Security Act has been mainly one of getting the states to enact unemployment insurance laws. While, fortunately, since this law was passed we have had no second "Great Depression," unemployment insurance has benefited millions of Americans and has operated as a built-in economic stabilizer. Even in the very prosperous year 1955, more than 6,000,000 Americans drew unemployment insurance during layoffs.

The other innovation was federal aid to the states for specialized public assistance purposes, originally related to old-age assistance, aid to dependent children, and aid to the blind, and has since been extended to include aid to the permanently and totally disabled. All these are state programs, established by the states and administered either by them or by local governments under their supervision. But the national government reimburses the states for a large part of their costs. Like general assistance (still exclusively a state and local responsibility), all the specialized forms of public assistance are financed from tax funds, with the benefits payable only to people in immediate need and in amounts determined by their needs—on what the British call a "means test" basis. Until the 1950's, larger in the aggregate than the social insurance programs, all the public assistance programs combined now are less than half as important, measured in the number of beneficiaries or in dollar expenditures. While critics condemn the Social Security Act because many people still need public assistance, this was not only anticipated when this legislation was passed, but the total expenditure for all forms of assistance are smaller now than in the 1930's when our population was a good deal less and there were many fewer old people, and that despite a halving of the purchasing power of the dollar. As the social insurance programs have become more inclusive and effective, the assistance rolls in this country have declined.

The third group of institutions for which provision was made in the Social Security Act is social services in which no cash payments are made to the beneficiaries but under which they receive services of a remedial and preventive type; this includes federal aid for public health services, vocational rehabilitation, crippled children's services, child welfare services, and maternal and child health service. Of these there had previously been aid for only vocational rehabilitation and maternal and child health services, and for the latter purpose no money was actually appropriated during the Hoover Administration. Quite a few new services of this type have since been given federal aid. They have become an important part of the social security institutions of the United States. Governments in the United States today expend for public health and medical care alone as much as they do for all forms of public assistance.

Almost from its inception the Social Security Act was very popular. No person of public importance has ever proposed its repeal. It has frequently been supplemented and amended, and most commonly in directions which have improved the law. It has benefited many millions of Americans and the entire economy. But it by no means is as generous a program as critics represent it to be nor as comprehensive and adequate as its champions would like to see it. People in more comfortable circumstances cannot understand how people can live on such low benefits as the present average of all benefits in the several social security programs. The average benefit paid a retired worker in the old-age and survivors' system is less than $62 per month; to dependents and survivors, only half of that. Old-age assistance payments throughout the country are around $53 per month; aid to dependent children, $87 a month per family, but only a little more than $30 per beneficiary. Unemployment insurance averages $26 per week—a little less than $125 per month. Workmen's compensation benefits are higher than unemployment insurance in some states and lower in others. No beneficiaries under any social security program can live in luxury from their benefits; many have great difficulty meeting even the cost of necessities.

None of the existing programs is as inclusive as is desirable. Old-age and survivors' insurance, the broadest in coverage, now applies to 85 per cent of our working force, but only half of the present old people have qualified for benefits. Unemployment insurance and workmen's compensation cover many less people. No provision at all is made for several great personal hazards whose consequences are poverty and dependency for millions. Aside from four states and a specific program for railroad men we have no governmental programs for partial compensation for wage loss in case of sickness, and nowhere have we any form of compulsory insurance against the larger costs of medical care; and voluntary types of health insurance meet only 40 per cent of the hospital bills and 20 per cent, or less, of other types of medical care services. We do not have invalidity insurance in this country as do most other nations making any claim to be at all advanced. Nor do we have family allowances, which now exist in all European countries, most of the Latin-American countries, and in Canada.

We have come a long way in social security, but still have a long way to go. But the objective of a minimum for a decent existence and for every family and unattached individual in all personal contingencies of life has become definitely an American ideal, if not fully a part of the American way of life.

No less important was the labor legislation of the 1930's. Under the intelligent leadership of the first woman member of the Cabinet, Secretary Perkins, the United States Department of Labor assumed something of its rightful place, although it remains to this day by far the smallest of the Cabinet departments. It became the leader in promoting improvement in protective labor legislation of the states. The years 1933 to 1937 were the period of greatest advances in protective labor legislation, second only to the ten years preceding World War I. In these years of the 1930's, great progress was made in the protection of child labor, the promotion of apprenticeship, improved safety and sanitation standards, and state minimum wage legislation. These advances were greatest in the South, which had decidedly lagged behind the rest of the nation.

During the 1930's, also, ... the most important protective labor law ever enacted by the national government, the Fair Labor Standards Act, was introduced. Forerunners of that law were the Bacon-Davis Act of 1932 and the Walsh-Healy Act of 1935, applicable, respectively, to contract construction for the national government and government purchases of supplies. The Fair Labor Standards Act of 1938 had broader application, applying to most interstate commerce and production for interstate commerce. It established a basic 40-hour week and minimum wage rates of from 25 to 40 cents per hour. It also restricted child labor in all such commerce and production. This major federal protective labor law is still in effect and its minimum wage rate is now $1.00 per hour. Its coverage, however, has been narrowed rather than extended, and that despite the recommendations of our Presidents, including President Eisenhower, again this year.

Closely akin to protective labor legislation—and often so regarded in other countries—is public housing. In the 1930's we got our first public housing legislation, which [is still the main part] of our housing legislation .... One such law was a bill enacted by Congress in the early New Deal period appropriating small amounts for slum clearance, undertaken by municipalities. The amounts appropriated for this purpose have remained scanty, with a result that many of our larger cities to this day have disgraceful slums. Of much greater practical value was the Housing Act of 1935, under which the government insured loans made by commercial financial institutions for the construction and modernization of small homes throughout the country. This has been supplemented by similar and even more generous housing loans to veterans. Without direct entrance of the government into the housing business or the loaning business, this legislation has been a major factor in the great private home building boom we have enjoyed in the postwar years.

Of great significance also was the action of the United States Congress in 1933 invoking this nation's adherence to the International Labour Organisation. This international agency was organized at Washington in 1919, largely at the insistence of President Wilson and the great American labor leader, Samuel Gompers. But Congress then refused to have the United States become a member, mistakenly regarding it as an agency of the League of Nations. In 1933 that mistake on our part was remedied and we have been a leading member ever since. Within the last two years, Russia has resumed membership in this organization—of which it was an original member—no doubt as another springboard for its propaganda to gain support from nations less fortunate than we are. The industry member of the American delegation to the ILO has recommended that we now withdraw, fearful that we cannot match Russia in propaganda. Fortunately the great business organizations of the country have delayed action on this recommendation for a year. It is to be hoped that it will never come to pass. Distressing as it must be to have to listen to the Communist propaganda, that clearly is less an evil than would be withdrawal from the ILO, which would be tantamount to a confession that we cannot match the Russians in arguments and are giving up to them all the world not yet committed in the struggle against communism.

Time will permit only brief treatment of most controversial of all the social welfare legislation of the 1930's, the National Labor Relations Act, popularly known as the Wagner Act. That legislation was designed to safeguard the rights of working men to belong to, organize, and be active in labor unions, and to make it possible for them to bargain collectively with their employers. Government did not promote labor unions, but protected the right of self-organization, and thereby encouraged unionism. Decisions of the Supreme Court in 1937 upholding the constitutionality of the Wagner Act and giving it broad application inaugurated the greatest advances in unionism and collective bargaining we ever had in this country. From less than 3,000,000 members in 1933, the American labor unions increased their membership to more than 8,000,000 in 1940; and by the end of the 1930's most of our great mass production industries, previously strongly anti-union, operated under union contracts.

Strong opposition to the Wagner Act, however, continued and increased when many great strikes developed in the first ten months following the end of World War II. The result was the enactment of the Taft-Hartley Act of 1947, which weakened the governmental protection accorded labor unions and made them subject to many restrictions. But the principal provisions of the original Wagner Act have been preserved. While unionism thereafter made slower gains, it has further increased its strength, having today 16,000,000 members in this country, and with nearly 75 per cent of all employees in manufacturing plants working under union contracts.

Near the end of the 1930's occurred a marked change in the attitude of the courts toward labor legislation. A committee of 58 of the most eminent corporation lawyers of the country named by the Liberty League, headed by John W. Davis, former Democratic candidate for President of the United States, acting as an unauthorized Supreme Court, in 1936 unanimously held that the Wagner Act was unconstitutional and advised businessmen to disregard this law. But in 1937, the Supreme Court provided for in the Constitution upheld the law; and this was a court on which there was not, as yet, even a single appointee of President Roosevelt. In the same year, the Supreme Court upheld the Social Security Act and state minimum wage legislation; soon thereafter, the Fair Labor Standards Act. Those great decisions settled once and for all the constitutionality of labor legislation and the broad powers of the national government in this field. These decisions are, perhaps, even more important than any of the specific laws of the 1930's, as they left no doubt that social welfare legislation is in accord with the Constitution of the United States and the duties of our government thereunder.

In concluding let me make these summary comments on the social welfare legislation of the 1930's:

The 1930's were a most trying time for this nation. They were a decade in which we did not advance our economic production. For businessmen, this was a decade of losses exceeding profits; for the workers, a period of widespread unemployment and much suffering for their families. But in the mysterious ways God has in carrying out His will, they were also a period of quickened social conscience, a time of great social advances, most of which have endured and have been of great value to this nation.

I am a man who by this time has lived almost the Biblical three score years and ten. It has been my lot, for good or ill, to have had a somewhat active role in quite a number of the developments of the period of my adult life. Of nothing I have done am I more reasonably satisfied than of the work I was privileged to do as Executive Director of the President's Committee on Economic Security, which sponsored the Social Security Act.

I shall ever remember gratefully the fine support the Social Security Act had from many leaders in all churches and, not least, the Catholic Church. Msgr. John A. Ryan of the Catholic National Welfare Conference, and author of the *Living Wage,* which was the intellectual forerunner of minimum wage legislation, was a most valuable member of the Advisory Council on Economic Security, with unlimited entry to the White House and a man who gave me much encouragement. Msgr. John O'Grady gave most valuable help in getting this legislation through the Congress. For their support and that of many other Church people, I will ever be grateful. The unfortunates in our society and all the common people of our nation —in fact, all Americans—owe them a debt of gratitude for what they did to advance social welfare legislation in the critical decade of the 1930's.

Security and
Economic Change

Excerpts from *Security in an Industrial Economy,* Eighth Annual Conference, Industrial Relations Centre, McGill University, Montreal, Quebec, Canada, April 16–17, 1956, pages 57–70

THIS IS AN AGE of rapid economic change. Nowhere has economic change been as great and continuous as in the two friendly neighbors, Canada and the United States.

Dealing primarily with the United States, in which I have lived for nearly 70 years, evidence of great economic changes is everywhere apparent. In my lifetime the United States has trebled its population. Its national income, measured in stable dollars, has increased more than fivefold. When I was born, half the people of the United States were still engaged in agriculture; an even larger percentage of the population was classified as "rural" in the Census. While by that time our economy had become predominantly a market economy—which it had not been in the early days of the nation—there was still much self-sufficiency, particularly in agriculture. At that time there was a good deal of concern about the trusts, leading to the enactment of the Sherman Anti-Trust Act in 1890, but the first billion dollar corporation, the United States Steel Corporation, was still 15 years off. More than half of all business in the United States was carried on by individual entrepreneurs and partnerships.

Much less than half of all products of industry today were then being produced by anybody. The first automobile came when I was a school boy, as did wireless messages; the airplane, radio, and television not until much later. All plastics and most of the present-day chemical products date from the present century, as does the widespread use of commercially canned foods. Electricity was beginning to be used for many purposes, but electric light was just coming into the larger cities and it was not until after World War I that electricity became the major source of power in industry. Radar and electronics were quite new as recently as World War II. Even the *term* "automation" is less than five years old.

These are only a few of the most spectacular of the material changes which have occurred in my lifetime. Equally, if not more significant, have been social changes of economic import. Among these I shall mention only changes in the labor force and in business organization. For one, the labor force has become much better educated. There are now many more students in colleges and universities than there were secondary-school pupils when I was in high school, and there are as many post-graduate students in the universities as there were undergraduates when I was numbered among them. Not less important has been the increase in the employment of women and the decrease in child labor. Very significant also has been the ever-increasing importance of associations and associational effort in the economy of the United States. More than 95 per cent of all manufacturing is now carried on by corporations and even higher percentages of finance, insurance, and rail and air transportation. Trade unions, coöperatives, farmer organizations, trade associations, and employer and professional organizations, all, veritably, have become a part of what we like to call "the American way of life."

These changes have given rise to many problems. But there can be no doubt that, at least in the economic sphere, they have represented progress—an improved standard of living, a better and longer life for the great majority of the people of our nation. In the fullest measure, ours has been a progressive economy—a striking demonstration of the possibility of continuous progress and of the soundness of a democratic, free enterprise economy.

Canada, for a considerable part of my life, appeared to be making economic progress more slowly than the United States. Since World War II your growth has been at a more rapid rate than that of our country. Second only to the United States, average per capita income in Canada has been increasing so rapidly that you may ere long surpass us. Both nations are far ahead of the rest of the world and widening the gap.

The promise of still more and even greater progress in the decades ahead seems bright in both Canada and the United States. During the Great Depression, the forecast of a declining rate of progress, with the approach of a static population and economy, seemed realistic. Since World War II, however, the rate of economic growth has exceeded that of earlier periods. The stagnation thesis has been replaced by a revival of the characteristically American optimism, which sees no limits to the possibilities for economic growth and improving living standards.

On the material side, this optimism is surely more than a figment of desire and imagination. Most frequently expressed are the expectations aroused by atomic and solar power. We are beyond the stage of demonstrations of the possibilities of these new sources of power. The major question regarding nuclear power has become that of bringing down its costs to make it feasible for great electric generating stations. The principal uncertainty now seems to be whether this will occur within ten years or in a somewhat longer period. As regards solar power—the concentration of energy in the sun rays upon small areas—present hopes center not so much on great power stations or military uses as on small heaters to boil water, cook simple meals, and to heat rooms. From reports of papers delivered at the world conference conducted at Albuquerque, N.M., last fall, it would appear that such household uses of solar energy are likely to be feasible, cost-wise, very soon and they offer a promise of a better life for the teeming millions in the impoverished southern countries of the world.

While the potentialities of nuclear and solar power loom largest in current discussions of the industrial future of our countries, many other technological developments of great significance seem likely. Among these, accounts which I have noted within the last few days mention greatly increased use of glass and plastics and new building materials of varied thermal properties and much more general use of year-round air-conditioning. Important to all areas of insufficient rainfall not too far distant from the ocean is the distillation of sea water to make its use feasible for irrigation. Processes for taking the salt out of sea water have been in use for several decades; now, according to reports, the costs have been reduced so that use of distilled sea water for irrigation seems likely ere long. Despite the meager success to date of cloud spraying to produce rain and to eliminate tornadoes, scientists working on these problems are not giving up their experiments. Finally, there is the even more far-reaching possibility of extensive food production for human consumption in water, without any use of land.

In appraising the possibilities for further economic growth in the United States, note must also be taken of automation. Without certain accepted meaning, I use this term to describe new machinery and processes which, in many productive and clerical operations, substitute mechanical controls for human judgment, just as the earlier mechanization represented the substitution of machines for human brawn and, to some degree, human skill. As automation in most fields requires large new capital investment, new knowledge and skills, it is probable that it will come much more slowly than many fear or hope. But automation presents possibilities for greatly reduced costs of production and for the wider use of many products.

As they have in the past, so in the future, nonmaterial developments are likely to operate not only to assure continued economic progress, but to speed its momentum. In this connection I shall only mention—and no more than mention—the greatly increased attention given to research by industry and government; the promise of improved industrial relations; improving knowledge and action in forestalling, mitigating, and ending depressions; the prospects of more and better trained scientists and professional and technical workers; and a slowly growing appreciation of the interdependence of all peoples, overshadowing differences of race, color, creed, and beliefs.

Allowing for all foreseeable developments, continued economic progress seems certain. This is in accord with our traditions and beliefs and is the great strength of our economies. Economic growth is, indeed, important. Production limits what can be done by way of security. Because our nations have the highest per capita incomes in the world, the best programs for security anywhere are possible here.

Our high per capita incomes, however, do not mean that there is no need in our countries for security institutions, both private and public. One reason why even in these wealthy countries there is need for security institutions is that averages do not tell the whole story. Averages obscure great individual differences. The high average per capita incomes do not establish that there no longer is any poverty or need in the United States or Canada.

During the nineteen thirties, President Roosevelt often referred to the "one third of all Americans who are ill-fed, ill-clothed, and ill-housed." Since then the percentage of the people of the United States who are in poverty has decreased, but the poor are still with us. The Bible states: "The poor, ye shall always have with ye." To get accurate information about the extent and causes of poverty and to suggest legislation to improve the existing situation, the Joint Congressional Committee on the Economic Report of the President in 1949 and in 1955, created Subcommittees on Low Income Families, which made extensive factual reports, based largely on Census data. From the latest of these reports, issued only a few months ago, it appears that there were 8.3 million families and 6.2 million unattached individuals whose money incomes were less than $2,000 in the year 1954. At this income level there were 20 per cent of all families and 64 per cent of all unattached individuals in the United States. The report is careful to note that if non-cash income, particularly among the rural families, were included, the situation, percentage-wise, would not appear quite so bad. Offsetting this is the fact that the cash incomes of the low income group include all social security payments and financial help from others.

One-fifth of the families living under conditions of poverty represents an improvement over President Roosevelt's "one-third of all American families" who are "ill-fed, ill-clothed, and ill-housed" of 25 years ago. In absolute numbers, however, there has been only a slight reduction in the extent of poverty. Half of the families and unattached individuals with cash incomes of less than $2,000 also had either no cash income at all or an annual income of less than $1,000. In this lowest income group there were, in 1954, 3.7 million families and 4.4 unattached individuals—considerably more people than were on all public assistance rolls. The families in this lowest income group—under $1,000 in 1954—constituted 9 per cent of all families in the United States, but got only 1 per cent of the total national income. In the next higher income group—from $1,000 to $1,999—were 12 per cent of all families, but only 3 per cent of the national income. This recent report revealed some trend toward greater equality of income, but in 1954 the highest two-tenths of the family units still received 44 per cent of the total national income, while the lowest two-tenths got only 4 per cent. Most disturbing was the fact that in actual numbers the lowest groups, arrayed in ascending dollars of income, had not decreased at all in total numbers and had barely retained their earlier inadequate share of the national income.

The study of the Joint Committee on the Economic Report dealing with money incomes in 1954 also reveals clearly who are the families at or below the poverty line and why they are in this situation. Most of the families who in 1954 had less than $1,000 of money income were families in which not even one member was in the labor force. Close to one-half of these families were headed by a man of 65 years of age or over. Another large percentage were families whose head was a widowed, divorced, or deserted woman; a smaller percentage, families in which the normal breadwinner was disabled. Also clearly revealed in this and earlier studies was the fact that most of the family units in the low income groups were those of people whose incomes had never been large. They include disproportionate percentages of the rural farm families of the South and those of our non-white population, and among the non-farm families those of laborers, service workers, and semi-skilled factory operatives.

Before the Great Depression, Americans generally ascribed poverty to the lack of enterprise and thrift of the individual. Later, when one-third of all Americans were out of employment and many of those who were employed were fearful that they next might experience the rigors of unemployment, this concept of the causes of poverty became less common. But it has come back in the last fifteen years of full employment and near full employment.

The available statistics and other evidence, however, establish that this view of the causes of poverty is only a half-truth, if not a complete falsehood. Most people are poor because they never had large earnings, or had an unusual amount of sickness, either themselves or in their families, are not now in good health, are members of minority groups, or live in areas which have not enjoyed the same measure of prosperity as the rest of the nation. Most people work and work hard so long as they can get and hold jobs. Nor is the problem one of lack of thrift and foresight. Both total and per capita savings have been increasing, not only in dollars but in purchasing power; and savings are today at an all-time high.

It is true that the unemployed include a high proportion of marginal workers, particularly in periods of high employment. Among the poor are many of the less well educated, the people not in good health, and those who were referred to in a harsher age as "the lower strata of society." But as Abraham Lincoln expressed it: "God must love the poor, because he made so many of them." The people who need public assistance are fellow human beings, much like all the rest of us. Not only considerations of humanity and religion, but of public safety and the general welfare, require that even those of the poor who can be said themselves to have been responsible for their plight must be provided with the minimum necessities of life.

Such a concept is the original and basic idea in social security. This is not a recent phenomenon. In its essentials it is age-old—as old as is civilization. Every religion worthy of being so-called has enjoined upon its believers that at least their own kin and kind must be taken care of when in need. Such an injunction occurs in Deuteronomy and was practised by the Incas in Peru when their civilization was brutally overwhelmed by the Spanish Conquistadores. In the European lands from whence came our ancestors, the Church and the religious foundations bore the major part of the burden of providing for the poor in the Middle Ages. After the confiscation of the monastic properties in the Reformation, this responsibility was shifted to the local governments in which the poor had their legal settlement. (On the Continent this remained much longer a Church function as it, largely, is in Asian countries today.)

In England this shift in the care of the poor found legal expression in the poor laws, whose purpose was both protection of society against the "sturdy vagabonds" and the humane objective of meeting the elemental needs of the "deserving poor." These statutes were codified, just before English-speaking settlement began on this continent, in the Elizabethan Poor Law of 1601.

The Poor Law was brought by the settlers to the Colonies, as were so many other English institutions. All Colonies and nearly every later State included the Poor Law in its earliest legislative enactments. Under the frontier conditions prevailing in America, workhouses were not established everywhere and poor relief was not always actually provided for those in need. But the principle that the local government is responsible for the care and support of all its poor has always been a legal requirement and part of the approved "American way of life."

The later development of social security institutions can only be sketched most briefly and in general terms. Poor relief was long an institution which differentiated little in the treatment of the poor on the basis of the causes of poverty or their future prospects. Such differentiation began in the late eighteenth century and was carried much farther in the nineteenth.

《《《《《《《《《《〇》》》》》》》》》

Very rapid in recent decades in the United States has been the development of social insurance institutions. These have much the same basic objective as public assistance, but with important modifications.

《《《《《《《《《〇》》》》》》》》

Social security continues to enjoy strong support among the masses in our country. There is no practical political possibility of its abandonment, but criticisms have been mounting and a powerful opposition has developed against extension and even liberalization of social security. Business interests are concerned about growing costs; insurance companies see increasing competition in the growth of social insurance. Even the charge that social security is a gigantic fraud which will never pay off, made in a recent book, is widely supported in the press, despite the fact that nearly 9,000,000 Americans at this time receive monthly old-age and survivors' insurance checks, with 100,000 additional people coming on the rolls each month. Every canard ever uttered in opposition to social security is still being repeated, despite its absurdity and volumes of disproof. As people are coming to realize that, as the advocates of social security have always told them . . . social security is not manna from heaven but involves costs as well as benefits, many who once applauded this development are less enthusiastic about it.

But, as I see it, the greatest difficulty in our country is lack of confidence in government, which, unfortunately, prevails among many Americans in the managerial group. Despite a more favorable political climate, management has been almost a push-over for union demands for industrial pensions, health and welfare plans and for increases in these programs. This has resulted from a widespread belief that whatever the government does is inefficient and that industry should provide all social security benefits for its employees.

Industry's payments into industrial pension, health, and welfare funds now approximate $5 billion per year—an amount greatly exceeding the total employer payments for social security purposes to the government. Industrial pension plans thus far exist in plants which have only one-fourth of all employees in urban industries. Only about 750,000 people in the United States now get industrial pensions, compared with the 8,500,000 people on the OASI benefit rolls. In many of the private social security programs, the overhead costs exceed one-half of the total, while the OASI system is operated at an administrative cost of less than 3 per cent of the tax take, and unemployment insurance at a cost of about 7 per cent of the contributions. If Uncle Sam did not foot half the costs of the corporation expenditures for economic security purposes, in the form of a deduction for income tax purposes, industry might be much more conscious of the waste represented by its preference for private to governmental social security institutions. As matters stand, it not only overlooks the much greater costs and the corruption which have developed in connection with many of the private funds, but also gives no thought whatsoever to the much greater burdens in the future it is assuming.

Back of such an irrational attitude, as I see it, is a still widely-held view that social security is inconsistent with free enterprise. To many, social security either is socialism or a long step toward it, for no more logical reason than that the word "social" occurs in both terms. Many Americans are allergic to "social" and "welfare," despite the fact that the Preamble to our Constitution sets forth that one of the four purposes for which our government was established was "to promote the general welfare."

Social security is not inimical to industry, thrift, and free enterprise, but a bulwark for these economic virtues, needed at home and most valuable for our safety in the troubled world in which we live.

This view was expressed nearly a century ago by John Stuart Mill, who formulated classical economics in its final form. Advocating *laissez faire* as the general policy the government should pursue in economic matters, he recognized that: "Energy and self-dependence are liable to be impaired by the absence of help, as well as by its excess." Winston Churchill, the grand old man of the British Commonwealth, in his youth, when he defended the British national insurance program in 1911, put it this way:

I do not agree with those who say that every man must look after himself, and that intervention by the State ... will be fatal to his self-reliance, his foresight, and his thrift.... If terror be an incentive to thrift, surely the penalties of the system which we have abandoned ought to have stimulated thrift as much as anything could have been stimulated in this world. The mass of the labouring people have known that unless they made provisions for their old age betimes they would perish miserably in the workhouse. Yet they have made no provision ... for they have never been able to make such a provision.... It is a great mistake to suppose that thrift is caused only by fear; it springs from hope as well as fear; where there is no hope, be sure there will be no thrift.

What will be the effects of social security programs depend upon what they propose to do and still more upon what they actually provide. It is possible to make of social security something of an unrealistic Santa Claus program. Emphasis in social security can be placed upon redistribution of wealth, or upon the much less radical concept of assuring a necessary minimum income for a reasonably satisfactory existence for the individual and the family on the occurrence of the immediate, personal hazards of life. The former has sometimes been represented as the objective of social security, even by some of its advocates, but the latter, much more modest aim underlies the social security legislation of the United States, and, I believe, that of Canada and Great Britain.

As institutions for the redistribution of wealth and income, social security programs have proven quite feeble. There are much more direct and effective means for redistributing income and wealth, such as tax policies. Santa Claus programs for social security have never gotten anywhere and are probably self-defeating, and the social security programs which actually have been established in the United States, Canada, and England have had but minor effects upon the distribution of income and wealth.

As I see it, social security institutions, also, do not have their principal justification in their effects upon purchasing power or in stimulating the prevention of the occurrence of the hazards against whose worst economic consequence they provide minimum protection, or in promoting full employment and economic stability. Social security institutions have some values in those important directions, but these have not been and, I think, cannot be their main objectives. Payments to replace in part income lost on the occurrence of the personal hazards of life keep purchasing from being reduced as much as it otherwise might be, but they alone will not suffice for full employment at all times. It is, of course, better to prevent hazards than to try to offset their effects. The maintenance of full employment, very properly, is now a major objective in all nations. But while we dream and plan for the abolition of poverty, we still have many poor in our midst. We must redress existing need while we dream and plan; and it remains sensible to make the best advance provision we can for meeting needs which we can anticipate.

Full employment does not render social security unnecessary. Some of the personal hazards are not directly related to general prosperity. When we attain ever-prevailing full employment, children still will not be able to support themselves and many of the old people and some not so old will still be unable to work. Progress and economic growth often actually increase the hazards confronting some individuals. Automation promises an increase in total employment, at least in the long run. But for many present workers, particularly the older workers, the not-so-well educated, and the less skilled and less adaptable, it is likely to mean more and longer unemployment. Because this is the age of economic change, we have even more need for social security than when progress occurred at a slower pace.

Social security is not all that we need in this day and age. It is not even all that we need for protection against the consequences of the personal hazards of life. The present great emphasis upon research and advances in the health field, the rehabilitation of the disabled, more employment opportunities for the aged, preparation for retirement, better utilization of the years in retirement, and similar programs—while serving as a lame excuse to some for keeping social security payments at an inadequate level—are basically sound and are definitely needed along with the older social security programs.

《《《《《《《《《〇》》》》》》》》

There is not just one sound governmental social security program. Social security programs, to be sound, must vary with and reflect the history, the traditions, and the total institutional pattern of the particular nation in which they are instituted. Canada has utilized British and American experience in formulating its social security programs, but has not blindly copied what these other nations have done. The United States has paid altogether too little attention to social security developments in your progressive, rapidly-growing nation. But I would not advocate that we adopt your policies because you have made a success of them, but only that the time has come for us to better understand what you have done and to give serious thought to adapting some of your devices to our needs. You have done many things by way of social security about which we need to know more than we now do.

The Objectives
of Social Security

Excerpts from address at the
meeting of the Catholic
Economic Association at
Chicago, December 28, 1958.
Published in the *Review of
Social Economy,* Volume
XVII, Number 1 (March,
1959), pages 23–33

My Concept of the Objectives
of Social Security

As with the meanings of the term "social security," widely differing statements have also been made as to the objectives of social security. I like Article 25 of the Universal Declaration of Human Rights, which was adopted by the United Nations in 1948:

Everyone has the right to a standard of living adequate for the health of himself and his family, including food, clothing, housing and medical care and necessary social services, and the right of security in the event of unemployment, sickness, disability, widowhood, old age or other lack of livelihood in circumstances beyond his control.

This statement links social security with the well-being of the individual and his family. The basic objective in social security is to assure the economic essentials to all people on the occurrence of the personal contingencies of life, which in the absence of such protection result in want and suffering and, in extreme cases, in starvation and death, for large numbers.

This does not mean that the government is to assume full responsibility for the support of all people. This may be considered desirable in a communistic nation, but not in a free society. Complete governmental responsibility for support carries with it governmental control of the allocation of all income, which leads to favoritism, corruption, and tyranny. It is not full support at all times with which social security is concerned, but with the essentials of life in circumstances beyond the control of the individual. It is not the objective of social security to provide an income sufficient for an acceptable standard of living regardless of what the beneficiary may do. Responsibility for his support and that of his family rests primarily on the individual. Social security is grounded in the philosophy that everyone must put forth his best efforts and rests on the assumption that in all normal circumstances most individuals, at least during the productive years of life, are able to support themselves and their families. Social security comes into play only in the personal contingencies which are enumerated in the Universal Declaration of Human Rights, as "unemployment, sickness, disability, widowhood, old age and other lack of income in circumstances beyond his control."

Social security is concerned with the essentials of economic well-being, with "food, clothing, housing and medical care and necessary social services." Social security does not contemplate maintenance in the style to which the beneficiary and his family have been accustomed. It does not seek to provide the luxuries or even all the comforts of an advanced society, but only an income adequate for living in accordance with socially approved standards.

What this means in terms of dollars and cents varies with the country and the time. In many nations, this is an income barely sufficient to keep body and soul together. In a wealthy and progressive economy, such as that of the United States, a minimum adequate income, in accordance with socially approved standards, is more than a subsistence income. A fundamental American idea—the strongest justification for our system of free enterprise—is that of the possibility and desirability of continuously improving standards of living. We, generally, have had and expect to continue to have increasing production, and it is part of our democratic ideal that all Americans should share in the benefits of progress. This includes the poor, as well as the well-to-do and the rich. They too, should have an American standard of living, which is well above a bare subsistence. It may be that in the great depression of the 1930's our economy could not afford a social security program more liberal than $30 per month, which was the approximate average for families on relief. Today, in view of our much more productive economy and the decreased purchasing power of the dollar, a much higher dollar figure is required to meet the test of a "socially approved standard of living." But today and in the foreseeable future, social security in the United States can provide only a minimum income sufficient for a standard of living compatible with prevailing concepts of needs and possibilities.

Providing such a necessary minimum income as a protection against the worst economic consequences of the personal hazards of life is the objective of social security, as I see it. The best possible protection against the personal hazards of life is the prevention of their occurrence. But this has never been done perfectly and to some extent is impossible. Some of the personal contingencies of life, for instance old age, are part of the life cycle. Others are partially preventable, as are accidents and some causes of unemployment, and should be prevented where this is possible. But they do occur, with terrible consequences to the individual and the family, and also, to society. So a minimum substitute income for wages and other earnings is very necessary.

Social security has important functions in the present-day society. But it is not a panacea or cure-all. It is not all that is needed to give us an ever-improving economy. It does not deal with economic growth and stability, which are at least equally important. It is not a substitute for increased productivity; rather the productivity of the economy is a limitation to what can be accomplished by way of social security. To some degree it may lessen the need for charity and social work, but mainly it changes the task they must perform. Social security does not satisfy all the economic needs of the individual, to say nothing about his even greater psychological, social, and religious needs.

But social security does matter and is very important. It is all to the good that we should plan and strive for a stable economy and one in which there is no poverty or dependency. But the fact remains that there are great fluctuations which result in unemployment and much distress for many Americans; and we still have many poor people who need protection against the most dire want. President Franklin D. Roosevelt in the 1930's often referred to the "one-third of all Americans who are ill-fed, ill-housed, and ill-clothed." In a quarter of a century, the percentage of the American people in dire want has been considerably decreased, but one-sixth of all our families are still in the income group of money incomes of less than $2,000 per year, and nearly one-half in that of incomes of less than $3,000. Included in the latter group are many who are fully self-supporting except when serious illness or some similar disaster strikes some member of the family. In the former group—the one-sixth of all Americans with money incomes of less than $2,000 per year— the great majority are below the line of complete self-support when any of the personal contingencies of life occur to them. Included in this group are a good many young people whose incomes can be expected to increase later on, but also many of the old people, and many of the families whose head is a woman; also a high percentage of all immigrant families and of all families in minority groups. Improved business conditions have somewhat reduced the percentage of the total population in these lowest income groups but they still number millions of people.

The hazards against whose worst economic consequences social security institutions are designed to provide protection, occur throughout life and are very great. A large percentage of all children are born in the homes of the poor and several millions of our children are in families without normal breadwinners. Industrial accidents cause a loss of far more working days than do strikes. Nonoccupational illness averages 6 or 7 days per year for our workers; and 10 per cent of the people have more than half of the total illness costs, while something like 2 per cent have medical care bills each year in excess of $1,000. An estimated total of nearly 3,000,000 Americans not yet 65 years of age are permanently and totally disabled. The number and percentage of people who are 65 or over is constantly increasing, and, while many of the "younger, old people" are still employed, old age is for most of them a period of greatly reduced earnings and of the cessation of all earnings for many. And old age is a period of life which for the people who reach that age averages about 30 per cent of their whole lifetime; this is a period so long that a person desiring $100 per month from age 65 on must, at that age, have accumulated, on the average, $15,000 if a man, and nearly $18,000 if a woman. Even death, while in a sense the end of the economic worries of the individual, often means economic distress for his dependents.

A civilized, Christian society must make provisions for minimum necessary income from all its members. We cannot condemn the aged and infirm to the gas chambers and let the unfortunate and the poor die in their misery. Such an inhuman policy violates all tenets of religion and morality; further, masses of the poor do not starve peaceably. Failure to insure the essentials of life, at least to substantially all people, breeds communism and revolution. Considerations of self-preservation, as well as the higher law, dictate that all people should be assured a minimum income adequate for an approved standard of living on the occurrence of all personal contingencies of life beyond the control of the individual. This is, clearly, an obligation of society. Society and the state are not synonymous; but, in a secular state, government must shoulder the main responsibility for insuring a necessary minimum income on the occurrence of the personal hazards of life.

Other Views as to the Objectives of Social Security

The statement of the objectives of social security I have presented agree pretty well with those made by the principle champions of social security the world over. But I would mislead you if I did not acknowledge that other views have wide support.

Among those who would turn back the clock or, at least, confine social security within its present scope, two views as to its proper place have been predominant. One of these is that the government should not do what can be done voluntarily. Holding this view, these right-wing critics believe that what are often called "the private social security institutions," such as voluntary health insurance and industrial pensions, are vastly preferable to governmental programs. They ignore the higher overhead costs of the private programs and worse, regard them as complete substitutes for governmental programs, although they do not cover many who most need protection. This preference for voluntary action and for private enterprise has deep roots in American thought and is not wholly without merit. Both the private and governmental programs have their proper sphere and complement each other. Public programs are needed to insure minimum necessary protection to all Americans against the worst economic consequences of the personal hazards of life. Private programs serve the socially desirable purpose of supplementing the public social security institutions. They do this, particularly, for workers to whom industry is under special obligations, affording them a better deal than is possible for the entire population.

The other right-wing critics of social security would restrict its scope to public assistance and vocational rehabilitation. They do not lack feelings of humanity and would give assistance to people in dire and immediate want. But they would eliminate the social insurance programs, reserving the term "insurance" to the several types of private insurance. Somewhat similar is the view that the principal effort in what the government should do should be directed toward restoring the victims of the personal hazards of life to self-support.

Both these views have had a good deal of influence in the development of social security in the United States. The private insurance companies have had a large role in the history of old-age, survivors', and disability insurance. Public assistance programs are more extensively developed in the United States than anywhere else, while we are behind other English-speaking countries and most of the western European countries in social insurance. Vocational rehabilitation has been the favored social security program in the present Administration.

Restoring the victims of the personal hazards of life to the fullest possible measure of self-support is, certainly, in the public interest. But by no means all of these victims are good prospects for rehabilitation. Public assistance, also, is essential, even when there are good social insurance programs. A first responsibility of government is to meet the dire needs of people without other means of subsistence and without first asking too many questions about the reasons for this state of affairs. But advanced preparation and budgeted methods of meeting the costs of the occurrence of the personal hazards of life are clearly desirable, whenever they can be utilized. So is wide resort to the contributory principle, not merely to keep down costs but to better preserve human dignity. My view is that costs must be given consideration, but I reject the concept that what should be done by way of social security must turn solely on costs.

Some supporters of social security and of its extension, also, have different views as to its objectives than those which I have presented. Among these are many Keynesian economists who approach social security from the point of view of the large costs and expenditures which it involves. They see in these costs and expenditures a powerful means of controlling the general level of business. Their interest in social security is in its total effects on the economy, rather than in individual and family needs.

Related is the more radical view that the basic purpose of social security is that of redistribution of income. The late Abraham Epstein, one of the foremost pioneers in advancing social security, often said that there is no value in social insurance unless it includes funds supplied by government and contributes to the redistribution of incomes. Some redistribution of income undoubtedly is involved in all social security programs. As I see it, however, this is only one of its results, not its principal objective.

A less radical-sounding statement of the purposes of social security is that it seeks to maintain the purchasing power of the victims of life's hazards. To some degree this is one of the effects of social security payments, but all such payments are smaller than the losses sustained. The degree to which purchasing power is maintained is one of the best by-products of social security but not its central purposes.

Very different and not reconcilable with the concepts of social security I have presented is what might be called the "hand-out" or "Santa Claus" theory. This is a view that little matters in social security except the size of the benefits. Costs are either altogether ignored or lightly dismissed. Quite to the contrary in the United States, the view has prevailed that costs must be considered along with the benefits. No more can be paid in benefits than is collected through contributions or premiums (called "social security taxes" in this country).

All the statements of the objectives of social security I have mentioned have respectable support. Many contain elements of truth. But I believe that the views I have presented square better with the actual development of social security in this country.

Needed Improvements in Social Security

That there is nothing revolutionary or even radical about social security appears most clearly when it is appreciated how meager are the social security payments on the average—although they are higher in the United States than in any other country.

«««««‹O›»»»»»

Few of you will think that these average benefits exceed the minimum necessary income for an American standard of living on the occurrence of the personal hazards of life, assurance of which I believe to be the objective of social security. As I see it, the level of benefits needs to be moderately increased to approximate this standard in all our social security programs. An average retirement benefit of $100 per month should be attainable in the not distant future. At least equally important is an increase in the widow's benefits and the development of genuine dependents' allowances in our old-age insurance system. In unemployment insurance, the maximum benefit should be increased to half the average prevailing wage in manufacturing. Half the normal earnings was the original objective in unemployment compensation, but the maximum is now far lower in most states. Similarly, nearly all workmen's compensation benefits need to be revised upward.

But increase in benefits is by no means all that needs to be done by way of the improvement of the existing social security programs. None of these programs applies to all who should have coverage under them. Many conditions governing eligibility are unduly restrictive and their administration is needlessly harsh. Except for proposals for the federalization of unemployment insurance or, as an alternative, the adoption of federal standards to govern this form of social insurance . . . there is not much controversy about the desirability of changes along these lines, but it remains to actually make these improvements rather than merely give them verbal assent.

Much more controversial is the establishment of forms of social security which we do not now have. Foremost among these is compulsory health insurance. We have cash sickness compensation established by law in four states and for railroad employees, but these laws cover less than one-third of the workers of the country; moreover (except for hospital insurance in California), they provide no protection against the costs of medical care, which, in the aggregate, are almost twice as large as the wage and earning loss resulting from nonoccupational illness. We have had a very great expansion of voluntary health insurance; but, as the years elapse, it is ever becoming more doubtful whether voluntary methods will suffice to give the protection needed against this hazard, which in times other than deep depression probably produces more poverty and dependency than any other. There are millions of Americans who have no voluntary health insurance at all and the protection afforded to those who have such policies is often inadequate. Only a little more than 40 per cent of the total costs of hospital care to patients is met today by insurance, and less than 20 per cent of the costs of surgical and medical care.

Compulsory health insurance, providing protection against both of the hazards connected with illness—the costs of medical care of all types and the loss of earnings due to sickness—is in operation in nearly all advanced countries other than the United States except those which have established complete systems of public medical care. For years the opponents of compulsory health insurance have been saying that voluntary health insurance will soon be expanded to provide satisfactory protection to substantially all Americans. Progress has been made by voluntary methods, but only to the extent . . . indicated. Many of those most in need of protection have either no health insurance or very limited and inadequate insurance. Surely, the time is coming when either we must solve the problem of protection against the heavy costs of medical care through voluntary insurance or we must come to compulsory health insurance or to virtually complete public medical care.

I include the last alternative—public medical care, on the model of England—because we have been moving quite rapidly in that direction. Thirty per cent of all medical care costs in this country are now met from tax funds. This percentage has been rapidly increasing. Rejecting compulsory health insurance on the cry that it is "socialized medicine," we have been moving apace toward socialized medicine, in the form of tax-supported public medical care.

I recognize that compulsory health insurance cannot be established at this time over the opposition of the American Medical Association and our strong American preference for voluntary action. It seems more likely that we will continue to increase tax-supported public medical care rather than consider the taboo, compulsory health insurance. The wisest course may be not to aim for a complete national system of compulsory health insurance, but to supplement voluntary health insurance by a governmental program of hospital insurance for old-age beneficiaries and by major medical expense insurance, as Senator Douglas has suggested. And we, clearly, should have cash sickness compensation in all states, now provided in only four states and for railroad workers. Whatever program or programs we may favor, it seems to me to be clear that we can no longer be satisfied that voluntary action will solve the problem of reasonably adequate protection against the consequences of nonoccupational illness.

Even more remote than compulsory health insurance appears to be the establishment of family, or children's, allowances. This institution exists in nearly forty nations, including most European and Latin-American countries and also our thriving neighbor to the north, Canada. In the United States, interest in family allowances has been restricted largely to Catholic Welfare people.

Much is to be said in its favor. Family allowances provide for some aid toward the support of all children. In some countries, this aid comes from social security funds; elsewhere, from the general treasury. It is always less than full support and is taxable income to the recipient families, so that the wealthy return a substantial part of the grants to the treasury. Lord Beveridge, on whose recommendation England provided for children's allowances, has said that children's allowances are the keystone to genuine social security. Economically, children are a source of costs to their families. Most children are born in the families of younger adults, whose incomes tend to be lower than the average of all families. A large percentage of all children are born in the homes of the poor. In this connection, I remind you that one-sixth of all American families now have annual money incomes of less than $2,000—and among them are many younger families. Family allowances do not relieve the parents of their obligation to support their children. The main burden of children's support still falls on them; but a family allowance may mean milk for babies who otherwise would not have it, and in Canada, family allowances have meant school attendance, which, generally, is a condition for the receipt of an allowance for children of school age.

The claim has been made that our aid to dependent children and the children's exemption in income taxes serve the same purpose as a family allowance and render it unnecessary. Our aid to dependent children, however, goes only to families having no normal breadwinner, the father being dead, invalided, or divorced, or having deserted. Children in such families are usually in need, but there are also many other children who are in need who are not eligible for aid to dependent children. And the income tax exemption for children benefits only the families with taxable incomes, and it is the children in the poorest families who most need to be helped from family allowances.

Concluding Remarks

The view I have presented of the objectives of social security is a conservative one. It does not look upon social security as a remedy for all economic ills or even a majority of them. This view restricts the immediate objectives of social security to the assurance of a necessary minimum income in accordance with prevailing American opinions and standards, on the occurrence of the immediate personal hazards of life. I am not oblivious to the side effects of social security, many of which are helpful in connection with other problems. But I would center attention on the central objective.

I do so because we still have much to do to reasonably fulfill this objective, conservative as it is. We have made considerable progress towards the attainment of social security. We need to make much further progress.

II

OLD AGE

I N THIS PART Witte reviews the questions of the changing nature and dimensions of the old-age problem in the United States and the need for a governmental program of old-age security. How should the federal government be related to the states in such a program? Should the basic approach be one of social insurance or public assistance? What are the dangers of the Townsend Plan? How can private plans for old-age security be integrated with public plans? Should such plans be contributory or not and should their benefit rights be vested with the individual worker?

Within the program of social insurance, the perennial questions are: What groups should be covered? What benefits should be paid and under what conditions? How should the program be financed?

Old-Age Security in the
Social Security Act

The Journal of Political Economy, published by the University of Chicago Press, Volume 45, Number 1 (February, 1937), pages 1–44

U P TO THE INTRODUCTION of the bill out of which developed the Social Security Act, the principal interest of nearly all committees and individuals concerned with its formulation was in unemployment insurance. Once this bill was introduced, however, the major interest, both in and outside of Congress, shifted to old age security. This has continued down to the present time.

Despite the numerous articles which have been written on the subject, and, to no small measure because of them, there is still a very general lack of information regarding the provisions of the Social Security Act relating to old-age security and their purposes. The two parts of the old-age security program are confused and many of the essential features have been grossly misrepresented. It is essential to grasp that there are two distinct measures for old-age security in the Social Security Act: old-age assistance, dealt with in Title I; and old-age benefits, dealt with in Title II, with which Title VIII is generally linked in public discussions.

《《《《《《《《〇》》》》》》》》

I. Old-Age Assistance

Title I of the Social Security Act authorizes Congress to appropriate not to exceed fifty million dollars for the fiscal year 1935–36 and "an amount sufficient" for subsequent years for federal aid to the states for old-age assistance.

《《《《《《《《〈〇〉》》》》》》》》

Grants under this title are to be made only to states which have a state plan for old-age assistance which the Social Security Board finds conforms with standards set forth in the federal act. These standards relate both to the substantive provisions of the state old-age assistance laws and to their administration.

《《《《《《《《〈〇〉》》》》》》》》

The authority of the Social Security Board, in the first instance, is limited to the approval or disapproval of the state plan for old-age assistance. Having approved the state plan, as conforming with the conditions specified in the federal act, the Social Security Board may discontinue federal aid only if it finds, after reasonable notice and opportunity for hearing to the state agency administering or supervising the state plan, that this plan no longer conforms with the requirements of Title I or that the conditions governing eligibility for assistance prescribed in the federal act are in actual administration being violated in "a substantial number of cases."

The original bill recommended by the Committee on Economic Security and the President gave more extensive authority to the federal government in the administration of old-age assistance and laid down more exacting conditions before the states would be entitled to any share in the federal aid. The major change made by Congress with regard to administration was the insertion of the proviso that the Social Security Board shall have nothing to say about the selection, tenure of office, and compensation of personnel concerned with the administration of old-age assistance in the states. In relation to the substantive content of the state legislation, Congress so rephrased the provisions of Title I relating to age, residence, and citizenship as to make it possible for the states to impose other restrictions upon eligibility for old-age assistance, while in the original bill these were specified as the only restrictions which the states might impose. It also struck out of the bill the requirement that the old-age assistance grants must be sufficient, with other income, to provide "a reasonable subsistence, compatible with decency and health" and failed to substitute for it any other standard governing the amount of the assistance to be paid. As the act stands the Social Security Board can neither review the old-age assistance grants in individual cases nor object to the administration in any state because its average grants are ridiculously low.

These amendments greatly weakened this part of the Social Security Act. Title I neither actually sets up nor renders certain adequate old-age assistance on a nationwide basis. It leaves it optional with the states whether or not they shall have an old-age assistance law. It insures uniformity between states having laws only in a few matters and leaves the two most vital points—the definition of need and the amount of the assistance—entirely to the determination of the states. It includes no safeguards against the selection of the actual administrators of the assistance on a political spoils basis.

It does, however, create a strong financial incentive for the enactment of old-age assistance laws conforming with the standards of Title I. This incentive has been very materially increased by the withdrawal of all federal aid for direct relief. Prior to passage of the Social Security Act the states received no aid toward the costs of old-age assistance, while they received aid from the federal government in amounts averaging 70 per cent of the total costs of direct relief. In consequence there was a great temptation for state and local authorities to get old people in need on relief rather than on old-age assistance. This situation has now been exactly reversed. It is now to the financial interest of the state and local authorities to get old people who are dependent upon the public for support on old-age assistance rather than outdoor poor relief.

While the Social Security Board was shorn of much of the power granted in the original bill, it, nevertheless, has still been able to assume leadership in the development of old-age assistance legislation and in the improvement of its administration. This has resulted from the fact that it must approve the state plans for old-age assistance and the quarterly allotments of aid to the states. The act expressly provides that the methods of administration must be satisfactory to the Board and, while it is expressly deprived of any voice in the selection of personnel, this provision affords ample authority for the policy which the Board has actually pursued of requiring the states to outline in detail their methods of administration in their state plans and of insisting that they live up to their plan once it has been approved.

The progress made has been much greater than seemed probable while the Social Security Act was under consideration. When this measure was introduced in January, 1935, twenty-eight states and two territories had old-age assistance laws on their statute books. Three of these laws were entirely inoperative and in only a few states were the laws actually in effect throughout the entire state, although only eight laws were in form optional with the counties.

《《《《《《《《《◎》》》》》》》》

Conservative and few as are the requirements in Title I of the Social Security Act prescribing conditions with which the states must comply to get federal aid for old-age assistance, none of the states had laws, when this measure was introduced, which complied with all these conditions. Every existing old-age assistance law had to be liberalized in some respect, many of them very extensively.

《《《《《《《◎》》》》》》》

Old-age assistance in this country, however, is by no means all that it ought to be. Very restrictive provisions remain in many states regarding the amount of property which old people may own without being disqualified. Particularly offensive to many old people are provisions requiring them to convey all their property to the state (or county) as a condition of getting assistance. Few states have liberalized the statutory provisions governing the amount of old-age assistance to be granted. But most serious of all is the unsatisfactory administration in many counties and in entire states.

Great differences exist between the states both in the percentages of all people over sixty-five who are in receipt of old-age assistance and in the amount of the old-age assistance grants. In most states less than 10 per cent of all people over sixty-five years of age were receiving old age assistance in June, 1936, but in six western states more than 20 per cent were on the old-age assistance rolls. The average of the grants for the entire country was $16.02 in this month, but the range between states was from an average of $3.62 to $25.26. In five states the grants averaged below $10 per month; in nine states, above $20.

A major factor responsible for such great variation is the confusion which still exists over the nature and purpose of old-age assistance. All old-age assistance laws restrict the assistance to old people who are dependent upon the public for support and with two exceptions all of these laws contemplate that the amount of the grants shall be determined by the needs of the individual. Popularly, however, old-age assistance is called "old-age pensions," and there is a widespread notion that everyone who reaches a specified age is entitled to a pension and a still more prevalent notion that all eligible persons should receive the same grants. These notions have influenced the actual administration of old-age assistance in many places, particularly where the Townsend plan has strong support. In quite a few counties and in some entire states nearly all old persons who have applied for assistance have been put on the pension rolls, only persons known to have a considerable amount of property or very well-to-do children being barred.

Practically everywhere high percentages on the old-age assistance rolls are associated with low average grants. Where old-age assistance is confused with universal old-age pensions every applicant who satisfies the age and residence requirements is granted a pension of the same amount which, however, is small because so many people must share the available funds. Such an administration is very wasteful and unjust. Small grants of this kind are adequate for old people who are housed and fed by their children but who need a little public assistance for clothing and spending money. They are very inadequate for the most needy old people—those who have no income or support from any other source and, moreover, have others who are dependent upon them. The Social Security Board is doing everything that it possibly can to correct these conditions, but it is not an easy matter to overcome the widespread confusion of old-age assistance with flat pensions for all old people, which the Townsend movement has done so much to create.

II. Federal Old Age Benefits

Federal old-age benefits are payable under Title II of the Social Security Act to all persons who are employed anywhere in the United States subsequent to December 31, 1936, with stated exceptions. The most important of these are persons engaged in agricultural labor, domestic service in homes, casual work, employment by the federal, state, or local governments, employment on any vessel, and employment by any non-profit-making religious, charitable, or educational organization. Self-employed persons, owners, and operators are likewise excluded. Persons who subsequent to December 31, 1936, are employed in included employments and who thereafter transfer to excluded occupations or industries do not lose their rights to benefits, but their benefits are based solely on their earnings in the included occupations.

The Committee on Economic Security estimated that of the 49,000,000 people reported gainfully occupied in the census of 1930, 26,000,000 would have been included in the federal old-age benefit plan. Excluded would have been 12,000,000 self-employed people, owners, and operators, 9,000,000 persons employed in excluded industries, 1,000,000 persons employed in included industries but over sixty-five years of age, and 500,000 casual workers. The 26,000,000 estimate still seems quite accurate for the initial number of included workers who benefit, although the potential number (if they had work) is closer to 30,000,000. This number is almost certain to increase in future years. Since persons once employed in industries to which Title II is applicable do not lose their rights by ceasing to be employed in such industries or being no longer employed, it is probable that the number of persons who will have some benefit rights under Title II will in the course of a few decades exceed the total number of persons gainfully occupied.[1] At the very outset more people will be included than are embraced within old-age insurance in any other country.[2] Unlike most other laws affecting

[1] This is likely to result because the majority of women employees drop out of gainful employment upon marriage. Married women who acquire benefit rights before marriage will be entitled to retirement benefits (usually at the minimum rate) on attaining age 65, although never gainfully employed after marriage.

[2] The coverage of the largest old-age insurance systems in 1934 (or other latest available year) was, in round numbers, as reported by the International Labour Office: The Soviet Union, 23,500,000; Germany, 21,000,000; Great Britain, 19,000,000; France, 8,000,000; Italy, 6,000,000; Sweden, 4,000,000; Netherlands, 3,000,000.

the relations of employers and employees in this country, there are no numerical exclusions in the federal old-age benefit plan. It applies to all employment other than in excluded industries or occupations, whether there is one employee in the establishment, or a thousand, or any other number.

The major benefit to eligible persons contemplated in Title I is a monthly retirement allowance. To be eligible [for] this monthly benefit the applicant must have worked for wages for at least five years subsequent to December 31, 1936, and have earned after this date a minimum total of $2,000 in employments other than those specifically excluded. He must also be at least sixty-five years of age and have retired from his usual occupation. The first retirement benefits will become payable in 1942 to persons then sixty-five or over who worked for at least five days in each of the years 1937 to 1941 in employments not specifically excluded and who earned a total of $2,000 during these years in such work.

The amount of the monthly old-age benefits is based upon the wages earned subsequent to December 31, 1936, and before attainment of age sixty-five, in employments not specifically excluded, disregarding, for this purpose, earnings in excess of $3,000 in any year. If the total wages earned are between $2,000 and $3,000, the monthly benefit rate is one-half of 1 per cent of the total wages. If the total wages exceed $3,000 the monthly rate is a sum arrived at by adding together one-half of 1 per cent of the first $3,000, one-twelfth of 1 per cent of the excess above $3,000 up to $45,000, and one twenty-fourth of 1 per cent of the excess above $45,000. The minimum monthly retirement allowance is $10, the maximum $85.

《《《《《《《《〈〉》》》》》》》》

This plan favors the workers who at this time are already middle-aged or over and those whose rate of pay is small. Every worker who earns more than another subsequent to December 31, 1936 (up to the maximum of $3,000 per year), will get higher benefits in absolute amount than such other worker, but the benefits of the worker with the smaller earnings will be a somewhat higher percentage of these earnings. In the early years after retirement benefits first become payable, most of the benefits will not be much greater than the average old-age assistance grants,[3] but they will tend to increase with the lapse of years subsequent to December 31, 1936. A young workman employed for forty years after Title II becomes effective can look forward to benefits on retirement at age sixty-five of $51.25 per month if he earned an average of $100 per month and larger benefits if his earnings were greater.

If eligible persons die prior to becoming sixty-five years of age a lump sum benefit is paid to their estates equal to 3.5 per cent of their total wages subsequent to December 31, 1936. The same benefit is paid to employees who on attaining age sixty-five cannot establish that they earned at least $2,000 subsequent to December 31, 1936, or who were not employed for at least five days in each of five years after this date. If employees die after retirement, but before they have drawn at least 3.5 per cent of their total wages in monthly benefit payments, their estate is entitled to the difference between this amount and the payments they received during their lifetime.

These benefits, all taken together, are such as can be paid for by 5 per cent contributions (or taxes), with interest at 3 per cent compounded annually, throughout an industrial lifetime on wages of $1,100 per year, which were taken by the actuaries as the average taxable wages of all employees to whom Titles II and VIII are applicable.[4] The benefits to workers earning less than this assumed average wage or who are not within the system throughout the entire period of their working lives cost more than 5 per cent of their

[3] The maximum benefit to anyone who is retired after having been within the old-age benefit plan but five years is $25 per month. The average benefits of all persons who will be retired in 1942 (the first year) will probably be somewhere between $15 and $18 per month. In each year thereafter, for two or three decades, the average benefits can be expected to increase, and, if present wage levels continue, are likely, ultimately, to exceed $50 and, perhaps, $60 per month. Should wage levels rise or fall the average benefits will be correspondingly affected.

[4] The actuaries also assumed that the average workman loses one-ninth of all working time through unemployment, accident, and sickness; also that, while under Title II he may retire at age 65, he will not actually do so until he is 67½ years old. These assumptions, and also the $1,100 average taxable wage figure, are reasonable in the light of the experience of industrial pension systems, but, of course, are very doubtful when applied to all the millions of workers who will be included in the federal old-age benefit plan and for all the years up to 1980 for which the actuaries made estimates. Should retirement occur earlier than assumed or the lost time be greater than one-ninth of all possible working time, contributions of more than 5 per cent will prove necessary unless there is a considerable increase in the average wage level.

For a complete explanation of the assumptions underlying the estimates on which the $47,000,000,000 reserve by 1980 is based, see Otto C. Richter, "Actuarial Basis of Cost Estimates of Federal Old-Age Insurance," *Law and Contemporary Problems,* III (1936), 212–30.

earnings, those of workers whose total wages are greater somewhat less, but in no case less than 3 per cent. The benefits, considered as a whole, are far more liberal than those of any compulsory insurance system in existence anywhere.

This old-age benefit plan is to be administered by the Social Security Board. The funds for payment are to come from the "old-age reserve account" which is set up on the books of the Treasury, to which Congress is authorized to appropriate annually "an amount sufficient as an annual premium to provide for the payments required under this title, such amount to be determined on a reserve basis in accordance with accepted actuarial principles, and based upon such tables of mortality as the Secretary of the Treasury shall from time to time adopt, and upon an interest rate of 3 per cent per annum compounded annually." These appropriations do not come from any special fund nor are they derived from any special taxes. There is no appropriation whatsoever in the title, but merely an authorization for an annual appropriation by Congress in the maximum amount determined on the basis above quoted. The language used clearly means that Congress can annually make any appropriation that it sees fit to the old-age reserve account, not exceeding the maximum estimated by the Secretary of the Treasury to be necessary to finance the old-age benefits on a reserve basis. In most discussions of the Social Security Act this provision has been interpreted as requiring financing on a reserve basis, but this interpretation has no foundation other than that this is the maximum authorized appropriation. Under the act it is possible for Congress to finance old-age benefits on a reserve basis, or on a pay-as-you-go basis, or any combination of these plans.

Any amount Congress may appropriate to the old-age reserve account in excess of the requirements for the immediate payment of benefits is directed to be invested by the Secretary of the Treasury in any outstanding United States securities or in special non-negotiable obligations of the government issued exclusively to this account and bearing 3 per cent interest. The Secretary of the Treasury is to include in each annual report to the President and Congress a complete statement of the actuarial status of the account, which means that he is to show not only the assets of the account but the present value of all contingent liabilities, assuming a continuance of the benefit plan without change.

The foregoing are all the essential provisions of the federal old-age benefit plan as set up in Title II of the Social Security Act. Since Title VIII, however, has been linked with Title II in all popular discussions, it is convenient to take note here of the provisions of this title.

Title VIII imposes two distinct taxes which came into effect January 1, 1937: an income tax on employees measured by the wages paid them and an excise tax on employers measured by their pay-rolls. The employees taxed are in the main the same people to whom benefits will become payable under Title II and the employers taxed are those employing these employees. For the first three years the tax rate is 1 per cent on the employer and 1 per cent on the employee, computed on the wages paid, but leaving out of consideration the excess over $3,000 paid to any individual in any year. In 1940 the tax rates will be increased to 1.5 per cent and every three years thereafter there will be another increase of 0.5 per cent until the maximum rate is reached in 1949. In that year and thereafter the rate will be 3 per cent on the employers and 3 per cent on the employees.

These taxes are popularly regarded as the source of the revenues for the payment of old-age benefits. They were loosely so described in the report of the Committee on Economic Security and by some members of Congress in the debates upon the Social Security Act. In the reports of the congressional committees, however, the complete separation of these titles was emphasized and structurally they are entirely distinct. The taxes levied in Title VIII may be amended or repealed independently of Title II. The revenues therefrom can be used for any purpose. While the United States government in simultaneously enacting both of these titles has assumed the moral obligation that the equivalent of the amounts collected under Title VIII, with interest thereon, shall be used for the payment of old-age benefits, there is no requirement that this amount shall be appropriated annually to the old-age reserve account.

That Title VIII would not have been enacted if Congress had not provided for payment of old-age benefits in Title II must be taken for granted. Title II established a policy which will involve very large expenditures. Very appropriately Congress made provisions for raising the necessary revenues to meet these anticipated expenditures. In doing so it levied taxes upon the persons who were expected to be benefited under Title II and upon their employers. But this is all that Congress actually did. The revenues raised through the taxes in Title VIII are not appropriated for the purpose of Title II nor segregated in any manner.

Before Congress acted there was much controversy over reserves and sources of revenues among the persons who were assisting and advising the Committee on Economic Security in developing the social security program. When Congress came to act, it did not write into law any of the conflicting theories. Contrary to the comments of most critics Congress carefully avoided writing into the Social Security Act either the reserve basis or a self-supporting plan of financing, but left future Congresses practically unrestricted as to the method of financing the federal old-age benefits.

What all this comes to is that the Social Security Act has not established an old-age insurance system, but only the closest approach to the European old-age insurance systems which anyone thinks is possible under the Constitution of the United States. No insurance policies or annuity contracts will be issued under Title II. This title does not legally obligate the federal government to pay the benefits therein stipulated for all time. There is no guaranty against amendment or repeal. In passing this legislation the country assumes a moral obligation to make good the hopes which it has aroused; in a democratic country it is inconceivable that this moral obligation to millions of citizens will not be observed, but there is no contract of any kind and there is no commitment as to how the plan shall be financed.

III. Objections to the Federal Old-Age Benefit Plan

The great majority of articles on the federal old-age benefit plan are very critical of its provision.[5] All legislation that imposes

---

[5] Among leading articles critical of the federal old-age benefit plan are M. Albert Linton, "Old Age Security for Everybody," *Atlantic Monthly*, CLVII (1936), 488–98, and "Reserve Provisions of the Federal Old-Age Security Program," *Transactions of the Actuarial Society of America*, October 3, 1935, pp. 363–80; Winthrop W. Aldrich, *An Appraisal of the Federal Social Security Act* (New York, 1936); Frank P. Stockbridge, "Social Security, or De Leevee Done Bust," *Saturday Evening Post*, March 7, 1936, pp. 10–11, 70, and March 14, 1936, pp. 27, 37–40, 43–48; Eveline M. Burns, "The Financial Aspects of the Social Security Act," *American Economic Review*, XXVI (1936) 12–22; and Abraham Epstein, *Insecurity: A Challenge to America* (New York, 1936), pp. 718–26, 734–38, 761–71.

new tax burdens is likely to be unpopular in the initial stages. This natural effect is aggravated in this instance by the fact that the retirement benefits under Title II will not be paid to anyone until 1942. But, more than anything else, misunderstanding of the plan has been responsible for the flood of adverse criticism. Much of this criticism is based not on the provisions of the Social Security Act, but on inaccurate secondary accounts.

Of all criticisms the ones relating to the methods of financing, which are supposed to be embodied in the Social Security Act, have been made most of. These center around the tax rates and reserves, and, specifically, include the claim that the reserve contemplated is so large that it will become unmanageable and will tend to increase rather than reduce costs, and also that the self-supporting feature will unjustly burden the younger and better paid employees.

Taking up, first, the most frequently urged objection of the large reserve, it is to be noted that insofar as this argument has any basis at all it arises from a table which was included in the report of the Senate Finance Committee on the estimated appropriations, benefit payments, and reserves under Title II.[6] This table indicated that by 1950 there would be a balance in the old-age reserve account of $14,000,000,000 and by 1980 of nearly $47,000,000,000. This table was prepared by the actuaries who assisted the committee and was based on the assumption that Congress would appropriate annually to the old-age reserve account the total of the revenues collected under Title VIII less costs of collection.

This assumption is one that has no warrant in any provision of the Social Security Act. In Title II, Congress is authorized to appropriate annually to this account "an amount sufficient as an annual premium to provide for the payments required under this title, such amount to be determined on a reserve basis in accordance with accepted actuarial principles." No possible construction of the language used [7] can make this authorization equivalent to the amount of the taxes

[6] *Sen. Rept., No. 628* (74th Congress, 1st session), p. 9.

[7] The most natural interpretation of this language would seem to be a level premium, as this term is used by insurance actuaries. This would require annual appropriations equal to approximately 5 per cent of payrolls from the very outset. Were Congress to make an appropriation of this amount it would have to supplement the revenues produced by the taxes under Title II by large additions from general tax sources until 1946, because until then the combined taxes under Title VIII will be less than 5 per cent.

collected under Title VIII. Moreover, this is merely the appropriation which Congress is authorized to make—that is, the maximum which it may appropriate in any year. It is not required to make this maximum appropriation and it is almost certain that it will not do so at all times. Yet, unless Congress, each and every year, appropriates the estimated total revenues under Title VIII, the $47,000,000,000 reserve will not actually develop. This reserve likewise will not develop if the actuaries underestimated the cost of the benefits or overestimated the tax collections, nor if in the course of forty-five years there are any important changes in either Titles II or VIII.

On the assumption that there will be such an enormous reserve, it is possible to conjure up all kinds of difficulties. Forty-seven billion dollars is more than the total debt of the United States at this time, and, if it is assumed that the debt will not be further increased, the matter of safely investing this reserve becomes a difficult problem.[8] Great fears are also expressed that this reserve will be an invitation for a constant increase in benefits.[9] Further, it is claimed that the reserve, even if maintained, will not reduce the tax burdens which must be borne in future years because taxes will have to be levied to pay the interest on the government securities in which the reserve will be invested. The conclusion drawn from these arguments is that the old-age benefit plan should be financed on a pay-as-you-go basis or, at least, that the reserve be kept down to a much smaller figure, and above all that the tax rates now in Title VIII be reduced.

The best answer to these arguments lies in the provisions of the Social Security Act. This act does not require financing on a reserve

[8] The $47,000,000,000 reserve is not expected to develop until 1980, by which time the debt of the United States may be much larger. Since the beginning of World War I the debt of the United States has increased by over $30,000,000,000 and approximately twenty-five times, and the entry of the United States into World War I is only twenty years past while 1980 is forty-four years hence.

[9] This danger is minimized through the provision in the Social Security Act that the Secretary of the Treasury shall include a statement of the status of the old-age reserve account in each annual report. Since the combined taxes under Title VIII will until 1946 be less than the 5 per cent of payrolls required to meet the costs of the old-age benefits under Title II, as determined on an actuarial basis, and Congress is almost certain not to appropriate a larger amount annually than the revenues produced by Title VIII, it is certain that for several decades this statement of the Secretary of the Treasury will indicate an excess of liabilities over assets. This should help to make it clear to Congress that there is no surplus which might be used for larger benefits.

basis; without any change in the law Congress may finance old-age benefits on the so-called pay-as-you-go plan.

Which of these methods Congress ought to adopt has nothing to do with the soundness of the old-age benefit plan, but may merit some comments. To answer this question a clear understanding of the nature of the reserve is essential.

The reserve arises because in the early years of the plan the current disbursements are small owing to the relatively small number of people who will be on the retirement rolls. For quite a few years to come the current costs could be financed without any increase in the present tax rates of 1 per cent on employers and 1 per cent on employees; in fact, even at these rates there would be an annual surplus for nearly a decade. But this is a very deceptive surplus, as the real cost of the benefits under Title II is 5 per cent of the payrolls. As the number of people on the retirement rolls increases the current costs will mount rapidly. Before 1970 they will exceed the tax collections under Title VIII at the then-prevailing combined rate of 6 per cent. By 1980 they will amount to approximately 10 per cent of the estimated taxable payrolls of that year. Thereafter, the actuaries estimate, the costs will increase further only slightly, but will continue at approximately 10 per cent of the taxable payrolls indefinitely.

To pay the promised benefits to the people who will be on the retirement rolls in 1980 and thereafter (who are the workers now young, and future workers), revenues equal to 10 per cent of the payrolls must be raised from some source whether the old-age benefit plan is financed on a pay-as-you-go or on a reserve basis. If the financing is on a pay-as-you-go basis, this entire amount must be raised through current taxes, either wholly on the employers and employees of that day or, in part, from the general taxpayers. If a reserve of $47,000,000,000 has been accumulated, as the actuaries estimated on the assumption that all taxes collected under Title VIII will each year be appropriated to the reserve account, the interest on this amount, equal to above $1,400,000,000 at the assumed rate of 3 per cent, will be available to reduce the revenues which have to be raised from current taxes to pay the old-age benefits. This amount of interest is equivalent to 4 per cent on the estimated payrolls of 1980 and will make possible the financing of the cost of old-age benefits at that time by levying only the combined 6 per cent tax on employers and employees, which is the present maximum rate in Title VIII, whereas under the pay-as-you-go plan taxes of 10 per cent would have to be collected to pay these benefits.

That a reserve will reduce the taxes which must be levied when the maximum costs develop under the old-age benefit plan would be obvious but for the complicating fact that the Social Security Act provides that this reserve be invested in the debt of the United States.[10] Were the reserve invested in other types of securities, no one would doubt that the interest earned would help to reduce the amount to be raised through taxes. If it is invested in the debt of the United States, however, taxes must be raised from general sources to pay the interest owed to the old-age reserve account, and so, it is argued, the situation is exactly the same as if the reserve did not exist.

This argument is fallacious because it loses sight of the fact that if the $47,000,000,000 of debt in 1980 were not owed to the old-age reserve account, they would probably be owed to private parties.[11] In that event the amount equal to 10 per cent on payrolls would have to be raised by current taxes to pay the cost of old-age benefits and, in addition thereto, the $1,400,000,000 interest on the $47,-000,000,000 of debt owed to private parties. If the debt is owed to the old-age reserve account, 6 per cent on payrolls in current taxes plus the $1,400,000,000 interest on the debt is all that has to be raised through taxes for old-age benefits and the interest on debt, a net saving to the government and the taxpayer of the $1,400,000,000 earned as interest on the reserve.

The term "pay-as-you-go" as used in other connections is applied to methods of financing in which all costs are met currently. As used

[10] Only a slight amendment will be required to authorize investment of the balances in the old-age reserve account in state and other municipal securities or in any other securities that Congress may consider advisable. That such an amendment may become necessary, if Congress actually finances old-age benefits on a reserve basis and if the debt of the United States is reduced to the predepression level, was recognized by the Committee on Economic Security. For at least a decade, however, such a problem will not arise and no safer investments can be made at this time than in obligations of the United States. When a different situation actually develops, the law can easily be amended accordingly.

[11] The argument here presented is not affected by the fact that the total debt of the United States in 1980 may be less than $47,000,000,000—which seems unlikely in view of the past history of public indebtedness in all countries. If the debt is less than $47,000,000,000 a part of the $47,000,000,000 reserve would have to be invested in other than United States securities, but the interest earned would be substantially as great. Whatever the interest earnings, they would reduce the amount which would have to be raised through current taxes to pay the cost of old-age benefits.

in relation to old-age insurance, however, the "pay-as-you-go" plan is the equivalent of the annual assessment method of some mutual fire insurance companies and benevolent societies. Because fire losses are fairly stable from year to year, this method of meeting costs has proven quite satisfactory in connection with fire insurance, but experience has established that it is very dangerous in life insurance, because the disbursements are certain to be much less in the early years than later on. This factor is fully as important in old-age insurance as in life insurance, as has been demonstrated by the experience of private employers with industrial pension plans. All the early plans of this kind were financed on the "pay-as-you-go" basis, with the result that the costs became so great in less than twenty years that the plans had either to be abandoned or placed on a reserve basis.

In a country as wealthy as the United States, it might be possible to finance a national old-age insurance system on a "pay-as-you-go" (annual assessment) basis. It is very certain, however, that the annual costs under such a plan would increase very rapidly, due to two factors: (a) the rapid increase in the number of old people, and (b) the fact that, on the average, men retired at age 65 live twelve years thereafter and women fifteen years. This phenomenon of rapidly increasing costs has characterized every retirement system ever established and will, undoubtedly, also occur in the national old-age insurance system.

In relation to old-age insurance, "pay-as-you-go" does not mean meeting all of the costs, but only the current disbursements, which in the early years are very much less than the real costs. It is essentially deficit financing, in which a large part of the costs computed on an actuarial basis are left unprovided for, to be met in the future as best they may. This method of financing has the advantage that in the early years a very low tax rate is possible, both for employers and employees. Later, however, higher taxes must be raised from some source or promised benefits be reduced. Most persons who argue for a pay-as-you-go plan suggest that the increased taxes be raised from the general taxpayers rather than from employers and employees, but there is no certainty that this will be done. When deficits developed during the present period of depression under the pay-as-you-go plan of financing in Germany, they were met, not through appropriations from general revenues, but through increases in the contribution rates and reductions in benefits. It is this factor of increased costs in future years and the uncertainty of how they will be met which has led all foreign countries except England to finance their old-age insurance systems on a reserve basis, at least nominally.[12] The pay-as-you-go plan is advantageous to present employers and present older workers, but is likely to prove very unfair to present younger workers and to future employers and employees.

This conclusion is very different from that of critics who condemn the federal old-age benefit plan as unfair to the younger workers. This criticism is premised upon the fact that persons with larger total earnings get monthly retirement benefits based upon smaller percentages of these earnings than workers with smaller total earnings.

The purpose of this sort of a benefit schedule is to make it possible for workers who are now middle-aged to get a sizable retirement allowance when they reach age sixty-five. Workers who are already past middle age will not have many years in which to make contributions, and compound interest on these contributions does not add greatly to the accumulations until after a lapse of years. The group of workers to whom retirement benefits will first become payable are persons who in 1937 are sixty years of age. These workers will be subject to the taxes under Title VIII for only five years. In these five years their total taxes, plus those paid by their employers, will produce an accumulation which at age sixty-five would purchase an annuity of less than $1.00 per month. Actually, they will get a retirement benefit of $10 per month as a minimum and, probably, $15 to $18 per month on the average. Similarly, all other middle-aged persons will get benefits which are in part "unearned," in the sense that the total taxes paid by them and their employers under Title VIII, with interest, will not be sufficient to pay the costs of the benefits they will get under Title II.

The critics of the federal act say that these unearned benefits are paid by the younger workers and the higher-paid employees. Actually, however, all or nearly all younger workers brought under the old-age benefit plan at the outset not only pay nothing toward the cost of the unearned part of the benefits paid to older workers, but will themselves receive some unearned benefits. This results from the fact, already noted, that the old-age benefit schedule is based on 5

---

[12] The revision of the German old-age insurance system in 1934 contemplates ultimate financing on a full reserve basis, but this basis will be reached only through gradual increases in contribution rates.

per cent contributions throughout an industrial lifetime. The combined taxes under Title VIII upon employers and employees will not total 5 per cent until the year 1946. Not all workers who become liable to taxes under Title VIII before 1946 will get larger retirement benefits under Title II than could be purchased from the combined taxes paid by them and their employers, but this will be true of a majority of these workers and, with the exception of workers with earnings of close to the maximum of $250 per month throughout their industrial lives, will be true of all workers who will be subject to the taxes under Title VIII from the outset.

Workers who enter industry in 1949 or thereafter will pay taxes under Title VIII of 3 per cent throughout the entire period of their industrial lives and their employers will pay an equal amount. This combined tax rate of 6 per cent is in excess of the amount required to pay the cost of the benefits under Title II. The taxes paid by the employees themselves, however, will in the average case be much less than sufficient to pay these benefits. For the employee earning average wages the benefits are such as can be paid for by 5 per cent contributions, while even these workers who enter industry in 1949 and thereafter will be paying taxes of only 3 per cent. For employees who have higher than average wages the advantages are less, but in all cases even workers who enter industry in 1949 or thereafter will get larger retirement benefits at age sixty-five than could be purchased from their own tax payments.

The same situation exists as to highly paid employees. Highly paid employees brought under the benefit plan at the outset will pay a larger part of the costs of their old-age benefits than do the lower-paid employees, but all of them and also highly paid employees brought under the plan in future years can look forward to larger retirement allowances than could be purchased from the taxes they pay, including interest.

Some critics, varying the argument, contend that the injustice to younger workers and higher-paid workers results because in the last analysis the employers' taxes will be taken out of the workers. This argument involves complex questions of the ultimate incidence of taxes imposed upon employers in proportion to their payrolls. This is a highly speculative and theoretical matter upon which real information is completely lacking. Very probably the ultimate incidence of taxes of this kind will vary in different situations and for different commodities. The courts have always refused to take cognizance of the possible shifting of taxes, and this seems to be the soundest rule in the development of governmental policies where the ultimate incidence of the taxes is obscure or debatable, as is the situation with reference to taxes upon employers under Title VIII of the Social Security Act. Further, it must not be lost sight of that, even if it is assumed that the entire taxes upon the employers will be shifted to the workers, the total combined taxes in the first nine years will be less than the cost of the benefits, computed on an actuarial basis.

Many of the critics who contend that the taxes upon the employers will be shifted to the workers at the same time claim that these taxes will prove ruinous to industry. It is natural that employers should be worried about the new taxes under Title VIII. All taxes are burdensome and this is especially true of new taxes. Many of the statements made regarding the tax burdens imposed upon industry, however, are false or misleading. Critics who attack the Social Security Act on this ground generally total the estimated taxes in the next fifteen, twenty-five, or even forty-five years, or, a little less unfairly, talk about the taxes which will become payable when the maximum rates take effect.[13] If a sufficiently long period of time is taken into consideration, the expenditures for any purpose can be made to look enormous; but as it is only present costs which are a real burden, such figures are practically meaningless. What taxes will amount to in 1949 is of some importance, but it is very misleading to talk about these estimated future taxes, as if they represented an immediate burden.

The tax rate upon employers under Title VIII in the three years 1937, 1938, and 1939 is 1 per cent of their payrolls. The Senate Finance Committee estimated that this tax would produce between $275,000,000 and $300,000,000 in each of these three years, and the tax on employees an equal amount. This is a large total, but very different from the figures bandied about by the opponents of the Social Security Act. These total taxes will increase as rates and the volume of employment increase, but even in 1950, and allowing for

[13] Even more misleading statements were made during the debate on the Social Security Act in the United States Senate. Large wall maps were displayed which totaled the estimated tax levies, benefit payments, and reserves in the next forty-five years as the costs of the federal old-age benefit plan. These figures were widely distributed among employers to arouse opposition to the Social Security Act and are still used in some articles attacking this legislation. By adding all these items together the gross cost is doubled, and no allowance is made for offsetting reductions in other governmental costs.

a very considerable increase in the total payrolls, the tax upon employers is estimated to produce less than $950,000,000. Taxes of this amount are nearly fifteen years off, and even so are only a little more than 20 per cent of the total present federal taxes.

That employers should contribute something to the costs of retirement allowances for their employees is generally conceded. Such contributions are quite similar to the amounts which employers include in their costs to cover depreciation of machinery and equipment. A charge for the depreciation of the labor element in production is just as proper as is a charge for depreciation of capital. A retirement system under which employers can humanely replace old workers with younger men is of great value to them. The exact proportion of the costs of such a retirement system which should be borne by the employers is a matter of opinion. The federal old-age benefit plan, under which employers pay as much as the employees, but in which the tax rates in the early years are kept at a figure below the true actuarial costs of the benefits, seems eminently fair and reasonable.

This brings us to the question whether the federal government should pay part of the costs of old-age benefits from general tax sources. This is a policy strongly advocated by many of the critics of the Social Security Act, but is at present a purely academic question. No one proposes that the government should begin to make contributions from general tax sources at this time. Not until 1965 or thereabouts will there be any need of government contributions, as the receipts from the taxes under Title VIII will until then exceed the current disbursements under Title II. Nor is there any way in which it could now be determined, as a matter of law, how the anticipated deficit in 1965 shall be financed when it arises. In the budget procedure which prevails in this country no appropriation could now be made to take effect in 1965 and an income or other tax levy to begin at that time would be ridiculous.[14]

[14] Most critics of the federal old-age benefit plan assume that the original bill included provisions for government contributions in 1965 and thereafter. This, however, was not the case, no provisions whatsoever being made for meeting the anticipated deficit at that time. In the report of the staff on old-age security to the Committee on Economic Security it was suggested that this deficit be met from general tax revenues, but there was, of course, no way in which this recommendation could be written into law. What the original bill did was to impose taxes at rates which rendered a growing deficit probable from 1965 on, leaving to the decision of the people in control of public affairs at that time how this deficit might be met.

Whether there should be contributions ultimately from general tax revenues toward the cost of old-age benefits is debatable. In opposition to such contributions it is to be pointed out that the entire costs of old-age assistance—the first part of the present program for old-age security—fall upon the general taxpayers. To make them pay a part also of the costs of the second part of the program—the federal old-age benefits—may well be argued to be burdening them excessively. Nearly half of all persons gainfully employed are excluded from benefits under Title II, but they would have to pay a large part of the costs if there are contributions from general tax sources. On the other hand, many good arguments can be made for ultimate government contributions.

The entire issue, at this time, is very remote. If all actuarial calculations are correct and if neither Title II nor Title VIII is ever altered, no contributions from general tax revenues will be necessary to finance the benefits under Title II provided that Congress will actually appropriate to the old-age reserve account an amount equal to all the taxes collected under Title VIII. Congress, however, is not required to make such an appropriation and, if past history is any guide, Congress will not make the maximum authorized appropriation in all years. The actuarial calculations involve assumptions as to the number of employees, their distribution by sex and ages, the volume of unemployment, and the wage rates which will prevail in years far ahead in the future. The actuaries frankly admit that if their estimates are no more than 25 per cent off they will have proved unusually accurate. Highly probable also are changes in Titles II and VIII if past experience with other legislation of comparable importance is any criterion. What all this means is that it cannot now be definitely stated whether the federal old-age benefit plan will or will not require contributions from general tax sources in future years. No one believes that such contributions should be made at this time and the people now in control of governmental affairs cannot determine what future legislators should do in this matter.

In the final analysis all of the arguments relating to tax burdens, sources of revenue, and reserves resolve themselves into the question whether the tax rates in Title VIII are too high. Very probably there would be less opposition if these rates were reduced,[15] but any tax

[15] This is by no means certain, as the opponents of this legislation could then be expected to argue that the anticipated, unprovided-for deficit would render it doubtful

reductions are at least premature. In the development of the old-age security program, I originally advocated pay-as-you-go financing and later concurred in the deficit financing plan incorporated in the original bill. That plan, however, could not be enacted into law and it became necessary to increase the tax rates [16] in Title VIII to lessen the chances of a large, unprovided-for deficit at the time when workers now young will be old. I now believe that this change was sound, as I have come to prefer, in the early years of the federal old-age benefit plan, tax rates higher than necessary to meet the current disbursements because the lowest possible rates leave it uncertain whether the younger workers of the present day will ever get the benefits they have a right to expect. The taxes which will be collected under Title VIII will not be anywhere near sufficient in the early years to pay the true costs of the benefits to which the workers brought under Title II will become entitled. Further to reduce the tax rates will increase the deficits which have to be met later on and will create a great hazard that promised benefits to present younger workers will be reduced when they are old. In 1946, when the combined tax rates become sufficient to cover the cost of the benefits of the workers then entering employment, there may be justification for stopping the further increase in rates contemplated in the present law. Until then, however, the tax rates certainly cannot be claimed to be too high and no large reserve will be created even if Congress should annually appropriate to the old-age reserve account the maximum authorized amount.

---

whether the promised benefits would ever be paid. This argument was actually made before the Congressional committees before the amendment increasing the tax rates was suggested by the Committee on Economic Security.

[16] In the original bill the initial tax rates were 0.5 per cent on employers and employees and the maximum rate of 2.5 per cent on employers and on employees was not to be levied until 1956. As the benefits were geared to a 5 per cent contribution rate, this meant that not only all persons, young and old, brought under the old-age benefit plan at the outset, but substantially all future workers who would attain retirement age before the year 2000, would have received partially unearned benefits. This plan of financing, on the actuaries' estimates, involved deficits beginning in 1965 and amounting to $1,100,000,000 in 1980 and annually thereafter.

This prospective large deficit was objected to by the President and by many members of Congress. To save the contributory old-age insurance plan, the Committee on Economic Security then proposed the increased tax rates which were included in Title VIII as finally enacted. This amendment was presented by Secretary of the Treasury Morgenthau and for this reason has been called the "Morgenthau Amendment." It was, however, not a proposal of Secretary Morgenthau alone, but was agreed to by all members of the Committee on Economic Security and was accepted by both congressional committees without a dissenting vote.

People who criticize the anticipated large reserve in the old-age benefit plan generally also argue that the benefits are inadequate. It apparently has never occurred to them that one sure way of avoiding the difficulties of a large reserve is to increase the benefits payable in the early years of the system. The benefits to people now middle-aged will not be sufficient for support in old-age unless they have income from other sources or receive old-age assistance in addition. These are arguments both for and against increasing the benefits in the early years, and I for one would not object to such an increase. If the fears of an unmanageably large reserve are genuine, it is vastly preferable to increase the benefits payable to people past middle age when the plan comes into effect to reducing the initial tax rates, which are not sufficient as they stand to meet the true costs of the plan.

The criticisms of the federal old-age benefit plan thus far noted which center around the tax rates are by no means the only objections urged by opponents. Limitations of space prevent consideration of many of the other objections, but some of them merit brief treatment.

Of these the limited coverage of the old-age benefit plan is made most of by the largest group of leftish critics, the Townsendites. Their argument is that the Social Security Act is discriminatory because nearly half of the gainfully occupied persons are excluded from coverage, plus housewives and other people who are not classified in the census as gainfully occupied.

Theoretically it would be desirable to include the entire adult population in the old-age benefit plan, as Sweden and three Swiss cantons are doing. The original bill had a much more inclusive coverage, excluding only self-employed persons and the employees of the federal, state, and local governments,[17] but Congress saw fit to adopt amendments greatly extending the exclusions.

Practically there is much to be said for the more limited coverage adopted by Congress. Even so, the federal old-age benefit plan will at the very outset include a larger number of persons than are included in the compulsory old-age insurance systems of any other

---

[17] The state and local governments could not be included because the federal government cannot tax the states and their political subdivisions. Federal employees were excluded because most of them already have old-age protection through the United States Employees Retirement Act, with higher contribution rates and larger benefits than the federal old-age benefit plan.

country. The excluded classes, moreover, are those which world-experience has shown are most difficult to bring under a compulsory old-age insurance system. In view of these facts the more restricted coverage is, perhaps, justifiable.[18] In any event extension of coverage can be brought about by amendments later on if the plan proves popular and successful.

In the meantime such discrimination as exists is very different from that claimed by the Townsendites. The excluded groups will not get any benefits under Title II, but are also exempt from the taxes under Title VIII. They, moreover, are not denied all old-age protection, but on the contrary will be eligible to old-age assistance on the same basis as persons who receive benefits under Title II. In fact, they will have the advantage, as but few persons receiving old-age benefits will be able to qualify for old-age assistance, although, as general taxpayers, the latter group will have to pay a large part of the costs of the assistance grants.

A related criticism is that the benefits paid to the persons who will be retired in the early years of the federal old-age benefit plan will be less than the amounts which other persons will get as old-age assistance without being required to contribute anything toward the costs. This criticism is based on the popular misinterpretation of the old-age assistance laws as fixing the amount of the assistance at $30 per month (or some other specified figure), whereas in all laws this is only the maximum assistance that may be allowed. The average grants throughout the country in August, 1936, were only a little more than $18 per month. This is approximately the same amount as the probable average of the retirement benefits to the persons who will first become eligible for these benefits in 1942. Moreover, it needs to be borne in mind that persons who receive old-age benefits will not be barred from old-age assistance if the benefits are too small for their needs. It is anticipated that in the early years of the federal old-age benefit plan there will be a considerable number who will simultaneously receive old-age benefits and old-age assistance. With the lapse of time, as the benefits increase, this will become rare, but in the early years it is unavoidable, unless it is deemed prefer-

---

[18] Some of the exclusions are indefensible. This is true, particularly, of the exemption of educational, charitable, and religious organizations, which was adopted on the plea that most of their professional workers already have old-age protection; but none of the church and educational pension funds include the large number of lay (non-professional) workers who most need protection.

On November 5, 1937, the Social Security Advisory Council gathered in Washington to analyze the social security law. Left to right, *seated:* M. Albert Linton, president of Provident Mutual Life Insurance Co., Philadelphia; Marion B. Folsom, treasurer of Eastman Kodak Co., Rochester, N.Y.; William Haber, member of the Unemployment Compensation Commission, Lansing, Mich.; G. M. Bugniazet (partially hidden), secretary of International Brotherhood, Electrical Workers of America; Theresa McMahon, University of Washington; A. L. Mowbray, University of California; Mary Dewson, member of the Social Security Board; Arthur J. Altmeyer, chairman of the Social Security Board; George E. Bigge, member of the Social Security Board; Lee Pressman, general counsel of the C.I.O.; Philip Murray of the C.I.O.; Harvey Fremming, president of the Oil Field, Gas Well, and Refinery Workers' International Union; George L. Stocking, University of Texas; Paul Douglas, University of Chicago. *Standing:* T. L. Norton, University of Buffalo; Matthew Woll, vice-president of the International Photo Engravers' Union of North America; Gerard Swope, president of General Electric Co.; Edward R. Stettinius, Jr., chairman of the Finance Committee, U.S. Steel Co.; Jay Iglauer, vice-president of Halle Brothers, Cleveland, Ohio; Henry Bruere, president of the Bowery Savings Bank, New York; Gerald Morgan, author of books on social security; Edwin E. Witte, University of Wisconsin; J. Douglas Brown, Princeton University.

Up the steps to his office on the campus of the University of Wisconsin, 1955.

Photo by Herb Kratovil
courtesy of *Business Week*

able to pay much larger unearned annuities to many persons who do not need them.

A different line of attack upon the federal old-age benefit plan is represented by the Clark amendment and the Jackson plan [19] for social security. Both of these received consideration when the Social Security Act was before Congress and the former came very close to adoption. Both are premised upon the thesis that industrial pension plans offer a much better solution of the old-age security problem than does the federal old-age benefit plan. The Clark amendment, accordingly, proposed to exclude employees who are covered by industrial pension systems from the federal old-age benefit plan, while the Jackson plan proposes to substitute for the federal plan the requirement that all large employers must establish industrial pension systems.

The major argument made for these proposals is that the Social Security Act will compel employers to abandon all industrial pension plans and thereby deprive their employees of more liberal retirement benefits than they will get under the federal plan.[20] This contention is now much less strong than it was while the Social Security Act was being debated because it has since been demonstrated that employers with industrial pension plans can convert them into plans supplemental to the federal plan without additional cost to the employers or loss of any part of the promised benefits to the included employees. A considerable number of employers with industrial pension plans have already so altered their plans, and the insurance company which has the largest number of group annuity (industrial pension plan) contracts has developed a standard form of contract for this coverage. Far from destroying the industrial pension systems, the Social Security Act has thus far operated to give a great stimulus to

[19] This plan was embodied in bill S. 2828 (74th Congress, 1st session) and was also offered as a substitute for Titles II and VIII of the Social Security Act, while this measure was under consideration on the Senate floor (*Congressional Record*, LXXIX, 9642–46). Its principal advocate is Mr. Henry E. Jackson, President of the Social Engineering Institute, New York City.

[20] The best presentations of the arguments in support of these proposals, particularly the Clark amendment, are the speeches made during the debate on the Social Security Act by Senators Clark and George (*Congressional Record*, LXXIX, 9510–27, 9541–43, 9628–29). Good statements of the case against these proposals are two articles by M. B. Folsom, "Company Annuity Plans and Federal Old-Age Insurance," *Law and Contemporary Problems*, III (1936), 231–35, and "Company Annuity Plans and the Federal Old-Age Benefit Plan," *Harvard Business Review*, XIV (1936), 414–34; and Paul H. Douglas, *Social Security in the United States* (New York, 1936), pp. 271–91.

the establishment of new industrial pension plans. At no time has the volume of new business done by insurance companies in this field been as great as during this period.

Industrial pension plans cannot be regarded as a substitute for the federal old-age benefit plan. Less than five million workers are now included in such plans and, while some further growth may be expected, there is no prospect that industrial pension plans will ever embrace a majority of all workers unless their establishment is made compulsory. Compulsory legislation cannot conceivably be applied to small employers; [it] would carry with it a degree of governmental regulation which most employers would regard as worse than the federal old-age benefit plan. Most serious of all is the fact that only a small percentage of all workers included in the industrial plans can look forward to ever receiving retirement allowances. Only employees who remain with the firm until they reach retirement age get any benefits under industrial pension plans. This means that the great majority of employees included in these plans really have no old-age protection, although the retirement benefits of the small number who stay on until they reach retirement age may be more liberal than those of the federal plan. On a basis supplemental to the federal old-age benefit plan, there is some value in industrial pension systems, but they cannot possibly be considered an adequate substitute for the federal plan.

Most of the objections to the federal old-age benefit plan considered up to this point are based upon misinterpretations of the provisions of the existing law or are merely arguments advanced by opponents of the entire legislation who could not be satisfied in any event. None of them presents any matters requiring immediate changes, although some are not entirely devoid of merit and may justify amendments at a later date.

The two matters which are of immediate importance are constitutionality and administration; and these are also the two most vulnerable points in the entire plan.

The objection of unconstitutionality is one to which it is not possible to give a dogmatic answer.[21] No similar plan has ever been

---

[21] Among many articles in legal periodicals discussing the constitutionality of the federal old-age benefit plan, the pro and con treatments of the subject by Harry Shulman and Charles Denby, Jr., in *Law and Contemporary Problems* (III [1936], 298–331) merit special mention. Favorable to the law, but fairly stating the issues

before the courts and there are no precedents directly in point. Whether the old-age benefit plan is constitutional, consequently, is at this time a matter of forecasting how the Supreme Court will look upon this legislation.

The question would seem to turn largely upon whether Titles II and VIII are severable. To the contrary can be cited the fact that, with but few exceptions, the people who get benefits under Title II are the same people who have to pay taxes under Title VIII. The benefits, while not based upon the taxes paid, are dependent upon the earnings subsequent to December 31, 1936, which are also the basis for computing the taxes. In support of the contention that the titles are severable, it is clear that each of these titles can be amended or repealed independently of the other. The proceeds of the taxes in Title VIII are not set aside for the payment of the benefits under Title II nor is Congress required to appropriate the amount produced by these taxes to the purposes of Title II. The taxes in Title VIII were, indeed, levied because the federal government launched the old-age benefit plan. But it is certainly not unconstitutional to make provisions for raising revenues to meet expenditures. Nor is there anything unconstitutional in placing new taxes upon those who will be peculiarly benefited by the new expenditures. The former is merely sound budget procedure and the latter a recognized principle of taxation.

Which of these lines of argument will prevail will probably depend, to a considerable extent, on the social viewpoint of the Supreme Court justices. Should a majority of the Court hold the federal old-age benefit plan to be unconstitutional, the decision would probably destroy both Titles II and VIII, although the former might stand while the latter was invalidated.

Such a decision would not necessarily mean the end of all attempts to establish a compulsory old-age insurance system or its equivalent in this country. The first workmen's compensation act passed in the United States was held unconstitutional and so was the first employers' liability law. Many decisions of the courts holding laws unconstitutional have merely operated to bring about some changes in the

_____

involved, are two articles by Barbara N. Armstrong, "The Federal Social Security Act," *American Bar Association Journal*, XXI (1935), 786–89, 792–97, and "The Federal Social Security Act in Its Constitutional Aspects," *California Law Review*, XXIV (1936), 247–74.

legislation to render it constitutional. Further, there is always the possibility of constitutional amendment, the amending clause being as much a part of the Constitution as any other. But no one can be certain that the damage done through an adverse decision could ever be repaired, and, in the most favorable circumstances, it would involve years of delay in getting a compulsory, contributory old-age insurance system started in this country.

Equally immediate and important is the matter of administration. This presents many difficulties primarily because the numbers involved are so very large. At the very outset the federal old-age benefit plan will directly affect several million employers and twenty-six million employees; and the number of the prospective beneficiaries will increase rapidly. Under Title II the benefits payable to each of these prospective beneficiaries (or their estates) depend upon their earnings subsequent to December 31, 1936. For some months it would have been possible to ascertain these earnings at the time of retirement or death, but ere long it would become absolutely necessary to get the record of earnings approximately currently. The Social Security Board, consequently, decided to institute at the very outset a system of permanent registration of all workers, involving the assignment of account numbers to all workers, many millions of such accounts and entries in all active accounts quarterly, or, at least, annually. Plus these there will ultimately be hundreds of thousands of claims to decide each year and millions of checks to send out each month. Assuredly this will become one of the largest of governmental business enterprises, requiring a large staff of employees.[22]

The administrative difficulties would be materially lessened if we had a flat-rate benefit system like that of England. This would eliminate the necessity of keeping track of individual earnings which is at least half of the total problem. But flat benefits, without regard to earnings, do not appeal to many Americans who are accustomed to wide differentials between urban and rural areas and in different parts of the country, and between occupations and races. This means that it is probably impossible to establish in this country as simple an old-age insurance system as prevails in England.

Difficult as is the administrative problem in this sort of an old-age benefit plan, it should not prove insurmountable. Twenty-eight countries of the world other than the United States are now success-

[22] In Germany there are nearly 10,000 employees in the compulsory old-age and invalidity insurance system.

fully administering compulsory old-age insurance systems. In all these countries other than England, benefits are related to earnings, and the same problems have had to be met which this country faces in keeping track currently of earnings. The administrative difficulties in this respect, in fact, are much greater in most of these countries than they are likely to prove in the United States, due to the fact that these foreign plans have introduced the further complicating element of wage classes. While, initially, there will be difficulties galore, it should be possible in course of time to develop an administration in this country which will work as smoothly and efficiently as do the old-age insurance systems of nearly all other major countries. An excellent beginning has been made in carrying through the permanent registration of all workers, which has been all but completed with surprisingly little friction.

IV. Alternatives to Federal Old-Age Benefits

Before passing judgment upon the federal old-age benefit plan, consideration should be given to the possible alternatives. It is conceded by nearly everyone that the United States can no longer avoid doing something about old-age security. Many persons, however, believe that old-age assistance is all that the government should attempt to do in the matter of old-age security. They are of the opinion that this is the cheapest way of meeting the problem and the one which involves the least difficulty.

Those who hold this view are very apt to underestimate the costs of old-age assistance in future years. It is natural to assume that present costs will not greatly increase, but such an assumption ignores the practical certainty of a large increase in the number of old people,[23] a probably even greater increase in the rate of dependency, and the tendency for a larger percentage of the old persons to get on the pension rolls—which has been manifested in every country which has a non-contributory old-age pension system. The actuarial consultants of the Committee on Economic Security estimated that

[23] The statistical and actuarial staff of the Committee on Economic Security estimated that the present number of persons who are 65 and over, of not quite 7,500,000, will be increased to 10,863,000 in 1950; to 15,066,000 in 1970; to 17,001,000 in 1980; and to 19,338,000 in the year 2000. The persons who are 65 and over now constitute approximately 6 per cent of the entire population; in 1970 they will be above 10 per cent of the population; in 2000 they will be 12.7 per cent. These estimates are based on the age distribution of the present population and the present life expectancy. They are much more conservative than the estimates of most population statisticians.

within five years old-age assistance in this country would cost the federal, state, and local governments $800,000,000. By 1960 this cost (assuming that old-age assistance is the only measure for old-age security) was estimated at $2,000,000,000 and at later dates at even higher totals.

The federal old-age benefit plan will not eliminate the necessity for old-age assistance, as nearly half of the population will not be included in the old-age benefit plan at the outset and for some years the benefits will be so small that in a considerable number of cases they will have to be supplemented by old-age assistance. In the course of time, however, the old-age benefit plan will materially reduce the need for old-age assistance, and there is at least a possibility that the total cost to the general taxpayers for old-age security will after a decade or thereabouts actually decrease despite the increasing number of old persons.

The principal reason why a program for old-age security offering nothing more than old-age assistance will not do, however, is not that it would mean greater costs to the general taxpayers than the Social Security Act, but that the American people will not be satisfied with such a program. Old-age assistance is urgently needed for persons who are old and are dependent upon the public for support. It is the best way now known for taking care of aged dependents. Beyond question, however, it is unsatisfactory in many respects. To the beneficiaries it means a distasteful inquiry into their mode of living, their property and income, and the possibilities of securing support from children and other relatives. More important still is the fact that many persons who are barred from receiving assistance will believe themselves the victims of unjust discrimination. As a general rule the persons who will receive old-age assistance are less thrifty and less industrious than those who cannot qualify for assistance. Many persons who pay taxes all their lives so that other persons may have old-age assistance will themselves be unable to get assistance when they are old. Another factor not to be overlooked is that military pensions have led the American people to look upon old-age pensions as a right and a reward for good citizenship. This same idea has been strongly inculcated by the Townsend movement which, moreover, has given millions of Americans the false notion that large pensions can be paid to every old person without costing the taxpayer anything.

The democratic traditions of this country, plus the Puritan heritage which places such a high value upon individual initiative and thrift, dooms a program for old-age security which offers no more than assistance on a needs basis to persons who are dependent upon the public for support. If such a policy is attempted, it is almost certain that ere long the old-age assistance laws will be modified to become free pensions to all persons who reach specified ages, barring, perhaps, the very small number who have large independent incomes.

The American feeling with regard to pensions has been one of the major factors accounting for the remarkable spread of popularity of the Townsend plan. This movement may now be somewhat receding, but the American people are by no means convinced that a free pension of a flat amount to everybody who reaches a specified age is not the best solution of the old-age security problem. Two hundred dollars per month is regarded even by many Townsendites to be an absurd figure, but many millions—perhaps a majority of all voters—believe that pensions of $30, $50, or $60 per month to everybody who is past sixty or sixty-five are entirely feasible. Most Americans will not be satisfied with a program for old-age security which merely gives them assistance on a needs basis if they are dependent upon the public for support in their old age. They want protection which comes to them as a matter of right, not by reason of need. This means that the real alternative to the contributory old-age benefit plan is not old-age assistance, but a system of free pensions to everybody who reaches a specified age of a flat amount regardless of need—a modified Townsend plan.[24] This alternative may include the additional feature that the income from other sources shall be deducted from the specified flat pension, but this will not alter its fundamental nature.

Any such plan would involve stupendous costs. A pension of $30

[24] A system of this kind can be established with only slight changes in the existing old-age assistance laws. The most important change is one which would merely strike out the provision that the specified pension (assistance) shall be the maximum grant or which would fix this amount as the minimum grant (e.g., instead of providing that the pension shall not exceed $30 per month, the law would then read that the pension shall be $30 per month or a minimum of $30 per month). Such a development has already occurred in California, in which a 1936 amendment has fixed the pension grants at a minimum of $35 per month, less income from other sources. It is reflected also in the order issued by Governor Johnson of Colorado in the summer of 1936 that the old-age pension grants shall be $30 per month in all cases and in the initiated measure adopted by the voters of this state in the November election increasing the pension grants to $45 per month and reducing the minimum age to sixty years.

per month to everybody over sixty will cost nearly four billion dollars per year at the outset. This is close to half of the combined federal, state, and local taxes now collected for all purposes. With the increasing number of old persons these costs will mount rapidly. By 1950 they will be 50 per cent greater than now; by 1970 double the present figure. Nor will the modification that income from other sources is to be deducted from the specified flat pension save the situation since but relatively few old people have any considerable income. It is only when children are held for the support of their parents that there is any large savings in costs, but this feature would make the alternative very much like the present old-age assistance laws and is entirely unacceptable to the critics of the Social Security Act.

Anyone who has a realistic understanding of American politics also will appreciate that under a system of universal free pensions there will be a constant tendency to increase the pensions and to lower the minimum age. The number of beneficiaries will be so much greater than that of the veterans that they will be able to exert much stronger political pressure and everybody knows that the veterans have been able to get pretty much everything that they wanted. No matter how high the age and how low the pensions at the outset, it can be taken for granted that ere long the minimum age will be reduced and the pensions increased; and this is apt to be repeated many times.

What this means is that free pensions of a flat amount for all people who have reached a specified age, even if reduced by their income from other sources, are a financial impossibility. No country has ever tried this experiment. The United States, of all countries, would seem to be the one in which it would be most likely to prove unmanageable. Despite the confusing hocus-pocus of the revolving transaction tax of the Townsend plan, it is very certain that universal free pensions must be paid for by the taxpayers, and the tax burden will soon become unbearable.

The impossible costs are by no means the only objection to universal free pensions. Pensions of a flat amount, if no more than adequate for the majority of the old people, are grossly inadequate for many who need special care or who have others who are dependent upon them. Old-age pensions can be given to persons who do not need them only at the cost of less than adequate assistance to persons who really need help. Even more serious is the danger that the promised pensions may not be paid. Anything that is given as a gratuity may subsequently be withdrawn. Millions of beneficiaries will make withdrawal difficult, but when the costs become unbearable the persons who are paying the bill may be expected to revolt. Free pensions may seem very desirable to the mass of the workers, particularly those past middle age, but the fly in the ointment is that a larger number of young people must pay most of the costs and there can be no certainty how long they will be willing to do so. Old-age insurance is a much safer proposition. Because it is contributory, the costs can be financed without excessive tax burdens. The contributory feature also will operate to render unreasonable increases in costs very unlikely, particularly if the principle is established that the entire costs shall be met through equal contributions of employers and employees. While the federal old-age benefit system is not contractual, its continuance is a moral obligation which no government is likely to regard lightly. If found to be constitutional it will accomplish all the purposes of European old-age insurance systems.

V. Next Steps in Old-Age Security

The present old-age security program of the United States is far from perfect. It has many shortcomings and doubtless will have to be changed in many respects in the future. Social security legislation everywhere has undergone many changes and the United States is not likely to prove an exception in this respect.

The old-age assistance laws are not as liberal as they ought to be and their administration in many states is still less liberal. It is my belief that the $15 per month limitation of the maximum aid which the federal government will pay in any case should be stricken from the federal act and so should the restriction that aid will be paid only for assistance to persons who are at least sixty-five years of age. To make the old-age assistance laws operate as they should, it may also be necessary to create a free fund from which the federal government can pay more than 50 per cent of the costs of old-age assistance to the very poor states or those which are temporarily in great distress due to some extraordinary emergency. Provisions probably should also be made for old-age assistance at federal expense to persons who cannot satisfy the residence requirements in any state but who have long been citizens of the United States.

In the state laws there are still many illiberal provisions. Many of the restrictions create injustices and are very much resented, particularly the requirement that dependent old persons must convey their property to the state (or county) to be eligible for assistance. Limitations of the maximum amount of old-age assistance, to be found in most of the state laws, are illogical and should be replaced by the more flexible standard of assistance in an amount sufficient for "a reasonable subsistence compatible with decency and health," which has for years been successfully applied in Massachusetts and New York. Above all, the administration of the state old-age assistance laws needs to be improved.

The federal old-age benefit plan is one which in course of time should be extended in coverage. Thought should be given also to the simplification of the benefit provisions and their liberalization in the early years of the plan. Old-age insurance systems everywhere have been modified in numerous respects as experience has demonstrated the necessity for changes. Beyond question the federal old-age benefit plan will in the course of time have to be similarly modified.

In the immediate future, however, it is far more important to get the old-age security program into full operation than to perfect it in details. The constitutionality of the federal old-age benefit plan is still undetermined; difficult problems of administration remain to be solved; the great mass of the people as yet have only the vaguest ideas about the entire program and are not at all certain that universal free pensions are not preferable.

A better understanding of the old-age problem and the alternative methods open to this country for dealing with this problem is the really vital need at this time. If the American people can get to understand the problem, no fears need be entertained about the future of the old-age security program. The Supreme Court may hold the old-age benefit plan unconstitutional but, if the American people prefer compulsory old-age insurance to a system of universal pensions supported by general taxation, a method certainly can be found under which an old-age insurance system or its equivalent can be established. When this has actually been accomplished it will be timely to consider changes and improvements.

Is the Continued Drive
for Universal Pensions
a Social Menace?

American Labor Legislation Review, Volume **XXXI,** Number 1 (March, 1941), pages 38–46

IMMEDIATELY FOLLOWING the 1940 election, the press read into it this interpretation: "Pension Panaceas Lose Grip on American People."

Dr. Townsend had endorsed Willkie for President, but the returns indicate that his support counted for no more in this election than did his endorsement of Lemke in 1936. At least 20 Congressmen who were pledged to the Townsend Plan went down to defeat, as did 40 signers of the discharge petition sponsored by the rival General Welfare Federation. In Arkansas, moreover, the voters rejected a radical pension proposal, while in California the "Ham-and-Eggs" group failed to get enough signers to its initiative petition to get on the ballot.

But it is now apparent that the report that the universal pension movement is dead, is premature. Offsetting defeats in other elections, radical pension groups scored in Colorado's rejection of a proposal to repeal the constitutional provision for a pension of $45 per month to everybody over 60, and in Washington's adoption of an initiated measure providing for pensions of $40 per month to everybody over 65. While there was less publicity about the endorsement of candidates for Congress by the Townsend and other universal pension groups than in 1938, a large majority of all Representatives and Senators recently elected had such endorsements. Dr. Townsend writing to his followers from Washington in December reported that the chances for victory for his Plan have never been better, and Mr. Johnson, of the rival General Welfare Federation—which in the recent House lacked but six signatures on its discharge petition—confidently asserts that it has increased strength in the incoming Congress.

Even more significant are indications of what the Administration is likely to do. I do not accept as gospel truth the report in two of our most widely read newspaper gossip columns that the President has made up his mind "to change the existing system of widely divergent state contributions to one of uniform Federal pensions, beginning at a lower age than the present 65." This report may be no more accurate than is gossip generally, but some action in relation to old-age security in the not distant future was foreshadowed in the Democratic National Platform and in one of the President's campaign speeches.

The Democratic Platform included the pledge:

To make the social security act increasingly effective, by covering additional millions of persons under its terms . . . by progressively extending and increasing the benefits of the old-age and survivors' insurance system, including protection of the permanently disabled; and by the early realization of a minimum pension for all who have reached the age of retirement.

Elaborating upon this pledge, the President said in his speech at the Teamsters' Union Convention:

Our old-age pension system must be improved and extended: the amount of the pension should be increased, and, above all, these pensions must be given in a manner which will respect the dignity of the life of service and labor which our aged citizens have given to the nation.

It is my hope that soon the United States will have a national system under which no needy man or woman within our borders will lack a minimum old-age pension which will provide adequate food, clothing and lodging—and I look forward to a system which in addition to this bare minimum will enable those who have faithfully toiled in any occupation to build up additional security for their old age which will allow them to live in comfort and happiness.

Whatever else these statements may mean, this is certain: the incoming administration is definitely committed to an extension of the old-age insurance system and to some sort of a minimum pension, although it is not clear whether this is to be a minimum pension for *all* who have reached retirement age, as the platform promises, or only for every *needy* man or woman, as the President envisioned.

Reasons for Universal Pension Sentiment

The reasons why universal pensions have so much political support are not far to seek. Foremost among them is widespread dissatisfaction with the way the existing measures for old-age security are working out. With the exception of the relatively small number of retired citizens who are receiving sizable military, governmental, industrial, or church pensions, the great majority of the people already retired feel aggrieved. One-fourth of them are receiving old-age assistance, but the percentages receiving assistance and the amount of the grants vary greatly from state to state and often within the same state. The federal government pays half of the costs, but this provision works out so that the largest amount of aid goes to the states which make the largest grants and which least need financial assistance. Few of the people receiving old-age assistance consider the allowances they get to be adequate and many of the grants are in fact very skimpy; moreover, there is constant complaint that applicants for old-age assistance are made to feel that they are paupers.

But if the old people who are receiving old-age assistance have a grievance, those who get no assistance—who are three times as numerous—are much more dissatisfied. Many of them are but little, if at all, better off financially, than those who get assistance. As our present laws work out, they seem to reward people who never amounted to much, while penalizing those who were industrious and thrifty. Such a result appears very unjust to those of our older citizens who cannot qualify for either old-age assistance or old-age insurance.

Nor are the retired oldsters the only people who feel that the present laws are very unjust. There are an even larger number of people still in the productive period of their lives who cannot look forward to any retirement allowances in their old age. This includes most of the housewives, the farmers, and other self-employed people, the employees in uncovered employments, and, also, although few of them are as yet conscious of the fact, the great majority of all women workers in industry. In these groups are our poorest people, who face the bleakest prospects in old age. True, they can look forward to old-age assistance should they be in dire want, but few Americans regard such aid as satisfying old-age protection. People who can look forward to nothing better than old-age assistance naturally are incensed because the steadily employed industrial workers are afforded the vastly better protection of the old-age and survivors' insurance system, plus old-age assistance, if they need it.

The millions who are excluded from insurance benefits and who need them most, moreover, believe that they are required to bear part of the costs of the old-age protection which covered industrial workers are enjoying. Most of them will contribute directly by reason of their employment during part of their lives in covered employments, and all believe that they contribute indirectly, in the form of higher prices for the goods and services they buy.

The 1939 Social Security Act Amendments did little to correct the justified grievances of the old people who are already retired and the millions who cannot look forward to any retirement allowances.

The maximum federal aid in old-age assistance cases was increased from $15 to $20 per month, but this aid may never exceed one-half of the grant in any case. Where assistance allowances are not more than $30 per month, the 1939 Act left the situation unchanged. And the latest figures indicate that in seven states old-age assistance grants average, not $30 per month, but less than $10, and in 28 states less than $20.

The 1939 Amendments slightly increased the total coverage, for tax purposes, of the old-age insurance system. National bank employees, maritime employees, and people who after they pass 65 years of age are employed in covered employments were brought into the old-age insurance system. Offsetting these was the exclusion of many workers previously covered, by unnoticed changes in the definition of "agricultural workers," which Dr. Andrews brought to light in the current issue of the *American Labor Legislation Review*.

The improvement represented by the slight net increase in the coverage of the old-age insurance system was more than offset by exclusion from benefits of large numbers of people who are required to pay taxes but who will get nothing in return. Under the original Social Security Act everyone who paid taxes also got benefits, and the provisions were such that within a generation practically our entire population would have been assured at least partial protection under the old-age insurance system. Under the 1939 Amendments, as under the original law, substantially all our people will have to pay old-age insurance taxes during a part of their lives, but probably close to half of them will never get benefits. This is the result of the introduction of definitions of "fully insured" and "currently insured" employees, and of basing benefits on "average wages." Under these definitions most of the people who shift between covered and uncovered employment, as well as most of the women who leave employment on marriage, will get no benefits at all, not even the return of the money they have paid in taxes; and many others will get only the minimum retirement benefit of $10 per month.

Other reasons for the continued popularity of universal old-age pensions are to be sought in the popular moods of the moment. There has been an alarming growth in the quest for governmental handouts and in the sentiment, "Let Uncle Sam do it." For this development, well-to-do conservatives, who "view with alarm," are quite as much responsible as the poor people who say with Jack Benny: "Isn't Roosevelt wonderful?" They have talked so much about the "economy of abundance" that the masses who do not have abundance are asking for what they believe to be their share. Increasingly, all elements in our population turn to government whenever they want something they cannot easily provide for themselves, but all groups are unwilling to foot the costs. Politicians promise the moon, but refuse to levy taxes. Even reputable economists see the solution of all or most of our problems in increased governmental spending. It is the federal government to whom everyone turns, to avoid the necessity of raising taxes locally. So it happens that the people often vote against radical pension plans to be financed from state and local funds, but elect congressmen who, at one and the same time, promise increased expenditures and reduced taxes.

Of similar character is the vogue of "pay-as-you-go," which as applied to old-age insurance means "letting the future take care of itself"—spending all moneys collected for old-age insurance purposes currently, without making any provision for meeting accruing liabilities. This is not the place to revive the controversies over the financing of old-age insurance, but note must be taken of the fact that "pay-as-you-go" has become the slogan of every radical pension group. It is not so much the comparatively slight changes in actual financing made in the 1939 Amendments which are threatening to destroy the entire old-age insurance system, as is the false propaganda which was launched to get taxes reduced. The mythical "reserve of 47 billions" and the notion that every dollar collected for old-age insurance should be spent immediately have become a part of the thinking of most Americans on this subject. Starting with such premises, we can very materially increase benefits and further reduce taxes. We can have our cake and eat it too; we can have a liberal universal pension, which costs us nothing; with the day of reckoning still some years in the future.

Alternative Approaches to Universal Pensions

Universal old-age pensions, or something akin to universal pensions, are well-nigh inevitable in this country. The situation being what it is, the most important question has become: What sort of a universal pension system shall we adopt? There are an almost infinite number of possibilities, if every minor conceivable variation is taken into account, but these five seem to me to be the basic alternatives:

1. We can extend the old-age insurance system to include all or most of the present uncovered groups, as proposed in the Wagner Bill, now pending in Congress.

2. Either in conjunction with the extension of the coverage of the old-age insurance system or independently thereof, we can improve the operation of old-age assistance, by removing from this institution the taint of pauperism and by distributing the federal aid so as to benefit most the states which have the greatest need for such aid, or at least so as to give the same amount of federal aid to beneficiaries living in poor as in rich states.

3. We can have the federal government take over complete responsibility for old-age assistance, as it now has for old-age insurance, but keeping these two institutions quite distinct, retaining need as the basis for old-age assistance and contributions as the basis for old-age insurance.

4. We can amalgamate old-age assistance and old-age insurance,

financing both from present payroll taxes, supplemented by such appropriations from general revenues as Congress may see fit to make.

5. We can scrap the present institutions for old-age protection and substitute for them a universal pension system, financed from general taxes, under which substantially all American citizens who have attained a specified age will get the same old-age pension.

The last of these alternatives—the adoption of a Townsend or "baby Townsend" Plan—is the one which has been most widely discussed. These plans have been presented by their advocates as having objectives of even greater importance than old-age protection. Time will not permit discussion of these objectives, but only to point out the weakness of these plans as measures for old-age protection.

Among these the most evident is the great cost they entail. There are 8,500,000 people over 65 years of age and nearly 13,000,000 over 60. A pension of $1 per month for everybody over 65 costs $100,000-000 per year; $1 per month for everybody over 60, $150,000,000 per year. Pensions of ten dollars per month cost ten times these amounts; $30 per month, 30 times these amounts, etc. Thirty dollars per month to everybody over 60 costs more than the total of all normal federal expenditures; $60 per month, as much as the total expenditures for all purposes; $200 per month, more than twice as much as the total of all taxes now collected by all governmental units.

Quite obviously, if we are to have uniform pensions for all old people, they will have to be of small amounts. Even so millions will be wasted, because their recipients do not need any governmental aid, the pensions paid them serving only the purpose of increasing the estates they leave their children. On the one hand, small pensions to everybody will prove inadequate for old people in need of assistance, necessitating supplementation of old-age pensions by relief. No matter how low universal pensions may be initially, there will be almost irresistible pressure for upping the pensions. This was very plainly stated in a recent issue of the *General Welfare News:* "It is child's play to raise the amount or lower the age limit once the principle of a general or flat pension based on age, retirement and citizenship is enacted into law"; and Dr. Townsend has told his followers that even $200 per month is only a beginning.

For these and still other reasons, enactment into law of the radical universal pensions proposals is unlikely, despite the large number of congressmen who have pledged their support. Much more likely is an amalgamation of old-age assistance and old-age insurance. The form such an amalgamation is most likely to take is the inclusion of the entire population within the old-age insurance system, including people already retired, with payment of $20 or $30 per month as a minimum retirement annuity.

There are many things to be said in favor of this sort of universal pensions. They will, admittedly, not provide sufficient income for all of the old people already retired, nor for many of the people who will reach retirement age in the future. But the states could supplement the inadequate pensions and, even if they did not do so, many needy old people would get more than they now receive.

Such a system, however, would also mean that large amounts of public moneys would be wasted, because they would go to people who do not need any financial aid. A minimum retirement annuity of $20 per month would cost at least $1,500,000,000 per year at the very outset, and the costs would increase rapidly.

At this point the question naturally arises: "Who is going to pay these costs?" I take it for granted that Congress will continue to appropriate from general revenues an amount equal to that now appropriated for federal aid for old-age assistance. There would also be available the current collections from the payroll taxes for old-age insurance purposes. These amounts combined, however, fall far short of meeting the costs of a combined system which would guarantee $20 per month to everyone over 65 who has retired from gainful employment—to say nothing about $30 per month to everybody over 60. If the reserve of nearly two billion dollars in the old-age and survivors' insurance fund is used up, no additional revenues will be needed for a few years, but such a raid upon the funds from which future pensions are to be paid will postpone the evil day, when additional taxes must be raised, by not more than five years.

The more consideration is given to the crucial question, "Who will pay the costs?" the more it becomes apparent that only needy men and women can be guaranteed minimum pensions. Thus limited, a universal pension system becomes a possibility financially, although the costs will still be much greater than at present.

There is a lurking menace, however, even in such a program. This is that the costs of old-age assistance may be shifted from general revenues to the payroll taxes on employers and employees. This will result, at least in part, unless the appropriation from general revenues to the combined old-age insurance and old-age assistance system considerably exceeds the present appropriation for federal aid for old-age assistance. If the old-age assistance costs are shifted to the payroll taxes, the people in the low income groups will be worse off than they are now.

As a practical matter the dangers inherent in combining old-age insurance and old-age assistance are so great that the soundest policy seems to me to be a combination of the first two alternative methods enumerated for getting universal old-age pensions in this country. I favor the extension of our old-age insurance system to include our entire population, and, at the same time, improving old-age assistance—retaining state administration, but removing the taint of pauperism, and distributing the federal aid on a fair basis.

I am convinced that it is administratively feasible to bring all people who are still in the productive period of their lives, whatever their occupation may be, within the old-age insurance system. That cannot be done if all people are required to make contributions on exactly the same basis. But there is no constitutional or practical reason for collecting contributions from all groups on exactly the same basis. Once this is recognized, the problem of complete coverage no longer is an insoluble one.

The improvement of old-age assistance is equally important. To begin with, the federal aid must be distributed so that every needy old person will get adequate assistance. To this end, the largest amount of federal aid should go to the states which need it most. If that is not politically feasible, at least the same amount of federal aid should be paid for each person on the old-age pension rolls.

But increased and better apportioned federal aid alone will not solve the problem. We must also make old-age assistance an institution "which will respect the dignity of the life of service and labor which our aged citizens have given to the nation."

I think that we can take a lesson from Europe in this respect, particularly from the non-contributory pension system of England and the universal pensions of the Scandinavian countries. To begin with, we should go back to calling this institution "old-age pensions," and make it clear in our laws that it is not relief. Like the democratic European countries, we should also provide that small amounts of earnings and other incomes should not be taken into consideration in determining eligibility for old-age pensions or the amount of the pensions. It may even be advisable to fix a minimum pension, with deductions therefrom only for fairly large amounts of income from other sources. Unless old-age assistance is thus improved, dissatisfaction with its operation will result in a universal pension system of a type which is a serious social menace.

Remarks at the American Economic Association

American Economic Review,
Volume XXXVII, Number 2
(May, 1947), pages 363–364.
Papers and Proceedings of the
59th Annual Meeting of the
Social Security Session of
the American Economic
Association at Atlantic City,
January, 1947

HOLDING AS I DO the view that our social security program is basically sound, although it should be broadened and liberalized and can be improved upon, I find myself in disagreement with both of the principal papers and the first discussant and generally in agreement with the last three discussants.

Mr. Swan has ably presented the fiscal policy approach to social security, which makes social security important only as it may contribute to or hinder economic stability. Fiscal policy considerations are important but by no means all that matters. Social security is a justifiable end in itself, not merely a minor measure for the attainment of economic stability. As expressed by the late Msgr. John A. Ryan: "Industry exists for man; not man for industry." Full employment, important as it is, is not the complete answer to the problems of destitution and dependency. Let us, indeed, consider the economic effects of social security measures, but while exploring the mazes of fiscal policy let us not forget our objective, the relief of need and destitution in all contingencies which confront individuals and families.

With Mr. Meriam I am pretty much in agreement up to the point where he makes proposals for basic changes in the social security system. I recognize, as he does, that what we can do by way of social security depends upon our total economic production. With the three basic conditions he set forth for the maintenance of a high level of production, which will make possible an adequate system of social security, I have no fault to find.

But I cannot follow Mr. Meriam and Professor Lutz in their proposal to finance social security from payroll taxes on the employed workers but to pay benefits only to persons in need. Behind this proposal is the assumption that such a system would result in keeping the costs at a minimum. That this is very doubtful is indicated by our own experience with old-age assistance, particularly in western states. Where social security payments are made dependent upon a showing of need, the definition of need will be broadened to include most everybody. To place the burden of supporting social security upon the workers and then not to pay any benefits to most of them is as politically unrealistic as it is basically inequitable.

In his criticisms of the basic concepts of the present social security system, Mr. Meriam revived the old canard, "Made in Germany." It is true that national social insurance originated in the Germany of Bismarck. But Mr. Meriam overlooks that the system he advocates, of benefits limited to people in need but financed from payroll taxes on all workers, was Hitler's plan of social security. I know that Mr. Meriam dislikes everything about Hitler and the Nazi regime as much as do all other right-thinking people. I do not suggest that he is consciously trying to imitate the Nazis, and I assume that he is not aware that Hitler abolished unemployment insurance benefits as a right and substituted for them relief payments on a needs basis. But if the fact that social insurance originated in the Germany of 65 years ago is used to condemn our system of social security, it needs to be appreciated that the proposal to convert social security into a relief program has been tried only in Hitler's Germany and ended with the downfall of the Nazis.

Let no one be in doubt about the relations of social security to a system of free enterprise. Social security is not a program inconsistent with freedom of enterprise or the principles of democracy. On the contrary, it operates to make our democracy the more valuable and to strengthen our system of free enterprise.

Unpublished paper

P ASSAGE OF THE Social Security Amendments Act represents an important forward step and an accomplishment of the national administration of real value to many Americans. The measure passed is not nearly as good, however, as the original Administration bill recommended by President Truman and the Social Security Administration. Despite this new law, much remains to be done to give us as good a Social Security Act as we should have.

The passage of the Social Security Amendments Act has come after years of recommendations to Congress by Presidents Roosevelt and Truman for improvement of our social security legislation. President Truman has made such recommendations in every one of his Annual Messages and, repeatedly, in Special Messages as well. The Senate Finance Committee of the Republican 80th Congress created a Social Security Advisory Council, most of whose members were businessmen, which recommended many improvements in the existing law. Instead, the 80th Congress passed an act restricting the coverage of the Act. In the present 81st Congress, the Administration came forward with a bill making great improvements in the present law as soon as Congress convened in January, 1949. The congressional committees devoted months to hearings and more months to the consideration of social security legislation. Amendment after amendment weakening the bill was adopted by the votes of the Republican members, aided by some Southern Democrats. But enough was left of the original bill to make it a distinct improvement over the present law. In the end, practically every member of both houses voted for the bill; in fact, there was but one vote against the measure as finally enacted, that being cast by Congressman Byrnes, a Republican from Wisconsin. But it is to the insistence of President Truman, more than to any other factor, that the Social Security Act has finally been improved—for the first time since 1939.

The new law extends the coverage of the federal old-age and survivors' insurance system to more than 7,000,000 Americans not previously included. The largest group among these are the nonfarm self-employed people, with the exception of some professions whose representative organizations insisted upon exemption. The grave injustice that small businessmen who have had to contribute to the old-age security protection of their employees have themselves been denied protection is now corrected, and they will hereafter get the same protection under the Social Security Act as the officers of corporations who work for them have always enjoyed. Also brought under the law for the first time are fulltime domestic employees and farm workers who work for one employer only, and the employees of private educational and charitable organizations. It is also made possible for the state governments to bring under the Social Security Act state and local government employees not covered by any state and local retirement system. As substantially all state and local government employees in Wisconsin have some sort of retirement systems of their own, this provision will not benefit many, if any, people in Wisconsin. Workers covered by private pension systems are included in the federal system, nevertheless, and get its benefits, but public employees are denied such additional protection—clearly a grave injustice.

The extension of coverage in the Social Security Act Amendments falls far short of the complete coverage provided for in the original Administration bill. It gives no protection to farmers nor to many farm workers and domestic employees, and to but a few public employees. Nothing short of complete coverage for all Americans is really satisfactory.

Great improvements are also made in the new law with respect to eligibility for benefits. The changes made will largely correct the restrictive conditions which were added to the original law in 1939. Under the amended law, many people will be eligible for benefits who heretofore have been ineligible although covered for tax purposes. For people who reach retirement age within the next few years, only very short periods of tax payments will be required. Anyone who is 65 years of age or over and who can establish coverage in half of the quarter years since January 1, 1937, or since January 1, 1951, whichever date is more favorable to him, is eligible for a retirement benefit. Under the amended act, some people will be eligible to benefits in 1952 on as little as 6 quarters of coverage, in each of which they had earnings in covered employments of as much as $100 per quarter. Except for the alternative date of January 1, 1951, for beginning to apply, the half-of-the-quarters rule for eligibility, introduced in 1939, is retained. That will require further changes later on.

The immediate effect of the inclusion of the alternative date, however, is to make eligible many older people who have not heretofore been eligible for benefits. The present 2,000,000 people over 65 who get retirement benefits is expected to be increased to 4,500,000 within a year or two. This will take many older people off old-age assistance and public relief rolls and mean a great deal to many retired workers and those unable to work. At the same time, the new amendments increase the amount retired workers may earn in covered employment without reduction of benefits from $15 to $50 per month, thus encouraging older workers who have lost or given up their former regular jobs to earn what they can by part-time or other employment—which is highly desirable for their own satisfaction as well as the nation's welfare in a tight employment situation.

The new act also materially increases the retirement benefits, although not as much as was recommended and as is desirable. Under a new formula for computing benefits, the average benefit on retirement, now $26 per month, will become $45 per month, and go somewhat higher in future years. Where the wife of the retired insured worker also is 65 or over, she is entitled to three-fourths of the husband's benefit in addition to his benefit; and each child under 18 is also entitled to a benefit three-fourths that of the father. If an insured worker dies prior to or after retirement, his dependents become entitled to survivors' benefits, which under the new law are also very nearly doubled. The maximum benefit to all members of any family is increased from $85 to $150 per month.

The amounts of $45 per month for single retired workers and even $150 per month for a large family of dependents are not sums enabling old people to live in luxury; the $45 amount is clearly inadequate for a decent existence. But the increases in benefits Congress has made at least correct the greatest inequity resulting from its failure heretofore to bring the original benefits into line with the changes in the price levels which have occurred in the meantime. That was that the benefits in the contributory old-age insurance system were below the average of the noncontributory old-age assistance payments under the state old-age assistance laws. Workers who have made no direct contributions to their old-age assistance grants have received far more than those who have made contributions to the costs of their retirement benefits. Under the new law, the average of the contributory retirement benefits will slightly exceed the average of the old-age assistance grants.

The increase in benefits under the new law is not satisfactory and far less than recommended by the Administration. But thanks to the changes in conditions of eligibility, plus the increases in benefits, the total amounts which the older people of this country will get under the federal old-age and survivors' insurance system will be increased more than threefold by 1952.

One other important improvement is made in the new act. This corrects the injustice to the veterans of the last war resulting from the 1939 conditions of eligibility. Under the law until now, the men and women who served with the colors got no credit toward old-age and survivors' benefits for their period of service. Instead, many of them lost the eligibility they had attained prior to being called into service, by reason of the fact that the quarters in which they were in service counted against them, in applying the 1939 rule for eligibility of coverage in half of the quarters after January 1, 1937. President Roosevelt recommended correction of this injustice when draft legislation was first enacted in 1940, and during the war repeatedly renewed this recommendation, as did President Truman after the war. But Congress never got around to doing this until the new Social Security Amendments Act. In that act, veterans are at least dealt with justly. Under the amended act, all service with the colors counts as employment in covered employment, with credited earnings for that time of $160 per month and more if the pay was greater. This will benefit men now called to the colors as well as the veterans of the last war and all men and women who have since served in the armed forces.

Altogether, the Social Security Act Amendments represent very real progress toward the sort of social security legislation we ought to have in this country. But much remains to be done. Besides the further improvements already indicated, major very necessary changes include the following:

1. The old-age insurance system should provide benefits to insured workers if permanently and totally disabled prior to attaining age 65. Such people are economically prematurely old and need assistance even more than many people over 65, as their costs often are even greater since they have heavy medical bills in addition to the expenses of their own support and that of their dependents. Benefits for the permanently and totally disabled were recommended by President Truman and included in the amending act as passed by the House, but were eliminated in the Senate. In nearly every other country, permanent and total disability is treated the same as old age, and our law should do likewise.

2. Our law should provide for a system of genuine dependents' allowance, replacing the present very inadequate benefits paid directly to some dependents. Our present law provides for no additional benefits to retired workers with dependents, but allows wives of such workers to claim benefits, at a reduced rate, in their own right when they themselves get to be 65; and the same rule applies to children under 18. This works out particularly badly in the case of married retired workers. Two-thirds of all men at age 65 have a wife dependent upon them, who on the average is more than 5 years younger. Such a married worker who has always supported his wife gets no additional benefit for her support on retirement. Apparently the concept is that the wife, who on the average is under 60 when the husband reaches 65, should then go to work to support herself until 65, when she may claim a reduced benefit in her own right. For this very inequitable arrangement, a system of genuine dependents' benefits should be included in the law.

3. The rank discrimination against women in the present law should be eliminated. This results principally from the 1939 conditions for eligibility. Women workers typically leave employment on

marriage. As the quarters elapsing thereafter count against them, but few women can establish coverage in half of the quarters on reaching old age, although many have paid substantial amounts in taxes for their old-age protection. Only if they marry the right man (a covered worker) can they claim any benefit when they get old, and then only at a reduced rate. Such a discriminatory provision is an absurdity in the present day and age.

A contributory old-age insurance system is the best possible plan for meeting the costs of old-age support beyond the provisions which people can and should make for themselves. Establishment of such a system in 1935 was a great forward step, and the amendments that have now been adopted a great improvement over what we have had heretofore. We need to perfect the present system and should not delay in doing so.

Contributory versus Noncontributory Industrial Pension Plans

University of Minnesota, Industrial Relations Center, Research and Technical Report 7, *Employee Welfare and Benefit Plans,* Dubuque, Iowa: William C. Brown Co., 1950, pages 20–22

I HAVE PREVIOUSLY on many occasions expressed myself as being strongly in favor of an all-inclusive governmentally established Social Security system, financed on a contributory basis. I have recognized that there is value in private programs established unilaterally by employers or under collective bargaining agreements between employers and unions. These values are limited but very real. Such private programs, however, do not lessen the need for an all-inclusive governmental program which will provide an assurance of a minimum income sufficient for a decent and reasonable existence in all major personal contingencies of life. It is above such a minimum degree of Social Security provided for all Americans that private welfare and pension plans have real value.

In an address I delivered at the Chicago meeting of the American Management Association in February, 1948, I took a definite position in favor of the joint financing of such private programs. My views on this subject have undergone some change but far from a complete reversal.

I am still strongly of the opinion that public Social Security programs, particularly in the health, welfare, and pension fields should be contributory. I hold this view, in part, because adequate programs, even if they do not provide anything more than a minimum income sufficient for a decent existence upon the occurrence of all major personal contingencies of life, are so costly that they cannot be carried on employers' contributions or from general tax sources alone. Beyond this, and even more important, is the consideration that it is only under a contributory system that benefits and costs can be kept within manageable limits.

I also have not changed my view that private health and welfare programs should be contributory. Such programs also are costly and many companies instituting these cannot bear the additional cost alone and continue to compete on even terms with firms which have not established such private health and welfare plans. More important, again, is the matter that health is not solely a responsibility of the employer. The 40 hours a week which American workers typically spend in the factory have something to do with their health, but so have the much longer number of hours during which they are not working for the employer. Health and welfare plans which provide nothing more than partial compensation for wage loss due to illness can be defended on a basis in which the employer pays the entire cost. The actual situation in this country to date, however, is that the employers pay none or only a small part of these costs; so the establishment of the principle of equal contributions in the financing of such plans represents a real gain for the employees.

In the collective bargaining negotiations of the past year the unions in most industries were satisfied with such joint financing of health and welfare plans. Only in the coal industry are such plans financed exclusively by the employers. Until last year labor generally also did not object to having the employees pay part of the cost of industrial pension plans, although there were many plans in operation which were financed exclusively by the employers. Traditionally, labor has viewed with great suspicion industrial pension plans established unilaterally by the employers. When employers were willing to make these plans matters of collective bargaining negotiations, labor was quite satisfied to pay half the costs or thereabouts.

Collective bargaining negotiations of the past year in the major mass production industries have seen the unions, principally CIO unions, change their position. The unions demanded that private retirement pension programs should conform to these three essential requirements: they must be jointly negotiated, jointly managed, and financed exclusively by the employer. Many plans conforming to these three essentials, as conceived by the unions, have been established since last summer. The pension program of the United Mine Workers was of that pattern earlier, with the modification that the actual management rested with the union rather than the joint board.

I have stated that my views on the question of employee contributions to retirement systems have undergone some change; upon further study stimulated by the developments of the past year, I have not come to supporting the unions' position. But I believe that whether an industrial pension plan should be contributory or not depends upon how the plan is set up.

Industrial pension programs established unilaterally by employers and which are not funded at all or very inadequately funded clearly should not be contributory. Such plans may be discontinued by the employer at will. Even when the employers obligate themselves to return the employees' money with interest, there are some objectionable aspects in plans to which the employees must make contributions but about which they are not consulted.

Where retirement plans are established under collective bargaining agreements—as they now must be if the collective bargaining representative so demands—there are still serious doubts about employee contributions unless employee pension rights are fully vested and funded. Pension plans of the kinds which have been established during the past year are very costly. Employers financing them alone will in time find them very burdensome. This consideration justifies contributions by the employees. On the other hand, the fact that the great majority of the employees covered at any given time have little real expectation of ever being able to get a retirement pension under the plan strongly suggests that they should not be contributory. Guesses as to the percentage of employees on the payrolls of the employers with industrial pension plans who will ever receive any pensions range all the way from only 5 per cent to possibly as high as 50 per cent. But unless there is a further great reduction in the mobility of labor, certainly the great majority of the younger workers included within such pension plans will not remain with the same employer until they attain the retirement age, which is usually 65. Workers who leave the employment and who have contributed to a retirement plan clearly should have returned to them the money they contributed, with interest. Should the percentage of the total employees who will get no pensions prove as great as past experience suggests, it will be so burdensome and costly to make the refunds that very little will be gained financially through employee contributions.

Merely returning the money employees have contributed, with interest, does not completely satisfy the situation. Employees who leave the employment—and that will probably prove to be the great majority of all the employees—who get their money back with interest cannot be said to have been robbed by contributory retirement plans. Likewise, however, such employees also will have no protection toward their retirement.

This consideration calls for vesting the retirement rights in the employees who have made contributions to an industrial pension plan. When they leave the employment instead of getting their money back with interest, the accrued rights to retirement pensions should remain with them. Vesting costs a great deal of money and will make industrial pension systems much more costly. But it is only when retirement rights are vested in the employees that the retirement plans can be said to be completely equitable and most valuable.

Where retirement funds are vested in the employees, contributions by them are sound in all respects. Where employers are not willing to vest retirement rights in employees, there is a much stronger case for a noncontributory system. There is still something to be said for contributions, but I have come to the view that, on balance, the case for a noncontributory system is the stronger where a hand-to-mouth system of financing is adopted and accruing retirement rights are not vested in the employees. Systems of that character still have some values although they manifestly have many limitations and present large potential dangers. But these values are such that the employers cannot reasonably demand that all employees should contribute to the costs of pension systems, from which only a small percentage of the employees will benefit.

What Is Needed for
Economic Security
in Old Age?

Papers presented to Second
International Gerontological
Congress at St. Louis,
September 11, 1951

THE TWO MAIN POINTS I have to make are both in the nature of antidotes to popular impressions which I fear are being created by many of the other papers at this Congress. They are, first, that adequate economic means, while not all that is needed, is an essential for a happy old age; and, second, that many different approaches are indicated to insure adequate income for decent living in old age; specifically, that increasing employment opportunities for older people is not a cure-all for the economic problems of old age. In developing these points, I can cite only data for the United States, as my knowledge of the situation in other countries is, unfortunately, very limited.

Concerning the first point, that older people must have a means of livelihood, I fear that the greatly increased attention to the non-economic problems of older people which the gerontological movement has produced may have the effect of minimizing the importance of their economic problems in our thinking about the rapidly growing number of older people. Fifteen years ago the reverse situation existed. At that time there was, perhaps, too much enthusiasm for the possibilities of measures and institutions for economic security in old age. Today, it is realized that there is much more to the problem of a satisfying old age than providing means of subsistence. This change in concepts is very much to the good. But there is danger that, in our enthusiasm for the progress made in the new approaches, we will overlook the important truths, that many older people even today lack economic means for a decent existence and that none of our institutions for economic security in old age, nor all of them combined, give assurance that we will no longer have dire want in old age in the years that lie ahead.

"Man does not live by bread alone," but food is an essential for life and so are clothing, housing, and many other wants which in modern societies can be gotten only through the command of money, taking the form of either accumulated wealth or current income. Prolonging life by conquering diseases which produce death in old age is a social benefaction, but does not of itself solve the problem of how the larger number of old people are to live. Improving the health of the older people increases their employability, but most people, if they live long enough, will reach a stage when they will no longer be able to support themselves by their earnings. The recent studies of the United States Bureau of Labor Statistics establish that the gap between life expectancy and work-life expectancy has been widening, even during the long period of near full employment we have enjoyed. It may be true, as representatives of the American Medical Association stated during the consideration of the Social Security Act Amendments of 1950, that doctors do not need old-age insurance protection because they keep on working until they die, but for the great majority of people old age is a time of reduced income from earnings and for many the complete cessation of earnings.

Economic costs continue to be large in old age. For most people old age is a period of somewhat reduced expenses. This is a consequence of the fact that they generally have fewer dependents, although many old people have dependents. In the United States, two out of three men over 65 are married and support a wife, on the average five years or more younger than they are and so not eligible for a wife's benefit under the Social Security Act. Something like 10 or 15 per cent of the men over 65 also appear to have children, grandchildren, or other dependents besides a wife whom they support. Conversely, only a third of the women over 65 are married and more than one-half are widowed. Moreover, some economic costs appear to increase with age, notably, the costs of medical and related care—a problem which is aggravated by the fact that generally voluntary insurance for the costs of medical and related care is not available to older people.

Further, old age is a long period for many people. For white males in the United States average life expectancy at age 65 is now more than 13 years; for women about three years longer. These are periods more than a fourth as long as what are often called the "productive years" of life. What periods as long as these mean in terms of the costs of economic support is perhaps best indicated by the fact that an insurance company annuity to provide an income of $100 per month from 65 on costs between $15,000 and $17,000 at that age. For many people the costs are greater, as average life expectancy figures, of course, mean that half of the people over 65 live longer than the indicated durations of life after that age—some of them twice as long and even longer. If medical advances result in a lengthening old age, the amounts required for economic support will be correspondingly increased. A similar but even worse effect will be produced by continued inflation, which for most old people means continually rising costs without increased incomes.

For the great majority of all people the best economic security is provided through employment. That is also true of older people. In discussions of the problem of increasing the employment opportunities of older people, it is often overlooked that a great many of the older people are now employed. In the United States, 45 per cent of all men, but less than 10 per cent of the women, over 65 are employed at this time. Criticisms directed against the Social Security Act because it permits retirement at age 65 obscure the facts that this law has no compulsory retirement age and that the average age of retirement under that law is 69, not 65. Retirement systems for public employees often have compulsory retirement ages, but the average ages in public employment appear to be much higher than in private employment. Industrial pension systems also generally have compulsory retirement provisions, but in times of keen demand for labor, like the present, many workers above the retirement ages actually are employed. Compulsory retirement provisions account to a minor degree for the fact that no more older workers have jobs, but are far less important than prejudices and habits which persist, although retirement for most workers is not compulsory.

Even more important, probably, is the fact that many older people are not able to work full time at their former occupations and cannot readily be fitted into new jobs. A study of the Social Security Administration reported on only this year indicates that between two-thirds and three-fourths of all recipients of old-age insurance benefits are disabled to the extent that they cannot do the work they formerly did on a full-time basis. Nearly one-half are unable to work at all by reason of sickness. Another recent study made by the Wisconsin Board of Public Welfare revealed that 27 per cent of the recipients of old-age assistance in that state not only are presently unemployable but require physical care from others.

The present enthusiasm for the increased employment of older people is most laudable. We need additional workers and the large number of older people who are not employed are, perhaps, the most promising source for meeting this need. But more than enthusiasm is needed to make a real dent in this problem. The account that the present problem arose because during the Great Depression it was public policy to encourage the early retirement of older workers, I believe, is more traditional than factual. A very disproportionate percentage of the older workers were unemployed in the early 1930's. The Committee on Economic Security in recommending the Social Security Act stressed that there was great need for better provisions for the unemployed older workers than poor relief, and did not even suggest that the remedy lay in getting older workers to retire earlier. Since then many more older workers have found employment and the number of the employed older workers is still going up, but the increase in the numbers employed has no more than kept pace with the increase in the total number of older people.

The impossibility of meeting the entire problem of economic support in old age through finding employment for older workers is best appreciated when it is recalled that women now exceed the men among the people over 65 and the percentage of the older women is rapidly increasing. Although the percentage of older women who are employed, unlike that of the men, has increased, it is still below 10 per cent. More than half of these older women are widowed and most of them have not worked in industry for years, if at all.

We need to increase the employment of older people. But even to hold our own, percentagewise, will not be easy. To increase the present percentages appreciably will require most careful studies where old people, now unemployed, can fit in, of the possibilities of changes in job content to make jobs more suitable for older workers, opportunities for part-time employment, and the like. Plus research and the publicizing of accurate, specific information on the subject, coöperation by industry, labor, and the government will be required actually to increase the percentages of the older people who are employed. That can and should be done, but realistically we should try to get the public to understand that employment is not a complete answer to the problem of economic support in old age, although earnings from employment are now the largest source of income for people over 65 and can be further increased.

Having dealt at such length with increased employment as a solution for the problems of economic support in old age, I have time to comment only very briefly in other aspects of the subject, "What is Needed for Economic Security in Old Age."

In doing so, let me first say that we still know but little about how older people actually get their livelihood.

《《《《《《《《◇》》》》》》》

What seems clear is that, despite the fact that we have a good many wealthy widows and quite a few older people with respectable incomes and considerable property, many older people have to live very skimpily. Large numbers exist, even today, under conditions of serious want or of demoralizing fear and uncertainty. The estimate of the Federal Security Agency that two out of five people over 65 need some form of assistance for decent subsistence from governmental sources is, probably, not far off; but we need to know much more than we now do about the actual situation as to how the economic needs of our older people are being met.

We must also know more than we now do about the reasons why some older people are in need while others are getting along very well economically. I suspect that one of two factors mainly account for this difference: the earnings received before age 65 and employment or nonemployment after 65. Very certainly, however, other factors also are of importance: unemployment and sickness prior to 65, long serious illness of some member of the family, disabilities of one kind or another, loss of savings, and, doubtless, such personal factors as debilitating habits, unwise spending, divorces, and many others. What we actually know about the reasons why many older people are in need is even more scanty than as to the actual situation with reference to how the economic needs of older people are being met today.

Equally great are the gaps in our knowledge as to the operation of the several institutions we now have which are designed for the purpose of improved economic security in old age. We know but little about the actual savings which older people have and what they do with these savings. Personal savings have greatly increased in the last decade. The people of the United States have not lost their habits of industry and thrift by reason of the existence of social security institutions. But certain forms of savings have been greatly reduced in value through the declining purchasing power of the dollar. Yet savings remain an important source of old-age support even if it may be true that they are the principal source of income of only 10 per cent of our older people.

Clearly, we also need to know more about support received from children and relatives. Every evidence seems to point to the fact that it is declining, but I suspect that it is a supplementary source of income for a good many of our older people who receive public assistance in one form or another. Conversely, a good many older people are secretive about accumulated savings because they want to leave an estate to their children.

Industrial pensions have been very much in the limelight in recent years, but what do we really know about them? We, vaguely, know that there are somewhere between 12,000 to 15,000 industrial pension plans and around 7,000,000 to 10,000,000 workers and executives who work where these plans are in effect. We know the provisions of a relatively small number of these industrial pension systems. But we lack information about how many people are actually receiving industrial pensions or what they get. Actual recipients seem to number only a few hundred thousand, and to date industrial pensions are not one of the large sources of old-age support, although employers are today putting into their industrial pension programs as much money as they pay into the federal old-age and survivors' insurance system. A majority of all industrial pension plans are of recent origin, but many have been in operation for a sufficient length of time so that we might be able to get from their experience a real clue as to the percentage of workers employed in plants with industrial pension plans who can reasonably expect ever to benefit from them, if the records of these older plans were opened for independent study by qualified outsiders. And the same thing goes for the records of insurance companies in their experience with various types of annuity policies.

Very definitely, also, much remains to be learned regarding the operations of the several public programs for old-age security. Least known of all are veterans' pensions and disability allowances and the liberal retirement system of our armed forces. But there are big gaps in our knowledge regarding the operations of retirement systems for public employees, the railroad workers, and the federal old-age and survivors' insurance system—the world's largest single social insurance program. The same situation exists with reference to old-age assistance and the older people who are on other assistance programs. We know something about total numbers of beneficiaries and total expenditures, but very little about the benefits paid individuals and their circumstances.

At this point let me also say that there is great need for more research and information, but, likewise, for making the public acquainted with the facts already known.

《《《《《《《O》》》》》》》

In stressing the defects in the present programs for economic security in old age, I do not belittle the progress we have made in less than two decades. Our older people, as a group, are better off economically than they were during the Depression and, quite likely, also than during the prosperous 'twenties. Our programs to assure a minimum of subsistence, however, have scarcely kept up with changing price levels and improvements are very necessary. How fast we should move in making these necessary improvements must take costs into account; but it needs to be brought home to the American people that the United States, the wealthiest country in the world, spends a much smaller part of its income for old-age security and for all forms of social security and welfare than any other western country, to say nothing about our friends "down under" and our progressive near-neighbor Canada.

My plea is for increased attention to social security and the economic aspects of the problems of an aging population. We need to know much more than we now do about these economic aspects and also must educate the public as to the facts and translate what we know into action. Despite the great importance that social security has attained, the attention given this subject in our colleges and universities and by research agencies is slight. Speaking of my own profession, that of the economists, less than 1 per cent have ever concerned themselves with these problems, and most of those who have done so have discussed the subject on the basis of assumptions which have but little relation to the facts. The prevailing ignorance regarding social security is astounding in view of the immense amount of discussion of the subject.

This situation is, at least in part, due to the fact that much of what is said and written on the subject is uninformed and misleading. Very wrong impressions have been created in the public mind. There is danger that further misinformation may be one consequence of the gerontological movement. That will be the result, along with the many good things it may do, if it lulls people into thinking that the economic problems of old age have been solved or will disappear if but employment opportunities for the older people are increased.

The Old-Age Problem
in 1953

Address at the Janesville
Industrial Relations Center
Institute, May, 1953

F IRST, THIS COMMONPLACE FACT: We have in the United States
a large and a growing old-age problem. Old age, of course, is difficult
to define—some people are old at fifty; others are vigorous at 85.
But the only available statistical data is based upon the traditional
age groupings of the Census, which classifies as the older citizens of
the country, the people who are 65 and over. Having attained that
age myself, I regard anybody who is only five or ten years older than
I am as still young. But the Census puts me in that class—65 and over.

We had on January 1 of this year, by estimate of the Census
Bureau, 13,400,000 people over 65 years of age. That is roughly 9
per cent of our population. There are four times as many people in
the United States today that are over 65 as there were in 1900, fifty
years ago. The population of the country doubled in this half-
century, while the number of old people increased fourfold. The
same ratio appears in the last census period. Between 1940 and 1950,
the population of the United States increased by 14½ per cent—the
number of people over 65 increased by 29 per cent—again, exactly
double. To make this perhaps a little more vivid and to bring out
more clearly what the problem is: At the present time, the number

of people over 65 years of age increases at a rate almost 2.5 per cent a year. That is our rate of increase and we know pretty well that that rate of increase will not, for quite some period, decline. From the Census, we know the ages of all our people and, by merely applying life expectancy tables, we can make a pretty good guess how many people over 65 we will have at the minimum at all foreseeable future dates—dates which are as far ahead as 65 years from now—because everybody who will be 65 years of age, 65 years from now, is now living in the United States, except for the few immigrants whom we will admit in the intervening years. The probability is that we will have a good many more people in this older age group in the years that lie ahead than we are now estimating.

This is an interesting fact: In each of the last three censuses, the preliminary estimates of the Census Bureau have been wrong by a very considerable margin and always in the direction of underestimating the number of older people. In this last census period, moreover, something quite significant happened in relation to our older population. Until 1950, while we had a great many more people who were getting into the old-age group, after they reached age 65 their life expectancy was just about the same as it has been for people over 65 ever since we have taken a census. In this last period, the ten years between 1940 and 1950, however, the life expectancy of people over 65 increased by a year and a half. Not only are more people getting into the old-age group, but they now have a longer life expectancy remaining to them. Present estimates are that within other generations—something like 25 or 30 years—average life expectancy at birth is likely to increase by another ten years. That may seem an extreme guess, but it needs to be appreciated that the child born in 1900 had a life expectancy of 48 years, while the child born in 1950 had a life expectancy of better than 68 years. For white women, the white girl-child, the life expectancy in 1950 was 71 years. The guess that by 30 years from now, average life expectancy will be 78, is, perhaps, not so far off.

Until fairly recently, the assumption was that you could not do anything about the diseases from which old people died. The assumption was they died from old age. Actually they died from diseases that are very prevalent in old age. That something can be done about these diseases is now a creed of substantially all the medical profession. The discovery of penicillin and the sulfa drugs, alone, is believed to have been mainly responsible for the phenomena that we've witnessed for the first time in this last census period—an increase in the life expectancy of older people. Where pneumonia used to be the second cause of death among older people only fifteen years ago, today it is way down to the seventh or eighth cause of death, because of the discovery of these wonder drugs. This whole family of drugs has made such a tremendous difference that medical men are hopeful that we're on the verge of coping successfully also with many of the other diseases which, if I may say so, cause older people to die prematurely.

《《《《《《《《《〇》》》》》》》》

Now let me say something about the composition of our older population. This may be of interest. The first thing that I would like to have you grasp—I am sure that when you think about it, you will appreciate it at once—we talk about people 65 years of age and over, but overlook that "the over" means up to 100 for some people in the group. The older age group includes people whose ages range from 65 to 100. Let me bring this to your attention, too. Almost half of the people who are over 65, and by the time the next Census rolls around, that figure will exceed one-half, are also over 75. For many purposes, you can classify the people who are over 65 into two groups: the younger old people, 65 to 75, and the older old people, 75 to 100, and, in a few instances, beyond 100.

Next I want to say something about sex distribution. Among the older people we have far more women than men. In the 1950 Census, for every 100 women over 65, we had only 89 men. Until 1940, the men over 65 exceeded the women over 65. In 1940 there were for every 100 women, 95 men. In 1950, the ratio is 100 old ladies to 89 old men. Present trends indicate that within 20 years this ratio will be 100 women to not more than 75 men. Women now have a life expectancy more than three years longer than men, and the gap is widening. The old-age problem is more of a problem of the old ladies than of the old men.

Let me also say something about geographic distribution of the older Americans. We all know older people who have gone to California or Florida. But when we examine the Census we discover this interesting fact: Both California and Florida are among the four states of the Union in which the percentage of the older people did not increase between 1940 and 1950. Many older people did move to California or Florida, but still more younger people also moved to those states. Both California and Florida have a smaller percentage of their population in the 65-and-over age group than the older states that have not grown so rapidly. Rapid growth is a matter of increase in population in the younger age groups much more than in the older age groups. The problem of an aging population is more of a problem for Wisconsin than for California. The percentage of the older people in Wisconsin at the present time is almost 1 per cent higher than in the nation as a whole and this disparity will increase, unless we have an unexpected growth in total population.

Next I want to say something about the employment of older people. There are many who are under the impression that the great bulk of people in the United States retire at the age of 65. That is a sort of a traditional age for retirement. As a matter of fact, a good many people retire before age 65. In our population of adult age, we have more than 2,500,000 who are disabled before they reach 65 to such an extent that they are unable to work. There are at least another 2,500,000 people who retire before 65 for one reason or another. On the other hand, we have 3,000,000 people above 65 who are now employed. The average age of retirement under the Social Security Act has been 69, not 65. The Social Security Act has no compulsory age of retirement. People are not required to retire at any specified age. They have retired in the typical case at age 69 and in the past year at age 70. The retirement age is going up slightly, not down. Of all the people between 65 and 70, 60 per cent of the men are still working. In the younger old age, from 65 to 75, you have a very high percentage of employment. On the other hand, you do not have much employment among the nearly one-half of the older people who are 75 years of age and over. The percentage of people employed goes down every single year of life after age 60. But for the entire group of the people over 65 years of age, employment is the largest source of income. Somewhat more than 40 per cent of all the men over 65 are in employment, holding down jobs, and most of them full-time jobs. The percentage of the women employed is increasing but is still very small compared with the men in employment—the Census does not classify the housewives.

This is an important item about the employment of the older

people. The trend in the percentage of the older people who are employed has been pretty steadily downward with the exceptions of the two world war periods. About 80 per cent of all men over 65 were employed as recently as 1870. More than 65 per cent were employed as recently as 1900. Only 41 to 42 per cent were employed in 1940, but during the war years this percentage went up to 50 per cent. Since then it has again decreased despite the general high level of employment we have enjoyed. The percentage of the people 65 and over decreased to 45 per cent by the time of the Census of 1950. It has declined farther since then and is believed to be down now to about the figure of 1940, 42 per cent of the men over 65.

The reasons for the trend toward a decreasing percentage of older workers who are employed are quite apparent. Very important is the shift in occupations in our population. The highest percentages of employment of older people are among the farmers, the railroad men, the coal miners, the retailers, and the self-employed. With the exception of retailing, these are all industries of decreasing total employment. The total number of people employed in these industries is going down as well as, along with these totals, the number of the older people who work in these industries. The 80 per cent of all the men over 65 who were employed in 1870 were mainly on farms; today the people living on farms constitute only a fifth of our population.

There are many other factors accounting for decreasing percentages of the older people who are employed. One is the difficulty the older people experience in getting other jobs once they lose their jobs. The problem of employment of older people is not mainly a matter of their being compulsorily retired, but that once they have lost their jobs they have much greater difficulty in finding other jobs. In part, that merely reflects the fact that with age there is a decrease in the capacity to perform many types of jobs—not in all lines, but it is an exceptional man who at 65 and, still more exceptional, who at 75, can perform the hard labor that he could perform at 35. It is also exceptional that the man of 65 is willing to take the same risks —for instance, on a public utility construction crew—of the man of 25. On the other hand, there also are some things that older people can do at least as well as, if not better than, younger people.

Also affecting the situation is the prevailing idea of retirement . . . that 60 or 65 is the age at which people should retire. Most people do not retire at 65, but people talk so much about retiring at 60, 65, or 70 that these are the most common ages for retirement.

《《《《《《《《O》》》》》》》》

Now, briefly, let me say something about what we must do in view of the old-age problem we face. A civilized society, a Christian society, cannot condemn the aged to the gas chambers. Hitler proposed that, but we will never do that in the United States. Every civilized society must take care of its entire population, including the old people. The old people have to be supported; they cannot support themselves and most of them are beyond the age of employment and the possibility of supporting themselves by employment. They have to be supported by someone else.

That someone else may be their children. Children's support is an important source of income for older people. I, for one, strongly believe that children should support their parents, if they can do so. Children's support in our society, however, is decreasing. There's every evidence of that effect. There are many reasons why this is occurring. One major reason is that children and parents in our present-day society are often separated—often by hundreds and thousands of miles. The children no longer are in close and immediate contact with their parents. Well-meaning as they may be, they often do not know the problems that their parents face.

There is an even more important factor explaining the decrease in the support of older people by their children, which the sociologists have developed. This is a change in the nature of the family itself, which is occurring in our present-day society. This change is expressed in the technical terms: "consanguinal" family and "conjugal" family. The old consanguinal family was (and that is still true of the Chinese family and a much greater extent true of the rural than of the urban family in this country) a family of blood relations, who often lived in the same dwelling, who had a close feeling of kinship, who supported each other. We still have something left of the old consanguinal family when deaths occur and to a lesser degree at births and weddings. All the blood relations of the neighborhood will gather as a clan. Some families do that also at Christmas time. But what we principally have at the present time is the conjugal family, which consists of a husband and wife and their immature children. When the children become mature, they leave the home; they settle elsewhere, often miles away; they have their own problems, their own families, and they no longer are members of the families of their fathers and mothers and often know little about them. They may still have tender feelings toward their parents, but they have their own family problems. That is the typical family situation of today, and in this change in the very nature of the family lies one of the reasons why support of the older people by their children has weakened, although it still is important.

Savings also are important for old-age support. On every occasion possible, I emphasize the value of personal savings, even in an age of inflation, but they are the principal source of income of less than 10 per cent of the total number of the older people. Savings are the most reliable source of support which people unable to work can have. Even in the Great Depression years, the main support of the unemployed and of the poor, generally, came from their own savings and those of their relatives, overshadowing the great expenditures for relief. Savings are greater now than they have ever been before in this country, whether you measure them in terms of money totals or in terms of real income. We are not a country that doesn't save; we do save. But the great majority of people cannot save the amounts of money that are needed for support for such long periods as we must deal with in old age. It is this fact which has operated to throw increased burdens on the public for the support of the aged.

It is an age-old concept in the United States that when people have no other means of support and are in need, the public must support them. This principle, which in the statutes of Wisconsin reads that every city, town, and village is responsible for the care and support of the poor resident therein, was written into our statutes when Wisconsin was a territory and our first legislature met at Belmont, in that little building some of you undoubtedly have seen. Wisconsin Territory copies this provision from Michigan Territory of which it had been a part. Michigan Territory copied it from Indiana Territory of which earlier we had been a part; Indiana Territory, from the Northwest Territory; the Northwest Territory from the state of Pennsylvania; the state of Pennsylvania from the Elizabethan Poor Law, which was enacted in England just before settlement in this country began. The concept that people who are poor must be supported by the public if they have no other means of support, is age-old and is in effect in every civilized society. The way any society takes care of its people in need is a mark of its civilization—a test of whether a nation is civilized or not.

What is new in this matter of public support for people who are without other means of support is the increasing number of people who have had to be supported by the public in one fashion or another. At the present time about 18 to 19 per cent of our people over 65 are getting old-age assistance. The bulk of the people on old-age assistance are the older-old people. Many older-old people supported themselves until they reached the stage when they could no longer be employed. Then they used up their savings and when the savings were gone, they had to turn to the public for support. There are some people in the younger-older group who are on old-age assistance, but this matter of getting public support in the form of old-age assistance is very largely a matter of age. Plus old-age assistance, we have in this country an old-age insurance system. Three and a half million people over 65 years of age now get benefits under the old-age insurance system on retirement from their regular employment. The average retirement benefit is $50 per month. This is large payment in comparison with the amounts which the beneficiaries have paid into the insurance fund, but affords only a bare minimum for existence, and under present conditions hardly that.

We also have industrial pension systems. Employers put into the industrial pension systems of this country at present more than 1.5 billion dollars per year. Five hundred thousand people are receiving industrial pensions—however, this is about 3 per cent of the old people. That percentage will go up. It's unlikely, however, to ever reach anything like, say 50 per cent of the total number of old people. It will be a long time before even 10 per cent of the old people will get industrial pensions. While there are something like 9 million people working in plants that have industrial pension systems, a large percentage of the total number of these workers undoubtedly will not be there when they get to the age for retirement—most workers in this country do not stay with the same employer throughout their working lives. Rights in industrial pension plans are seldom vested. When workers leave or lose their jobs in plants with industrial pension systems, they lose their accumulated pension rights.

Public old-age security programs are of much greater importance. Employers and workers are putting 3.5 billion dollars a year into our old-age insurance system. We are paying benefits now of 1.5 billion dollars. We are putting two billion more into the reserve, which is not an adequate reserve but something for contingencies at least. We are spending nearly two billion dollars for old-age assistance. On the other types of public pension plans, especially public employees' retirement systems and the railroad retirement plan, we are putting in more than a billion dollars a year. Almost half of all older people now get some sort of benefit from a public old-age security system, most of them fortunately under an insurance plan to which they have themselves contributed.

It is obvious that just about everybody would be benefited if we could increase the employment of our older people. . . . Clearly, the older people themselves would be benefited. The retired men feel left out. From a psychological point of view, employment for the older men who can work is certainly a great advantage. From an economic point of view it is even more to their benefit that older men who still can work should do so. We will never provide, and certainly not from public funds, any pension comparable to that which a person who can work can earn, and we should not try to do that. Payments such as we make under old-age assistance, now about $55 in Wisconsin, or under old-age insurance of $50 per month on the average throughout the country, are sufficient, at the most, for the barest necessities of life. That we are doing this for our older people is decidedly worthwhile, but these payments fall short of providing a satisfying life. If workers can continue in employment, they will be better off economically, and the longer they continue in employment, the more likely they are to tide over the period that we call old age without experiencing real economic suffering.

From the point of view of the general public, an important consideration is the production that the older workers can provide. Social security and industrial pension systems must come out of the current production. The more production we have, the more there will be to distribute. Plus this there is the matter of the costs to the public of unnecessarily supporting anyone in idleness. It is a safe prediction that the public costs for old-age support will continue to rise and rise very rapidly, unless we can materially increase the percentage of the older people in employment.

The reverse side of the picture, however, must also be taken into consideration. Employment is not a cure-all for the problems of old age—nor even the problems of economic support in old age. I call attention again to the figures I have given you. Almost half of the people over 65 are also over 75. There are considerably more women among those who are over 65 than there are men. Less than 10 per cent of the women over 65 are now employed, although that percentage, fortunately, is increasing, unlike that of the men over 65 who are employed. It takes a lot of doing to even hold our own in this matter of the percentage of older people who are employed. The number of older people in this country is increasing by 2.5 per cent a year. To just hold our own and not continue to slide back farther, as we have been doing, we must provide employment for 2.5 per cent a year more people over 65 than we have been providing. At least two-thirds of all the people over 75 are in an age group where employment is out of the question. Of the people on old-age assistance in Wisconsin, a survey made in 1951 disclosed that 27 per cent are people who need physical care to exist, to say nothing about employment.

Old age is a period of increasing disabilities and infirmities. We will probably be able to further prolong life, but I for one do not believe that life will ever terminate in the way of the wonderful one-hoss shay of Oliver Wendell Holmes in the *Autocrat of the Breakfast Table,* which was in perfect condition for 100 years and then on its hundredth anniversary, all of a sudden, a puff and it disappeared from earth. That is not the way most of us will terminate our lives. There will be periods of infirmity and a period in the last years of life in which we no longer will be able to work. The total length of life after 65 may increase and quite considerably, but how much working life will increase is quite another question. Since 1900 the average period that our American citizens have spent in retirement has more than doubled. It is now more than 5 years; it was only 2.5 years in 1900. As life expectancy has improved, maximum working life expectancy has decreased. The percentage of people employed after 65 has gone down. We certainly want to reverse this trend, but that will not be easily accomplished. To accomplish this much-to-be-desired result, coöperation of industry, labor, and government, of the entire community, and of the older people themselves will be necessary. Industry faces the old-age problem in two major aspects: the hiring of older people, and the retaining of older people who are employed.

The question of retaining older people gives rise to the further question of a fixed or a flexible retirement age. A majority of all employers of the country have no fixed retirement age. There also is no fixed retirement age in the Social Security Act; in fact, no compulsory retirement. In public employees' retirement systems and in some companies, particularly those with industrial pension plans, we have fixed retirement ages. In many such companies in private industry, the fixed retirement age is often departed from. In public employment, in contrast, when you attain a given age, that is the end.

A fixed retirement age has many advantages . . . as well as disadvantages. Not an industrialist, I am quite sympathetic with the employer who faces the problem of older workers whose efficiency is decreasing. When there is a fixed retirement age, arguments over the retirement of particular workers are greatly reduced. A fixed age is not merely a subjective test, a whim of the employer or the foreman. It is something that every worker can understand, and about which there is little dispute. On the other hand, we undoubtedly waste manpower in that way, because people differ in their capacities at age 65, as they do at age 55 or any other age. Some existing retirement ages are too low. They date back to the Depression years when we had great surpluses of manpower. They are not suitable under present conditions. I hope that better objective tests of ability can be developed than we now have. Some companies have done pretty well with flexible retirement ages. Others have found them unsatisfactory because the workers regard all subjective tests of ability to be arbitrary, depending upon the whim of the man who makes the decision.

Many other problems arise in this connection. One is the possibility of shifting workers to less arduous jobs and to jobs better suited to them, which are generally less well-paying jobs. This is something industry, generally, would like to do, but the workers themselves often resist and the unions often do not permit it. Then there is the matter of part-time work. . . . This is a possibility in some plants and for some lines of work, but it also calls for a lot of working-out. The knowledge we have about jobs suitable for older workers is still pretty limited, as is knowledge about the possibilities for part-time jobs. It will take a great deal of study and research and application to the work to be done in the particular plant before intelligent transfers of older workers can be made and more part-time jobs created.

There is also the problem of preparing workers for retirement. Many companies are doing a good deal along that line, including Wisconsin companies. The problem is one the worker himself has to face, but in which the employer certainly has an interest. Many employers are pursuing very intelligent policies in that respect.

Then there is the problem the entire community faces, industry included, that of accepting the older people as part of our society, giving them a sense of usefulness, affording them opportunities, treating them as the senior citizens that they are in our society. The older people have limitations, just like all other human beings, but they also have a great deal to contribute to our society.

I have talked so long that I must conclude. I do so by repeating that the old-age problem is more than an industry problem, although industry has grave responsibilities in this connection. Unions also have responsibilities towards the older workers; and we will not get decent solutions unless unions recognize their responsibilities. The community also has great responsibilities. The great majority of the senior citizens of any community will not go to California or Florida. They will continue to live in your midst. In the smaller towns you will have an actual increase in people coming to live with you at that stage of their lives.

But first and foremost, old age is not merely an industrial, a labor, and a community problem, but an individual problem. Old age is a part of the life cycle and one which most younger people will experience before their lives are ended. At the present time, of all people who get to be 20 years of age, 7 out of 10 will also get to be 65. Old age will confront the great majority of all our people. It is, hence, a problem in which everybody has a direct interest. Like many other problems it gives rise to many difficulties. But America can solve this problem by understanding and intelligent action.

Old-Age Security:
The National Picture
in 1954

Excerpts from address at the
Conference on Social Security
in a Free Society, Pomona
College, Claremont, Cali-
fornia, October 2, 1954

WHILE THE CHANGES made in the federal old-age and survivors' insurance system by the Social Security Act Amendments
of 1954 were less far-reaching improvements than the Social Security
Act Amendments of 1950, they were distinctly in the right direction.
This is particularly gratifying because only a year ago it seemed
likely that the 83d Congress would do nothing to improve the law
and might completely destroy the contributory old-age insurance
system. That, instead, progress has been made is very much to the
credit of the Congress, which passed the new law by a large majority
from both political parties, and of the President and the Department of Health, Education, and Welfare, which sponsored the legislation.

The major improvement made lies in the extension of the coverage of the old-age and survivors' insurance system. The claims from
Washington that 10,000,000 additional people have been brought
under the protection of old-age and survivors' insurance appear
exaggerated. The 10,000,000 figure may be approximately accurate
for the number of people who might conceivably be brought under
coverage. But it overstates the number who are likely to gain pro-

tection within the next year or two. As to several large groups included within the 10,000,000 figure, the new law is in effect elective. It is probable that by no means all who might be brought into the system will actually enjoy its protection for quite some time to come.

The largest such group, totaling 3,500,000, are state and local government employees who have heretofore been excluded because they are covered by state and local retirement systems. The recent amendments make it possible to correct this rank discrimination against public employees, as compared with private employees who, from the beginning, have enjoyed the protection of the old-age and survivors' insurance system, although many also are covered by industrial pension systems. But the new law still does not put them on an equal footing. Private employers and employees are covered compulsorily; public employees only if the employing unit so elects. Beyond that there is the farther hurdle that before state and local government employees can be brought under the law they must so vote by a two-thirds majority.

The new law also continues the exclusion of doctors, dentists, and lawyers, contrary to the recommendations of the President. In doing so Congress yielded to lobbying pressures from the professional associations in these occupations, without allowing their members a vote whether they desire coverage. But while yielding to the pressures from the American Medical Association and the American Bar Association in excluding doctors and lawyers from the protection of the old-age and survivors' insurance system, it is to the credit of Congress that it did not pass the special privilege bill relating to private retirement programs which was promoted by these associations and which a year ago seemed likely to be enacted. Under that bill, practitioners in the enumerated professions would have been allowed tax exemption on payments they might make to retirement plans set up by these associations up to $7,500 per year and $150,000 in a lifetime—an amount which would provide an annuity of $1,000 per month—to a very great extent at the expense of Uncle Sam.

Despite the failure of the Congress to go the whole way with the Administration in the extension of coverage, very substantial improvements have been made in this respect. Most important is the extension of coverage to the farmers—the largest group heretofore excluded—and the broadening of the coverage of farm laborers. The 1950 amendments brought farm laborers who work for one employer the year around under the law, but not the farmers or the migratory workers. Now substantially all farmers and farm laborers will be covered, beginning January 1, 1955. We still do not cover all employed people, as the Committee on Economic Security which sponsored the original Social Security Act recommended, but we again have come closer to that ideal. In addition we now cover most of the self-employed, whom, it was believed in 1935, it was not feasible administratively to bring under old-age insurance.

To people who are now receiving old-age benefits or who are not many years away from eligibility for retirement benefits, the most important improvements in the old-age and survivors' insurance system in the 1954 amendments will seem to be increase in benefits. Without going into details, this amounts to an increase for people now receiving old-age (retirement) benefits ranging from a minimum of $5 per month to a maximum of $13.50, the larger increases going to the people with the presently higher benefits. For survivors there are smaller, but proportionate, increases. For people not yet on the benefit rolls, the increases will be greater. For those who will not retire until some years from now, the old-age benefits may be as high as $108.50 per month, at the maximum; and the minimum hereafter will be $30 per month. The combined total of the benefits to all members of one family from now on may go as high as $200 per month. Average benefits will continue to be between the minimum and maximum limits and, for some time to come, probably will be close to midway between these limits. Wives', children's, and survivors' benefits will be paid at the same percentages of the primary beneficiary's benefit as heretofore, and will all be increased somewhat, although not as much as those of primary beneficiaries. Averaging all benefits, I estimate that an increase of around $6 or $7 per month in old-age and survivors' insurance benefits is likely in the next few years, and larger increases in later years.

It is at this point that I register publicly a criticism I often have expressed privately about the publicity released from Washington on the average size of the old-age and survivors' insurance benefits. This publicity always stresses, and sometimes gives exclusively, the combined benefits of husband and wife where both are on the OASI rolls. So we have the figures that married recipients now get benefits up to $127.50 per month, and will get $162.80 under the new law, and up to $200, if they have children under 18. These figures are correct for a small percentage of the couples on the OASI rolls, when all the benefits going to one family are combined. But they are very misleading. For three-fourths of all the retired workers on the rolls there is no benefit to the wife, although there are often wives dependent upon the retired workers. The typical old-age benefit is a single person's benefit. That averaged $51.62 in April and, doubtless, is still very close to that figure. Under the new law that average figure, certainly, will not increase by as much as $10 per month for many years to come.

This highlights one of the outstanding defects of the old-age and survivors' insurance system of the United States, about which nothing has been done in the new law. This is the absence of allowance for dependents, particularly wives.

«««««‹‹‹O›››»»»»»

While the administration proposed nothing and the Congress did nothing to correct this great defect in our old-age and survivors' insurance system, the benefit provisions in the federal old-age and survivors' insurance system have been materially improved in several important respects. These improvements involve more than the increase in the amount of the benefits resulting from changes in the benefit formula and increases in the statutory minimum and maximum benefits. Other definite improvements affecting benefits are: (1) the provisions under which up to four years may be omitted in determining the average wages on which benefits are to be based; (2) the increase in the earnings retired workers may have without resulting in a reduction of their OASI benefits; (3) the provisions freezing benefit rights when workers are permanently and totally disabled before attaining retirement age; and (4) the increase in the maximum tax base from $3,600 to $4,200 per year.

Ever since 1939, benefits have been based on average wages, computed by dividing the total wages on which taxes have been paid by the number of months which have elapsed since the starting date, which now most commonly is January 1, 1951, but may be January 1, 1937, and many years from now, the date on which the insured became 21. As the divisor in this formula includes periods in which the worker may have had no earnings, this formula for computing average wages results for many people in average wages for benefit purposes far below their full-time wages. The new law retains the average wage formula, but permits dropping consideration of the years of lowest earnings, up to as many as four years. This change will operate to considerably increase retirement benefits of many people retiring hereafter and will bring the computed average wages more nearly into line with what the worker believes his wages to be.

Of benefit to a considerable number of retired workers will be the changes in the amount of earnings such workers may have without losing current retirement benefits. The OASI system has never had provisions for compulsory retirement at any age, nor has it ever prohibited any worker from earning as much as he could from employment. But it has had an earnings test to determine whether a worker has retired. Such a test has been included in the law because it has been assumed that the basic purpose of retirement benefits is to provide income after retirement. The retirement test prior to the 1954 amendments has been earnings from covered employment not exceeding $75 per month, unless the worker is past 75, after which there is no longer any earnings test for retirement. Under the new law, earnings up to $1,200 per year from employment, whether in covered or uncovered employment, are permitted without affecting the right to retirement benefits, and the age after which any amount of earnings are disregarded is reduced to 72. These changes are not likely to have much effect on the employment of older people, but should operate to increase the total income of many older people who are able to get part-time employment.

The new provisions "freezing" the benefit rights of workers who become totally and permanently disabled will probably not affect many people, but are fair and right. Such freezing of the benefit rights of the totally disabled is not the same thing as the invalidity insurance protection provided for in most foreign countries; it is hardly even a step in that direction. Probably only a few of the 2,500,000 people under 65 we have in this country who are permanently invalided before they attain age 65 will ever benefit from this new provision. But some of these unfortunates, who were fully insured when they became permanently and totally disabled, will now retain their rights to old-age benefits on becoming 65, without having the period of disability counted against them in determining their right to benefits and the amount thereof.

Direct increases in benefits will result for people retired under the new law by reason of the increase in the maximum amount on which old-age insurance taxes are payable from $3,600 per year to $4,200. The people who will benefit are those whose earnings exceed $300 per month. As many workers now have earnings above that figure, the change will benefit not only executives and other people with large salaries but close to half of all workers.

This increase in the tax base is sound for still another reason besides its effects on benefits. This is that it is a step, although not a sufficiently long step, toward correcting a grave defect in the tax levies for old-age and survivors' insurance purposes. When the Social Security Act was enacted, the then existing maximum of $3,000 of wages and salaries subject to the old-age insurance taxes gave partial exemption to less than 10 per cent of all wage earners and salaried employees and a much smaller percentage of the total payrolls. At present wage and salary levels, the $3,600 upper limit of the Act, as it stood before the recent amendments, affected close to one-half of all covered people and operated to exempt a third of the total payrolls from having to contribute anything toward meeting the costs of old-age and survivors' insurance. The equivalent of the original upper limit of $3,000 per year is now $6,000. President Eisenhower recommended to Congress increasing this limit from $3,600 to $4,800. Congress did not go that far, but made the limit $4,200. This is a step in the right direction, but at least a fourth of the total payrolls of the country will still be exempt from taxation for old-age insurance purposes.

This exemption occurs at the wrong end of the payroll schedule. There is a good deal to be said in favor of exempting very low earnings from contributions for old-age insurance purposes. But the exemption we have is one enjoyed only by people with well-above-average earnings.

There are no good reasons why covered employees should not be required to pay old-age insurance taxes on all their earnings. In the recent debate on this issue, the specious argument was advanced that it is unfair to collect taxes on earnings above $4,200 per year because workers who only now are entering employment, and who will contribute on more than this amount of earnings each year from 20 to 65, will not always get back as much in benefits as they will pay in taxes. This obscures the fact that for decades to come at every wage level covered people will on the average get back far more than they pay in taxes. And the people with the largest earnings get back the largest amounts in benefits, although, percentagewise, the system favors the low-paid workers. If it is thought that people who pay old-age insurance taxes should always get back at least as much as they pay in taxes, provision to that effect can be included in the law. This was included in the original 1935 law but taken out by Congress, because it adds to the costs. To exempt the larger incomes from the tax levies is a special privilege for the more fortunate, contrary to all principles of equity and, in the long run, will add to the burdens which the lower-paid workers or the general treasury will have to bear. In this connection it is important, also, to have in mind that in our system the employers pay equal amounts in taxes with the employees. The maximum limit on which taxes are payable operates to make the basis of financial support something which falls far short of a general payroll tax. The maximum tax limit is a special privilege to executives and other highly paid people and to the corporations that pay the high salaries, which should be stricken from the law. If that is politically not feasible, the maximum tax base should be raised at least to $6,000—the present-day equivalent of the $3,000 figure of the original law.

Further changes are necessary also in the present law to correct inequities that have developed in the system. The most serious inequity is that many workers who have paid old-age insurance taxes for many years get considerably smaller benefits than people newly covered who paid far less in taxes. This results from limited coverage and harsh eligibility conditions in effect from 1939 to 1950 and from the action of Congress in striking out any additional allowance for years of tax payments. It was right that Congress in 1950 and again this year extended coverage, reversing what earlier Congresses did in this respect. Congress in 1950 also needed to adopt a new "starting date," to offset the 1939 amendments providing new rules for eligibility for benefits, which operated to deny all benefits to a large percentage of all taxpayers. But the combination of liberal eligibility conditions with the elimination of any credit for the number of years of tax payment has created the present inequity that newly covered workers get larger benefits than people who have long paid taxes and in much larger total amounts.

I am not one who believes that considerations of equity need to be taken into account only in private insurance, not social insurance. To the contrary, I believe that a social insurance system cannot survive unless it satisfies the concepts of the beneficiaries and the public generally as to what is fair and right. To pay larger benefits to the newly covered than to those long covered, who have contributed a much larger share of the cost of their benefits, is inequitable and is a condition that remains to be corrected.

The remedy does not lie in the proposal presented to Congress this year by the Chamber of Commerce of the United States that all old people not now on the OASI rolls be paid minimum benefits of $25 or $35 per month out of the old-age and survivors' insurance fund, and that these payments take the place of the federal aid to the states for old-age assistance, which comes out of the general fund. It is greatly to the credit of the Administration and of the Congress that, after first appearing to react favorably to this proposal, they saw it in its true light, as a scheme to shift a considerable part of the share of old-age assistance now borne by the national government to the states, and the remainder from the federal income tax to the payroll taxes. It would not have corrected the existing inequities in the OASI system, but would have destroyed that system and, in the end, probably would have left us nothing but old-age assistance on a needs basis financed from state funds.

To correct the existing injustice of higher benefits to the newly covered, we need to restore the increments in benefits for years of tax payment which were part of our old-age and survivors' insurance up to 1950. Removing this increment was a backward step; it should have been increased. Still to be done, which the present Congress did not do, is the correction of the inequities which have developed by reason of failure to take into account the length of the period in which workers have paid taxes. This is peculiarly necessary to deal fairly with the younger workers of today, who will contribute far more in taxes than the favored oldsters who have been benefited so greatly by the amendments of 1950 and since that date.

As must be clear from what has been said, I am not satisfied with the old-age and survivors' insurance system we now have, improved as, undoubtedly, it has been by the 1954 amendments. I do not see its greatest defects in what is often referred to as the meagerness of its benefits. Benefits such as we now have will not of themselves provide a satisfying living. But that is not the objective of social security legislation. That objective does not go beyond trying to guarantee a minimum income sufficient for all essentials in all major personal contingencies. It is grounded upon the premise that the primary responsibility for support rests upon the individual and the family. It is the individual himself who must provide the essentials, at a standard approved by public opinion and made possible by the productivity of the economy.

The present level of retirement benefits for single persons may not be high enough; in this state of high incomes, compared with the rest of the country, most people will be of that opinion. Doubtless, the present old-age (primary) benefits will again have to be increased ere long. But as I see the situation, increases in the primary benefits are less urgently needed than are the other improvements I have discussed. It is less necessary to increase the benefits to single retired workers than to provide dependents' allowances to married retired workers with wives to support who are less than 65 years of age.

Also very necessary is the correction of the inequities that have resulted from giving no credit whatsoever for years of tax payment, under which higher benefits are now paid to those who have been but newly covered and who have contributed very little toward the cost of their benefits. Assuredly, also, the exemption of wage and salary payments above $4,200 from any contributions to the costs of old-age survivors' insurance should be ended. If that cannot be done, the evil arising from the special privilege now accorded the recipients of high wages and salaries and the corporations making these payments should be lessened by increasing the maximum wage for tax and benefit purposes to $6,000 per year—the present-day equivalent in purchasing power of the $3,000 limit included in the original law. And it seems to me most desirable to do what most other democratic countries have done long since in providing invalidity insurance protection along with old-age and survivors' insurance protection. Finally, I strongly believe in President Eisenhower's recommendation, which Congress has carried out only in part, that all employed and self-employed persons should be brought under the coverage of the OASI system.

These are all badly needed further improvements. But with all its defects, the old-age and survivors' system we have now provides substantial economic help to large numbers of the older people of the United States and to many of their dependents and survivors. The beneficiaries are steadily increasing in numbers and percentages. The basic principles on which this system is grounded are sound and should be preserved.

Five million of our fourteen million people of 65 and over are now receiving old-age and survivors' insurance benefits, plus 1,500,000 surviving younger widows and dependent children of deceased insured workers. The number of beneficiaries is increasing at the rate of 100,000 each month, despite the fact that 3,000,000 people over 65, otherwise eligible, are still working. As recently as 1952, more old people were on old-age assistance in the United States than were on the OASI rolls. Now the latter outnumber the former group two to one. But for the restrictive provisions governing eligibility to benefits, which were introduced by the 1939 amendments and were in effect until 1950, the percentage of the presently retired older people who would be getting OASI benefits would be much greater. Even so, nearly half of all Americans who are now in retired status are receiving OASI benefits. In the years ahead the great majority—quite likely at least 90 per cent—of all retiring older workers will get such benefits.

Reliance upon a contributory insurance system as the main public institution for necessary minimum economic security in old age is sound and in accord with our system of free enterprise. Paying benefits only to old people in immediate need, as some conservative critics of the insurance system advocate, may seem cheaper. As some of the experience of California with old-age assistance has abundantly illustrated, however, need is such a flexible concept that the costs of an old-age security system based on need may well exceed those of an insurance system. Conservative critics, also, should realize that contributions based on payrolls can be justified only where all contributors get benefits.

Some private insurance people have been most anxious that public old-age security should not be based on insurance principles. That too, I believe, is a bad mistake. The more social security institutions utilize insurance principles, the better it will be. Under insurance principles, it follows that when benefits are increased contributions must also be increased. This operates as a restraining influence against unwarranted increases in benefits. A contributory insurance system further preserves the feeling of self-reliance and independence and operates as a stimulus to industry and thrift. Contributory social insurance not only is consistent with our system of free enterprise, but, under present conditions, is a very necessary part of such a system.

This brings me to the relation between old-age insurance and old-age assistance. In recent years there have been many statements to the effect that because many old people are still on old-age assistance rolls nearly fifteen years after OASI benefits first became payable, the old-age insurance system is no good. These critics assert that old-age insurance was sold to the country on the claim that ere long it would render old-age assistance unnecessary. Such a claim was never made by the advocates of the Social Security Act. To the contrary, the Social Security Act inaugurated federal aid for old-age assistance, as well as old-age insurance, in anticipation that old-age assistance is needed for a satisfactory system of old-age security as well as old-age insurance. Congress was told that old-age insurance would not benefit people already retired and that some old-age insurance beneficiaries would also need old-age assistance.

A sizable percentage of the present old people were retired before the Social Security Act came into operation. Many others who in 1937 were not yet 65 were adversely affected by the fact that Congress provided for considerably narrower coverage in the original law than was recommended by the Committee on Economic Security and the President, and that Congress in 1939 and again in 1946 further narrowed coverage. Even worse was the insertion in 1939 of restrictive eligibility conditions, which originated outside of the Administration and were not even taken up with the then-functioning Advisory Committee on Social Security. These had the effect that a majority of the people who retired before 1951 were ineligible for OASI benefits, although many had some credits in the system, through tax payments. This unfortunate result was partially remedied by the liberal eligibility conditions enacted in 1950. These gave many of these older people an opportunity to qualify for benefits, but many of them could no longer work or find employment. The older people are themselves getting older. Nearly one half of the people now of 65 and over are also 75 or above; and nearly 15 per cent, 85 and over. As people get older and retirement lasts longer, resources they have accumulated are exhausted and the likelihood that they will have to have assistance increases.

It remains true also, as was explained when the Social Security Act

was under consideration, that at all times some people who get
OASI benefits will need supplementary old-age assistance. Throughout the country, one-sixth of all OASI recipients now also get OAA;
in California, due at least in part to the unique special needs provision in its old-age assistance law, twice that percentage. Some old
people have unusually great needs, due to large medical and hospital
bills or a great number of dependents. Social security benefits cannot
be geared to the man with unusually great needs. To do so would
make social insurance impossibly costly and very wasteful. For the
old person with extraordinary needs and no means, we will continue
to have to have old-age assistance, as well as old-age insurance. But I
doubt whether the percentage of the OASI beneficiaries who really
need supplementary old-age assistance is as great as the California
figures suggest.

The liberalization of conditions for eligibility to benefits and the
extension of coverage in 1950 had the effect of materially reducing
the old-age assistance rolls throughout the country. The total number of old people on old-age assistance is now lower than four years
ago, despite an increase of at least 10 per cent in the total number
of old people and the gradual increase in the average age of the old
people. As the old-age and survivors' insurance system is improved,
the need for old-age assistance will decrease. But we will continue to
need old-age assistance for the people who were old before old-age
insurance could benefit them and for those old people who have
extraordinary needs.

Costs and Benefits in OASI

Excerpts from "Some Un-
solved Problems in the
Economics of Welfare,"
an address at the
Economics-in-Action Program
of the University of Wisconsin
Extension Division, July 28,
1955, broadcast over WHA
and other stations of the State
Radio Network

RECENT ESTIMATES publicized by officials of the United States Department of Health, Education, and Welfare are that more than 3 billion dollars per year goes into industrial pension funds and nearly as much into health and welfare funds. Much higher figures are given by industry groups as to the total cost of what they call "fringe benefits," which are principally welfare payments. For life insurance the American people are now paying annual premiums of 11.5 billion dollars. Very certain it is that employers pay considerably more to private agencies for welfare benefits to their employees than the total of their contributions to all governmental social insurance programs. To date, the number of beneficiaries under these private programs is much smaller than the number of beneficiaries in the social insurance programs and the total benefit payments are much less. The explanation of this situation, that the private welfare programs cost more in the aggregate but pay for less in total benefits than do the social security programs, lies in part in the recency of the establishment of most industrial pension, health, and welfare plans, and in part in their considerably higher administrative costs, but above all in the larger reserves they have accumulated. In contrast to a total reserve of 20 billion dollars in the federal old-age and survivors' insurance fund and 9 billion dollars in all unemployment insurance funds combined, the life insurance companies now have total reserves of 71 billion dollars and the industrial pension funds of 20 billion—and the reserves of private economic security institutions are growing much more rapidly.

This phenomenon of the much greater growth of the reserves in the private security programs has pretty much laid to rest what critics originally represented as the most serious problem confronting the federal old-age and survivors' insurance system. The reserve of 47 billion dollars which they estimated would exist in the old-age security fund by 1980 was represented as likely to be larger than the total public debt and completely impossible. So there was a great outcry for so-called pay-as-you-go financing, which in connection with old-age security really means paying no attention to accruing liabilities. This outcry led to the reduction in contribution rates from 1942 to 1950—at a time when higher contributions would not have been burdensome and would also have tended to keep down the then-occurring inflation. In 1950, Congress put itself on record to the effect that "pay-as-you-go" would not do; since then we have returned to a program of financing designed to assure that there will be enough money in the fund to pay all promised benefits, which is impossible unless sizable reserves are accumulated in the early decades of the system. Today, despite the mistaken tax reductions of the 1940's, the reserve in the old-age and survivors' insurance trust fund is considerably larger than the critics estimated it would be by this time. But there is little concern about the fact that 20 billion dollars of our 280 billion national debt is owed to the old-age and survivors' insurance trust fund. It is now more generally realized that instead of too large a reserve, the present 20 billion dollar reserve is almost 50 billion dollars less than there would have to be were our OASI system financed on a full reserve basis—which is the method of financing followed by the commercial insurance companies.

The financial problem in old-age insurance, whether it be publicly or privately operated, is not that of collecting too much money in the early years, but of not having enough money on hand in the future years when the system matures. If the present method of financing is adhered to and benefits are not increased without providing adequate additional revenues, this will not be any problem; but the OASI system is sure to be in trouble if we reduce contribution rates or increase benefits without correspondingly increasing contribution rates. The benefits now promised in the OASI system are estimated by the actuaries to cost more than 7.5 per cent of taxable payrolls on a flat rate basis. We now collect only 4 per cent—2 per cent from employers and 2 per cent from employees. But the actuarial deficit we have developed in consequence of the low contribution rates of the first decades is offset under the present plan of financing by provisions that will give us a combined contribution rate of 8 per cent beginning in 1975. This higher-than-necessary average rate twenty years from now, if left undisturbed, together with the interest earnings on reserves, will keep the OASI system solvent despite the fact that, in all old-age insurance systems, costs increase for many decades. But if benefit costs are increased—as I believe they should be in some respects—contribution rates must also be increased.

These statements assume that the OASI system will continue to be self-financed, without drawing upon general tax revenues. From the outset there have been a good many people who have advocated that the financing should, at least in part, be from sources other than the so-called payroll taxes, which are contributions, measured by a part of their earnings from the prospective beneficiaries, and matching contributions from their employers. This proposal has never gotten much political support for two reasons: (1) the demands upon the general revenues of the United States government have been so great that neither the administration in office nor Congress has been willing to put this additional burden on income taxes or any other general tax; and (2) so long as millions of Americans were excluded from possibility of getting benefits, it was manifestly unfair to burden them with a part of the costs, as they would be were a part of these costs met from general taxes. As the coverage of the OASI system has been considerably broadened and conditions for eligibility to benefits has been liberalized, the second of these objections now has lost much of its force, and pretty much will disappear altogether if we get universal coverage. But the first objection remains and makes the only safe course to increase contribution rates as benefits are increased.

This brings me to the problem of broadened coverage and improved benefits.

In the matter of coverage, there is little difference of opinion at the present time. In principle, few people will question that all social security systems should extend to all people who are exposed to the hazard against which these systems are designed to afford protection. The practical difficulty in getting this principle enacted into law has been that all insurance is two-sided, involving contributions (or taxes) on the one hand and benefits on the other; and the contributions come before the benefits. So long as only the benefits are talked about, just about everybody wants extended coverage; but the question, as it comes to Congress and the state legislature, is one of broadening the coverage for contribution or tax purposes. It is at that stage that political considerations enter and selfishness asserts itself. At this moment, the acute questions concern the exclusion of certain professional groups from OASI and the discriminatory treatment of public employees in that system; also the exclusion from other social security programs of the employees of small establishments and of most farm workers, particularly migratory workers. Progress is gradually being made toward universal coverage, but much remains to be accomplished before this becomes an actuality.

Is the Social
Security Fund
Solvent?

Reprinted from *Challenge:*
The Magazine of Economic
Affairs, published by the
Institute of Economic Affairs,
New York University, Volume
VI (August–September, 1958),
pages 25–29

U NTIL 1957 the critics of our social security system insisted that it was overfinanced. They advocated reduction in the contribution rates and the adoption of what they called "pay-as-you-go" financing. By this they meant that we should disregard accruing liabilities and collect only enough taxes (contributions) to meet the current payments.

But in the winter of 1957, the Social Security Administration issued a statement which showed that the benefit payments for the old-age, survivors', and disability insurance system (OASDI) in the first half of the fiscal year exceeded tax collections by several hundred million dollars. The critics then shifted their ground and argued that the social security system was near bankruptcy!

Such criticism overlooked some important facts in the situation. Tax receipts are largest in the final months of the fiscal year, while the benefits are fairly stable month after month. For the *entire* fiscal year of 1957, disbursements for old-age and survivors' insurance exceeded the tax collections set aside for this purpose by 125 million dollars. This difference resulted from unexpectedly large demands when women were given the choice of claiming an actuarially reduced benefit at age 62 instead of a larger benefit at 65, and when many more farmers retired than had been anticipated. In the same year, in the portion of the tax funds set aside for disability payments, there was an excess of 650 million dollars over benefit payments, plus administration costs.

But the critics made an even more serious error by ignoring the reserve fund and the interest of that reserve. The reserve fund today exceeds 23 billion dollars, and the interest on the reserve, which must be added to the fund, exceeded 550 million dollars in 1957. Adding the interest to the tax collections we find that there was a net increase of 425 million dollars in the old-age and survivors' insurance fund in 1957.

Tax Increase

Least excusable was the failure of critics to take account of the express provisions in the present law for an increase of one-half per cent in tax rates for both employers and employees every five years, until 1975 and thereafter, when a maximum rate will be applied. The next increase will become effective January 1, 1960, when the current rate for old-age and survivors' insurance of 2 per cent on employers and on employees will become 2.5 per cent. In 1975 and thereafter the old-age and survivors' insurance tax rate will become 4 per cent on employers and a like amount on employees. In addition, there is since 1957 an additional levy of .25 per cent on both employers and employees for disability payments. The proceeds of this levy are set aside in a separate fund, but can be combined with the old-age and survivors' insurance fund whenever Congress deems this advisable. Self-employed people now pay one-third less than the combined rate for employers and employees, but will likewise have their rates increased by the same amounts and at the same time as others.

The old-age, survivors', and disability insurance system is not now and never has been financed on what private insurance people refer to as "full reserve" principles. Neither is it operated on what mis-leadingly is called the "pay-as-you-go" plan—which more appropri-ately should be referred to as the "owe-as-you-go" plan, since it ig-nores all accruing liabilities that are not yet due. The financing of the present system might be said to rest between the full reserve and pay-as-you-go plans. But it is actuarially sound.

Reserve Financing

Under the present law the rate of benefit payments is such that a full reserve plan of financing would have required a combined tax of nearly 8 per cent (instead of the current 4.5 per cent) collected from the beginning, and the reserve would by now be many times greater than the 23 billion dollars we have. The present law does not provide for collection of 8 per cent until 1975. That year and thereafter a combined 8.5 per cent will be collected. Nor will the reserve ever be as large as under full reserve financing. The interest on the reserve, which in 1957 changed a deficit into a surplus of 425 million dollars, will help to keep the system solvent in future years at much lower tax rates than would otherwise have to be collected.

The costs of financing any retirement system, public or private, inevitably increase for many years after the system has been established. For years the number of beneficiaries will grow cumulatively because most of the people who are placed on the rolls in any year survive for many years thereafter. For people of 65, the average remaining length of life is now approaching 13 years for men and 16 for women, but half will live longer. While they stay on the benefit rolls, new people are put on each year, with similar and gradually improving life expectancies. This cumulative growth will continue until the number of beneficiaries who die equals the number placed on the rolls. Apart from any other cause, this means an annual increase in the number of beneficiaries for 35 to 40 years.

The number of new people who are placed on the rolls also increases each year. This is a consequence of an aging population. The number of Americans who become 65 now totals more than 1,000 per day, 400,000 each year. This is an annual increase of nearly 3 per cent.

Finally, our national system makes no provisions for past service credits. As a result, the benefits are small in the early years, but increase over the years. The same effect has been produced by the gradual extension of coverage in the national system. Average benefits per individual have also been increased—somewhat more than the decreased purchasing power of the dollar.

As a result, total benefit costs have increased more than the number of beneficiaries. At the end of the first year in which retirement benefits were paid out (December, 1940), the number of beneficiaries was 222,000 and the benefit payments totaled 35 million dollars.

Seventeen years later, in December, 1957, there were 11.2 million beneficiaries, while benefit payments totaled 7.4 billion dollars. Both the number of beneficiaries and the total benefit payments have increased year after year; and the increase has never been less than 15 per cent higher than the preceding year. While the total disbursements were less than 0.1 per cent of the taxable payrolls in 1940, they are now almost exactly equal to the 4 per cent tax we are currently collecting.

Both the number of beneficiaries and the total disbursements will increase in the years that lie ahead, although at a slower rate. Because we have a growing population, a rising life expectancy, and a lengthening period of old age, the numbers on the benefit rolls will not be stabilized until the year 2020, or even 2050. Actuaries estimate that benefit costs and administrative expenses will take 12 per cent of the taxable payrolls of that time. While the maximum tax rate provided for in the present law is 8.5 per cent, the difference between this rate and the 12 per cent which may be required in 60 years or so is expected to come from the reserve and the interest on the reserve.

These estimates are based on the law as it stands and on assumptions as to the growth of the population, the number of beneficiaries, the wage level, and other elements which are admittedly uncertain. That is why the law provides for an annual report on the financial soundness of the system by the trustees of the old-age, survivors', and disability insurance funds. An actuarial estimate of the expected costs and revenues has been prepared for the congressional committees whenever changes have been made in the law. A more comprehensive study of the entire problem of the financing of the system is now being made by the Social Security Advisory Council organized in the autumn of 1957 pursuant to congressional legislation.

Self-financed System

This study may disclose that the system is either slightly overfinanced or slightly underfinanced. But this would not be a serious matter, since any possible excess or deficiency relates to a situation that may develop in the next century. Erroneous computations or forecasts can be corrected as they are discovered by slight changes in future tax rates.

What is important is that the central principle on which the system is financed be preserved. This is the principle of a contributory self-financed system. This means that whenever benefits are increased beyond any existing surplus, contribution rates must also be increased, since such benefits can only be financed by tax collections and reserve. Thus a powerful safeguard is provided both against runaway benefits and against diversion of old-age, survivors', and disability funds for other purposes.

This has been the central thought behind the financing of the system from the beginning. Every dollar collected for old-age, survivors', and disability insurance has been used for this purpose only. Hard-pressed as the government has been to balance its budget, it has never been proposed that the old-age, survivors', and disability insurance funds be diverted. Conversely, not one dollar expended for benefits and administration costs comes from general tax revenues.

Congress has also faithfully observed the principle that when benefits are increased the tax rates must also be increased, unless it is clear that such an increase is unnecessary to keep the system fully financed. When it substantially increased the benefit costs in 1950, it increased the tax rates correspondingly. In 1952, it slightly increased the benefits, but on the actuaries' advice left the tax rates undisturbed, because the 1950 law produced somewhat more revenue than had been forecast. In 1953, the President, new to the problems of old-age insurance, endorsed pay-as-you-go financing. But the Congress refused to go along with him; instead, it wrote into the law that the system should remain self-financed. In the Social Security Act Amendments of 1954, and again in 1956, benefits and also tax rates were increased.

Not only is our old-age, survivors', and disability insurance system clearly solvent, but it promises to remain so throughout the foreseeable future. To this end, however, the principles upon which it rests must continue to be observed.

III

ISSUES IN
UNEMPLOYMENT

THE BASIC QUESTION in the field of unemployment is, of course, the nature and extent of unemployment and the character of income losses associated with it. How much unemployment is there, of what duration are typical periods of unemployment, and what are the several causes of unemployment?

To what extent and in what ways may unemployment compensation be preferred over relief programs? Can unemployment compensation be expected to prevent a considerable amount of unemployment? Will this preventive effect be maximized by a system of reserve financing and experience rating?

How should the federal-state relationship in unemployment compensation be structured? How can coverage and benefits questions be resolved to realize more fully the purposes of unemployment compensation? Is it possible to achieve a more completely integrated approach to unemployment problems by better use of the employment service along with retraining and rehabilitation services?

Unemployment Insurance

Address at the Milwaukee
County League of Women
Voters' Public Welfare School
of Citizenship at Milwaukee,
March 2, 1928

I The Unemployment Problem

IT IS GENERALLY RECOGNIZED that unemployment is the most serious of present-day industrial problems. Herbert Hoover has said:

No waste is greater than unemployment, no suffering is keener or more fraught with despair than that due to inability to get jobs by those who wish to work.

In the same vein the committee on business cycles and unemployment of President Harding's Conference on Unemployment, whose chairman was Owen D. Young of the General Electric Company, said in its report made in 1923:

Nothing is more demoralizing for wage-earners than the feeling of insecurity of employment. Unemployment and the fear of unemployment are powerful causes of discontent.... Loss of employment not only eliminates income but lessens the ability of wage-earning men and women and their families to make purchases, thus intensifying the period of depression.

The National Industrial Conference Board in its research report on the unemployment problem in 1921 estimated that 1,800,000 persons are normally out of work in the United States. During the

215

great industrial depression then on, the total number of the jobless rose to around 5,000,000, representing one-seventh of all persons gainfully employed. Of factory workers alone, one-third were jobless in the worst period of the depression. Since then the number of the unemployed in this country is estimated to have never been less than 1,500,000 at any time. In recent months there has been a great increase in unemployment. Exactly how many persons are unemployed, no one knows, because we have in this country only imperfect statistics upon the number who are employed and none at all upon the number who are unemployed. That there is now an unusually large volume of unemployment, however, is shown not only by the reports of the public relief agencies throughout the country, but also by the index numbers of employment published by the United States Bureau of Labor Statistics and state labor departments. In this state, according to the monthly employment statistics of the industrial commission, the total number of persons employed in December of 1927 was lower than in any December since 1921. In the entire United States the number of persons employed in manufacturing industries was lower than in any December of record, including even 1920 and 1921.

This widespread unemployment is now generally recognized as being mainly an industrial, rather than an individual, problem. There are some causes of unemployment which are personal—unsteady working habits, sickness and accidents, strikes, and yet others. These causes, however, are responsible for probably less than 10 per cent of the total unemployment. Ninety per cent is due to causes wholly beyond the control of the worker, principally these four: (1) the many casual and short-time jobs in industry; (2) the seasonal ups and downs of practically all industries; (3) the recurring periods of acute business depression; and (4) the displacement of men by machines and the increase in productive efficiency. The first three of these have long been recognized as the principal causes of unemployment, but the last is no less important, although not so well understood.

Only a few years ago there was great clamor for increased production and many people thought this to be the solution of all labor questions. We have had a marvelous increase in production, particularly in the last five years. The factories of this country last year turned out 70 per cent more goods than in 1914, and 20 per cent more than in 1919, which was the peak year prior to the last great depression. While the total product, however, has increased 70 per cent since the base year 1914, the number of wage-earners employed has increased only 15 per cent, and since 1919 has actually decreased 14 per cent. More than a million less workers are now employed in manufacturing industries than in 1919, and there have also been corresponding decreases in the number of employees on farms, in railroading, in coal mining, and other industries. These men thrown out of work by the improvement of machinery and processes, and the greatly increased output per man, have to a great extent been absorbed in the building industry, by the filling stations and garages, in trade, and in other channels. There, however, have been more men out of work at all times during recent years, which have been, on the whole, the most prosperous that industry has ever known, than during any previous period of prosperity. Now that the building industry is contracting instead of expanding, this problem is even more acute. What is to become of the workmen who are thrown out of employment by changing habits of consumption, by new processes, and by the increased output per worker?

Perhaps all this means that we are bound to have as much chronic unemployment as has long prevailed in Europe, in addition to having the more extreme and rapid fluctuations in employment than any other country. This is speculative, but the fact that unemployment is mainly due to industry is undeniable. While the older and less efficient workers are the ones who find it most difficult to get and keep jobs, they are by no means to be described as unemployables or derelicts. On the contrary, the men are not only willing to work but their labor is at times required by industry, although at other times they cannot find work.

The Commons (Wisconsin) Proposal for Unemployment Insurance

This fact that most unemployment is a direct product of modern industry, which is the central idea in the plan for unemployment insurance, was worked out by Dr. John R. Commons and has been introduced in each session of the Wisconsin legislature since 1920, usually referred to as the "Huber Bill."

The essential provisions of this plan can be stated briefly: Employers are to share the costs of industrial unemployment with their workers, in much the same manner as they bear a part of the cost of industrial accidents under workmen's compensation. Whenever an employee is laid off and cannot find other suitable employment, and provided that he has worked at least six months during the preceding two years, the employer must pay him unemployment compensation at the rate of $1.00 per day, but for not more than 13 weeks. (In seasonal industries employers are liable for compensation only for the normal season.) This law is to be administered by the industrial commission, through the public employment offices. Provision is also made for the organization of a statewide mutual employment insurance company, to be controlled by the employers, with which all employers must insure their risks, unless they are clearly financially responsible, so that there will be funds from which to pay the unemployment compensation, even if the particular employer is caught in the throes of depression.

The idea behind this plan is not so much that of giving a little help to the unemployed workmen as that of preventing unemployment. It is thought that when the employer knows that if he expands his working force, he also runs the risk of having to pay unemployment compensation when he needs again to reduce his force, he will be less likely to recklessly expand, which everyone recognizes as one of the great causes of industrial depressions. If the individual employer is not sufficiently deterred from reckless expansion, it is thought that his banker will withhold credit, because he also must count upon the possible consequences of recklessly taking on additional employees. In a similar manner, this plan for unemployment compensation is expected to help to iron out the seasonal peaks and depressions in employment. Finally, it is urged that when employers are faced with the possibility of having to pay unemployment compensation, they will leave no stone unturned to find work for employees they must lay off and will really tackle the problems of unemployment in dead earnest. It is believed that when American employers really do this, they will solve this greatest and most difficult of industrial problems, as they have solved so many other problems.

Unemployment Insurance Abroad

Nowhere in this country is there any law providing for unemployment insurance. Most European countries, however, have such laws. Compulsory unemployment insurance on a nationwide basis exists at present in eight countries: Great Britain, Italy, Austria, Russia, Queensland, Poland, the Irish Free State, and Germany, which has been added to the list within the last year. In addition nine other countries give subventions from the national treasuries to unemployment funds maintained voluntarily by employers, employers' associations, or trade unions: Denmark, France, Norway, the Netherlands, Finland, Spain, Belgium, Czechoslovakia, and Switzerland.

The most widely known of these foreign unemployment insurance laws is that of Great Britain. In this country, and among certain classes in England, this law is spoken of as a system of paying "doles" to the unemployed and is blamed for all of England's present troubles. It is significant, however, that no serious attempt has ever been made to repeal this law and that every one of the many investigating commissions has reported in favor of its retention. First enacted in 1911 by the Liberals, over Conservative opposition, and applicable only to a few industries, it was extended when the Conservatives controlled Parliament in 1920 to practically all industries. It was further liberalized when Labor was in power in 1924, and now under Conservative rule a new law making extensive amendments has been enacted, which, while objected to by Labor, certainly does not abandon unemployment insurance and, at this distance, would seem to improve the law in many respects.

The derisive term "doles" is really applicable to poor relief rather than to unemployment insurance. Long before Great Britain had an unemployment insurance law, unemployed workmen in distress received doles—enough to keep from starving—from the poor commissioners. In no civilized country are the unemployed nowadays allowed to starve, and whenever unemployment becomes acute large amounts must be paid in doles. That has happened also in the United States, and is being witnessed at this very time in the increased demands for relief upon public welfare organizations. This in time has always been followed by the bread line and frantic attempts to create work for the unemployed at public expense—doles in their worst forms.

Unemployment insurance was introduced in Great Britain to get away from doles, as far as possible. Under a plan of uniform contributions from employers, employees, and the state, it was proposed

to create reserve funds, for the payment of benefits to unemployed
workmen in times of depression. Up to 1920 this law, by general ad-
mission, worked admirably. It then applied to some 4,000,000 workmen and the reserves in the unemployment insurance funds totaled
22,000,000 pounds. In that year the unemployment insurance act
was extended to practically all industries, some 12,250,000 workmen
being brought under the law at one stroke. No sooner had this been
done than the great industrial depression set in, from which England has never entirely recovered. For seven years now England has
had an unusual volume of unemployment—probably, at present,
not a greater percentage than the unemployment in the United
States, but much more serious, because largely confined to the ex-
port industries, particularly coal mining, which has been hard hit
ever since 1920. With millions of workers who had just been brought
under the law thrown out of work before they had contributed very
much to the unemployment insurance funds, these funds were soon
overdrawn and the public treasury had to come to their rescue with
advances.

On top of this, the further burden was thrown on unemployment
insurance funds of having to pay benefits to workmen not entitled
thereto. This was done by parliamentary act, first to give benefits to
returned soldiers in dire need, and then so-called "extended benefits" to unemployed workers who had exhausted their credits under
the unemployment insurance law. In this manner unemployment
insurance became mixed up with doles (poor relief). In every other
European country the same problem arose at the same time, and
large amounts had to be paid from the public treasuries to take care
of the worst victims of the unprecedented depression, those who had
exhausted all claims to unemployment insurance. Elsewhere, however, unemployment insurance and poor relief were kept distinct.
Failure to do so in Great Britain caused a lot of needless trouble,
and has only recently been remedied in the Unemployment Insurance Amendment Act of 1927, which cuts off all "extended benefits."

Despite these great handicaps, the British unemployment insurance act has not worked out so very badly. This is the opinion not
only of all official commissions which have studied the working of
this law, but also of all British writers on the subject. The unemployment insurance fund is still "in red," but has been reducing its
indebtedness to the treasury in the last two years. The total indebtedness, moreover, is not much more than $100,000,000 in our money

—a small amount as compared with the sums we have already spent on the federal farm land banks and other forms of agricultural relief, or the amounts called for by the McNary-Haugen act. The cost of administration has proven low, and is now about 8 per cent of the total contributions—not a large overhead. Above all, the system of unemployment insurance has spared many British workers the extremities of want and despair. Deterioration of the morale of the unemployed there has undoubtedly occurred, but certainly not as much as would have occurred had no aid been given them.

On the other hand, the British act has had little value in preventing unemployment. In England, public funds are set aside in times of prosperity to make possible the expansion of public works in times of depression, while we merely talk about such a system, or pass unenforcible laws along this line, like the Wisconsin law of 1923. Aside from this, however, there is little to suggest in the British situation that the unemployment insurance act has tended to prevent unemployment. The fundamental causes for the prolonged depression that England has had to face apparently have no connection with the unemployment insurance system, but, on the other hand, this system has not tended to right business conditions.

In this connection it should be noted that the British unemployment insurance act differs from the proposed Wisconsin law in several important respects. In the British law, the employer, the employee, and the state all make contributions, while the Wisconsin law contemplates payments by the employer only. Still more fundamental is the fact that the British law does not make payment of unemployment benefits an obligation of any employer, or, for that matter, of any industry. The contributions of all employers are equal, regardless of the amount of unemployment they or their particular industries may have. This, of course, means that there is no particular incentive to employers to reduce unemployment; and such a result has never been claimed for the British act.

Observations on the Wisconsin Proposal

With this digression to foreign systems, I return to the proposed Wisconsin unemployment insurance bill. It is not my intention to either advocate or condemn this proposal, but only to explain the same. I will, however, make some observations, which

I hope may be helpful to an understanding of the question that is raised by this bill.

One of the strongest arguments in favor of this proposal is that it emanates from Dr. John R. Commons. Even those who believe that Dr. Commons is wholly wrong in advocating this bill, recognize that he is one of the great, if not the greatest, constructive geniuses of this state. To him, more than anyone else, we owe our workmen's compensation law and our industrial commission act, both of which laws have satisfied the employers as well as the employees. He also has to his credit the advocacy of the idea that high wages promote prosperity and that good industrial relations are good business, which when he first presented them seemed to many to be extremely radical, but are now a part of the creed of every forward-looking employer.

Next, it is evident that this Wisconsin proposal must stand or fall mainly upon its value, or lack of worth, as a measure for preventing, or at least reducing, unemployment. The unemployment compensation of $1.00 per day is so low that it clearly is inadequate to support an American workman and his family. The other limitations in the bill, moreover, are such that it is certain that a large percentage of the unemployed in periods of prolonged depression will be deprived of benefits. In this connection, moreover, it is worthy of note that there is less need for unemployment insurance as a relief measure in this country than in Europe, because the financial reserves of working men are greater. This factor explains how it is possible for as much unemployment as prevails at present to exist without most people knowing anything about it.

A factor worthy of serious consideration, but likely to be overlooked, is the problem of administration. This undoubtedly is more difficult in Wisconsin than in England, due to the sparser population and the greater labor turnover. We must develop an administrative system that will fit not only the conditions in Milwaukee, but in Park Falls, Crandon, and hundreds of other places—yes, rural districts as well. Then we must somehow keep track of men who are today in Milwaukee, next week in Butte, and next month in Superior.

That this is a new proposal, it seems to me, alone should not condemn it. Wisconsin, of course, is only one of forty-eight states, and not one of the large states at that, and there are decided hazards in pioneering. On the other hand, there are also profits, if pioneer proposals are sound. There is almost as much need for experimentation in government as in industry. The fathers of this country were not appalled at the thought of experimenting and we are the gainers because they did experiment.

On the other hand, governmental intervention is only justified when there is real need therefor. That unemployment is a really serious problem, the most pressing of all industrial problems, cannot be denied. It is a problem that industry cannot afford to neglect. As Dr. Commons and others have pointed out, the workman is first of all interested in security. Unemployment is the most serious indictment and the greatest menace to the existing industrial system.

That we have only scratched the surface in the matter of solving this problem is my belief. We have had many articles upon using public work to stabilize private employment, but throughout the country we are no better set for putting such a plan into operation than we were long ago. The public employment offices are doing good work but certainly are still far from really centralizing the labor market. Seasonal fluctuations in employment seem greater than ever.

Individual employers, however, have been pointing the way. There are now a considerable number of employers who have apparently solved the problem of seasonal fluctuations. Some employers even went through the last great depression without having to lay off a man. There is, moreover, a growing list of employers who are voluntarily maintaining unemployment insurance systems—the men's clothing industry in Chicago, the ladies' garment industry in Cleveland, the fur industry in New York City, Dennisons, the Lackawanna Railroad, the Johnson Company at Racine, and still others. Only this month the Metropolitan Life Insurance Company announced that it is prepared and anxious to write unemployment insurance on the group plan, as soon as insurance laws are amended to allow it to do so.

It is in this connection that the Wisconsin unemployment insurance bill has already had a good influence. Probably as much as anything that has occurred, this bill has brought home to industry that unemployment is primarily its problem. If industry will solve this problem there is no need for legislation; otherwise, the state is bound to intervene.

Job Insurance:
Its Limitations and Value

Economic Forum, Volume 2,
Number 4 (Winter, 1935),
pages 411–424

As RECENTLY AS 1931, numerous articles were appearing in this country in which the British unemployment insurance system was derisively referred to as a dole, and England's economic difficulties were pointed to as a warning that this country must never embark on any similar policy. Now that our direct relief expenditures are more than five times as great as the amounts which the British government is expending for unemployment insurance and relief, an equally large number of articles are attributing England's alleged rapid progress toward economic recovery, in large measure, to its unemployment insurance system.

This remarkable change in opinion probably derives far more from the seriousness of our problems than from an intelligent analysis of unemployment insurance and its consequences. Though long, and still, a staunch believer in the value of unemployment insurance, I must protest against expecting too much from this social device. Unemployment insurance has definite values, but also, like all other manmade institutions, distinct limitations.

I

To deal with this subject honestly and realistically, it is well to begin with some of the limitations. Unemployment insurance will not solve the problem of the business cycle. It is not a cure for depressions. Unemployment insurance may, as apparently it did in England, help in a measure to sustain consumer purchasing power during a period of depression. It cannot prevent the depression.

Unemployment insurance will not give jobs to the millions of wage-earners now employed, nor will it make relief unnecessary. It is conceivable that the majority of those now on relief might be covered by an unemployment insurance system and given extended benefits from the outset, but such extended benefits would have to come from the public treasury and would still be essentially relief payments, although under a new name.

Unemployment insurance will not directly benefit any group in society other than the wage-earners and salaried employees. This excludes the 20 per cent of our gainful workers who are farmers, merchants, professional men, and other self-employed persons. Among the employees, moreover, there are many who cannot easily be included in any unemployment insurance system. This holds true for nearly all of the more than 3,000,000 wage-earners employed in agriculture, forestry, and fishing; for the great majority of the 4,500,000 people who are employed in domestic and personal service; and also, for the 2,300,000 "executive and professional" salaried employees. Furthermore, any unemployment insurance system must almost certainly have numerical exclusions, in that it pertains only to employers with a specified number of employees—three, five or ten—whatever number may be chosen. In England, despite its relatively higher degree of industrialization, nearly 7,000,000 persons gainfully employed are excluded from the benefits of the unemployment insurance act, as compared with the little more than 12,000,000 who come under the provisions of the law. It is probable that in this country not more than half the 50,000,000 gainfully occupied persons could be covered by any unemployment insurance system.

Unemployment insurance, moreover, is not well suited to many groups of industrial workers who can legally be brought under its provisions. British experience has proven that the inclusion under the act of part-time workers and of short-time and casual employees creates serious problems. These groups are probably the source of a majority of the cases arising under the unemployment insurance acts and the benefits payable to them constitute a heavy drain on the funds. It may be that such workers should, nevertheless, be provided for under the unemployment insurance system. However, some more suitable device, possibly a dismissal wage, is worthy of consideration as a means of furnishing a degree of economic security to these intermittently or irregularly employed wage-earners.

II

With all these exclusions there remains for consideration the largest group in our total population, the steadily employed industrial workers and the majority of the clerical employees. In our concern for the 20 per cent or 25 per cent of the wage-earners who are unemployed, there is danger of neglecting the 75 per cent to 80 per cent who are employed. Real progress is made not by depressing all to the lowest prevailing level, but rather by raising the submerged to higher standards. No one denies that those who are at present unemployed need help very badly; but it is equally true that the steadily employed, those who held their jobs throughout the Depression or were the first to be reëmployed, are in need of a greater degree of security than they now have.

The employed and the unemployed are not, of course, entirely distinct groups. There is constant interchange between them. Even in the worst stage of the Depression some of the unemployed were able to secure work, and in very prosperous times some of the steadiest workers would lose their jobs and suffer comparatively long periods of idleness before they were reëmployed. From such rather meager data as are available, it appears that from 20 per cent to 25 per cent of the unemployed in this country have been out of work less than six months. In England this percentage is considerably higher; 55 per cent of all the registered unemployed in January, 1934, had been out of work less than three months, 67 per cent less than six months.

While there is constant interchange between the employed and the unemployed, it is unfortunately true that there are many among the unemployed who, at least for the present, cannot be classified with the great mass of the steady workers. A third or more of all of the unemployed have not had a real job for over two years. The best of these are now "soft" and have lost much of their former skill. A great many are young men who have never had a job. Many others never worked steadily even in boom times. To call even this latter class "unemployables" is an unjustified stigma; during World War I even the inmates of poorhouses found employment. But under prevailing conditions the problem of restoring many of the unemployed to self-support is one of rehabilitation quite as much as of employment. Those who have long been unemployed require public assistance not only for their immediate needs but to enable them to recover their former status.

The much larger group of the employed (including in this group those who have no jobs but who have excellent work records and have retained their skill) likewise need greater economic security, but along quite different lines. Unquestionably the best cure for unemployment is employment, at least for workers of this class. This largest group among the wage-earners would be benefited more by a restoration of private employment to 1929 levels than by any other measure. Until we are back to this level, our major objective must continue to be increased production and economic recovery; and until private employment takes up the slack, we must have large emergency work and employment programs. Economic policies which tend to stabilize employment at a high level and which insure automatic expansion of public employment when private employment slackens are of more fundamental importance for economic security than any device which merely provides a means of support when unemployment occurs.

President Roosevelt, in his radio address of September 30, very properly stated that we must not gauge our economy on the assumption of a large permanent army of unemployed. We cannot permanently have one group who are employed supporting another large group who are unemployed. Our economic system cannot endure unless it can be so organized that there exists only a small residuum of unemployed wage-earners.

As far as can now be foreseen, however, there always will be such a residuum. There was unemployment even during World War I; no country has ever been without it. In the years immediately preceding the Depression, unemployment among industrial workers in this country averaged close to 10 per cent of the total. So long as we have seasonal industries there is certain to be some loss of time in the off-seasons. Changes in technology and in market demand, as well as numerous other factors, inevitably cause dislocations which result in much unemployment for many of the best workers. Nor have we found a cure for the most outstanding of all causes of unemployment—cyclical depressions. We may hope that, out of our present experience, we will develop machinery and policies which will render serious depressions less likely in the future; but it would be folly to assume that this is the last depression we will ever have.

Many workers suffer no unemployment whatsoever for long periods of time. Of all persons who, in December, 1932, had been insured under the British unemployment insurance system for at least eight years preceding, 2 per cent had never drawn a shilling in benefits during this entire period. Yet any wage-earner runs the risk of losing his employment through no fault of his own. Few people, indeed, a quarter of a century ago expected that either the railroad or the coal industries would be on the decline by this time. No one can be certain which of the great industries will be the next to suffer a similar decline. Even while an industry flourishes there are always certain companies, or plants in certain localities, which go under. Only a minority of all plants operate with even reasonable steadiness.

III

Insurance alone cannot meet the hazard of unemployment for any group of workers. For one thing, unemployment insurance, as distinguished from a "dole," is of limited duration, with benefits in definite proportion to contributions or length of employment. It is premised on contract, not on need. Again, unemployment insurance cannot solve the problem of the old worker who has lost his job and is unable to secure other work. In normal times, in industries that are declining, and in periods of depression in substantially all industries, many men with the best work records who become unemployed are certain to exhaust their contractual benefits. In England there are at this time more insured workers who are receiving "transitional" (uncovenanted) benefits than "standard" benefits. In Germany, eight times as many able-bodied workers are in receipt of "emergency" benefits or poor relief as are receiving "regular" unemployment insurance benefits. Unemployment insurance does not eliminate the necessity for relief or emergency employment. It affords limited protection only and it must often be supplemented. But unemployment insurance is for the regularly employed steady industrial workers a valuable first line of defense. Unemployment may not be an insurable risk in the sense that death, old age, and accidents are definitely insurable risks. It is impossible definitely to forecast what the rate of unemployment will be in any industry and still less [to predict] the hazard to any employee not merely of losing his employment, but also of being unable to find another job. It is possible, however, to create reserves which can be drawn on when unemployment occurs.

At any given time our entire population must be largely supported from current production. It is impossible to store in periods of prosperity more than a very limited quantity of consumption goods to satisfy wants during periods of depression. What is possible, through the device of reserves, is to give to workers who are currently not producing because unemployed, a legal title to a definite share in the current production. Reserves accumulated while employees are working to be paid out to them when they are unemployed are essentially savings, serving much the same purpose as other savings. In this depression, as in former depressions, individual savings have proven the salvation of many a worker who has lost his job. It is probable that in the aggregate, savings have furnished a larger part of the support of the unemployed and their families than the great expenditures for public relief. Even now, after five years of depression, only half of the unemployed are on relief. At this point the objection will be raised that what is needed, from a social as distinguished from an individual point of view, is spending by the wage-earners rather than saving. All savings necessarily represent a decrease in current consumption. Depressions result from insufficient mass purchasing power and this difficulty, it is argued, will be aggravated by the accumulation of unemployment reserves, particularly if the workers are required to contribute.

Granting a considerable element of truth in the mass purchasing power theory of the cause of depressions, this argument overlooks the fact that unemployment reserves may represent not additional savings, but rather directed savings. Successful industries are always piling up great reserves for all kinds of purposes. The regularly employed better class of wage-earners save vast sums in periods of prosperity. Even during this depression, large amounts are being saved by those wage-earners who are employed. True, the recent Brookings Institution study, *Our Capacity to Consume* [Leven, Moulton, and Warburton, 1934] indicates that in 1929 the total net savings of families in the lowest income group were negative—the total amount spent exceeding the current income. Even among people in this group who, in any event, are largely outside of the unemployment picture, there are many who regularly save a part of their income through industrial insurance and other means.

A compulsory unemployment insurance system, with contributions from all insured employees, will undoubtedly represent additional savings for some of the insured workers. But for many it is likely to represent, in the main, merely one form of savings as compared with others which they regularly and voluntarily build up. It may even be that the net effect of unemployment insurance will be to reduce the total savings of wage-earners. Workers save primarily because of the uncertainty of the future. In giving wage-earners a degree and a sense of economic security they do not now possess, unemployment insurance may well operate to reduce the net total savings rather than to increase them. Similarly, the employer's contribution to unemployment insurance funds may, at least in part, come from monies which would otherwise be "saved" for other purposes.

During the period of the 20's, industry in this country enjoyed a great boom, while industry in England, if not depressed (in the sense in which we have used this term since 1929), was distinctly dull. England had unemployment insurance; we did not. In our period of prosperity, savings increased apace. Billions of dollars of workers' savings went into the purchase of homes, insurance, bank deposits or mortgages, bonds, and even common stock equities. These savings did not prove altogether worthless when the Depression came, but the realization upon them certainly fell far short of 100 per cent. Total savings in England were far smaller, even allowing for the much smaller total production. As it actually worked out, unemployment insurance in England did not lead to the piling up of any large reserves. The contributions collected went almost immediately into current consumption. They operated to keep large numbers of the unemployed somewhat above the mere subsistence level of relief and thereby tended toward increased consumer purchasing power.

Professor Alvin H. Hansen of the University of Minnesota has recently estimated that if a nationwide unemployment insurance system had been in operation in this country throughout the seven prosperous years from 1923 to 1929, with 4 per cent contributions, a four-week waiting period, and a $15 per week maximum benefit, the actual reserve accumulated by 1929 would have amounted to a little less than $4,000,000,000. This is a very substantial amount, but not a large percentage of the total savings during this period. How much of this $4,000,000,000 would have represented additional savings and how much merely directed savings is debatable.

In any event, the net effect upon total savings would have been slight. Had unemployment insurance been in operation during the prosperous 1920's, it is doubtful whether it would have had any great effect either on mass purchasing power or on general business conditions. It would, on the other hand, have been beneficial to many workers during seasonal layoffs and still more to the workers in declining industries. Coal miners, even in the boom period, experienced prolonged unemployment. It is at the onset of the Depression, however, that the chief value of the unemployment reserves would have been demonstrated. Four billion dollars of reserves converted into unemployment compensation payments would have unquestionably had a pronounced effect toward sustained purchasing power in the period of decline. Whether, as a result, our present situation would have been better, no one can positively say; but, as a minimum, workers' savings would have lasted just that much longer.

IV

The foregoing description of what might have resulted, had we had unemployment insurance in the 20's, assumes the investment of unemployment reserves in such a way as actually to be available when needed and capable of liquidation, when the Depression set in, without increasing deflationary tendencies. This is a vital point in the consideration of any unemployment insurance system. Unemployment reserves which are so invested as to be no more liquid, in a crisis, than savings put into real estate, or no more secure than savings invested in securities, are of no real help in meeting a depression. But it is certainly possible to avoid investing unemployment reserves in this manner. This is a point which President Roosevelt has thoroughly grasped. In speaking of unemployment insurance today, he has been specific only upon two points: he favors a nationwide (although not necessarily a nationally administered) unemployment insurance system and he has made it very clear that he wants all reserves to be within control of the same agency which is responsible for the credit policies of the country.

Reserves as large as those which might have been built up in the 20's, while relatively unimportant as compared with the total volume of savings, bulk large in their possible effects upon the monetary situation. The sudden uncontrolled liquidation of several billion dollars of reserves might well offset all attempts of the national government to maintain the credit structure. Handled as President Roosevelt suggests, however, any such possibility is guarded against as completely as is humanly possible. Barring unintelligent handling of the funds by the controlling board, these reserves can be made a valuable stimulus to expansion, when expansion is in the public interest, and can be used to check inflation, when such a policy becomes desirable. In times of depression, the funds can be liquidated (through purchase of the securities held by the Treasury or the reserve banks) in such a way that not only will every dollar of the funds be available, but also that deflationary tendencies will be counteracted and the purchasing power of the wage-earner sustained. If this can be done—and there is no reason why it cannot be done—unemployment insurance becomes equally as important to the general public as it is to unemployed wage-earners themselves. Although it is not a solution of the problem of the business cycle, unemployment insurance can be made a factor of considerable value in maintaining economic stability. Intelligently handled, it will benefit the merchant, the professional man, and the farmer, as well as the wage-earner.

What are the effects of unemployment insurance upon the employers? Initially, at least, it will probably increase costs. In this connection it should be noted, however, that even without a formal unemployment insurance system, most employers make some payments to their employees which amount to a haphazard unemployment compensation. Old employees are retained for long periods after their services are not really needed. In this depression many large firms and some small ones have been paying a dismissal wage of some sort to employees they have been forced to discharge. The total costs of such haphazard types of unemployment compensation may well approximate the cost to employers of a genuine system of unemployment insurance, with fixed conditions and regularized benefits. Unemployed wage-earners and their families must be maintained by someone. The costs of their maintenance, if not derived from industry, can come only from their savings or those of their relatives and friends, or from private or public relief. The latter has become a tremendous burden which must ultimately be paid through taxation; and it is industry which will have to bear a large part of these taxes.

Unemployment insurance, if developed along the right lines, may actually mean reduced costs in the long run. Such a result is to be expected if it encourages the regularization of industry. Unemployment insurance in England has had little, if any, effect in this direction and prior to the correction of the so-called "anomalies" in 1931, actually operated to subsidize irregularity in some industries. But this is not a necessary result of unemployment insurance. Where the individual employer has to pay all or a substantial part of the benefits to employees whom he discharges, a strong incentive is created to eliminate all avoidable turnover. Employers cannot possibly eliminate all irregularity in employment, nor even the major part of irregularity, but they can do something, as evidenced by the greatly varying rates of turnover among different plants in the same industry.

V

Unemployment insurance should not be considered a cure-all. There is quite as much danger in overstating its values as in refusing to consider its merits open-mindedly. It will directly benefit perhaps half of the population of the country. It does not afford complete or unlimited protection, even for those who come under its provisions. It is however, of great value, particularly to steady, regularly employed industrial workers who are unemployed for short periods because of seasonal layoffs or any of the other numerous minor industrial disturbances. It can be of service to them, also, in the early stages of a depression. It is of value to the general public because it serves as a first line of defense for the largest group in our entire industrial population. Correctly handled, it can be made to operate toward stability and sustained purchasing power.

Unemployment insurance does not eliminate the need for other measures for economic security and it in no sense conflicts with them. Increased industrial production is, at this time, more vital than any other need; and all measures for economic security must be timed so as not to impede recovery. Emergency employment programs will always be necessary when there is much unemployment, whether we have unemployment insurance or not. Old-age pensions and mothers' pensions serve entirely different groups in the population. Unemployment insurance on a national scale will stimulate rather than retard the enactment of those additional measures which are necessary to give the individual a reasonable degree of protection against the many hazards of our modern economy.

At this stage our entire population, or at least a large part of it, has reached a point of emotional exhaustion where it is looking for a panacea—a simple formula—which will solve all of its present problems. The problems confronting us, however, are too complex to be solved by any one remedy. A great variety of measures are necessary to meet the complex unemployment and relief situation and to give our people an adequate degree of economic security. Unemployment insurance is only one of the many steps necessary to this end, but one which is urgent and most valuable. Failure to act now on this essential step toward more complete economic security would be inexcusable. The consequences would very likely be legislation much more costly to industry and far less sound in principle.

Major Issues in
Unemployment Compensation

The Social Service Review,
published by the University
of Chicago Press, Volume IX,
Number 1 (March, 1935),
pages 1–23

O N THE VERGE of the nationwide adoption of unemployment insurance, there is a very widespread lack of definite understanding of the issues and objectives involved. Unemployment insurance has been in operation in England since 1911 and more recently has been adopted in most other Western European countries. In this country it has been the subject of much controversy for more than a decade, but outside of some twenty voluntary plans and the Wisconsin law, which came into operation only last July, there has been no actual experience with this institution. Within a limited circle, there is intense debate over details; outside of this small group, only a vague concept of what the implications are.

Place of Unemployment Compensation in a Program for Economic Security

For a better understanding of the problem, it seems appropriate to begin with the place of unemployment compensation in a comprehensive program for economic security. On this, as on all other questions relating to unemployment compensation, there is much disagreement, but there is little dispute over facts.

The present popularity of unemployment insurance is, to a considerable extent, due to the prevailing notion that it is a substitute for relief. This is a very erroneous impression. In no country has unemployment insurance replaced relief. In England only half of the unemployed insured workers are now receiving unemployment insurance benefits. The others have exhausted their benefit rights and are being supported by public assistance grants or local poor relief. In Germany only one-eighth of the unemployed insured workers, according to the latest available figures, are in receipt of standard unemployment insurance benefits. Every plan for unemployment insurance in this country except the Lundeen bill (which is so vague upon this point, as upon most others, that it is impossible to say what it does provide) applies only to workers who become unemployed after the system has been in operation for some time—usually two years after collection of contributions is begun. Unemployment insurance has little direct relation to the present depression. It will not lessen the relief load for several years, nor give people now on relief any increased allowances.

Every plan (except again possibly the Lundeen bill, which is essentially a relief rather than an unemployment insurance measure) also strictly limits the periods during which benefits can be paid to unemployed workers. In England the benefits are flat sums varying with the number of dependents, but range between 30 and 40 per cent of the average earnings of the industrial workers. These benefits are payable for a maximum period of twenty-six weeks, which is increased to a full year if the unemployed insured worker has not drawn any benefits for five years previously. In Germany standard benefits are paid for only six weeks, after which a means test is applied to determine eligibility for extended benefits. Actuaries of the Committee on Economic Security have estimated the probable operation of a national system of unemployment insurance in this country. Benefits of 50 per cent of wages and not exceeding $15 per week, with a four-week waiting period, can be paid for a maximum of only sixteen weeks, if the contribution rate is 3 per cent of payroll; for twenty-two weeks on a 4 per cent contribution rate; and for thirty-nine weeks on a 5 per cent rate—and these figures assume that the system should not be expected to remain entirely self-supporting during a prolonged depression.

During the present depression all countries with unemployment insurance systems increased contribution rates and decreased benefits, and, in addition, most of them made loans or outright grants to the unemployment insurance funds. Where, as in Germany and Italy, they did not do so, the benefits were reduced to a point where little remains of unemployment insurance except the machinery. In all unemployment insurance bills in this country, authority is given for the reduction of benefits when the funds run low, and such reductions are inevitable in prolonged depressions unless the government comes to the rescue.

Unemployment insurance, then, should be regarded merely as a front line of defense against the hazard of unemployment. It is of value principally during the period just after the loss of a job when the worker has a reasonable expectation of returning to his old line of work within a short time. At this stage, the unemployed worker is, naturally, very reluctant to accept unaccustomed work which will remove him from immediate consideration for reëmployment when hoped-for new orders come in. The great majority of all workers who are laid off go back to work within the short periods during which unemployment compensation can be paid, but inevitably some workmen—and more of them in depression than in normal times—will still be without work when benefit rights are exhausted. For such workmen, something beyond unemployment compensation is needed. That something more may be direct relief or work relief, both of which differ fundamentally from unemployment compensation in that they are based upon need rather than a contractual right.

Unemployment compensation and relief can be combined, but, as shown by England's experience from 1924 to 1931, the results are almost sure to be disastrous. Unemployment compensation works best when it is given as a matter of right in such limited amounts and for such limited periods as the receipts and the reserves warrant. These amounts and periods can be increased with higher contribution rates, but cannot possibly be made to cover all unemployment. Unemployment compensation is indispensable in a program for a reasonable degree of economic security, but should be conceived of as merely one of several measures needed for protection against the hazard of unemployment. It is complementary to, and not a substitute for, public assistance and public employment.

Federal Versus State Administration

Withal, unemployment compensation is indisputably worthwhile. Had a nationwide system of unemployment insurance with a 3 per cent contribution rate been in operation in this country from 1922 on, above $10,000,000,000 would have been collected by 1933 and disbursed to unemployed workmen, mainly during the first years of the depression. Such disbursements would have had great value in maintaining purchasing power at a critical period, preserving morale, and lessening relief. Although not well adapted to many groups of workers, it is peculiarly valuable to the largest element in our entire population, the industrial workers who are ordinarily steadily employed.

The present is, moreover, clearly the opportune time for a real beginning with unemployment compensation. We are now, fortunately, on the upswing of the business cycle. While there is still a terrifying amount of unemployment, the people who have jobs are no longer losing them in abnormal numbers. From the point of view of building up reserves, which is essential to a good start, no more favorable period will probably present itself for a long time. Politically, also, this is the time for action. Not only do we now have a national Administration which is earnestly desirous of establishing safeguards against the major hazards and vicissitudes of life, but public opinion is well prepared for such measures. When unemployment is less prevalent, it will be much more difficult to secure action on unemployment compensation. In the depression of 1920–21, President Harding named a commission to study methods of preventing unemployment and mitigating its evils. That commission made an excellent report, but not until the depression was over. There is good reason for believing that if the recommendations of this commission had been adopted, some of the worst mistakes made in the present depression would have been avoided. As it was, the commission's work resulted in precisely nothing, because the favorable time for action had passed.

Conceding that unemployment compensation should be established on a nationwide basis now, what sort of unemployment compensation system should be adopted? Ought we to have federal or state administration?

Prior to the New Deal, no advocate of unemployment insurance would have hesitated to answer: "Under the Constitution unemployment compensation must necessarily be established along state lines." The Democratic national platform of 1932 specifically committed the dominant party to "unemployment insurance and old-age pensions through state legislation."

The New Deal has altered all this in the minds of some sincere advocates of unemployment insurance. While some of the support for a federally administered system of unemployment compensation represents merely the old game of opponents playing federal and state action against each other in the hope of defeating both, there can be no doubt of the sincerity of some of the recent converts to a federal system. They are people who have become disheartened because it is so very difficult to get one state to act, let alone forty-eight states. The prestige of state governments is at a low point, while the present national Administration commands utmost confidence. Further, it is undeniable that a uniform, federally administered system would have great advantages both to corporations operating in several states and to employees whose work takes them into different states. The difficulty of providing unemployment compensation for such workmen under state systems of administration is the strongest argument for an exclusively federal system.

But there are also strong arguments on the other side. To begin with, despite the New Deal legislation, there is grave doubt whether the federal government has authority to establish a national system of unemployment compensation. There is no constitutional basis for such action except the taxing power and the welfare clause. The latter has never been regarded by the Supreme Court as conferring any powers on the Congress not granted specifically, and the former, while broad, cannot be employed where the Court deems the tax a mere subterfuge for unauthorized regulation. Should the Agricultural Adjustment Act and the National Industrial Recovery Act be sustained, the Court's decisions may be broad enough to warrant setting up a federally administered unemployment insurance system (provided that they do not hinge upon the emergency character of these acts), but at present the only safe course is still state administration.

To many who have had experience with both federal and state administrations, moreover, the assumed vast superiority of federal over state action seems debatable. Federal personnel is on the whole undoubtedly superior and federal salaries are distinctly higher. On the other hand, the very size of the federal administrative machine is a great handicap. Its vast amount of red tape and its extreme centralization often paralyze action. There is probably no less friction between federal bureaus and departments than between states. The Seventy-third Congress was more ready to pass forward-looking legislation than any state legislature has ever been, but that was probably due more to the extreme emergency confronting the nation than to the normal superiority of members of Congress over state legislators. In this connection it is not amiss to call attention to the fact that Congress did not enact a workmen's compensation act for the government's own employees or for the District of Columbia until ten years after all progressive states had taken such action.

What sort of unemployment compensation act would emerge from the present Congress were it to attempt to write a complete law is entirely a matter of conjecture. The truth is that conditions are so diverse in this great country that no single act could meet the situation unless it delegated broad discretionary powers to an administrative agency, and the present Congress has indicated that it is in no mood to follow the example set by the preceding Congress in this respect. In all probability a federal unemployment compensation act would prove very disappointing to the more progressive industrial states, if for no other reason than that the nonindustrial states have the largest number of senators.

These and still other reasons seem to throw the balance against an exclusively federal system. An exclusively state system is even more out of the question. States cannot go it alone in this respect. The failure to secure state unemployment compensation laws is conclusive proof of this. While the subject has been agitated for years, while many bills have been introduced in practically all legislatures, and numerous interim committees and commissions have reported favorably, only one state has passed an unemployment compensation law, and that, quite naturally, is a very meager law. States will not enact unemployment compensation laws if it means placing their industries at a disadvantage in interstate competition. To make it possible for the states to act, the federal government must protect them from the unfair advantage enjoyed by states that do not act. That can be accomplished only through a uniform tax on employers in all states, with an offset or refund of the tax to states which have set up unemployment compensation systems.

The President has characterized the desirable relationship of the federal and state governments with respect to unemployment compensation as a "coöperative federal-state system"—a New Deal in government, in which there is not a conflict over the respective rights of the federal and state governments, but a joint attack on the grave problems of insecurity. In such a coöperative federal-state system it is clearly the function of the federal government to make it possible for the states to act, to encourage them to do so, and to help them with their problems. It alone can equalize competitive costs and it alone can invest and liquidate reserve funds in such a manner that they will promote industrial stability, rather than the reverse. It must also assume responsibility for the compilation of nationwide statistics of unemployment and give guidance to the states in the difficult problems of administration. Beyond that, wide latitude to the states in meeting their peculiar conditions seems desirable. By this means both uniformity, where it is essential, and diversity, where necessary, can be secured.

The Committee on Economic Security, its staff, and the two major advisory groups, the Technical Board and the Advisory Council, gave much attention to two other functions which the federal government may very properly perform in a coöperative federal-state system of unemployment compensation. These are re-insurance and transfer of compensation rights where workers move from one state to another. The desirability of such arrangements is at once obvious, but the difficulties in working them out practically are so great that every group which gave them consideration concluded unanimously that much further study will be necessary before anything along this line can be included in the federal act. Such study should be one of the major duties of the federal administrative agency.

Tax Offset Versus Tax Refund

Accepting the view that a coöperative federal-state system of unemployment compensation is best and safest under existing conditions, considerable controversy has developed, within the circle of people who have been employed or consulted by the President's Committee on Economic Security, over the type of federal law which should be enacted. This is the controversy which within this inner circle has been referred to as "the Wagner-Lewis versus the subsidy plan."

The "Wagner-Lewis" plan was incorporated in the unemployment insurance bill indorsed by the President in the Seventy-third Congress and is also included in the Administration's economic security bill in the present session. It provides for the levy of a payroll tax on all employers subject to the act, with a credit (in the present bill up to 90 per cent of the federal tax) for the contributions paid by any employer during the taxable year to the proper state authorities under the provisions of state unemployment compensation acts. When first announced it was hailed by all advocates of unemployment insurance (to quote Professor Paul H. Douglas) as "a truly brilliant method" and as representing "federalism at its best." Now, however, many of its former champions, along with the opponents of unemployment insurance, are very critical of this method.

The explanation of this change in opinion is the suggestion in the interim of a new method for inducing the states to enact unemployment insurance laws. This method has been called the "subsidy" or "grant-in-aid" plan, but is more accurately described as a tax-return plan. It proposes that the federal government shall levy a payroll tax on all employers throughout the country and then return to states which enact approved unemployment insurance laws all or a stated percentage of the payroll taxes collected from the employers within these states.

This is not a subsidy or grant-in-aid as these terms have been understood heretofore. No prior subsidy has ever been based upon the taxes collected from the state to which the grant-in-aid is made. Rather than a subsidy, this is an earmarked tax which is returned to the states from which collected. The only essential difference between this plan and the Wagner-Lewis proposal lies in the collection of the payroll tax. Under the present Wagner–Doughton–Lewis bill the states collect the contributions required from employers for unemployment insurance purposes and then deposit the monies collected in the United States Treasury, to the credit of the state. Under the subsidy plan the payroll tax will be collected by the federal government and the monies from a given state credited to the account of that state in the United States Treasury. Aside from this difference in the way in which the monies credited to each state in its unemployment insurance account reach the United States Treasury, there is nothing that can be done under the subsidy system that cannot be done under the Wagner-Lewis plan, or vice versa.

The advocates of the subsidy plan have advanced many reasons for this preference. Many of them believe that it is but a stepping-stone to a national system of unemployment insurance; in fact, one of its leading advocates always refers to it as a "national plan." Since under this plan, as well as the other, each state will have its own unemployment insurance system, it clearly does not eliminate the greatest weakness of state systems, the difficulties arising out of the shifting of workmen from one state to another. Under this plan, each state will have its own law and its separate fund, which presumably would lead to the same resistance against the subsequent establishment of a national system as might arise under the Wagner–Doughton–Lewis bill.

Many advocates of the subsidy plan believe that it lends itself more readily to the insertion of numerous standards in the federal act with which the state laws will have to comply, and that this will bring about a desirable uniformity in these laws. Whether or not this is a valid argument is certainly debatable. Keen students of federal legislation have noted the very strong feeling in this country that the federal government should give aid to the states without trying to dictate to them. This sentiment seems to be particularly strong in the present Congress, and it is not at all improbable that a bill based on the subsidy plan would wind up with fewer standards than are included in the Wagner–Doughton–Lewis bill.

There also are arguments that the subsidy plan is sounder constitutionally. As neither the Wagner-Lewis nor the subsidy plan has come before the courts, this argument is clearly speculative. The Wagner-Lewis device has in its favor a direct precedent in the unanimous decision of the United States Supreme Court upholding the provision in the federal estates tax law allowing credit up to 80 per cent of the federal tax for the amounts paid to the states under their inheritance tax laws. On the other hand, it has been held that a taxpayer cannot question a subsidy payment paid out of general revenues. Both methods of securing state action give rise to the same question, whether the payroll tax is in fact a tax or a disguised method of regulation. Both are probably valid and attorneys differ as to which is safest.

This leaves the more direct method of getting the unemployment compensation funds into the United States Treasury as the chief advantage of the subsidy system. There appear to be no constitutional obstacles in any state to the deposit of moneys collected for unemployment compensation purposes in the United States Treasury, but it must be conceded that the Wagner–Doughton–Lewis bill requires two operations to get these moneys into the Treasury and the subsidy plan only one.

[One of] the strongest arguments on the other side [is] that the subsidy plan would leave the states entirely dependent upon the federal grants, since their unemployment compensation laws would not include any revenue-raising features. There would, thus, be danger that the entire structure of unemployment insurance in this country might be wrecked through an adverse court decision or the failure of Congress to renew its annual appropriation for this purpose.

Another consideration which carried great weight with Administration and congressional leaders in their decision in favor of the Wagner-Lewis rather than the subsidy plan was the use of the term "subsidy" to designate the tax-return method. While it does not contemplate a subsidy from general revenue, there is a danger that the federal grants will come to be regarded as such and that there will be great pressure upon the federal government to come to the rescue of states when they fall into difficulties. If the subsidy plan is accompanied by requirements for high and uniform minimum benefits throughout the country, as most of its advocates urge, then many states will certainly get into serious difficulties. The subsidy plan, consequently, may turn out to be a most dangerous device from the point of view of the United States Treasury. It presents the dangers of a system under which the United States government may be called upon to underwrite the state funds, without having any control over them.

Quite frankly, these arguments against the subsidy plan are matters of judgment and opinion, as are the arguments in its favor. The truth seems to be that the differences between these methods of bringing about state action have been exaggerated. Either method will accomplish the purpose of removing the disadvantages to which states at present must subject their employers if they enact unemployment compensation laws.

At this point, it should be noted that a subsidy of the usual kind will not accomplish this most essential purpose. Suggestions for such a subsidy from general tax revenues have been made from time to time and are now being renewed. Such a subsidy, if of a sizable amount, would, it is true, operate as an inducement to the state legislatures to enact unemployment insurance laws, but would still have the employers in these states at a great disadvantage in interstate competition as against employers in states which have no such laws. It is only through a uniform payroll tax that this greatest obstacle to state action can be removed.

Source of Funds

The suggestion that a subsidy from general revenues should be used to induce the states to enact unemployment compensation laws comes at this time from members of Congress who object to a payroll assessment against employers as a sales tax. This is also the argument against the pending economic security bill used by advocates of the Lundeen bill, which has a surprisingly large support despite its extreme vagueness. According to this view, the costs of all unemployment compensation should be met from income and inheritance taxes, rather than from contributions of employers and employees.

This argument has a strong appeal to liberals who do not like sales taxes. But is a contribution by employers to an unemployment insurance fund really a sales tax? In what essential does it differ from accident (workmen's) compensation? Certainly no one proposes that accident compensation shall be paid from income or inheritance taxes, any more than that the wage bill shall be so paid. Instead, accident compensation is regarded as a proper charge to be included in the cost of production, to be passed on to the consumers. Unemployment compensation, likewise, should be so regarded, particularly when it is limited to the period following the loss of a job while the employee has a good chance of returning to work soon and often is encouraged to wait for his old job by the employer himself.

Many, perhaps most, advocates of unemployment insurance who do not sympathize with the view that unemployment compensation should be paid for entirely from income and inheritance taxes nevertheless believe that the government should make large contributions to the unemployment insurance funds. In England there is a triparty arrangement, the government, the employers, and the employees all contributing equally. A similar arrangement is strongly urged by many of the dyed-in-the-wool advocates of social insurance in this country.

If unemployment insurance is considered a form of relief, there is much to be said for government contributions. If it is set up merely as a first line of defense, the argument for government contributions becomes much less strong. Under such a concept, government contributions should be used to provide work or public assistance to those whose unemployment benefit rights have been exhausted or who are excluded from the system entirely, rather than to increase unemployment compensation benefits. Particularly at this time when 10,000,000 workers are without employment, there is every reason to urge that whatever funds can be provided from general revenues should be used to give work and assistance to the unemployed, rather than to be paid into reserve funds from which benefits will be paid some years from now to those who may be out of work at that time.

This is the position taken by the Committee on Economic Security and the President. The pending economic security bill is a companion measure to the four-billion-dollar appropriation for public work. While the economic security bill carries no government contribution to unemployment compensation, the administration program contemplates the largest contribution ever made from general revenues toward meeting the costs of unemployment. In contrast with the proposed four-billion-dollar appropriation for public work, plus eight hundred million more for relief prior to July 1, 1935, the British government contributed and loaned to the unemployment insurance fund a total of 355 million pounds in the fourteen years ending in March, 1934—considerably less than one-half the contemplated expenditure from general revenues in this country in one year to provide work for the unemployed. Certainly, the American government cannot fairly be charged with being penurious if it prefers to use its funds to aid those now without employment, rather than to contribute to reserve funds to pay unemployment compensation in the future.

Apart from the government, the possible sources of funds for unemployment compensation are the employers and the employees. Except for those who hold that unemployment compensation should be paid for entirely from income and inheritance taxes, there are none who would excuse the employers from contributing. With reference to employer contributions, there is no serious question other than how high the contribution rate should go.

On first thought it might appear that it makes little difference how high a rate employers are compelled to pay, so long as all must pay the same rate. By and large, the employers shift their contributions to the consumers; but they cannot always do so. A high rate may seriously curtail consumption and, also, has some tendency to encourage the replacement of labor by machinery. At this time some consideration may very properly be given to the fact that recovery is still incomplete and that industry cannot stand as high a contribution rate as in more normal times. In England the employer contributions average about 1.5 per cent of payroll; in Germany, about 3 per cent. In this country, the Wisconsin act provides for a 2 per cent contribution. The Wagner-Lewis bill as introduced in the Seventy-third Congress provided for a 5 per cent rate, but, as revised by the Ways and Means Committee, for only a 3 per cent rate. This is the highest employer contribution rate proposed in any state bill. How high the rate shall be, however, is largely a matter of judgment, to be decided by practical considerations, rather than abstract theories.

Regarding employee contributions, the main issue is whether or not employees should be required to contribute at all. Most of those who advocate employee contribution believe that it is immaterial how much the employees contribute so long as they are required to contribute some part of the costs. Those who hold this view argue that if the employees contribute they will have a greater interest in conserving the reserve funds and also in resisting unreasonable increases in benefits, since, presumably, increases in the contribution rates of employers would be paralleled by increases in the contributions of employees. Further, it is claimed that employee contributions are needed to assure the employees a real voice in the administration of unemployment compensation.

On the other hand, it is urged that employee contributions are a tax on wages, imposed at a flat rate and without exemption even of the lowest paid wage-earners, whose income is often insufficient. Moreover, such a tax on wages, unlike the payroll tax on employers, cannot be shifted to the consumers. In fact, the wage-earners, as consumers, pay part of the tax imposed on employers and with employee contributions would have to pay still another tax.

The Committee on Economic Security and the pending Administration bill leave the question of employee contributions entirely to the states. No employee contributions are required in the federal act, but the states are left free to add employee contributions if they wish. Through employee contributions the benefits that can be paid can be increased. There may also be something in the argument that employee contributions will give labor a better claim to participation in the administration of the system and an interest in conserving the funds. On the other hand, employee contributions certainly are a tax on those least able to pay and represent a departure from traditional principles in this respect.

Coverage

Who should be brought under unemployment compensation? This is a practical question to which no dogmatic answer can be given. The natural course for people who believe in unemployment compensation will be to include everyone who can possibly be included. Administrative difficulties and, above all, the obvious fact that if some groups of employees draw an undue share of the total benefits, others will receive less than they should, are, however, countervailing considerations which render it desirable not to attempt maximum possible coverage, at least at the outset.

In European countries there are no numerical limitations in the social insurance laws such as are included in all but one of the American workmen's compensation acts. Such numerical limitations are illogical but are certain to be urged on both traditional and practical grounds. They greatly reduce the number of employees included within the scope of the law. More than one-half of all manufacturing establishments have five or less employees, but employ only 3 per cent of all employees engaged in manufacturing; 85 per cent of all retail establishments fall in this class but have only 25 per cent of the employees in this industry.

Traditionally, in this country, agriculture, domestic service, and employment "not in the usual course of the trade, business, or profession of the employer" are exempted not only from the workmen's compensation laws but from practically all labor laws. Agriculture has been exempted from the British unemployment insurance act until now, when, finally, a special compensation scheme for agricultural workers is under consideration. Inclusion of these groups of workers is difficult administratively and, for short-time and intermittent workers, is of relatively little value, since they seldom accumulate any substantial benefit rights. Unquestionably, it is desirable to include commercial agriculture and large domestic establishments, but as realists we must recognize that legislative bodies will probably prefer the traditional complete exemption.

In the Wisconsin law, regular part-time workers are excluded. This was an exemption strongly opposed by the champions of this legislation and is without any justification; in fact, a difficult administrative problem is created through exclusion, while none arises through inclusion. Part-time workers should, of course, be compensated only on the basis of the wage loss they actually sustain, rather than on the basis of full-time work; but to deny them any protection is both unjust and troublesome.

With regard to seasonal industries, also, there is sure to be considerable demand for exemption. As British experience has demonstrated, there is danger that employees in such industries will draw a very undue share of the total money available for unemployment compensation unless the special restriction is introduced that only unemployment occurring within the actual season of work can be compensated. With such a provision, however, there is no good reason for excluding seasonal industries.

Quite often religious, charitable, and educational institutions are likewise exempted. Aside from tradition there is no good reason for such an exemption, and it seems little short of hypocritical that organizations which have urged the enactment of social legislation, as have many of these groups, should themselves ask to be excluded. To their credit be it said that but few such organizations are asking for an exemption at this time.

In any federal law the employees of the states and their political subdivisions must necessarily be excluded, since the federal government cannot tax the states. It is utterly illogical that governments should impose obligations on private employers that they will not themselves assume, but the inclusion of any public employees must necessarily be left to the states.

Benefits

The benefits which can be paid, manifestly, depend primarily upon the rates of contribution. The higher the contribution rates, the more liberal the benefits can be. There are some important questions regarding benefits, however, which are independent of the contribution rate.

A fundamental question is whether the benefits should be designed to cover primarily short-time or depressional unemployment. Either of these purposes is quite logical. If the former is deemed the major objective, a shorter waiting period and a longer maximum duration of benefits are warranted than if the system is primarily designed for depressional unemployment. In either case, the benefit rate should be high enough to sustain the unemployed worker and his family while benefits are being paid. In this country, benefits of less than 50 per cent of the wage are not likely to be satisfactory, but an absolute maximum limitation of possibly $15 per week is justified. All states also need a minimum benefit, which obviously should vary from state to state, to conform with differences in costs of living and economic standards.

Available data indicate very great differences in the past unemployment rates of the several states, the range in the average rates for the years 1930–1934 being from a minimum of 17 per cent to a maximum of above 34 per cent. It may be that over the entire business cycle these extremes would be less pronounced, but it would seem clear that benefit rates cannot be the same everywhere, unless the contribution rates are higher in the states with greater unemployment or the government is willing to underwrite the funds. The most comprehensive calculations of the benefits which can be paid are those which were made by the statistical staff of the Committee on Economic Security, based on the average unemployment throughout the country in the 'twenties and in the depression period. Most states would seem to be reasonably safe if they base their benefit schedules on the experience throughout the country in the years 1922–1931, as indicated in the report of the Committee on Economic Security; but states with very unstable industries should either increase their contribution rates or reduce their maximum benefit periods. While uniformity in benefit rates throughout the country is desirable from the workers' point of view, any attempt to impose such uniformity from Washington will almost surely result in the insolvency of many state funds.

Benefits for partial unemployment are a special problem which the authors of any unemployment insurance legislation must face. Such partial unemployment results most frequently from a policy of spreading the work, through reducing the hours of labor when orders diminish. This policy has always been advocated by organized labor, but only within limits. It involves a wage loss for which many workmen will feel that they should be compensated. To compensate all partial unemployment, however, may result in encouraging industries to maintain a large surplus labor supply, through using unemployment compensation to supplement inadequate wages. This has occurred in England and should be avoided in this country. At the other extreme a policy may be adopted under which no compensation is paid for partial unemployment until the earnings of the workers are reduced to less than the amount they can receive as compensation for total unemployment. This is objected to on the grounds that it gives the workers nothing more if they work than if they do not do so. To overcome this objection and yet not throw the doors wide open to such abuses as have developed in England, it has been suggested that partial unemployment be compensated only to the extent that the wage loss exceeds a stated percentage which is slightly higher than the percentage of the wage paid as compensation for total unemployment (i.e., if the compensation rate is 50 per cent of the average wage, only partial unemployment causing a wage loss in excess of, say, 40 per cent is compensated).

Pooled Funds Versus Industry and Plant Accounts

The most heated controversy which has developed in this entire field concerns individual industry versus plant accounts. In European unemployment insurance laws all contributions are placed in a central pooled fund, from which benefits are paid without regard to the employer for whom the unemployed person last worked. (It is to be noted, however, that in England the banking and insurance industries have separate funds and that in Belgium, while there is a central pooled fund, the contribution rates vary by industries in accordance with their respective unemployment rates.) In this country, most, but by no means all, of the advocates of unemployment compensation strongly favor pooled funds on the European model; many of them refuse to recognize plant funds or accounts as being insurance at all. On the other hand, most employers who know anything about the subject strongly favor separate plant funds, or "unemployment reserves" as distinguished from "unemployment insurance."

The employers' preference for unemployment reserves is based mainly upon two considerations: (1) their desire to deal directly with their employees, and (2) their strong feeling that they should not be asked to pay for some other employer's unemployment. The principal argument advanced for permitting employers to have such separate accounts is that when they must pay for their own unemployment they will keep unemployment down to the unavoidable minimum.

Organized labor, at first uncertain as to its preference, is now definitely committed in favor of pooled unemployment insurance funds. Its objections to separate plant funds are also twofold: (1) a belief that they are essentially "a company union device," inasmuch as they tie the employees closer to the company, and (2) a fear that many workmen will, under such a system, fail to receive benefits when unemployed, because the fund of their particular employer will have been exhausted.

It is difficult to appraise impartially these opposing claims because there has been little experience to test their validity. That the separate plant account system should furnish some incentive to reduce unemployment would seem unanswerable, but how effective this will prove, no one can be certain. How much employers can do to stabilize their employment will vary in different industries and, manifestly, many causes of unemployment are beyond the control of the individual employer. The relatively small number of employers in this country who have voluntarily set up unemployment reserve systems, on the whole, have not done anything so very striking in stabilizing employment, although some of them have a fine record in this respect. There is much reason to believe that what employers can do most effectively to keep down their unemployment compensation costs under a plant account system is not stabilization of their employment but distribution of available work among all of their employees when slack times come. But upon this point also the evidence from actual experience is scanty.

Opponents of individual industry and plant accounts say that this is a system which attempts to differentiate between good and bad employers and to reward those who have a stable employment record. Besides this, however, there also is the factor that the risk of unemployment differs greatly between industries. Industries like building construction, coal mining, and the capital goods industries generally have much more unemployment than, for instance, retail trade, public utilities, and the consumer goods industries. In all other lines of insurance there is some attempt to adjust the rates to the risk, and this seems but equitable also in unemployment insurance. Such an adaptation of the rates to the inherent risk is possible under a pooled state fund system, but not automatic as under a system in which each employer bears the cost of his own unemployment. That a plant account is of advantage to employers with better than average stability of employment is obvious. But what of the employees? Clearly an individual account system is disadvantageous to the employee when he leaves one establishment to enter the employ of another unless he can take his unused benefit rights with him, which is difficult to work out. The most serious question of all, however, concerns the danger of the inadequacy of many plant funds. A single establishment cannot have the advantages of average exposure, which is fundamental in all true insurance. Under a system, such as has been set up in Wisconsin, where each employer, however small, has his own account, it seems certain that many of these accounts will be exhausted when their employees most need protection. Of course, pooled state funds may also be exhausted, and if such funds become insolvent all employees in the state will suffer, while under the plant account system some employers, at least, will be able to meet fully all obligations. If plant accounts are allowed only to employers who furnish adequate security to guarantee payment of all promised benefits, all arguments directed against such individual accounts on the score of the inadequacy of the protection afforded would seem to be completely answered. There would still remain, however, the fact that the employers permitted to have such accounts would probably be the ones having less than average unemployment and their withdrawal from the central pooled fund would lessen its chances of remaining solvent.

Unemployment reserves, as distinguished from unemployment insurance, were advocated by champions of unemployment compensation when the British unemployment insurance system was generally believed in this country to be a failure. Now that the British system is regarded as a great success, sentiment has swung very strongly in favor of pooled state funds, although most employers continue to favor reserves systems. The question has become whether any state should be permitted to establish a plant account system of unemployment compensation or allow any establishments or industries to contract out of the central pooled funds.

The Wagner-Lewis bill of the Seventy-third Congress permitted states complete free choice in these matters. The Committee on Economic Security and the pending economic security bill permit states to set up an individual plant account system of the Wisconsin type, or to allow "contracting out" from pooled funds, or variations in the rates of contributions to pooled funds, but only under drastic restrictions. In all such cases the employers given such privileges must pay at least 1 per cent of their payroll into the pooled state fund and they cannot reduce the contributions credited to their own accounts until they have built up reserves of at least 15 per cent of their payroll (which few of them will be able to do in less than ten years). These provisions are of a compromise character and have been assailed, on the one hand, because they do not definitely outlaw plant funds and, on the other, because the restrictions are so drastic that employers will lack all incentive to reduce unemployment.

Guaranteed Employment

Raising some of the same questions which are involved in plant accounts are the contractual arrangements between employers and employees known as "guaranteed employment." In such arrangements employers contract to furnish their employees a specified number of weeks of employment during the year and can legally be held for payment of the full wages for the guaranteed amount of work. Such contracts are quite common in England and have been experimented with in a number of voluntary unemployment compensation plans in this country and under the Wisconsin law. Persons interested in continuing these experiments demand that the federal act recognize such guaranteed employment contracts and exempt the employers from making any contributions to central unemployment compensation funds for any employees thus protected.

Guaranteed employment is clearly of advantage to the employees if they are guaranteed sufficient work to give them larger earnings than they would probably get without such a guaranty. Guaranteed employment, however, could also be used as a device to cheat employees out of their unemployment compensation rights. It is only when the guaranty covers most of the possible working period and some provision is made for compensation to employees whose contracts are not renewed and who lose their jobs, that adequate safeguards are provided to make certain that guaranteed employment will truly benefit the employees.

Administration

The final major question arising in unemployment compensation concerns administration. On this subject there is no clash of interests between employers and employees, but a problem of keeping the administration as far removed from politics as possible.

The actual administration must be placed in the local employment offices. Only involuntary unemployment is to be compensated. World experience has demonstrated that the best way to test willingness to work is through requiring the unemployed workman to register at the nearest employment office and to keep constantly in touch with it. It is through the employment offices everywhere that unemployment compensation claims are passed upon in the first instance and benefits paid. To this end a nationwide, efficient, public employment office service, as contemplated in the Wagner-Peyser act, is an absolute essential.

Besides the local employment offices there must be a central state office through which contributions are collected and at which records are kept. A procedure for the settlement of disputed claims is also essential. Advisory committees representative of employers and employees should prove very helpful.

In a coöperative federal-state system, there also must be a federal administrative agency. This federal agency must pass upon whether the state laws meet the prescribed requirements which entitle employers in these states to an offset against the federal payroll tax. It should also collect statistics upon unemployment experience throughout the country, so that rates may be established on a more scientific basis. It should assist the states in setting up unemployment compensation systems and in devising methods for dealing with such difficult problems as interstate transfer of employees and re-insurance.

Regarding the federal administrative agency, the only serious question of policy is whether this should be an independent agency or attached to the Department of Labor. Every argument would seem to favor the latter arrangement. Not only is there now strong sentiment against the creation of any additional permanent independent federal agencies, but the administration of unemployment compensation is so inextricably interwoven with that of the employment offices that the United States Employment Service would have to be transferred from the Department of Labor to this agency. As the Department of Labor is the smallest of the cabinet departments, any such step would be most illogical; moreover, unemployment compensation is clearly a labor problem.

The Federal Government's Role in Unemployment Insurance in 1938

Excerpt from memorandum prepared for Dr. Arthur J. Altmeyer, Chairman of the Social Security Board

W ITH REGARD TO CHANGES in Titles III and IX relating to unemployment insurance, four different courses of action might be considered:

1. The substitution or the establishment of a federally administered system of unemployment insurance.

2. Institution of the so-called "subsidy" system of unemployment insurance, under which the federal government would collect all taxes for unemployment insurance purposes, but the states would continue actually to administer unemployment insurance.

3. The continuance of present methods of tax collection and administration, but with a change in the basis of the federal aid for the administration of unemployment insurance and, perhaps, the insertion of additional standards with which the states would have to comply to get any federal aid.

4. The repeal of Title IX, with transference of the standards now included in this Title (or rather such of these standards as it may be considered advisable to retain) to Title III. This would take the federal government out of the picture as far as the taxes for un-

employment insurance purposes are concerned, but would retain federal participation through aid for administration.

In reaching a decision between these fundamentally different proposals, a number of possible objectives need to be considered, particularly (1) the convenience of employers in reporting; (2) the convenience of employers and employees in having uniform provisions with regard to unemployment throughout the country; (3) protection of employees whose employment takes them into more than one state and who now get little or no benefit from unemployment insurance; (4) lessening of the danger that some state unemployment insurance funds will become insolvent; (5) more efficient administration of unemployment insurance than now prevails (or is likely ever to prevail) under state administration.

All these considerations, and particularly the last three, seem to point toward a federally administered system of unemployment insurance. To me, however, these considerations do not furnish a sufficient reason for attempting to establish such a federally administered system of unemployment insurance at this time. While there is a likelihood that in the course of time some of the state funds may become insolvent, none of them are now insolvent. While many states have failed to administer unemployment insurance even reasonably efficiently, state administration is improving, and it is not at all certain that direct federal administration would be much more efficient. The difficulties of giving protection to employees whose employment takes them into more than one state are very great under state-administered unemployment insurance laws, but the number of people thus situated is not so great that for this reason alone a federal unemployment insurance system should be established. If greater uniformity in the state laws is desirable, such uniformity can be secured through inserted standards in the federal act with which the states must comply, provided that Congress can agree upon what the standards shall be. If Congress cannot agree upon standards to be inserted in the federal law, it is obvious that it would be equally as great a difficulty, if not more, in agreeing upon any federal act whatsoever.

Regardless of the merits of federal versus state administration, it seems to me that a federal system of unemployment insurance has no possibilities of enactment at this time. The Executive Council of the American Federation of Labor has come out for a federal unemployment insurance law, but the members of Congress pay quite as much attention to what their state federations of labor want as they do to the wishes of the American Federation of Labor, and the state federation people generally are not in favor of a federally administered system of unemployment insurance. Aside from organized labor, only a few large employers want a federal system. On the other side are the local officeholders and the popular sentiment against federal centralization. When a considerable number of state systems actually break down, the establishment of a federal system of unemployment insurance may become possible. At this time there is more sentiment for a federal system than there was when the Social Security Act was passed. But at that time practically no member of Congress was for a federal system and it is probable that a large majority of the congressmen would still line up against such a proposal.

Considering next the "subsidy" system, it is evident that this is not a mere extension of the long-established federal policy of grants-in-aid to the states, but a proposal for the collection of taxes by the federal government for the states. This proposal has the advantage that it will eliminate the reports which employers must make to the states in connection with the collection of state unemployment insurance taxes. It also would insure complete uniformity in the taxes levied throughout the country for unemployment insurance purposes. It is subject to the difficulty, however, that it involves a constitutional question which has never been passed upon by the Supreme Court—whether the federal government can collect taxes for the states. As a practical matter also, it involves the necessity of having Congress determine at the time of the enactment of the law whether there shall be employee contributions and merit rating and what shall be the provisions of the merit-rating scheme. It seems to me that this would lead to such a controversy in Congress that it is doubtful whether the bill could be gotten through at all.

In this connection, also, it needs to be remembered that if the "subsidy" system is adopted, there must be some way in which the states can get the wage data they need for the payment of unemployment insurance benefits. If all states would adopt a separation basis for reporting benefit data, a subsidy system would be much more easily workable than in a situation where most states insist upon current wage reporting. It may be possible to combine a subsidy system with a current wage-reporting basis for handling benefit claims, and even possible to have a subsidy system and varying state merit rating and other tax provisions. Very certainly, however, a subsidy system would give rise to many difficulties in state administration, which should be very carefully considered in advance.

A further important consideration in this connection is that the subsidy system could not well be instituted except on the basis of its coming into effect not earlier than 1941. Forty-two states hold the regular sessions of their legislatures next winter and in these states no regular sessions will again be held until 1941. It is a practical certainty that any comprehensive act which the Congress may pass amending the Social Security Act will not be passed until fairly late in the next session of Congress. This will be after the state legislative sessions of 1939 have adjourned. The states cannot repeal their tax levies for unemployment insurance purposes until a federal law is enacted under which they will get corresponding revenues from the taxes collected by the federal government.

This means that if a subsidy system of unemployment insurance tax collection were enacted by Congress in the spring and summer of 1939, the states would still have their taxes on their statute books until their legislature changed the state laws. They could, of course, do so in special sessions, but it is doubtful whether Congress will pass another Social Security Act under which the states will again be compelled to hold special sessions of their legislatures in order to comply with the federal act. Accordingly, it will probably be necessary to provide that any subsidy plan which may be adopted should not take effect until, say, July 1, 1941, so that the states will have an opportunity to make the necessary changes in their laws without being compelled to convene their legislatures in special session. (This factor that a federal act amending the Social Security Act in a comprehensive fashion will not be passed, in all probability, until the regular sessions of the state legislatures of 1939 have adjourned, should also be borne in mind in connection with any other material changes which the states will have to make in their laws by reason of changes in the federal act; if possible, the necessity of holding such sessions of the state legislature should be avoided and this can be done through postponing the time of the taking effect of changes in the federal law which necessitate changes in state legislation.)

Considering next the proposal to repeal Title IX and to leave the collection of unemployment insurance taxes entirely up to the states, this change would have the same effect as the adoption of the subsidy system insofar as the simplification of the reports by employers is concerned. Moreover, it would have the effect of somewhat reducing the total taxes collected for social insurance purposes. On the other hand, it would somewhat lessen the revenues of the federal government without reducing its expenses (if it is assumed that the federal government would continue to give aid for the administration of unemployment insurance). It also would lead to the danger that some states might repeal their unemployment insurance laws. Whether they would do so would depend upon the local popularity of these laws and the incentive created by the federal aid for administration. It is my belief that no important state would repeal its unemployment insurance law if Title IX were repealed, and it is entirely feasible to insert in Title III a standard that states must collect a tax of at least 2.7 per cent (or 3 per cent) from their employers to get any federal aid for the administration of unemployment insurance, which would operate to retain the feature of the present system of a uniform tax rate for unemployment insurance tax purposes on employers throughout the country. I am nevertheless of the opinion that the repeal of Title IX would not be advisable at this time. It has little to commend it except a reduction in the number of reports which employers must make, and of all the reports which employers must now make, the reports which they make to the states in connection with the payment of unemployment insurance taxes are the least troublesome.

This brings me to my conclusion that the most feasible plan is to make only relatively minor changes in Titles III and IX at this time. The major change I think should be to make the federal aid under Title III payable on an automatic formula basis, rather than have the federal government reimburse the states for all their expenditures for the administration of unemployment insurance. The present system inevitably leads to a vast amount of friction between the Social Security Board and the state authorities, and is very likely to lead to much unnecessary expenditure. A formula under which the states would get aid for the administration of unemployment insurance in a lump sum would eliminate this friction and ought to result in a reduced cost of administration. It may also be advisable to insert a few additional standards to which the states must comply in their unemployment insurance laws. If anything along this line is done, I suggest that the standards now in Title IX be transferred to Title III, with the elimination of such of the present standards as are now obsolete.

The program I suggest with reference to unemployment insurance is one calling for few modifications in the federal legislation and a continuance of all basic principles of the present law. With all the dissatisfaction there has been this year concerning the administration of unemployment insurance, there is little prospect that Congress will consent to an abandonment of state administration. If this is a correct analysis of the situation, it follows that the big task is to improve the state laws and the state administration. In this connection the simplification of the state laws is very important.

This matter is one of the most important of the tasks now confronting the Social Security Board. The state laws, with few exceptions and with but minor variations, were copied from the model bills promulgated by the Board. It has become evident that many of the provisions in these state laws are too complicated and the Board cannot escape some share of responsibility for this situation. Having suggested to the states that they adopt these provisions, it is now a duty of the Board to suggest other provisions which now seem to be preferable.

I know that the Board is thinking along these lines and has the work of trying to simplify the state laws and their administration well in hand. What I wish to suggest is that this matter is one which needs to receive much more attention at this time than possible amendment of the federal law. Simplification necessarily involves a change in the state laws, and the state legislatures will convene in January. If there is to be simplification, consequently the new model bill (or bills) should be ready before January, so that they can be taken up with the state unemployment insurance authorities whose support is vital to get these changes through the state legislatures. If the new model bills are not available until the state legislatures are well into their work, little will be accomplished in the coming sessions toward simplification of state laws. Such simplification, moreover, cannot possible be brought about as a mere production of standards written into the federal act—if for no other reason than that there will be no new federal act until the state legislatures have adjourned.

Whither Unemployment Compensation?

Address at the Regional
Institute on Employment
Service and Unemployment
Compensation Procedures,
University of Minesota,
April 10. Somewhat condensed
in *The Social Service Review,*
published by the University
of Chicago Press, Volume
XIV, Number 3 (September,
1940), pages 421–437

U NEMPLOYMENT COMPENSATION has now been in operation for some time in every part of the United States. The majority of the states have had more than two years of benefit experience, none less than nine months' experience. It is timely to ask: What has been accomplished? What remains to be done? Whither unemployment compensation?

In retrospect, the outstanding fact about unemployment compensation is that most of the predictions made prior to the enactment of this legislation have proved false. While the Social Security Act was under consideration, and after its passage, the "experts" who claimed to know most about the subject predicted that the tax-offset device would fail and that only a few states, at the most, would enact unemployment compensation laws. The American Liberty League promptly proclaimed both the tax-offset provision and the state laws to be unconstitutional. On every hand there were predictions that once benefit payments began, the state funds would soon be bankrupted. The administrative problems were said to be impossible of solution. A complete breakdown of unemployment compensation was predicted by its enemies and feared by its friends.

What happened? In less than two years after passage of the Social Security Act, every state had enacted an unemployment compensation law. The Supreme Court found both the provisions of the Social Security Act relating to unemployment compensation and the state laws to be constitutional. Instead of exhausted state funds, the problem has become one of excessive reserves.

The administrative problems, while not completely licked, have been met reasonably well as they have arisen. Benefit payments were started in most states at the worst possible time—during the very severe depression of the winter of 1937/38—with untrained staffs, and with very inadequate preparation. In a considerable number of states, there was something akin to a complete breakdown in administration for some months and, naturally, much complaint from claimants whose payments were delayed. But everywhere the administration of unemployment compensation improved rapidly. Before the end of the first year—and much earlier in most states—benefits were being paid on time in nearly all uncontested cases, and contested cases were being disposed of expeditiously. Once caught up, no state has ever again fallen behind. In the matter of costs of administration, the record in many American states has been truly remarkable. In England it was ten years after the enactment of the 1920 act before administrative costs ever were as low as 10 per cent of the collections. In many states this low figure has already been attained, and the minimum is now around 7 per cent.

Very certainly, however, all problems have not been solved, and unemployment compensation is not all that it ought to be. It is almost a certainty that important changes will have to be made in unemployment compensation before long.

Foremost among the major issues now to the fore is the question of what should be done about the large and increasing reserves, the proposal for the insertion of benefit standards in the Social Security Act, and the problem of experience rating. These issues are interrelated but justify separate treatment.

Basic in the present situation are the large reserves in the state unemployment compensation funds. Up to the close of 1939, all states combined had collected nearly $2,400,000,000 for unemployment compensation purposes and paid out but $825,000,000 in benefits. The reserves totaled $1,550,000,000 and constituted 63 per cent of the entire collections. In no state was there the slightest danger

of the early exhaustion of the reserves. In only one state—Idaho—
did the benefit payments in 1939 exceed the tax collections of the last
calendar year. In only five states did the benefit payments total as
much as 80 per cent of the current collections. Taxes collected in
1939 in all states amounted to $800,000,000; benefits paid to $430,-
000,000—but 54 per cent of the current collections.

For a correct understanding of this situation, it is important to
remember that approximately half the present reserves are accumulations of the period before benefits became payable. Another
important factor is that it takes considerable time before all who
are entitled to benefits actually claim them and know enough about
the procedure to take promptly the necessary steps to get all that is
coming to them. This was the experience under workmen's compensation and has been repeated under unemployment compensation. Probably even more important is the fact that, with the exception of the first three months of this year, the general trend of
employment has been upward. The total volume of the unemployment compensation benefits at any given time or during any given
period does not depend upon the total number of people who are
unemployed, but upon the number of workers recently discharged
or laid off. People who have been long unemployed have no benefits
coming under unemployment compensation laws. Millions may be
unemployed while unemployment compensation benefits run very
low. It is at times when unemployment is increasing that benefits
will run high. Since benefit payments began there has been only one
quarter in which this has been the situation. A prolonged period
of declining employment will give us the first real test of the extent to which present reserves are too large, and there has been no
such test to date.

But while there are these factors which explain why the reserves
are now very large, it is my conviction that the present tax rates
are higher than they need to be under the present benefit scales.
Expressed the other way, present benefits can be materially increased
without necessitating an increase in tax rates.

I hold this view, not only because of the experience to date, but
because I believe that the costs of unemployment compensation were
greatly overestimated by the statisticians and actuaries who advised
the Committee on Economic Security and the Social Security Board;
and the benefit schedules included in most of the state laws are those

which were recommended by the Social Security Board in its model draft bills.

These overestimates resulted, in part, from the supercaution of the actuaries. After computing what unemployment compensation would have cost, on the basis of the available data regarding unemployment during the last complete business cycle, 1922–1933, the actuaries added a 33⅓ per cent loading for unexpected contingencies. I do not say this by way of criticism of the actuaries. Everybody interested in unemployment insurance was at that time greatly concerned lest the collections should be insufficient for payment of the promised benefits, with resulting discredit to the entire movement. But it remains a fact that if the actuaries had not arbitrarily added a 33⅓ per cent loading, to be absolutely sure that promised benefits could be paid, the general scale of benefits could have been increased correspondingly, on the basis of the American unemployment experience from 1922 to 1933.

It is very clear now, also, that the basic data used by the actuaries in their estimates—which were the only data available to them— overstated the volume of compensable unemployment. These data were derived from the Unemployment Census of 1930, corrected for its admitted failure to record all the unemployed, and numerous local counts of all the unemployed taken at some time between 1922 and 1933. All such censuses of all the unemployed are overweighted with the people who have been long unemployed and who have no rights to unemployment compensation. There has been much misunderstanding as to the unemployment which is compensable under unemployment compensation laws. Not all unemployment, but only recent unemployment, is compensable. At times, other than those in which employment is decreasing sharply, it is probable that more than half of all compensable unemployment is represented by layoffs, in which the worker returns to the job that he left, after a period of but a few weeks or months. In times of sharply declining employment, discharges probably account for most of the compensation claims, but even at such times there is no direct relation between the total volume of unemployment and compensable unemployment. But before we had unemployment compensation laws, the costs of unemployment compensation had to be estimated on the total volume of unemployment, which meant that, even apart from the 33⅓ per cent loading, costs inevitably were overestimated.

There is still another reason why estimates of unemployment compensation costs based on the unemployment of the last complete business cycle are now too high. This is the decrease in the labor turnover. Total unemployment has greatly increased, but turnover has greatly decreased. Voluntary quitting of jobs has become a rarity and, in this day and age of restrictions upon discharges and seniority rules, discharges are far less common than formerly. It needs ever to be borne in mind that unemployment compensation compensates only comparatively recent unemployment. It is the layoff and turnover rates which determine the total volume of the unemployment compensation payments, not the total amount of unemployment. While total unemployment is greater than in the 'twenties, compensable unemployment is much less than was estimated on the basis of the 'twenties.

All these factors lead to the conclusion that existing contribution rates and benefit scales are out of line. They should clearly be brought into closer correspondence. There is need for a revision of the unemployment compensation laws. The question remaining to be answered is whether benefits should be increased or taxes reduced.

There are some things to be said in favor of tax reduction. Reduction in unemployment insurance contribution rates would probably result in somewhat increased profits. Very certainly, a reduction in tax rates would yield immediate unexpected profits to many entrepreneurs who calculated their costs on long-time, uncompleted contracts on the basis of the existing tax rates. Such unexpected and increased profits might have a stimulating effect upon investment, and we need more investment.

How much of a beneficial effect tax reduction would have, however, is uncertain. The desirability of an investment depends less upon the immediate rate of profits than upon the long-time prospect for profits and, above all, on the security of the investment. It is my belief that it is far less the low return on investments than the danger of losing them altogether which retards investment. In the long run, security of investments depends upon social stability. It may well be doubted whether keeping down unemployment compensation benefits tends toward social stability; almost certainly, such a policy has the opposite effect. The long-time interests of the investor and of business generally may be better served by making unemployment compensation a more satisfying institution than by the unexpected, immediate profits resulting from tax reduction.

To me, the case seems overwhelming for an increase in unemployment compensation benefits. The present benefit provisions are extremely illiberal, judged by any standard whatsoever. They are illiberal as compared with the English benefits. They are illiberal as compared with workmen's compensation benefits. They are below WPA wage rates. They are barely sufficient to keep most workers who are normally regularly employed off relief for the few weeks during which they are payable. It has often been said that unemployment compensation can never become anything more than a first line of defense against the ravages of unemployment. As now functioning in the United States, it is a very weak first line of defense—one that needs strengthening at many points.

To me a comparison of the benefits payable under the unemployment compensation with those recoverable for temporary disability under workmen's compensation is most illuminating. The workmen's compensation laws were passed by the states, without any pressure from Washington whatsoever. Each state has acted as it has seen fit in fixing the cash benefits recoverable when workmen are injured. The benefits payable for temporary disability under workmen's compensation laws represent what the legislators of each state have deemed necessary to enable injured workmen and their families to live while they are unable to work—and they are not intended to cover anything else.

I recognize that there are important differences between unemployment compensation and workmen's compensation—between a man who is unemployed because he has been discharged or laid off and a man who has been hurt in an industrial accident. The latter has additional costs for medical and surgical treatment; and under all workmen's compensation acts, injured men get their doctor and hospital bills in addition to the cash compensation, which alone may fairly be compared with unemployment compensation. If they suffer any permanent disability by reason of their accident, they receive additional compensation for permanent injury. But the cash compensation for temporary disability is given for exactly the same reason as is unemployment compensation in cases of involuntary unemployment due to discharges or layoffs. Clearly, a man needs just as much to support himself and his family when he is involuntarily unemployed although able to work as he does when temporarily unable to work because of an industrial accident (always bearing in mind that under workmen's compensation the injured worker gets all necessary medical, surgical, and hospital treatment in addition to his cash compensation). And I remind you that the states determined for themselves what compensation is necessary in periods of temporary disability.

I cannot give you a comparison between the cash compensation payable to injured workmen, while temporarily deprived of their usual wages, and the compensation recoverable under our existing unemployment compensation laws. I suggest that you make such a comparison for your own state. I did so for Wisconsin and found that for most imaginable periods of unemployment, the cash benefits under workmen's compensation were more than twice the unemployment compensation benefits.

A comparison of typical benefit provisions in workmen's compensation and unemployment compensation laws must first consider the waiting periods. In unemployment compensation, they are either two or three weeks; in workmen's compensation, seldom over seven days, and with three days not uncommon. No unemployment compensation law has a compensation rate of above 50 per cent of the full-time wages, while only a very few workmen's compensation laws have so low a rate of compensation; most of them have either 60, 65, 66⅔, or 70 per cent. In many states, also, both the maximum and minimum compensation rates are higher under workmen's compensation than under unemployment compensation. In a considerable number of states, partial unemployment is not compensated at all.[1]

But it is especially in the limitations upon the duration of benefits that unemployment compensation is illiberal. All American laws have two sorts of limitations upon the duration of benefits: absolute limitations and ratio provisions. The absolute limitations prevent anyone from drawing unemployment compensation for more than thirteen, fifteen, or sixteen weeks in any year. The ratio provisions restrict the duration of benefits to one week of compensation for every three, four, or five weeks of employment during the preceding

[1] An excellent brief presentation of the limitations of the existing unemployment compensation laws is the article by Dr. Arthur J. Altmeyer, chairman of the Social Security Board, "Liberalizing Unemployment Compensation," in the *Social Security Bulletin*, III, No. I (January, 1940), 3–5.

year, or limit the total compensation benefits which may be received in any year to one-half of the earnings in the highest quarter of the preceding year.

To date we have but little information on the way these limitations on the duration of benefits actually work out. Enough data are available, however, to leave no room for doubt that they are the most restrictive of all the illiberal provisions in the existing unemployment compensation laws.[2] A large percentage of those who draw benefits do so only for very short periods, not because they return to their old jobs or get other work—as, of course, many beneficiaries do—but because the ratio provisions cut them off from compensation while they are still unemployed. The absolute limitations are deceptive in that most claimants who do not return to work before exhausting their benefit rights are cut off from benefits long before the thirteen, fifteen, or sixteen weeks which are, theoretically the maximum periods for which benefits can be drawn in any year. In Michigan, under one of the most liberal of unemployment compensation laws, the average duration of benefits for employees who exhausted their benefit rights before getting back to work was not the theoretical maximum of sixteen weeks but only eleven weeks. In other states the average duration of benefits for employees who exhaust their benefit rights—a large percentage of all claimants—is probably less than in Michigan, perhaps not more than eight weeks, and almost certainly not above ten weeks.

It is at this point that unemployment compensation is most strikingly less liberal than workmen's compensation. There are limitations to the duration of compensation for temporary disability, but there are four or six years of compensation payments under the workmen's compensation acts. I do not argue that similar durations of benefits should be established in unemployment compensation. In unemployment compensation, as in every other type of insurance, only as much can be taken out in benefits as is put in in contributions. The benefits which can be paid from 2.7 per cent of contributions are distinctly limited. In the period of the last complete business cycle, 1922–1933, unemployment among industrial workers is estimated to have averaged 15 per cent in the United State—8

---

[2] Some of these data are presented in the article by Daniel Creamer and Marion Bloom, "Some Data Indicative of the Need for More Liberal Unemployment Benefits," in the *Social Security Bulletin*, III, No. 1 (January, 1940), 6–9.

per cent in the eight years of prosperity, 35 per cent in the four years of depression. In the business cycle we are now in, total unemployment is apparently much greater than the average of 15 per cent for the last complete cyclical period. With contributions limited to 2.7 per cent of payrolls, manifestly not all the 15 per cent or more of working time lost through unemployment can be compensated. In England, where the combined contributions of employers, employees, and the government amount to about 4½ per cent of the total payrolls in the covered employments, the benefit scales can, of course, be more liberal than in this country, although even in England only a part of all unemployment (less than half) is compensated. But we can pay better benefits from the 2.7 per cent contributions we have than we are doing, and we can have better benefits if we retain the 2.7 per cent contribution rates than if we reduce the contribution rates to 2 or 1.7 per cent. To reduce the contribution rates is certain to freeze benefits at their present low level and, in many states, would even necessitate a reduction in the present very inadequate benefits. This would render unemployment compensation almost worthless and would amount to selling the unemployed down the river for the sake of unexpected, and only slightly larger, profits. What we need to do, instead, is to increase our benefits as warranted by the existing 2.7 per cent contribution rates; but even so we can compensate only a part of all unemployment and have to determine to whom among all of the unemployed the relatively small amounts we have available for benefit payments shall go. World-experience has demonstrated that unemployment compensation cannot be made to serve even reasonably adequately the needs of people who are only very irregularly employed and cannot be extended at all to people who have no employment in private industry. It can be made a fairly adequate first line of defense, however, for the largest group in our entire population; the urban workers who are normally fairly regularly employed. With our 2.7 per cent contribution rates, this first line of defense can be made much better than it now is and, clearly, should be strengthened. With reduced contribution rates, it would hardly be worth maintaining at all.

This brings me to a discussion of the methods through which unemployment compensation benefits can be increased. There are two alternative methods: (1) voluntary action by the state legislatures to increase the benefits in their unemployment compensation laws; and

(2) the inclusion of minimum benefit standards in the Social Security Act, which the state legislatures would be compelled to adopt to entitle the employers in their states to the 90 per cent offset against the federal 3 per cent tax for unemployment insurance purposes.

Of these alternative methods, I consider the first preferable, provided that the state legislatures will actually voluntarily increase benefits as warranted by the present contribution rates. There is danger that the coercion of the states will be carried to a point where there will be such a strong reaction against federal intervention that we may lose even the federal tax—which is still very important to enable us to maintain unemployment compensation throughout the country. I am doubtful, also, about the sort of benefit standards which can be gotten through federal action. Most people who talk about federal standards assume that Congress would prescribe minimum standards such as are considered reasonable in the leading northern industrial states. But there are many more rural states than there are industrial states. Standards which might be set by the present Congress would very probably prove disappointing to many of the people who are relying upon Congress to liberalize unemployment compensation benefits; and the next Congress may be much more conservative.

If federal benefit standards are adopted, they must either be set at so low a level that the states with the worst records with regard to the intermittency of employment can maintain solvent funds, or some of the state funds will be bankrupted, or some sort of a re-insurance fund must be instituted. If a reinsurance fund is financed from general federal revenues, such a fund will be all to the good. In the present state of the federal finances, however, I see little prospect that federal revenues will be made available for the maintenance of a reinsurance fund, to enable states with an excessive amount of compensable unemployment to pay the same benefits as states with less unemployment. The alternative is to take the money for the reinsurance fund from the contributions collected from employers in states which have average or less than average unemployment. This amounts to "robbing Peter to pay Paul"—to penalizing industries with little unemployment in order to subsidize industries which have an excessive amount of intermittent unemployment.

The other possibility that the federal benefit standards may be set at a high level and no reinsurance fund created, with the resulting bankruptcy of some of the state funds, seems to me still more hazardous. There are sincere supporters of unemployment compensation who believe that everything possible should be done to bring about the establishment of a federal system of unemployment compensation at the earliest date possible. Some of these sincere people think that the way to bring about the establishment of a federal system is to bankrupt some of the state funds; accordingly, they favor high federal benefit standards, without any reinsurance fund. I grant that it is a possibility that, when a considerable number of state funds are bankrupted, a federal system of unemployment compensation may be substituted for the present state systems; but I suggest that it is at least as likely that, if a considerable number of state systems go bankrupt, unemployment compensation may be done away with entirely in this country.

Finally, I have doubts about either the need for or the desirability of complete uniformity in unemployment compensation benefits throughout the United States. Almost certainly, if minimum benefit standards are inserted in the Social Security Act, it will be extremely difficult in all states to get the legislatures to adopt more liberal benefits, in any respect, than those prescribed in the federal law. If a reinsurance scheme accompanies the federal standards, it will be absolutely necessary to limit the benefit payments which may be financed from the reinsurance fund to the minimum benefits required by the federal act. In such circumstances, the minimum federal standards will become the uniform standards throughout the country. I have already expressed my belief that, at least in the long run, these minimum federal standards are more likely to suit the situations in the states which would naturally have low benefit standards than in the smaller number of industrial states in which higher standards have the support of public opinion.

At this stage, moreover, we know relatively little about what are the best standards in all situations. For instance, I incline to the view that a flat maximum duration of benefits is desirable, such as is proposed in all the bills now pending in Congress for minimum federal benefit standards; but a flat maximum duration of benefits can only be provided for if there are high qualifications for eligibility to benefits. It will not be possible anywhere to pay more in benefits to unemployed workmen than they earned in wages in the preceding year. As the experience of California and other states which have established flat maximum durations of benefits clearly indicates, such action must be accompanied by a raising of the qualifications for eligibility to benefits. The net result is that many workers who are now entitled to unemployment compensation benefits for short periods will be denied unemployment compensation at all. A flat duration of benefits will improve the compensation for the workers who are fairly regularly employed, but will operate to cut off from unemployment compensation altogether a considerable number of workers who now have some protection. As I have stated, my personal preference is a flat maximum duration of benefits, but I do not think that we know enough about the effects of such a provision to be warranted in saying to the states, "Although you prefer to compensate a larger part of your workers to improving the compensation for those who are fairly regularly employed, you must come to a flat maximum duration of benefits because Congress thinks this advisable."

This brings me to the final major issues in unemployment compensation today—experience rating. No other question is more of a headache to the administrators or has provoked more controversy among the theorists.

There are good theoretical arguments on both sides of this question. To me the weight of the theoretical arguments seems to be in favor of experience rating. I hold this view not so much because I believe that experience rating will operate to reduce unemployment, but because I believe that the adjustment of contribution rates to the varying risks of unemployment of different industries and establishments is in accord with prevailing American concepts. In all other "insurances" in this country, rates are adjusted to the risk. Our private economy is grounded upon the concept that each industry should stand on its own feet. Honest cost accounting requires that all costs be ascertained and properly allocated to the commodities produced or services rendered. An industry which operates intermittently occasions great costs to its employees and to society through its methods of operation. Whether it can or cannot operate more regularly, the unemployment which arises by reason of its intermittent or irregular operation is a cost which should be charged to the establishment producing the goods or services and which gets the profits of the enterprise. Every reason can be advanced for contributions from employers only—and in all but six states all contributions come from the employers—logically leads to variable contribution rates, rates adjusted to risk and costs. In a socialistic economy it might be proper to have all industry collectively bear the costs of unemployment; in a private economy, where the profits go to particular entrepreneurs, all costs of production should be borne by the particular establishments, and these should include the unemployment compensation costs, as well as all other costs.

Can the employer reduce unemployment? I think it is a defeatist, antisocial attitude to say that he cannot do so. Of course, he cannot prevent all unemployment. But numerous employers have demonstrated that they can eliminate a large part of the extreme intermittency and irregularity of operation which characterizes many American industries. Charles A. Myers,[3] who certainly was not biased in favor of the Wisconsin system, found, after a year of field investigation which took him into a very large number of Wisconsin plants, that one-fourth of these plants had made efforts at stabilization with some degree of success. He further found that many more employers had reduced unemployment compensation costs by following the policy of "sharing the work"—when orders declined, reducing hours of labor instead of laying off men. He did not consider this stabilization of employment, but it is the most widely prevalent of all methods of stabilization. Professor Emerson Schmidt[4] of the University of Minnesota and the Employment Stabilization Service, which has been set up by Mr. Hormel and the American Legion and which is doing a notable work in interesting employers in stabilization and in advising them what they can do to stabilize, has concluded that practically every large employer in Wisconsin has done something to regularize his operations since our unemployment compensation law was enacted. I am satisfied that the Wisconsin law had greater effects in this respect because it has been so savagely condemned by critics from outside the state. But whether a similar record can be made in other states, whether a particular industry or establishment can or cannot reduce intermittency in its operations, does not affect the soundness of the adjustment of the contribution

[3] "Employment Stabilization and the Wisconsin Act," *American Economic Review*, XXIX (December, 1939), 708–23.

[4] "Easing the Payroll Tax Burden" in *Barron's*, January 1, 1940, and in the publications of the Employment Stabilization Service, Minneapolis.

rates to the compensation costs. Charging its own unemployment compensation costs to each industry will furnish at least some incentive for regularization; but whether it does or does not reduce its costs, these should properly still be allocated to it. There are enormous differences in the amount of unemployment compensation costs occasioned by different industries and among different establishments in the same industry. At least so long as employers have to pay all these costs, there is every reason for trying to distribute these costs equitably among them, which leads, inevitably, to adjustment of the contribution rates to the unemployment compensation costs of the particular employer.

But while I believe that the weight of the theoretical arguments is decidedly in favor of experience rating, I am also of the opinion that the experience-rating provisions of the existing state laws are very defective.

Before going into this matter, let me say, parenthetically, that the usual experience-rating provisions in the state laws were not copied from the Wisconsin law. They come from the model "pooled fund" bills of the Social Security Board, which, in turn, copied them from the "pooled fund" bill of the Ohio Commission of 1932, which was the great rival to the Wisconsin plan in the days before any state but Wisconsin had an unemployment insurance law.

A basic defect in experience rating under the existing state laws is that the contribution rates which employers must pay depend not upon how much unemployment they have, but [upon] the volume of their compensable unemployment. There is a difference between the unemployment caused by discharges and layoffs by a particular firm and the amount of the resulting compensable unemployment. A minor factor producing such results is that there may be great differences in the length of time it takes discharged workers to get other employment, so it is largely a matter of chance how much a given volume of unemployment due to discharges will cost in unemployment compensation. More important and more serious is the fact that under all experience-rating provisions now in the unemployment compensation laws, including the Wisconsin law, it is possible to reduce compensable unemployment without reducing unemployment, through taking advantage of the qualifications and exclusions of these laws so as to throw most of the unemployment into the groups among the employees who have no benefit rights.

So long as this loophole exists, experience rating is very defective, and in actual operation will fail to secure the theoretical advantages of variable contribution rates.

Whether experience rating can be made to work equitably is still debatable. I am satisfied that the present provisions will be found to have many "niggers in the wood pile" and will have to be changed in many respects. Nevertheless, I am strongly of the opinion that the state should not only be permitted to have experience rating if they so desire, but should be helped by the Social Security Board to make experience rating work as equitably as possible.[5] I hold this view, not only because the Board suggested the present experience-rating provisions to the states (except in Wisconsin), but because employers believe variable contribution rates to be equitable and are willing to accept unemployment compensation, if it is accompanied by experience rating.

I believe that the point of view of the employers should be taken into consideration in the development of unemployment compensation; further, that if this is not done, unemployment compensation may be swept away entirely. It is very probable that once experience rating is tried, division will develop among the employers, particularly if experience rating works both ways—that is, if contribution rates are reduced when an employer has a good record and are increased if he has much compensable unemployment, which is what experience rating should do and how it actually works in Wisconsin. In our state, the contractors' association has this year come out against variable contribution rates and asked for an amendment to make the rates the same for all industries and all employers. A similar development can be expected elsewhere. Employers in industries which have a high rate of compensable unemployment, in the long run, are almost certain to favor flat contribution rates. But until experience rating is given a fair trial, the great majority of the employers will favor experience rating and will feel very aggrieved if they are not given an opportunity to reduce their unemployment compensation costs.

Legislation by Congress which would make it impossible for the states to have experience rating would, in my opinion, be most un-

[5] A beginning in work of this kind has been made by the Social Security Board in its studies, *Administration of Automatic Merit Rating under Pooled Fund Laws*, September, 1938, and *Current Experience Rating Research*, April, 1940, but much more active assistance will be necessary if experience rating is ever to have a fair test.

wise. But there is a much stronger case for standards in the Social Security Act to provide a safeguard against the danger that some states may keep their unemployment benefits so low that their employers will get reduced contribution rates not because they have decreased unemployment or have very little unemployment in their plants, but solely because these states have abnormally low benefit scales. It must be conceded that in the absence of minimum benefit standards, below which the states may not fall, there is a distinct incentive for the states to keep their benefits abnormally low. The strongest argument for federal action in unemployment compensation was that only through uniform tax rates throughout the country could states enact unemployment compensation laws without penalizing their manufacturers from states without such laws. The same argument can be made for minimum benefit standards as a condition which the state must meet before they can permit any of their employers to pay less than the standard contribution rate of 2.7 per cent. As matters stand, the uniformity in contribution rates is being destroyed. That is quite proper, it seems to me, if the rates reflect differences in the amount of unemployment, but very inequitable if it is merely the result of low benefit scales in a particular state. Accordingly, while I am not in favor of minimum benefit standards which Congress forces all the states to adopt—at least, until it has been demonstrated that the states, without federal coercion, will not provide decent benefits—I believe that the Social Security Act should include provisions for minimum benefits which states should have to insert in their laws before any employer could claim as an additional credit against the federal tax a reduction in contribution rates allowed to him under the experience-rating provisions of the state law.

Summarizing my views as to what should be done in the matter of changes in our unemployment compensation laws, I believe that the time has come for materially increasing benefits, as can safely be done without necessitating increases in present contribution rates. I would prefer to have the increased benefits come as a result of voluntary state action, but if the states neglect to act, the federal government must act. Unsatisfactory as the present experience-rating provisions are, I am opposed to federal legislation which would prevent the thirty-five states which have experience-rating provisions in their laws, but as yet do not actually have experience rating, from putting these provisions into effect, as four states have done. But I think that Congress may properly amend the Social Security Act by making reduction in contribution rates under experience rating conditional upon inclusion in the state law of minimum benefit standards, to prevent employers from getting reduced rates merely because a state has unwarrantably low benefits.

Experience Rating and Other
Forms of Incentive Taxation
to Promote Employment

Concluding remarks at a
round-table conference on
"Incentive Taxation with
Special Reference to
Unemployment," held on
October 14, 1941, as part of
the National Tax Association's
annual conference on
taxation. Published in
pages 479–483 of the 1941
Proceedings of the Association

Concluding this session, it may be apropos for me to briefly state my views on the subject we have been discussing, particularly as several of you have directed questions to me.

As I have always looked upon unemployment compensation as an insurance institution, designed to give workers normally employed a partial wage for a limited period after being laid off, until they find other work or, more commonly, are called back to their old jobs, I must confess that I have found the approach to experience rating as incentive taxation, which we have been pursuing tonight, somewhat strange. I recognize, however, that it is an entirely proper one.

The employer's "contributions" to unemployment compensation funds (as they are called in the laws of most states) may be, as I believe, more in the nature of insurance premiums than taxes, but they are popularly called a "payroll tax" and the recent tendency has, undoubtedly, been to emphasize the tax aspects of unemployment compensation more than the insurance aspects, which was the original concept.

Professor Schmidt opened vistas of the use of taxes as an incentive to private industry to provide increased and more regular employment which are much broader than experience rating in unemployment compensation, although this is the only such incentive device now in operation. I am not prepared to discuss the several possibilities to this end outlined by Professor Schmidt; much less to suggest still other incentive taxes which might be utilized to increase employment, although I am satisfied that there are other measures that might profitably be considered. I merely want to record my agreement with the general line of thought which Professor Schmidt developed in the early part of his paper.

I agree with Professor Schmidt that it is doubtful whether this country, and particularly its democratic institutions, could survive another such period of mass unemployment as we experienced in the Great Depression. Despite the present boom, the problem of insuring full employment on a lasting basis remains our number-one domestic problem, which is likely to break out again in an acute form following the war.

Unemployment insurance, as well as every other institution for the benefit of the unemployed or which affects employment opportunities, needs to be judged on the basis of what it can contribute to the solution of the fundamental problem of securing and maintaining full employment.

Unemployment insurance, with or without experience rating, is not the complete answer, but, I believe, is an essential step toward the solution of the unemployment problem. Quite obviously other measures are also necessary. Incentive taxation, including devices yet untried, merits consideration in this connection and seems to me to be sound, at least in theory.

Incentive taxation is in line with the older progressive philosophy in this country. This philosophy aimed not at the displacement of our so-called "private capitalistic economy" by a governmentally directed economy, but at the revitalization of our economy of free enterprise. In this progressive philosophy, indirect incentive devices, utilizing the profit motive of the entrepreneurs, were deemed more desirable than direct control measures, while governmental operation was thought of as suitable only within very limited fields and as a last resort.

More recently, there has developed strong support in the country, particularly in Washington circles and among economists serving as advisers to government agencies, for what is called "a planned economy." This is an economy controlled in all essential details by the national government. While retaining private property and some degree of freedom of choice of occupations and investment, it contemplates central direction of all enterprises.

In such an economy indirect incentives can be of but little value. They are too uncertain to be useful for the detailed direction of industry. For a centrally controlled economy, resort must be had to such direct measures as extensive governmental investment and employment priorities, price controls, the rationing of consumption, and ultimately, as I see it, the conscription of both labor and capital.

In such a "planned" or "controlled" economy, individuals have little free choice, yet are important to the state because no economy can be maintained without the labor of the men and women of the nation. So while they approach all problems from the point of view of control of the entire economy, they, too, believe in social security measures as essential to the productive efficiency of the nation. But to them social security means nothing more than the maintenance of the working population to insure maximum efficiency. Unemployment compensation is but another form of relief, and society as a whole should pay the costs.

This approach to social security has a strong appeal to labor and to many of the underprivileged. "Work or maintenance" is the slogan of the British socialists, and in this country there are many people who put "maintenance" ahead of "work." Interestingly enough, one of the slogans on which Adolf Hitler rode into power in Germany was "Volksversicherung nicht Sozialversicherung"— maintenance of the population, not social insurance. This is, indeed, an appealing concept; at first sight, it seems to be all in favor of the underdog.

This is not the concept of social security of the people who had most to do with giving us the Social Security Act. Among the early advocates of social insurance, none was more conspicuous than Dr. John R. Commons and the late Justice Louis D. Brandeis. These two men were the very people who first advocated varying contribution rates in unemployment insurance, to the end that this institution might serve as not a mere relief measure, but as an incentive to the regularization of employment. This idea came not from reactionaries or business leaders, but from outstanding progressive thinkers.

When the Social Security Act was under consideration in Congress, President Roosevelt urged that any provisions made for unemployment insurance should be directed toward stabilizing employment, not toward mere maintenance of the unemployed. That was the position also which the American Federation of Labor took when, in 1932, it reversed its former stand in opposition to unemployment insurance. The provisions in the Social Security Act permitting experience rating were vigorously supported at the time by the present chairman of the Social Security Board, and the sections on this subject in the laws of most of the thirty-eight states which provide for experience rating were copied verbatim from model bills prepared by the Social Security Board.

Some of these may have changed their ideas since, but it is worth remembering that the concept of experience rating in unemployment compensation came from progressives and was pushed to enactment by them. Very definitely, it is in line with what might be called the progressive thought and traditions of this country.

It may be that progressivism is now outmoded, that we should aim not at revitalizing our economy of free enterprise, but at substituting for it a governmentally controlled economy. In wartime we, undoubtedly, must have a large measure of governmental direction of our economy. We have to accept such things as defense unemployment at the very time when we need to utilize all the labor and capital we have to defeat the Nazis, because economic planning has been defective. Great as may be the risks of such errors and the costs which government control of our economy may entail, nearly everyone will agree that to defeat Hitler we must adopt at least some of his methods. But an economy which, in peace as well as in wartime, is controlled in all respects by the national government is quite another matter.

The glowing picture, painted by the planners, of an economy in which there is always full employment and maintenance, at an American and rising standard of living, is very attractive. But what has happened in Germany may well give us pause. Hitler's planned economy, with its "Volksversicherung" (maintenance of the entire German population by the state) was attractive alike to the great industrialists, the petty shopkeepers, the farmers, and many of the workingmen; but it has meant the wiping out of all real distinctions between private and public property, compulsory labor, and the complete loss of personal freedom, as well as plunging the entire world into a holocaust of war.

I do not suggest that the advocates of a planned economy want to create such conditions as prevail in Germany. I grant their sincere patriotism and their desire to make this a still better country for all our people. But I cannot go with them in seeing the solution of the employment problem in complete governmental control or in looking upon social security as maintenance at public expense.

To me social security remains a group of institutions to take care of the needy, but, above all, to decrease the need for relief by making the widest possible use of insurance principles and encouraging industry to do its utmost to provide employment. Indirect incentives may seem less certain than direct measures of control and extensive participation in industry by government itself, but they seem to me worth trying in the fullest degree possible.

《《《《《《《《《◇》》》》》》》》

Viewing unemployment compensation as basically an insurance institution, I believe that experience rating is necessary to equitably distribute compensation costs.

《《《《《《《◇》》》》》》》

In theory at least, also, experience rating is justified as a measure of incentive taxation. It is socially highly desirable that employers should stabilize their employment. They cannot do so perfectly, some of them perhaps not at all; but there is ample evidence that many employers acting separately can do a great deal to reduce the intermittancy of their employment, and, as Professor Schmidt has suggested, we cannot know what might be accomplished by something like a concerted effort to regularize employment, if employers were encouraged to make such a concerted effort. The statements made by the opponents of experience rating that employers try in every manner possible to keep down their contribution rates, is clear proof that the incentive in this case is very strong and that experience rating does make a difference in employment practices.

Justified doubts about experience rating arise, not from its theory, but from its operation. . . . Some results of experience rating in concrete cases have no logical justification. That experience rating does not work perfectly is not surprising considering its newness. In all insurance, the rates are never perfectly adjusted to the risks. But while defects are understandable, they deserve serious attention. Experience rating as thus far developed is defective in that it does not accurately measure differences in costs and in making it possible through various devices, most of them antisocial, to reduce compensation costs without decreasing unemployment.

If experience rating is to continue, it needs to be improved. The Social Security Board should furnish leadership to this end; but all who believe in experience rating should be on the alert to make it a better instrument for making the contribution rates equitable and [for developing] incentive to reduce not merely compensable unemployment, but all unemployment.

It is my hope that experience rating may be given a real trial and that a major effort will be made to make it a fairer and more serviceable institution. Its abolition by action of Congress would be strongly resented by employers and would be grossly unfair to stable employers and industries and to the states in which such industries predominate. It will work, not to promote national unity, but to create resentments interfering with our maximum defense effort.

To destroy experience rating, by fiat from Washington, would be a sad mistake; to improve experience rating is a vital need. As an old-fashioned progressive, I believe in incentive taxation, although more direct measures to insure full employment may be more appealing.

Federalization of
Unemployment Compensation?

*American Labor Legislation
Review,* Volume XXXII,
Number 1 (March, 1942),
pages 41–48

I N THE United States unemployment compensation has been set up on what is called a federal-state basis. It is established and administered by the states, but the national government, through the Social Security Board, has final control in most respects.

While under the Social Security Act the states were free to pass pretty much any unemployment compensation law they might desire, nearly all of them copied the model bills prepared by the Social Security Board. More variations have developed since, but at all times the Social Security Board has powerfully influenced the provisions of the state laws. Even greater has been its influence in matters of administration. Differing from all other federal aids, the aid for the administration of unemployment compensation is a one-hundred per cent grant. Moreover, the Social Security Board has never allotted this aid on the basis of any formula, but has insisted upon detailed budgets which it must approve and from which the states may not depart.

This system has been under attack from the beginning. In nearly all foreign countries unemployment insurance is administered by their national governments. When the Committee on Economic Security was formulating the Social Security Act, several of its most important staff members tried to work out a similar plan for the United States, although we have in this country a federal and not a unitary form of government. Instead, the committee recommended the present "federal-state" system. One reason for this decision was the inability of the "experts" to agree upon the provisions of a federal law. More important were the considerations that few people then believed that an unemployment compensation system established and administered by the national government would be sustained by the Supreme Court and that there was no support in Congress for such a system.

The first of these reasons has never satisfied the advocates of an unemployment compensation system exclusively controlled and administered by the national government. They have never had any doubt that Congress would write into the federal law the provisions they individually favor, and so they have not been concerned that other people have different ideas as to what these provisions should be. The second reason—that of unconstitutionality—has disappeared altogether with the about-face of the Supreme Court in the great decisions of 1937 and the many changes in the personnel of this highest court. The third reason, however—that of lack of support in Congress—until recently operated to confine discussion of the entire question to academic and administrative circles.

No bill to substitute a nationally-administered unemployment compensation system for the present federal-state system has even been introduced in Congress since enactment of the Social Security Act. When, late in the past summer, newspaper stories from Washington [indicated] . . . that the Administration would propose "federalization" of unemployment compensation, and [this] seemed to be borne out in speeches by Federal Security Administrator McNutt, such an outcry arose from every section of the country that it seemed unlikely that Congress would do anything along this line very soon. The President at this stage made a statement to the effect that while the Administration was very anxious that the coverage of unemployment compensation should be extended and benefits liberalized, no decision had been reached as to how this could best be done.

The treacherous attack of the Axis Powers upon the United States has completely altered this situation. On December 19, the President telegraphed all governors asking that they turn over the control, facilities, and personnel of all public employment offices to the national government. In this telegram a specific statement was made that unemployment compensation was to remain with the States and it was implied that the transfer of the employment offices was to be for the duration only. To this request, all states have complied promptly and on January 1 all public employment offices came under the direct and exclusive administration of the national government. Following this, the President in his budget message of January 7 recommended—along with an increase in payroll taxes, extension of old-age and survivors' insurance, and the establishment of disability compensation and hospitalization payments—the "liberalization and expansion of unemployment compensation in a uniform national system." He also suggested that Congress give precedence to the increase in payroll taxes above all other recommendations in the message.

Whether Congress will comply with this request of the President is still uncertain and no details have been revealed as to what sort of a "uniform national system" will be proposed. What is certain is that these new developments have made the issue of "federalization" a practical political question, upon which Congress is likely to act one way or another.

Arguments For and Against Federalization

The case for "federalization" as made before Pearl Harbor rested basically upon the argument that unemployment, in its most important aspects, is a national problem and, hence, should be the exclusive responsibility of the national government. Supplementing this major argument were claims that the divided control under the federal-state system violates all principles of public administration; that this system entails duplicate tax reporting and often deprives of compensation those workers who migrate or are regularly employed in more than one state; and, above all, that the benefits under the state laws are inadequate and that, by reason of experience rating, we do not now have uniformity of tax burdens among competing employers. Attention was also directed to the wide variance in the reserves of the several states, some being apparently very excessive, while the fear was expressed that others would be exhausted early in the next period of widespread unemployment.

To these arguments the opponents of federalization have replied that national problems do not necessarily have to be dealt with exclusively by officials of the national government. The United States, under its federal system of government, has dealt quite as effectively with national problems as have the unitary governments of Europe. Our national and state governments should not be regarded as hostile and warring governments, but as integral parts of a coördinated federal system of government, such as was contemplated by the founding fathers.

Contacts with the unemployed workmen and with at least the small employers must necessarily be made on the local level. While it may be preferable for large employers operating in many states and the national unions with headquarters in Washington to be relieved of the necessity of dealing with the state as well as the national governments, this is more than offset by the remoteness of the national capital to the small employers and individual workmen.

There is no present danger of the exhaustion of the reserves in any state and benefits can be liberalized under the present system. The inadequacy of the present benefits is mainly attributable to the extreme conservatism of the model bills of the Social Security Board; moreover, benefits have been very materially increased in the few years we have had unemployment compensation. Whether in the long run benefits will be more liberal in an exclusively nationally administered system of unemployment compensation than they would be in the industrialized states under a federal-state system is doubtful. As for experience rating, this is an issue quite apart from federalization. With 39 states now having experience rating, it seems probable that any new law passed by Congress would include provisions for experience rating applicable to the entire country, but no one can be certain what may happen in this respect.

Finally, as regards principles of public administration: the test is whether benefits have been paid promptly and accurately and whether the costs of administration have been unnecessarily high. Much friction has developed between state administrators and the Social Security Board, but as stated by Chairman Altmeyer in a speech to the Interstate Conference of Unemployment Compensation Agencies in 1938: "The Board is of the opinion that a national system would have broken down under the initial impact of the administrative difficulties you have been able to surmount with such a considerable degree of success." Moreover, as developed by Raymond C. Atkinson in his comprehensive study, "The Federal Role

in Unemployment Compensation Administration," the friction between the two groups has been decreasing, and, while trying upon
both, has not harmed the unemployed workmen, and may very well
have resulted in greater progress than would have been made had
control been centralized in Washington. Certain it is that costs of
administration have been low and that the insistence of the Social
Security Board upon selection of the state staffs on a merit basis has
had a most wholesome effect upon state government generally.

Effects of War

The recent developments have strengthened the case for
federalization of unemployment compensation. For the duration we
have not only a national economy but a governmentally-directed
economy. As the founding fathers foresaw, the conduct of war must
necessarily be controlled in all respects by the national government.

The priorities unemployment we now have results from actions of
the national government. The taking-over of the public employment
offices has increased the difficulties of continuing the federal-state
system of unemployment compensation. While heretofore the Social
Security Board has insisted upon the complete integration of the
employment service and unemployment compensation, they are now
under divergent ultimate controls. The segregation of functions
seems to have been intelligently made, but there is a strong likelihood of increased friction as a result of the federalization of the
employment service.

But it is particularly the situation after the war, when our industry will have to be shifted to again serve primarily civilian needs,
which affords the strongest of all arguments for the federalization of
unemployment compensation. Much unemployment can scarcely be
avoided at that stage and the pooling of all unemployment compensation reserves, which now total $2,500,000,000, would help materi-
ally to relieve the situation.

Fairness and Good Faith

While these are telling arguments, much is to be said on
the other side. Very important is the matter of good faith. Conceding
that the national government can legally take over the reserves in

the state unemployment compensation funds, its action in doing so would constitute a violation of the conditions under which these monies were collected and deposited in the Treasury in a special trust fund, and would be regarded by many Americans as a steal. Similarly, the federalization of unemployment compensation represents a direct departure from the promise the President made to the Governors when he asked them to turn the state employment offices over to the national government.

There is also the matter of the fairness of federalization as between different states and different industries and their employees. Unless additional revenues are provided from some new source, the pooling of the unemployment compensation funds, while it will make possible the payment of larger total amounts in benefits in some states, will result in smaller total payments in other states than could otherwise be made. The states which are likely to gain are those with relatively small reserve funds at this time and those in which war production contracts are concentrated. Similarly, pooling is likely to benefit the employers in industries which have more than average unemployment: at this time, the plants and industries which were slow in converting to war production and those adversely affected by priorities; in the transition period after the war, the war industries; and in normal times, industries operating intermittently. While no real studies of these effects have been made, scattered available information indicates that the industries which will benefit most are those in which profits and annual earnings are highest, while the states benefiting will be mainly those with the highest per capita incomes. If large amounts are contributed from the general treasury to the unemployment compensation fund, these larger benefits may not adversely affect anyone, but unless this is done, they are likely to be at the expense of the poorer states, the less profitable industries, and the less well-paid employees.

The question can also be raised whether the costs of the unemployment resulting from war should be borne from the unemployment compensation funds. All other war costs are paid from the general treasury. The unemployment we now have is largely attributable to the war, and the unemployment likely to occur when peace is restored also is properly to be regarded as a part of the costs of the war. While the present reserves are large, they almost certainly will prove insufficient, whether pooled or not, if unemployment compensation is burdened with the entire costs of the unemployment attributable to the war. The British attempt to use unemployment compensation for this purpose after the first World War all but wrecked the British system.

Various methods can be employed to make the costs of relieving unemployment attributable to the war a part of the war costs, as would appear to be logical and equitable. I shall mention but one of these, which is to continue unemployment compensation pretty much as at present but to have the national government pay supplemental compensation (and a dismissal wage, in appropriate cases) to the victims of unemployment due to governmental action in connection with the war. Such supplemental payments could be made through the state agencies and could be financed, in part, from a special assessment on the war contractors and their employees. As the President has large funds at his disposal for the conduct of the war, such a system could probably be put into operation at once, without necessity of any Congressional legislation, if deemed necessary to take care of the expected large volume of priorities unemployment of the next months.

Possible Alternatives

Whether any consideration will be given to alternatives to "federalization" remains to be seen. It should be noted, however, that the President's budget message does not preclude these alternatives. "Federalization" is not the only means for carrying out the President's recommendation for the "liberalization and expansion of unemployment compensation," nor even for "a uniform national system." Nor is there evidence that the President has changed his mind since he recommended in his first message on social security of June 8, 1934: "I am convinced that social insurance should be national in scope, although the several states should meet at least a large portion of the costs of management"—a specification he particularized in his message of January 17, 1935, in recommending a system in which the "states will largely administer unemployment compensation, assisted and guided by the federal government."

At this time, federalization of unemployment compensation is in the offing; many people treat the matter as already settled. There is no certainty, however, even that it will make its appearance on the stage—that is, that it will be proposed by the President. Still less is there information about the form "federalization" might take.

Should federalization come in the near future, all who are interested in unemployment compensation should do everything that they can to make it a success. At this stage, however, there appears to be no need of rushing into such a radical change and careful study of all implications of the proposal would seem to be called for. If the necessity of converting our industries rapidly into full war production requires provisions other than those we now have for taking care of the resulting extensive but short-time unemployment, more immediately effective measures can be adopted to take care of the situation than would be afforded through a proposal to federalize unemployment compensation—which, at the minimum, would involve long delays. Aside from these first months, unemployment during the war period should be at a very low level. This allows ample time for a thorough study of the possible ways of meeting the anticipated large volume of unemployment . . . compensation in the postwar period.

[Addendum]

Since the above article was written, the President, in a letter to Congress on January 20, has recommended the prompt enactment of temporary and emergency legislation appropriating $300,000,000 from the Treasury for supplemental compensation to workers temporarily jobless by reason of plant conversion to war production. Such compensation is to supplement unemployment compensation payable under state laws, with a maximum of 60 per cent of the prior wages or $24 per week for 26 weeks from both sources combined. As a condition of being paid supplemental compensation, the temporarily idle workers must use their time to learn the new war production skills.

The merits of this proposal depend very largely upon the detailed way it is worked out. It can be developed in such a way that it will be a backdoor method of federalizing unemployment compensation. Any such action would be a breach of faith by the national government and would retard rather than promote our victory effort.

Anything of this sort, however, would not seem to be the President's intent. While everything depends upon the details which still have to be supplied, the President's proposal is sound in principle. Workers who are thrown out of work because of actions of the national government necessitated by the war may well be compensated from the general treasury. Basically sound also is the suggestion that compensation paid from the Treasury should be linked with training for war production.

The President's proposal would seem to be one which may well serve also as a precedent for meeting the costs of the expected large volume of unemployment during the period of adjustment after the victory has been won. It renders unnecessary any hurried action on the federalization of unemployment compensation. It would seem to offer a method through which the national government can avoid breaking its promise to leave unemployment compensation undisturbed, which it made to the states when it took over the employment offices for the duration of the war.

How Economic Progress Is Related to Employment Security

Excerpt from *Proceedings*
of the 1956 Educational
Institute presented in co-
operation with the University
of Wisconsin Extension
Division, by the Wisconsin
Chapter, International
Association of Personnel
in Employment Security,
pages 9–14

B OTH MAJOR ASPECTS of employment security—the public employment service and unemployment compensation—were originally established because of widespread unemployment in times of depression. To a very great extent both are still associated in popular thinking with depressions. So both may seem to be far less important today in a period of long-continued near-full employment than in the depression years; and, in the view I have expressed that continuous progress is possible, they will become increasingly less significant.

This concept of the purposes and values of the employment security institutions is far from correct and does not fit actual developments. The public employment service had its beginnings in the 19th century in emergency offices established by municipalities or charitable organizations to help the large number of unemployed workers find jobs in times of widespread unemployment. Established when the emergency was already upon the community, staffed by totally inexperienced personnel, and at all times up against the basic difficulty that employment offices cannot create jobs, these first free public employment offices accomplished very little. But out of this emergency, municipal offices developed the state public employment offices, the state public employment services, the free employment offices connected with the Immigration Service, and, at the time of World War I, the United States Employment Service.

In what is generally referred to as the "Progressive Era" in the first decades of the present century, high hopes were entertained that the public employment offices might become central labor markets, to which the man needing work would come and also the man needing workers, bringing together buyers and sellers of labor, thereby eliminating the wastes involved in unorganized labor markets.

That these high hopes of forty years ago have not been realized must be evident to everybody. Neither in the United States nor any other free country do the majority of all employees get their jobs through the employment offices, and employers do not come to these offices to find the bulk of the men whom they hire. Some employers do so, but certainly not the great majority. Two years ago, in England, I learned that the same situation prevails in that country. Long functioning and efficiently organized as are the British employment exchanges, they have not become the central market for all or substantially all labor, any more than have the public employment offices in this country.

It is now pretty well realized that the central labor market concept of the functions of the public employment offices is unrealistic in a free economy—although it may fit in with a controlled economy, in which production is centrally planned and directed, and in which freedom of choice of occupations and of movement of labor must be restricted. That a central labor market, as conceived forty years ago, is neither possible nor desirable in a free economy, I very much doubt. In periods of great labor shortage a central labor market has distinct advantages, but human nature being what it is, it is natural that employers will believe that they can make better choices of workers than anyone else. Doing what employment offices have always had to do—referring but not hiring workers—destroys at least part of the expected economies of a central labor market, and many employers will not see any advantage in going to the employment office when they can get the workers they need through references from men they already employ or by men seeking work coming to their gates in large numbers. When jobs are not easy to get, good applicants also will try other methods of finding work, in addition to applying at the public employment office. Not often recognized, but I believe to be a fact, even in this country, there are large untapped sources of labor supply to be drawn on when demand for labor is keen and wages rise greatly. We are not an underdeveloped country, with a large volume of chronic unemployment, but we too have many workers who do not work all year 'round, but are ready to do so, when the incentives become sufficiently great.

With the central labor market ideal now appearing unrealistic, the place of the public employment offices in a balanced program for employment security has become something quite different. Employment office people often say that they are always getting the hard employment situations to deal with. Employers give orders to employment offices which they cannot fill through their usual methods of recruiting. Conversely, a high percentage of the workers who come to the employment offices to find jobs are men and women hard to place.

But precisely because this is the character of much of the work public employment offices have to do, they are indispensable. Nearly forty years ago when I had just become secretary of the Industrial Commission of Wisconsin, I gave a report on employment office work in Wisconsin at a meeting of the Association of Public Employment Offices. In it, I stressed that our state then had an unusually low cost per placement. Dr. Royal Meeker, then the United States Commissioner of Labor Statistics, jumped all over me for these statistics. He said that if Wisconsin had such low costs per placement, this indicated that we were doing a poor job—that low placement costs reflected mass service for casuals and domestics of but limited value to either employers or workers. He pointed out that the greatest service employment offices can render lies in the more difficult and costly work of helping employers find hard-to-get employees and in finding jobs for the older people, the handicapped, and other hard-to-place applicants for work.

And Meeker was right. It is in helping employers get workers whom they cannot get through their own efforts, in ascertaining the needs of employers in advance, in carefully selecting the workers referred to them, and in gathering and correctly interpreting data on the business situation and employment prospects, that employment offices are of the greatest value to employers. It is in ascertaining through testing and other methods and in wisely counseling the hard-to-place workers and often getting them into training programs, that the employment offices are most valuable to labor. From the public point of view, the more the work of the employment offices becomes, not mere claims-taking and routine referral to jobs for which orders have been received, but a service concerned with the total employment problems of the community, integrated with all related services, on the community and to some extent the state and national levels, the greater will be the value of the service. And I am not forgetting the need for and value of courtesy and human kindness in dealing with the man who has lost his job and is down on his luck. Beyond help in finding jobs, the big task of the employment service is to help rescue the hope and self-respect of many whose morale is in danger of being completely undermined and destroyed.

Coming to the other major employment security institution, unemployment compensation or unemployment insurance, as it is interchangeably known in the United States, let me first say something about the relation of unemployment compensation and the public employment office. Going back to the beginnings of unemployment compensation in the nineteen thirties, the relation envisioned between the two employment security institutions is clear from the fact that one of the few standards prescribed in the Social Security Act of 1935, which state laws must satisfy to entitle employers to credits against the federal employment tax for payments made to state unemployment insurance funds, is that the compensation payments to unemployed workers must be made through public employment offices or such other agencies as the Social Security Board may approve. This alternative provision led a few states to seek approval for payment of unemployment compensation through other agencies than the public employment offices. The Governor of Ohio in office when the unemployment insurance law of that state took effect proposed to the Social Security Board that it approve payment of unemployment compensation through the state liquor stores, his argument being that liquor stores were to be found in all communities in the state and that they could assume the responsibility for unemployment compensation payments with but little additional expense. The Social Security Board turned down Governor Davey, and has never authorized any other agency to make unemployment compensation payments than the public employment offices.

The thought underlying this provision, which is still part of the

Social Security Act, was that unemployment compensation payments should go only to workers involuntarily unemployed. Whether unemployment is voluntary or involuntary is difficult of determination, apart from the objective tests of exposure to job offers and non-refusal of suitable jobs when offered. So the Social Security Act required that in order that employers may avail themselves of tax offset credits, the state law must require registration for work at a public employment office and provide for the cessation of unemployment compensation when a worker refuses a suitable job open to him.

As for the purposes to be accomplished through unemployment compensation, it is very clear that we now have unemployment insurance laws because of the Great Depression. With many millions of workers without jobs, it was necessary to make public provisions for their support and that of their families. Relief was degrading, uncertain, and very costly. Unemployment insurance came in as a better and less costly method of providing minimum necessary income to unemployed workers and their families.

Experience to date with unemployment insurance on the whole has been quite good. When unemployment insurance was under consideration, it was feared that the promised benefits would prove impossibly costly. The benefits then provided were for maximum periods of 13 or less weeks, and dollar maximum less than $15. So great was the fear that the promised benefits could not be provided at tax (contribution) rates of 2.7 per cent, that practically all states wrote into their original laws provisions for reducing benefits if the reserve funds should run low. Such reduction of benefits has never been necessary in any state. Instead of too small reserve funds, the problem in most states has been one of larger reserves than necessary—in spite of the fact that the taxes collected have averaged only a little more than half of the statutory rate of 2.7 per cent. Benefits have been liberalized in many respects, even when account is taken of the reduced purchasing power of the dollar. This liberalization has been most significant with respect to the maximum duration of benefit, now averaging more than twice as long as that provided for in the original state laws. A fairly large percentage of the insured workers have exhausted their benefit rights before returning to work or finding other jobs, but that percentage has not been nearly as great as English experience led us to expect. There have occurred a

good many scandals and outcries over chiselers who have drawn unemployment compensation when not entitled to compensation.
Nearly all these situations have come to light in large urban centers
where effective policing is most difficult. But in the majority of the
states there never have been such scandals, and great vigor and even
severity has been displayed in dealing with chiselers. To me it is
also significant that by far the most common form of cheating has
taken the form that workers who were unemployed have collected
compensation after they were working in other jobs. The much
dreaded danger, that unemployment compensation would encourage
idleness, appears not to have materialized. In the economic ups and
downs we have had in the 15 years of actual experience with unemployment insurance, this institution has proven a bulwark in our
economy, operating toward stability and the maintenance of a high
level economy. It has also enabled most workers who have experienced unemployment to tide over such adverse periods without having to go on relief.

But the limitations of unemployment insurance have become
equally clear. Unemployment insurance is of no value to unemployed people who have had no employment or only very little
employment in the past year or who have exhausted their benefit
rights. Unemployment compensation has not obviated the need for
relief. The people benefiting from unemployment insurance and
those on relief have been fairly distinct groups. Most of those on
relief have little employment save in periods of greatest employment.
For them, unemployment compensation is not adequate to keep
them off relief. But unemployment compensation is a valuable safeguard to the man or woman who is normally regularly employed.
At times these groups overlap. The people often on relief rolls at
times get quite steady employment, thereby qualifying for unemployment compensation when they lose their jobs. Conversely, when
either the general business situation or the economic conditions of a
particular industry become such as to produce long periods of unemployment, people who normally are regularly employed qualify
for unemployment insurance; and in such situations that unemployment compensation has proven of undoubted value.

In better times—such as fortunately have prevailed during most
of the time unemployment insurance laws have been in effect—unemployment compensation has fitted best the laid-off worker. When

the unemployment insurance laws were enacted most of the discussion centered around the workers who had lost their jobs and were seeking other employment. In operation there have been many more claimants for unemployment compensation who have been laid off but expect to return to their old jobs than workers who have been discharged and must look for other employment. And for the laid-off worker, unemployment insurance has proven a godsend and reasonably adequate.

But it has become very clear that unemployment compensation is not all-sufficient for employment security. At present only slightly more than half of the unemployed are receiving unemployment insurance. The other half of the unemployed include some agricultural workers, domestics, and others who are in employments or establishments to which unemployment insurance laws do not apply. Around 200,000 may be insured workers who have exhausted their benefit rights. The large number are marginal workers who have only a slight or tenuous connection with the labor force. They have jobs in covered industries when employment conditions are very good, but are the first to be let go when the business situation takes a turn for the worse.

Long ago Lord Beveridge, who is the world's greatest authority on the subject, pointed out that while unemployment insurance is most necessary and desirable for the man who has a reasonably good prospect of getting back into employment quite soon, the man long unemployed or who has never been able to get or hold a job for any length of time needs something more than unemployment insurance. That something more is often re-orientation and training, assistance in moving, and similar measures. Unemployment insurance —in which I thoroughly believe—is not alone sufficient for employment security. It is but one program for a reasonably satisfactory approach to this great problem. Particularly in periods of business decline and still more in deep depression, it must be supplemented by other measures, such as training, the creation of new jobs, and adequate stimuli for full employment.

In recent years there has been growing recognition that what we must have is a total approach to the problems of employment security. We have come to the time when the problem is seen as one of employment security, not of unemployment compensation and the placement of unemployed people. These are still very important aspects of employment security, but not all there is to employment security. Included within the concepts of employment security are not merely unemployment compensation and employment services, but also continuous studies of the employment situation and the gathering of information for anticipation of employment needs and opportunities. There is also a realization that employment security is closely related to, if it does not include, training and retraining of people needing such services to improve their employment possibilities, and testing and guidance to help job seekers to make the most of their opportunities. Attention is being given increasingly to special groups in the total labor force whose employment problems are distinctive, the young workers, the older people, the handicapped and disabled, the veterans, the part-time workers, and still others. The entire job is seen as one of high level employment for the society and employment suited to the needs and capacities of the individual, and of developing these capacities to their maximum possibilities. Nowhere is this complete job now being done, but there is a better appreciation now than we had earlier of the nature of the problems of employment security and of the far-reaching objectives of the governmental programs in this field.

This is a much broader concept than prescribed when the public employment offices were established and when unemployment compensation was instituted. And it is one which is in complete harmony with the American concept of economic growth and progress.

IV

ISSUES
IN HEALTH

I N THIS PART we come to an involved set of hazards to economic security associated with illness and disability. There is the possibility for every family of short- or long-term loss of income; beyond this there is the risk of extraordinary costs of medical and hospital care. Measures to alleviate these economic losses are separable from private and public measures to minimize or prevent illness and disability. Witte asserted that "in normal times more Americans sink to the poverty line and become dependent by reason of sickness than for any other cause."

The first question in any discussion of these hazards is apt to be: What is the nature and extent of the several parts of the problem? The second is: What approaches can we take to them?

The approach of workmen's compensation is identified by Witte as "a scheme for dividing the cost of accident, on a predetermined equitable basis, without reference to fault, and justified upon the principle of least social cost."

Can this "principle of least social cost" be the basis for a system of general compulsory health insurance? Is there a better alternative in either direct public provision of health care or in private, voluntary health insurance? Should health insurance concentrate upon the wage loss problem or upon the cost of care?

The Theory of
Workmen's Compensation

---

*American Labor Legislation
Review,* Volume 20,
Number 4 (December, 1930),
pages 411–418 [1]

THE DICTIONARY defines a theory as "the act or result of looking into or contemplating any object or group of objects, or any series of events; a mental plan or scheme framed to agree with the observed facts and designed as a rational explanation of them." In this sense, there is no adequate theory of workmen's compensation. Like Topsy, workmen's compensation has "just growed," and everybody has been too much concerned with immediate practical problems to give much thought to theory. A broad and valid constitutional foundation has been developed; but the usual economic explanation and justification of the compensation laws, I submit, is crude and untenable.

This generally accepted theory has two parts, one an explanation of workmen's compensation, the other a social justification. Workmen's compensation is described as a system for placing the cost of accidents, or the resulting economic loss, upon industry. In justification, the second part of the usual theory asserts that industry adds the compensation it pays to the costs of the product and shifts this cost to the consumers.

[1] Address, Twenty-third Annual Meeting, American Association for Labor Legislation, at New Orleans, December 28, 1929.

This theory was derived from the German system of social insurance, but was carried over to the American laws, although these departed far from the German system. It occurs in the reports of most of the state commissions which drafted the original compensation laws of 1910 and 1911, and has survived, practically without dissent, to this day. While often reiterated, it has, however, apparently influenced very little the actual course of compensation law and practice. From its inception, it has represented rather a sugar coating to make workmen's compensation palatable than the true content of the remedy.

Does Industry Pay?

The first proposition in this theory, that the purpose of the compensation acts is to place the economic cost of industrial accidents upon industry, perhaps expresses the ideal, but certainly is not a rational interpretation of the existing compensation laws.

To begin with, workmen's compensation does not place the *entire* cost of accidents on industry. The most liberal of our compensation laws allow the injured workman two-thirds of his wage loss, and even these laws limit the period during which compensation is payable and prescribe a maximum wage for purposes of computing compensation. The effect of these limitations appears in a study of the Wisconsin law, made by the chief statistician of the industrial commission of Wisconsin. Although this law is rated by insurance companies as standing third highest in its aggregate benefits, employers in Wisconsin pay only about 30 per cent of the total loss sustained by injured workmen; and some compensation laws pay less than one-half the Wisconsin benefits.

Even if this first proposition in the usually accepted theory is modified to the extent of placing *a part only* of the economic cost of accidents upon industry, it still does not fit most of the existing laws, since they make the employer, not industry, liable for the statutory compensation. True, most of these laws require the employer to insure, but, except in California, it is only when insurance is carried in a state fund that the employer is thereby relieved from liability. When an employer carries compensation insurance, the liability of the insurance company is primary; but the employer remains secondarily liable. When the insurance company fails or for any other reason defaults in payment, the employer must come to the rescue.

The responsibility of the individual employer is increased by provisions in the compensation laws for payment of additional compensation in certain contingencies: when the accident is due to a violation of a safety law or order, when the injured is a minor illegally employed, when payment of compensation is unreasonably delayed, and in still other situations. Such provisions invariably include a prohibition against all insurance of the liability for increased compensation, the underlying idea being to penalize the employer who is at fault. The same consideration has led to the widespread adoption of schedule (merit) and experience rating in the determination of compensation insurance rates, as a result of which the rate of any given employer depends to a very great extent upon his own equipment, activities, and record in accident prevention.

These features, which represent mainly recent innovations, have extended the liability of the individual employer. On the other hand, there have been some other new features which look toward liability on an industry, rather than an individual employer, basis. Most of the existing compensation laws do not proceed exclusively upon either of these bases, but use both; however, of the two, the liability of the individual employer is emphasized distinctly the more.

Does the Consumer Pay?

Let us now consider the second part of the usual statement of the theory of workmen's compensation: That the employer adds the compensation paid injured workmen to the cost of production and shifts this cost to the consumers. Does this concept agree with the known facts?

There is within each state a wide range in compensation costs among employers in the same industries. In a Wisconsin industrial city there are two large aluminum goods factories, one with a good, the other with a bad, accident record. The first has a compensation insurance rate of $1.15; the second, of $3.00. In another Wisconsin city is a third large aluminum goods factory. A few years ago, after years of self-insurance, this concern insured with a mutual insurance company. Because of its highly favorable accident experience, this company received a rate of $1.00. At the end of the year it was paid back 20 per cent of its premiums in dividends; yet the insurance company in that year made $15,000 on the risk. This company is now again a self-insurer, and its accident cost in 1929 probably will not exceed 50 or 60 cents per $100 of payroll. Which compensation cost of these three factories is shifted to the consumers of aluminum goods: $3.00, $1.15 or 50 cents per $100 of payroll?

This is not an unusual situation; on the contrary, it is what happens right along under schedule and experience rating. Last year, experience rating was extended to three-fourths of the entire compensation insurance premiums in Wisconsin, and schedule rating to three-eighths of the total. Besides, employers who insure with state funds or with mutual insurance companies have an appreciably lower rate than those who insure with stock companies, because the overhead expenses of these carriers are less than those of the stock companies. Self-insured employers pay no overhead to insurance companies at all, and many of them have such a good accident experience that what they pay in compensation is but a small fraction of the cost falling upon insured competitors.

To these differences within each state must be added differences between states in compensation benefits. On January 1, 1929, the New York law was rated by insurance companies as having a general level of benefits of 1,000; those of Massachusetts and Pennsylvania at 714 and 715, respectively. Arizona's law was rated at the top, 1,031; New Mexico's law at the bottom, 484. These are neighboring mining states; but which compensation cost was reflected in the price of copper or silver: the cost of the New Mexico operators, under a law rated at 484, or the cost of the Arizona operators, under that rated at 1,031?

Varying costs do not necessarily mean that the payments made by employers for compensation or compensation insurance are not shifted to the consumers. Economic theory teaches us that, both under conditions of competition and under conditions of monopoly, these costs *may* be shifted, in whole or in part, depending upon the elasticity of demand and other factors. It does not assert, however, that the entire cost is necessarily or usually shifted, nor does it answer what part is passed on to the consumers in any concrete case. Similarly, the extent to which compensation costs are shifted is not statistically measurable. It is probable that a part of the costs are normally shifted; but all employers, with their greatly varying costs, certainly do not escape painless. If employers were able to shift all their costs, they would have no reason to be concerned about the level of compensation benefits. In fact, they are very much concerned; and who would say that their concern is foolish?

"The Least Social Cost"

So much by way of destructive criticism; now for an attempt to formulate a more defensible theory. Workmen's compensation does not place the cost of accidents upon industry, but provides for a sharing of the resulting economic loss between employers and employees on a predetermined basis, without reference to fault, under a plan designed to insure prompt and certain recovery, at minimum expense. Its justification is not that the consumers in the end pay the bill, but that workmen's compensation reduces the economic loss resulting from industrial accidents to a minimum. This is the principle of "the least social cost," a phrase coined by the late E. H. Downey in his book on workmen's compensation—the philosophy of eliminating industrial waste, which President Hoover and his fellow engineers have made familiar in recent years.

This theory makes the prevention of accidents the foremost objective of an adequate compensation law. The remarkable records made by some plants show the possibilities of sincere, practical efforts at accident prevention; the failure to materially reduce the total number of industrial acidents points to the need for redoubled efforts in this field, and, perhaps, calls for new methods and devices. We need particularly to reach the small employers, who seem thus far to have been practically untouched by the safety movement. The compensation law which does not encourage accident prevention and the compensation commission which does not interest itself in this problem miss the most important of all their opportunities.

Next, this principle of the least social cost demands that workmen who are accidentally injured shall be restored, physically and industrially, as completely and promptly as possible. In this respect, genuine progress has undoubtedly been made. Medical benefits have been distinctly liberalized, and most states now give at least some attention to vocational rehabilitation. That the majority of the compensation laws still limit medical benefits, however, proves that the possibilities of preventing needless waste through measures of this kind are even now not fully appreciated.

Equitable Distribution

With reference to the cash indemnity, the principle of the least social cost does not demand that the *entire* economic loss due to accidents should be placed upon the employer. Rather, it suggests an equitable distribution of the costs between the employer and the employee, with benefits adjusted so that, on the one hand, there will be an incentive to the injured workman to return to work as soon as he can safely do so, and, on the other, assurance that his standard of living will not have to be lowered while he is disabled. Further, it calls for eliminating the wastes involved in slow and uncertain benefits and in unnecessarily high overhead costs.

This consideration condemns court administration of workmen's compensation, which invariably has meant shortchanging, delay, and expense. The enforcement of compensation laws is an administrative, rather than a judicial, problem, and it is a sad mistake to burden the courts with this duty. It is, also, a mistake for compensation boards to assume the attitude that they are judicial bodies and have nothing to do with enforcing payment, unless there is a dispute and the case is brought to them for decision.

The principle of the least social cost, further, suggests caution in the introduction of refinements in benefits which, while tending toward more exact justice, result in an increased number of contests, with their inevitable delay. It requires that the costs to employers and their competitive conditions be given consideration as well as the needs of the injured employees. Lastly, it raises the question whether it is really necessary that forty cents out of every dollar collected from employers for compensation insurance by the stock companies go to overhead.

As a final conclusion to be drawn from the principle of the least social cost, I submit the thought that there is nothing sacrosanct in the existing compensation laws or any of their features. This theory of workmen's compensation demands neither that industry nor that the individual employer shall be held liable for compensation. Either basis is possible, or a combination of the two, as is being developed in this country. The test is not whether industry or the employer is made responsible, but which works best and results in the least cost to society, including in this term the employers, the employees, and the general public.

Likewise, as the United States Supreme Court has held, compensation does not have to be based upon wage loss. And certainly there is nothing in the theory of workmen's compensation that recovery be allowed only for results attributable wholly to accidents, and not for consequences in which the injuries sustained are merely contributing factors, or that only accidents be compensated to the exclusion of other injuries directly traceable to the employment. The "dangerous tendency toward liberalization," which F. Robertson Jones has denounced, is not a departure from the theory of workmen's compensation, but a logical and necessary extension, to better carry out its true purposes. Workmen's compensation, even now, is far from being perfect, and no provision of the existing laws is so sacred that it should not be changed if something better is offered.

A Social Theory

The theory suggested is a truly social one. Any individualistic basis for workmen's compensation is manifestly untenable. Workmen's compensation does not place the entire cost of accidents upon the employers, but it does make them liable in many cases without fault on their part. A requirement that even one dollar of compensation must be paid for any accident for which the employer was not to blame cannot be justified upon principles of individual liability; neither can payment of anything less than full damages when the employer is at fault without negligence on the part of the injured employee.

This problem has been met, on the legal side, by the courts' development of a constitutional justification resting upon social grounds. This is the police power, the most social of all powers of government. Some state courts, having to deal only with elective laws, have regarded workmen's compensation as a contractual arrangement, voluntarily entered into by both the employer and the employee. The United States Supreme Court, confronted by compulsory as well as elective laws, has found a much broader basis for workmen's compensation, namely, the police power, the right of the public, in the interests of the general welfare to place restrictions upon freedom of contract and rights of property. Its conception of workmen's compensation appears in Cudahy Packing v. Parramore, 44 Sup. Ct. 153 (1924):

Workmen's compensation legislation rests upon the idea of status, not upon that of implied contract; that is, upon the conception that the injured workman is entitled to compensation for an injury sustained in the service of an industry to whose operations he contributes his work as the owner contributes his capital—the one for the sake of wages and the other for the sake of profits. The liability is based, not upon any act or omission of the employer, but upon the existence of the relationship which the employee bears to the employment because of and in the course of which he has been injured.

Here, we have not only a broad and sound constitutional foundation for workmen's compensation, but one that rests upon truly social considerations. The court does not proceed on the unproven assumption that compensation costs are shifted; there never has been one line in a decision of the United States Supreme Court to this effect. Instead, it bases its argument upon the progressive position that industry exists, not for the benefit of the stockholders alone, but also of the employees.

Unfortunately, the economic justification of the compensation laws has not been developed to the same point; in fact, there has been little progress here since workmen's compensation was first discussed.[2] The generally accepted theory of compensation will not bear examination. Further, putting forward the indefensible proposition that the employer should bear the entire cost of accidents makes it more difficult to secure an equitable division of the cost of accidents. When we cease talking about industry's bearing the entire cost of accidents, we may get support for a program of splitting the total costs on something like a fifty-fifty basis, which would represent an immense gain over existing standards, even in the best laws.

Similarly, the theory of workmen's compensation suggested serves to bring out clearly the relation of workmen's compensation to other forms of social insurance. The opponents of health insurance and

[2] Notable exceptions are the discussions of the theory of workmen's compensation by two eminent legal writers: Ernst Freund in *Standards of American Legislation* and Roscoe Pound in his *Theory of the Common Law*. The conception of workmen's compensation and the views expressed as to its social justification are in substantial accord with those presented in this paper, although the approach and emphasis are somewhat different.

unemployment insurance have stressed the thought that these forms of social insurance differ fundamentally from workmen's compensation. As long as the purpose of compensation is presented as being to place the entire cost of accidents upon industry, because industry is responsible therefor, this argument has great force. Clearly, industry is not responsible for all sickness or unemployment among its employees; and it is unjust and socially unwise to throw the entire cost of sickness or unemployment among wage-earners upon industry. When, however, compensation is presented in its true light, as a scheme for dividing the cost of accidents on a predetermined equitable basis, without reference to fault, and when it is justified upon the principle of the least social costs, it becomes apparent that workmen's compensation is a form of social insurance and rests fundamentally upon the same basis as do other types not yet adopted in this country.

But whether you agree with me or not, may I express the hope that you interest yourself in the problem of developing a theory of compensation which will be both sound and progressive?

Compulsory Health Insurance

Excerpt from "The Social
Security Act and Proposed
Changes" presented to the
Association of Clinic
Managers, Sheboygan,
Wisconsin, *Proceedings,
Twelfth Annual Conference,*
September 23 and 24, 1937,
pages 32–37

How [IS] THE SOCIAL SECURITY MOVEMENT likely to affect the medical profession? In discussing this subject permit me to state my conclusions at the beginning:

I think there is a remote possibility, but only a remote possibility, that health insurance may become a major issue in the next session of Congress, or in the session following; and a much lesser chance that a health insurance bill will be enacted into law. Not quite so remote, but still very unlikely, is the possibility that some state may actually experiment with health insurance. On the other hand, there is a strong likelihood of the continuance of the present, very marked trend toward socialized medicine. I expect this trend toward socialized medicine to continue, but believe compulsory health insurance to be quite unlikely.

Health insurance is the oldest and most widely prevalent form of social insurance the world over. The first social insurance law enacted in any country was a compulsory health insurance law. Health insurance is in operation in more countries than any other form of social insurance. It exists, in one form or another, in every European country, as well as in many South American countries and in

Japan. Health insurance in all the countries where it has been tried seems to be successful at least to the degree that there appears to be no likelihood of its abandonment. During the Depression, when health insurance systems and all other forms of social insurance, in fact, all economic institutions, were subjected to a very severe trial, health insurance not only survived but was extended in many coun- tries.

Health insurance is an institution—and I am speaking of health insurance as it exists in foreign countries—which serves two major purposes: (1) that of providing partial compensation for wage losses due to illness; and (2) medical care for people in low income groups. The original purpose in health insurance, and still the major pur- pose in European countries, is the former of these objectives. In the course of the years, however, there has been increasing emphasis upon the medical care aspects. Health insurance is now, in European countries, something of an institution for medical care for people in low income groups, as well as an institution to provide partial com- pensation for wage losses due to illness. Yet even today, practically every country pays more for cash benefits than for medical care. While the medical care aspect has been growing in European coun- tries, the wage loss aspect is still the largest part of health insurance practically everywhere.

Now I want to discuss briefly the health insurance movement in this country. We have had two major health insurance movements, one during the years 1915 to 1919, and the other since 1932. In the first period, the agitation for health insurance was an outgrowth of the workmen's compensation movement. Workmen's compensation was started in this country in practically all states from 1911 to 1915, and the people who had pushed workmen's compensation quite naturally thought of health insurance as the next step in the same general direction. When this movement started, the advocates of health insurance were mainly social workers and reformers, but they received considerable support from organized labor and progressive employers. The medical profession at the outset was neutral. This is indicated by the fact that the American Medical Association em- ployed as its expert on this subject the late Doctor I. M. Rubinow, who, for many years, was one of the leading advocates of health in- surance in this country. At that stage, the opposition came principally from the casualty insurance companies, who felt that compulsory health insurance would result in a lessened sale of commercial health insurance policies. In the end, the movement for compulsory health insurance in the years 1915 to 1919 came to nothing, despite favorable reports by a number of state legislative commissions. It came to nothing because the cry was raised, "Made in Germany." We entered the World War in 1917 and health insurance, which like all other forms of social insurance started in Germany, was doomed when its opponents branded it a product of the Kaiser's machinations.

By 1920 the compulsory health insurance movement, which started so auspiciously in 1915, was dead and throughout the 'twenties there was but little agitation for health insurance in this country. Another health insurance movement, which still continues, however, began in 1932 when the Committee on the Cost of Medical Care filed its report. This present movement began when the doctors who constituted this committee adopted several different positions on health insurance and to this day doctors are the group in the population who have been most interested in the proposal.

After the Committee on the Cost of Medical Care made its report, the next important development in connection with health insurance was the appointment of the President's Committee on Economic Security in June, 1934, following a message of the President, in which he said that at the opening of the next Congress in January, 1935, he would present for its consideration a comprehensive program for social security. In creating this committee, of which I was named executive director, the President expressly instructed it to study all aspects of the problems and to make recommendations to him for the comprehensive program for social security he was pledged to present to Congress.

These instructions made it obligatory upon our committee to study health insurance along with other methods for providing social security. Our committee, at the outset, however, did not regard health insurance as being of comparable importance with old-age security and with unemployment insurance. But such was the ferment among the doctors following the report of the Committee on the Cost of Medical Care that they would not let our committee treat health insurance as if it were a subject of secondary importance. The President of the United States received more telegrams on the subject of health insurance than on any other aspect of social security, barring only telegrams in support of the Townsend old-age pension plan. The members of the committee and I, personally, as executive director, had to devote more time to people interested in knowing what we were going to do about health insurance, than we were able to give any of the major lines of inquiry.

When it became apparent that health insurance would have to be given much more attention than we had contemplated, we created a Medical Advisory Committee, composed of some 15 leaders in the medical profession, including the presidents of three major medical organizations of the country. Because this Medical Advisory Committee had not completed its deliberations, the Committee on Economic Security in its report to the President and Congress in January, 1935, merely stated that it would make a later report on the subject of medical care; but that it had already reached the conclusion that, if we are to have health insurance in this country, it must be compulsory.

This statement in the report of the committee led to the special meeting of the House of Delegates of the American Medical Association held in Chicago in February, 1935, the first and only special meeting of this association since the World War. At that convention, the American Medical Association adopted a new statement on its attitude toward health insurance—one of unyielding opposition to compulsory health insurance, but support for voluntary health insurance under the control of the medical associations.

At the same convention, other resolutions were adopted which were very critical of the Social Security Act as introduced in Congress. One of these recited that compulsory health insurance was about to be foisted on the country. There was nothing in this bill about health insurance except that the Social Security Board should study the subject along with other problems of social security. This provision had been inserted because the Committee on Economic Security was doubtful whether it was timely to do anything about health insurance, but felt that, as a minimum, it should recommend further study of the subject.

I recall vividly the effect which the resolutions of the American Medical Association produced in Congress. The Social Security Act was then under consideration in executive sessions of the Ways and Means Committee. On the morning following the adoption of these resolutions, I was besieged by members of this committee who wanted to know, "What is there about health insurance in this bill? Are you putting something over on us? If the doctors resent the clause about studying health insurance, why not strike it out to appease them?"

So the Ways and Means Committee struck out of the bill this direction that the Social Security Board should study health insurance, but kept in the bill the instruction that the board shall study all aspects of social security. Pursuant to this direction the Social Security Board has studied health insurance along with other social security problems, but has never made any report on the subject.

This is the story down to this year. I think some of you may know what has happened this year better than I do. As to that, I cannot give you any inside information. I can only recite what has been reported through the newspapers.

At the American Medical Association Convention which was held in June of this year at Atlantic City, Senator J. Hamilton Lewis of Illinois who heads the Subcommittee on Social Security of the Committee on Labor of the United States Senate, stated that he had conferred with the President prior to his appearance on the Atlantic City program, and that the President had suggested to him (Senator Lewis) that he should challenge the American Medical Association to advise the Administration what the doctors believe can and should be done to improve the medical care received by people in the low income groups. Following this speech the American Medical Association adopted a resolution accepting this challenge and pledging co-operation to the President.

Based upon Senator Lewis' speech, many people have jumped to the conclusion that some sort of a health insurance bill will be presented by the Administration in the next session of Congress. As I have said, I have not the slightest information whether it will do so or not. I believe, however, that if such a bill is to be presented, it is very strange that the President should have announced it in such a round-about way. Besides this incident, a leading Administration senator, Senator Wagner, has recently stated that he believes that health insurance is the next step toward more complete social security. This indicates that there is some sentiment among members of Congress for health insurance. Whether that sentiment is sufficiently strong to render likely any action in the next session looking toward health insurance, however, is very doubtful.

On this entire subject, the thinking among people interested in social security is, I believe, undergoing considerable change. In the first movement for health insurance in this country, the emphasis was upon the wage loss due to illness, health insurance being urged as a method for providing partial compensation for this wage loss. In this more recent movement for health insurance, the emphasis has been upon medical care; in fact, many health insurance proposals have left out all provisions for cash benefits. Illustrating this tendency, the health insurance that has been enacted in the Province of British Columbia provides only for medical care, and the health insurance bills in most of the state legislatures this past winter, likewise, left out all cash benefits.

Among people interested in social security, there is a strong feeling at the present time that it may be advisable to treat separately the problem of compensating wage loss due to sickness and the subject of better medical care for people in the low income groups. Sickness is among the most important causes of unemployment. It accounts for approximately seven days of wage loss per year for the wage-workers in the country. In a normal period, sickness is responsible for approximately one-fourth of all unemployment, and over an entire business cycle for one-eighth of all unemployment. Clearly, sickness is one of the major causes of unemployment. Accordingly, it has occurred to some of the people who are interested in improving social security in this country that the logical thing to do is to compensate the wage losses due to sickness under the unemployment compensation acts, rather than to set up a new compulsory health insurance system. No concrete proposals along this line have been worked out, but a number of people who have given thought to the problem are inclining toward this method of dealing with the wage losses due to illness.

Such a solution would leave unsolved the problem of more adequate medical care for the people in low income groups, which is the aspect of health insurance about which the doctors have been most concerned. As to this aspect of the problem, I believe that health insurance will not be established unless a substantial number of doctors want it to be established. The medical profession has apparently turned thumbs down on any insurance device for medical care, at least of a compulsory nature; and so long as it persists in this attitude we will not have health insurance.

Instead we will probably have increased public medical services. I think you are all aware that there has been for some years a strong tendency in that direction. Already in 1929, of all the money expended for medical care, one-sixth came from general tax sources. During the Depression there has been a great extension of these public medical services, with the general approval of the medical profession. In view of this trend and the attitude of the profession there are many thinking people—for instance, Surgeon-General Parran—who believe that the greatest progress toward more adequate medical care can be made through the extension of public medical services. Insurance plans are out because they have been labelled in the medical profession as "socialized medicine," but because of this fact we may get real socialized medicine.

There is one more aspect of this entire problem which I had not appreciated until I visited British Columbia this summer. In this country, as in Canada, a large portion of the population are today expecting medical services to be furnished to them gratuitously because they have been getting their medical services at the taxpayers' expense for some years. In British Columbia working people are saying: "Why make contributions to the cost of medical care as is required under compulsory health insurance? Why should we pay any part of the costs? Let the taxpayers provide the care." I think this will be the reaction also of the millions who have gotten medical care without cost to them, if compulsory health insurance is seriously pushed in this country.

I have talked very frankly to you. I have presented my own views only. I am not speaking for anybody. I have no connections with the national government at this time. I have given you my ideas only as a student of this problem and I may be very mistaken.

But this is as I see the situation: There will be bills on compulsory health insurance in the next session of Congress, as there have been for years. There will be continued agitation among groups in the population who believe in compulsory health insurance. There is likely to be continued interest in this subject in the medical profession. But, I think, there is not much likelihood of the early adoption of compulsory health insurance anywhere in this country. On the other hand, I expect a continued trend toward increased public medical services to be supplied to the people in the low income groups at general taxpayers' expense.

Whether my forecast will prove correct, I think, will depend very largely upon the medical profession, that is, upon what the profession wants. Does the profession want a contributory insurance plan for providing medical care for people who alone cannot finance adequate care? Does the profession want tax-supported medicine for people in low income groups? These questions have to be decided by the profession itself. I have the highest regard for the profession. No other group of people has a better record of service to society than the medical profession. I am willing to let the profession decide what it wants to do about health insurance, but I urge the doctors to face the realities of the situation. Those realities are that profound changes are occurring at this time in the economic aspects of medical care and that, through doing nothing, this country is rapidly drifting toward socialized medicine. What the medical profession decides should be done will be given great weight by the American people, but if it offers nothing constructive, present trends will probably continue and be accelerated.

Address at the Iowa Conference for Social Welfare, at Des
Moines, April 20, 1940

Health is of vital importance both to individuals and to
society. Without good health the individual is seriously handicapped.
He cannot pull his own load and becomes a drain upon his family
or the community. To society, illness is a major cause of economic
loss; prior to the Depression it was by far the most important cause
of dependency and, while now overshadowed by unemployment, is
still one of the principal reasons why so many people become public
charges.

Health security involves four related but distinguishable matters:
the prevention of disease, medical and related care, payment of the
costs of disease prevention and medical care, and provisions for the
support of breadwinners who are ill and their dependents. The last
two of these matters are exclusively economic problems; the first
two are primarily medical problems, but both have important economic aspects. In discussing health security, I shall, of course, deal
only with the economic aspects, which, while basically not as important as the medical aspects, are the principal barriers which keep
many millions of Americans from getting adequate medical care and
which account for the fact that preventable diseases, annually, still

take a vast toll, despite all our knowledge about how to prevent these diseases.

The prevention of disease is the most important aspect of health security. In this respect there has been very gratifying progress and the United States has a better record than any other major country. Gratifying as has been our progress, however, there is still a great volume of preventable and postponable disease which is not being prevented or postponed. To illustrate: 70,000 people die from tuberculosis each year; 150,000 from pneumonia. Medical opinion is unanimous that 30,000 lives could be saved annually if cancer in easily accessible parts of the body could be given early attention. One-half to two-thirds of 14,000 maternal deaths each year are preventable; one-third to one-half of the 70,000 deaths of infants in the first month of life; two-fifths of the 75,000 stillbirths. Even diseases like typhoid and smallpox, which can be entirely eliminated, still claim many victims. We have only begun to seriously tackle the problem of stamping out venereal disease, which the Scandinavian countries have proven to be an attainable objective.

Further progress in preventing disease and thereby saving lives is not merely a matter of increased appropriations for public health services. The total expenditures for all public health services on all governmental levels in the United States, and including the entire costs of food and drug inspection, are $130,000,000 per year—$1.00 per capita. For this small expenditure the American people have been getting more real value than probably from any other expenditures of like amount. With somewhat larger expenditures for public health services, a great deal more could be accomplished. But at the stage we have now reached, further progress in disease prevention depends not only upon the amount of money expended, but upon the orientation of our public health services.

In the past, public health services have been concerned mainly with such matters as sanitation, quarantine, public health education, and statistics. To an ever increasing degree, public health services now involve actual treatment of disease and the correction of conditions likely to result in disability. Preventive public health services and public medical care are becoming inseparable. Further rapid progress in preventing illness depends very largely upon making the right kind of care and treatment available to those who otherwise would be without it. To translate the examinations of school children into effective means for the early correction of health defects, it is necessary to give actual corrective treatment to the many children whose parents cannot afford the costs of such treatment. To make headway against syphilis and other venereal diseases, long expensive treatment of the infection is necessary, and that is possible for many of these unfortunates only at public expense. Even vaccination and immunization treatments cannot be extended to all Americans, unless those who cannot pay the costs can get the services gratis. These are but a few illustrations of the very evident fact that public health services are increasingly coming to involve much direct medical care, and that further progress in preventing diseases is very largely dependent upon further extension of what alone may properly be called "socialized medicine"—medical care at the taxpayers' expense, rather than at the expense of the patients, the doctors, or private charity.

It is not generally appreciated how large a part of the cost of medical care in this country is now being provided from tax funds. Many people who discuss the problem paint an alarmist picture about the dangers of socialized medicine. The truth is that we have long had a considerable volume of socialized medicine in the United States. In 1936, at least $516,000,000 was paid by the government of the United States for health services. Today that total is considerably greater. At least one-sixth—more likely a fifth—of all expenditures for health services are now met from tax funds. Less than one-fourth of these governmental expenditures for health are devoted to what are ordinarily called "public health services." The remainder goes for the care and treatment of people who cannot pay their own care, or who can pay part of the costs only, and for treatment of expensive or contagious diseases. More than half of all public expenditures for health goes to hospitals. Seventy per cent of all hospital beds and 77 per cent of all hospital patients are in publicly supported hospitals. Most of these beds and patients are in hospitals for mental diseases or for tuberculosis, but 37 per cent of all beds in general hospitals are in governmentally owned and operated hospitals. Moreover, during the period 1923 to 1935, the beds in publicly supported hospitals increased by 57 per cent, while those in private hospitals increased but 17 per cent.

The United States does not now have an exclusively private system of medical care. What we have is a mixed system of private and socialized medicine. Usually the same practitioners are engaged in both types of medical practice. The doctor who gets most of his income from private practice does not hesitate to collect from the state, city, or county when he treats an indigent patient or a public charge— although this is socialized medicine. What is, perhaps, most significant is that for some time past there has been a pronounced tendency toward an increasing percentage of socialized medicine. To cite but one item: last year 24 per cent of all relief expenditures in my home county, Dane County, the second largest county in population in Wisconsin, went to physicians and hospitals and these funds all came from tax sources, and Dane County is not exceptional, and medical care for indigents is not the largest item in the cost of the socialized medicine we now have in the United States.

There are many reasons why the trend toward a greater degree of socialization in our mixed system of private and socialized medical care is likely to continue. To begin with, the costs of adequate medical care are increasing. Adequate medical care has been defined as the sort of medical care which is practiced by the leaders of the profession and is taught in the reputable medical schools. The sort of medical care that met this standard 25 years ago may cost little more now than it did then, but the great advances in scientific knowledge have made that care very inadequate today. Further progress is being made at a rapid rate. Not every new discovery increases medical costs, but this is a frequent concomitant. There is the further factor that with the advances in medicine, many more people are in the older age groups than formerly. Sickness increases with age; moreover, the typical sicknesses of old age are of a chronic character requiring care and treatment for a long time. Adequate medical care costs much more today than it did formerly, and the probability is that these costs will continue to increase with the advances in scientific knowledge.

The increasing costs of adequate medical care make it impossible for many millions of Americans to pay the costs of such care, at least on the still predominant, post-service, fee basis of paying for such care. There have always been a considerable number of Americans who have gotten medical care without being able to pay for it. This number has been enormously increased by the Depression. The most recent comprehensive study of the distribution of incomes in the United States, that made by the National Resources Committee in

Consumer Incomes in the United States: Their Distribution in 1935–1936 arrived at the conclusion that 32 per cent of all of the families in this country had incomes of less than $750 in that year, although only one-third of these families were on relief. Forty-seven per cent had family incomes below $1,000; 69 per cent below $1,500; 82 per cent below $2,000; 93 per cent below $3,000. There are now considerably more than 20,000,000 people who are receiving public assistance in one form or another and 20,000,000 other Americans, not on relief, with family incomes at below $800 per year.

In considering what are the possibilities that families with incomes such as we have in the United States have for meeting the costs of adequate medical care, it is necessary to bear in mind both that there is much sickness and that the incidence of sickness is very unequally distributed. About 2 per cent of all the American people are sick on an average day. The total annual costs of sickness in the United States approximate $10,000,000,000. Medical, hospital, and related care, alone, cost between 4 and 5 per cent of the total national income. Employed wage-earners lost on the average about 7 days per year from work by reason of illness.

Total and average figures on the costs of sickness and medical care, however, mean very little in connection with the ability of individuals and families to pay for adequate medical care on the predominant, post-service, fee basis. Nearly one-half of all Americans do not consult any physician in any particular year; another fourth are not in bed because of illness even for a single day. Most of the time lost from illness is concentrated in less than 10 per cent of the population. The Committee on the Costs of Medical Care revealed that the average expenditure of white families with family incomes under $1,200 was $43 per year and that 65 per cent of these families spent less than $30 for this purpose; but 10 per cent had costs of $400 to $700 for medical care; and 2 per cent over $700.

As Dr. Hugh Cabot, one of America's most eminent surgeons points out in his very illuminating recent book, *The Patient's Dilemma:* One of the most striking facts about medical care in the United States is the difference between the medical care which is available and that which patients actually get. Part of this difference is accounted for by lack of information on part of patients as to the availability of medical care and means of judging its quality. A large

factor, however, is the uncertainty of the cost and fear that it will
prove too great. Patients do not know what necessary medical care
will cost; do not want to go on charity; and so avoid going to a
doctor or clinic. The real problem is not what medical care is theoretically available, but what they actually get. The major problem
is not that medical care is refused to the people with small incomes,
but that they do not seek it, because they fear the costs and do not
want to be dependent on charity.

Moreover, most poor people, when they go to a doctor, naturally
go to one whose charges are low. Such physicians perforce are driven
to hit and miss methods of diagnosing illness, instead of the best
known laboratory and clinical techniques. In this respect, the complete indigents often fare better than the "medically indigent," who
are self-supporting but cannot pay the costs of adequate medical
care. Particularly distressing is the situation of many of the "new
poor," who previously had more adequate incomes and who are fighting desperately to keep off relief and are avoiding all medical costs
until they are down with very serious illnesses and often have irre-
parably injured their health.

Add to these factors of the increasing costs of adequate medical
care and the inability of millions of Americans to meet these costs
from their slender incomes and their abhorrence of pauperism, the
fact that today Americans, very generally, are coming to think of
health as a matter of major public concern, and you have the reasons
why I believe that further great changes in the economic side of
medical care are very probable. There is now general recognition
that health is not solely a private matter. The public has an interest
in the health of all citizens. A concept is developing among the
American people that everyone has a right to necessary medical care
and that it is a responsibility of the government to establish conditions under which this right will become an actuality.

What needs to be done to meet this responsibility is debatable and
differing views may honestly be held by people equally well inten-
tioned. Many people see the solution in compulsory health insurance,
while others label all proposals to this effect as "socialized medicine"
and denounce those who make such suggestions as "reds."

Of course, health insurance is not completely "socialized medicine," but an alternative to completely socialized medicine. It is

essentially a method of getting the costs of what might be called "ordinary medical care" on a preservice, budgeted basis. It is not medical care at public expense, but mainly at private expense, with possible regular contributions from government to match those of the beneficiaries. It is a method through which people with but small incomes may be able to get adequate medical care on a basis where they can avoid charity and pay at least part of the costs. It contemplates not governmental but the private practice of medicine, and mainly private financing. If it met the problem, we could arrest and, perhaps, stop the trend, which is so pronounced and is continuing toward socialized medicine.

That it will, at least, not completely meet the problem, I think, cannot be gainsaid. A preservice, budgeted basis of meeting the costs of medical care, obviously, will not enable the man who has no income to meet any part of these costs. Those who have only very small incomes must put food, shelter, and clothing first, and can contribute little, if anything, toward defraying the costs of providing themselves with adequate medical care. Even people with average incomes and above cannot pay the costs of the care required for treatment of the most expensive diseases, which include many of the most common and serious diseases. Compulsory health insurance has had demonstrated value in Europe, as indicated by the great popularity it enjoys both in the medical profession and among laymen. It is a possible alternative to socialized medicine for a large segment of our population and has great merit as a measure for meeting the costs of the adequate medical care required on ordinary occasions, but it alone will not meet the needs of all our people nor those of the groups it covers for the care they need in cases of diseases requiring long hospitalization and other very expensive types of treatment.

I agree with Dr. Cabot and Surgeon-General Parran that no single approach to the problems of meeting the costs of adequate medical care is self-sufficient. For some people there is no such problem, because they can pay for adequate medical care under present methods. Others can meet the costs of the care required in all but the most expensive diseases, through voluntary and, more certainly, through compulsory insurance. For many millions of Americans, adequate medical care can be provided only at taxpayers' expense, and for many more millions financial help from the government is necessary if we are to continue to make progress against the serious diseases that we know how to combat, but whose treatment is so very expensive.

Remaining to be mentioned is the aspect of health security which relates to the support of the family when the breadwinner is ill. In the aggregate the costs of medical and related care are much greater than the total of the wages lost because of illness. The latter total is in the neighborhood of three-quarters of a billion dollars for our employed population, but a third of this total loss falls upon 7 per cent of the wage-earners. Existing measures of protection against this hazard are very scanty. Unemployment compensation is nowhere given to the man who is unemployed because he is ill. Five million people only have health and accident insurance policies and most of these 5,000,000 people are in upper or middle income groups. Three-million, five-hundred-thousand people are members of mutual benefit associations, trade unions, or fraternal organizations paying cash benefits for sickness. The great majority of all wage-earners get nothing when they are ill to take the place of their lost wages. Not only must their families get along, for the time being, without income, but they have additional expenses for medical and related care. Clearly, there is need for insurance protection to give wage-earners when ill partial compensation for wage loss. That was the original purpose of compulsory health insurance in European countries and, while increasing attention has been given in recent years to services in kind—to making health insurance an instrumentality for providing more adequate care to the insured wage-earners and their families —the cash benefits to compensate for wage loss, in nearly every country, still represent the largest part of the total costs of compulsory health insurance.

So much for the needs for further measures for health security and my ideas as to how these needs can be met. Now let me discuss the progress to date and the future prospects for health security.

I shall devote but little attention to compulsory health insurance, because there is little to report. Health insurance was, prior to the passage of our Social Security Act, the most widely prevalent form of social insurance. Now there are more people who are included in old-age insurance systems, but health insurance is still much more common than unemployment insurance. Literally every country of Europe has some form of governmentally controlled health insurance, as also has Japan. Not only has no country ever given up health insurance after it has once had it, but there is every evidence that it is everywhere very popular. Both physicians and laymen are asking for its extension in England and in many other countries.

But compulsory health insurance has never made any headway in the United States. During the years 1915 to 1917 it seemed that health insurance would be the next step after workmen's compensation. Legislative committees reported favorably upon compulsory health insurance; even the American Medical Association was not then unalterably opposed. But our entrance into the World War and the cry "Made in Germany" killed the promising health insurance movement. After the war only the American Association for Labor Legislation and a few social workers and other "intellectuals" continued to urge the enactment of compulsory health insurance laws.

Widespread popular interest in health insurance revived when the Committee on the Cost of Medical Care made its report in 1932. That committee was dominantly a committee of medical men, and it split widely in its report. Only a small minority favored compulsory health insurance; even fewer members wanted socialized medicine; the largest group recognized that some form of group practice and insurance methods of payment for the costs of medical care were inevitable and urged that the AMA take the lead in organizing voluntary medical and hospital insurance plans. A strong minority, embracing the members of the Committee who were of the controlling group in AMA, condemned every form of group practice and even voluntary insurance. This report provoked a ferment among the medical men which has kept up ever since.

When the American Medical Association at the Special Meeting of its House of Delegates at Chicago in February, 1935, partially reversed its position and came out for voluntary health insurance under the control of the medical societies, while strongly condemning compulsory health insurance, it seemed for a time that all groups among the doctors would accept the new program and again present a united opposition to compulsory health insurance and socialized medicine, which has not proven true. The ferment among the doctors has continued. Opposition to the controlling group in the AMA has increased. Many of the most eminent of our medical men have publicly called on the AMA to recognize the handwriting on the wall and to assume leadership in a reorganization of the economic side of medical care, with the end in view of actually giving to the American people the adequate medical care which is only theoretically available to many millions.

I have been surprised at the continued interest in compulsory health insurance and the strong support which it has been getting, in the face of the relentless opposition of the AMA. It now has the endorsement of both major labor groups, of leading farm organizations, of most of the women's organizations, of the social workers, and many other organizations with large memberships. Compulsory health insurance is by no means dead. Were it submitted to a referendum vote of the American people, it might be adopted.

Realistically, however, it must be recognized that the prospects for the early establishment of compulsory health insurance in the United States are not rosy. Not only do we not now have compulsory health insurance anywhere in this country, but I doubt whether any state will soon make the experiment. We very much need experimentation and the state which is willing to pioneer will render a real service in line with the democratic and progressive traditions of this country. But states are not now in a pioneering mood and the demands upon public funds are so heavy that there is little prospect that the funds for health insurance can be gotten from this source. The fact that we have but recently placed upon employers the costs of unemployment insurance and half the costs of old-age insurance render it very difficult, if not impossible, to get the needed revenues from additional payroll taxes.

Looming greatest as an obstacle to compulsory health insurance is the attitude of the medical profession. Beyond question, the AMA reflects the views of the majority of its members on compulsory health insurance. To a layman it seems strange that the profession is so strongly opposed to health insurance on the score that it is socialized medicine—which it is not—and yet accepts without hesitation public funds for the care of people on relief, which is a form of socialized medicine. But whether this attitude is reasonable or unreasonable, the American people have such confidence in the doctors that we will not establish compulsory health insurance so long as the majority of the doctors are opposed—at least not immediately.

Detrimentally affecting the chances for compulsory health insurance legislation in the near future is the position which the AMA is taking on voluntary insurance. I take it for granted that the AMA is acting in good faith, that its leaders think that the problems of providing adequate medical care to all Americans can be met through voluntary insurance, and that the organization is doing everything possible to further this end. I consider the position which the AMA has taken since the Special Delegate Meeting of February, 1935, a distinct forward step. I welcome the progress which has been made with voluntary medical and hospital insurance.

As regards voluntary medical insurance plans promoted by medical societies, however, there can be no question that they are still numerically very small. No comprehensive figures have ever been published regarding their membership. All of them together do not have 1,000,000 members, and that figure is probably an overstatement by five or ten times. Many of the plans proposed and sought to be put into operation, moreover, are little more than "glorified collection agencies," which, through installment methods of payment, seek to lessen the shock of high costs to the patients, with a resulting larger percentage of actual collections by the doctors. Voluntary medical insurance plans not sponsored by the medical societies have been relentlessly fought by organized medicine. The entire record of voluntary medical insurance since its endorsement by the AMA has been disappointing, but I doubt whether the American public is as yet prepared to recognize in the failure of the AMA to make good its implied promises the strongest possible argument for compulsory health insurance.

Voluntary hospital insurance has worked out very much better. The first voluntary hospital insurance plan was launched in 1932. As recently as January, 1938, all hospital insurance plans had but 1,500,000 members. Now such plans have 5,000,000 members and by the beginning of 1942, at the present rate of growth, there will be 10,000,000. There will, probably, be some growth, ultimately, even beyond that figure.

Very certainly, voluntary insurance will not alone prove sufficient to give all Americans adequate medical care. Viewed as an all-sufficient measure, voluntary insurance has even greater limitations than compulsory insurance. It cannot reach the poorest strata in our population and will be taken advantage of only by some of the people who are economically so situated that they could get adequate medical care for all but the most expensive diseases on a preservice, budgeted cost basis, such as insurance makes possible. But the fact that the AMA is supporting voluntary insurance and that its inadequacy has not become evident operates to make it almost impossible to get compulsory health insurance at this time. Expressed differently, further experimentation with voluntary health insurance is necessary before compulsory health insurance will become politically feasible.

Next, let me say something about the prospects of the National Health Program, which was formulated by the Interdepartmental Committee to Coördinate Health and Welfare Activities, transmitted to Congress in January, 1939, and given legislative form in the Wagner Health Bill, introduced soon thereafter. Extensive hearings were held on this bill by the subcommittee of the Senate Committee on Education and Labor, of which Senator Murray of Montana was the chairman. During the closing days of the first session of the present Congress, in August, 1939, the committee presented a report to the Senate, which, at least in form, was a report of the entire Committee on Education and Labor and not merely of the subcommittee. That committee includes in its membership senators with as diverse views as Thomas, Murray, La Follette, and Taft. In its report, the committee stated that legislation "along the general lines" of the Wagner Bill "is necessary to strengthen the health services of the nation and to make provision for the progressive and effective improvement of health conditions in all parts of the country and among all groups of people." It concluded:

We have not yet had adequate time to make exhaustive study of all the problems involved in the legislation proposed by S. 1620 (the Wagner Bill). The committee will continue its study of S. 1620 so that a definitive report on the proposed legislation can be submitted soon after the beginning of the next session of Congress.

Despite this very definite promise, no report has been made on the Wagner Bill in the present session and it is improbable that such a report will be made. There is little above-board opposition to the National Health Program, but there is much sniping and underground tunneling. Most important, there is little active support for the measure. True, it has been endorsed by national organizations whose total membership is very impressive: the AFL, the CIO, the National Farm Bureau Federation, numerous women's organizations, and many others. But to all these organizations the National Health Program and everything relating to health security is but of secondary interest, while the AMA is doing everything possible to delay action, although it has expressed approval "in principle" of most of the program.

In this situation, the national Administration has assumed what can, perhaps, best be described as a "hands-off" attitude. Last December, the President announced that he would suggest to Congress a $10,000,000 appropriation for the construction of hospitals in areas where they are needed. This was at once heralded by the AMA as a scuttling of the National Health Program, while suggesting the adoption of a small part of that program. The President promptly denied this and reconstituted the Interdepartmental Committee to Coördinate Health and Welfare Activities, with Miss Josephine Roche as chairman, and instructed that committee to continue to work on the National Health Program with a view to perfecting the measure and securing its early enactment into law. The committee has, at least, done something along this line. Miss Roche has several times called upon Congress for prompt action. But there the matter stands. Not even the $10,000,000 hospital construction bill has been reported to the floor, although all commentators say that it will still probably be passed. But none of them see any chances for the Wagner Bill in its entirety, although the announcement has recently been made by Senator Wagner that the bill is being revised to meet the objections of the medical groups.

Whether the bill could have been passed, if the President had thrown all his influence behind the measure, is doubtful, in view of the support given by members of his own party to the opposition. Engrossment in the European war and, perhaps, the lack of active support for the Wagner Bill, despite all its endorsements, probably explain his failure to fight aggressively for the bill. The opposition, perhaps naturally, has had even less of a positive program. In the report of Dr. Glenn Frank's Republican Program Committee five pages are devoted to the health problem. There are many sentences that recognize the need for action, but the controlling group in the AMA might well have written the recommendations.

As a participant in the National Health Conference and an advocate of the National Health Program, I cannot view the prospects—or rather the lack of prospects—for the early enactment of the National Health Program with any degree of satisfaction. The National Health Program has been grossly misrepresented in the sniping attack to which it has been subjected. To quote again the report of the

Senate Committee on Education and Labor on the Wagner Bill filed last August:

It may be emphasized that the operation of health and medical care programs under this bill is a State and not a Federal obligation. The bill does not propose to set up a Federal system of medical care; it undertakes only to encourage and aid the States in setting up their own programs. Neither—as seemed to be thought by some witnesses—does the bill set up a Federal system of health insurance or of State medicine or of socialized medicine, nor does it require any State to set up any particular type of medical service. The role of the Federal government remains—as it is now—to give financial aid to the states.

Every part of the National Health Program is concerned with increased federal aid to the states for public health activities, to be performed by state and local public health agencies, with only a minimum of federal supervision. Federal aid is proposed to be given to the states for five types of health services: (1) child and maternal health services; (2) general public health services and investigations; (3) construction of hospitals and health centers; (4) general programs of medical care; and (5) insurance against loss of wages during periods of temporary disability. The total of the appropriations authorized for these purposes is $80,000,000 in the first year—a large amount for public health purposes when compared with present appropriations, but not much more than the cost of one battleship. After 1942, an appropriation of a "sum sufficient" is authorized, which means that each Congress must annually determine how much shall go for federal aid. All these federal aids must be matched by the states, on what is generally called a "variable grants basis." The poorest states will be reimbursed 66⅔ per cent of their expenditures; the richest, 33⅓ per cent; and the others between 33⅓ per cent and 66⅔ per cent.

In this entire program I see nothing that is radical—only further development along lines which have been tried and have worked well in this country. It is a program which would continue our present mixed system of private and socialized medicine, with only a slightly increased degree of socialization, which is necessary to provide adequate medical care for the people in low income groups. Whether it would encourage or retard the enactment of compulsory health insurance laws in the states is debatable.

Adoption of a national health program is a vital need at this time, when dictators are amuck in the world and the Communists and Nazis have joined forces, with danger to democracy everywhere. Like the great majority of all Americans, I want this country to stay out of the war, but I agree with the President that we cannot disregard what is going on in Europe. It is imperative that this nation must get itself in the strongest possible position to repel attack and to preserve our precious heritage. To this end few things are more important than the health of our citizens. We need to prevent and cure disease to the fullest extent possible; and this important public need cannot be left either to the chance circumstance of enough individual income to pay for all necessary care or to the uncertainties of charity.

Despite the great need for the enactment of a national health program, I expect no action in the present session of Congress. In the political campaign, both parties will probably talk about the need for a national health program, but offer little that commits them to any particular program. What will happen after the election—when a new Congress will be in office and 44 states will hold their regular legislative sessions—is pretty much anybody's guess. This can be said very certainly, however: unless much more active support develops for the National Health Program than thus far manifested, very little of that program will be enacted into law. And it will be a great advance if even one state enacts a compulsory health insurance law.

I am not entirely pessimistic about the outlook. Progress at times seems to be slow and the outlook for the immediate future seems none too bright. In retrospect, however, what has been already accomplished looms large, and factors that I have discussed render inevitable further basic changes in the economic aspects of medical care. The principle that all Americans are entitled to adequate medical care has not been stated in any law and I doubt whether it will be thus stated for some time to come. But that is what the great majority of Americans believe; and what the people want they ultimately get.

We have made great strides in providing more adequate medical care for the people in the lowest income groups. It will not be overlong before better provisions will also be made for people who are not indigents but who are unable to meet the costs of medical care on a post-service fee basis.

On its economic side, medical practice is now undergoing rapid changes in the United States. The extension of medical, including hospital, care to at least a majority of the people on relief and those receiving other forms of public assistance, larger appropriations for preventive public health services, the rapid growth of hospital insurance, the endorsement of voluntary health insurance by the American Medical Association, the increase of contract practice in medical clinics, the emergence of insurance policies written by commercial insurance companies which provide not cash benefits to compensate for wage loss, but payments to cover the costs of medical and surgical care, all illustrate the changes that are occurring.

It is no longer a question whether there should be changes in the economic organization of medical care. It has become a question of how far we shall move in the direction of socialized medicine and whether we should try to check the strong trend toward more and more reliance upon tax funds to pay for the costs of medical care. In a very real sense, the major issue has become whether we should endeavor to have people of small incomes, but above the poverty line, pay for at least a part of the cost of their medical care, as they can do on a dignified insurance basis, or whether this total burden shall fall upon the taxpayers, with medical care for this large group in our population being provided on a charity basis. Looking ahead, we can be sure that we will have more adequate medical care than is possible under the existing economic organization of medicine. What remains uncertain is whether the cost is to be defrayed exclusively from tax sources or in part from insurance funds, also whether the general public is to have any voice in the economic organization of medicine.

I do not expect the United States ever to come to a completely socialized system of medicine. Such a system exists only in the Soviet Union, and, as with everything else about the Soviet Union, I want none of it. In all foreseeable time, I think, we can look forward to a continuance of our present mixed system of private and socialized medicine. Very probably the percentage of socialized medicine will somewhat increase, and I think that is desirable. The great uncertainty is whether we will also have a wider application of insurance principles in this field than have thus far been developed or is likely ever to develop on a voluntary basis. The long-time alternative is compulsory health insurance or much more socialized medicine than we would otherwise have to have. I would prefer compulsory health insurance, but concede that it now seems much more likely that we will get increased socialized medicine rather than compulsory health insurance.

All changes which are occurring, however, are gradual and are certainly no more rapid than the needs of the situation require. Completely socialized medicine is not desired by any large group in the United States, and all differences of opinion about what should be done are primarily questions of degree. There is little reason for an emotional attitude toward the problems facing us in this field, but much need for an intelligent understanding of those problems. I think we are making some progress in that direction.

1944–1945 Programs for Postwar Social Security and Medical Care

Reprinted by permission of the publishers from *The Review of Economic Statistics,* Volume XXVII, Number 4 (November, 1945), pages 171–188, Cambridge, Mass.: Harvard University Press, copyright, 1945, by the President and Fellows of Harvard College

S *Earlier Postwar Social Security Programs*

OCIAL SECURITY and "full employment" are looked upon, in all Allied Nations and also in most neutral countries, as the keys to economic well-being in the postwar era. "Improved labor standards, economic advancement, and social security" are the economic objectives of the Atlantic Charter. All these terms are somewhat vague in meaning, but they express the hopes of hundreds of millions of people and are central in all postwar planning.

Even while the war was in progress, considerable improvement was made in the social security legislation of many countries.[1] This is not true of the United States, in which there was no social security legis-

---

[1] No comprehensive account has been written to date of the progress made in social security legislation the world over during the war. The author dealt briefly with this subject in his chapter, "Post-War Social Security," in S. E. Harris, *Post-War Economic Problems* (New York, 1943), pp. 266–70. A much more complete account, but dealing only with developments in the Western Hemisphere, is Arthur J. Altmeyer's article, "The Progress of Social Security in the Americas in 1944," in the *International Labour Review,* LI (June, 1945), pp. 699–721. The complete story of the developments in other countries can be gotten only from the items in the *International Labour Review,* the monthly periodical of the International Labour Office. On the progress in Latin America, the *Provisional Bulletins* of the Inter-American Committee on Social Security, a subsidiary of the *International Labour Organisation* which was organized in 1943 with headquarters in Montreal, are most valuable.

lation whatsoever on the national level during the five years between the enactment of the Social Security Act Amendments of 1939 and the passage of the Servicemen's Readjustment Act (the GI Bill of Rights) in 1944, except for the adoption of annual riders to appropriations acts which provided for freezing of the old-age insurance tax rates. Some advances were made in the states, particularly in the liberalization of unemployment compensation benefits. But the only law in this country which broke new ground was the Rhode Island Act of 1941 for cash disability benefits. In many other countries, in contrast, the war period brought forth much new social security legislation. The advances in this respect have been greatest in the Latin-American countries. Very significant new social security legislation also has been enacted in England, Canada, and Australia, while in New Zealand the comprehensive national health insurance and medical care program adopted shortly before the outbreak of hostilities has been put into full operation.

More important even than the new legislation are the comprehensive programs for social security which were developed during the war. Prior to 1944, such postwar programs were formulated and publicized in England, the United States, Canada, Australia, and South Africa—all of them under governmental auspices.[2]

The most famous of these was the Beveridge Plan in England, which made its appearance late in 1942.[3] Beyond question, this has been the most widely discussed social security program ever advanced anywhere in the world. In this country it has brought forth far more articles than were written about the Social Security Act during the entire year that this major American social security measure was in

[2] The programs presented in Australia and South Africa are not further discussed in this article. On the Australian programs, see "Planning for Social Security in Australia," *International Labour Review*, XLV (1942), pp. 458–60, and "The Planning of Medical Services in Australia," *International Labour Review*, XLVIII (1943), pp. 731–45. On the program for a national health and medical care service in the Union of South Africa, consult the *Provisional Bulletin* of the Inter-American Committee on Social Security, IV (October, 1943), pp. 25–29, and Raymond Burrows, *Social Security and the National Income* (Johannesburg, 1944). Sweden should, perhaps, also be included in this list. On this, see "Social Planning in Sweden," *International Labour Review*, XLVIII (1943), pp. 308–15.

[3] Among the best articles dealing with the Beveridge Plan which have been published in this country are E. Wight Bakke, "America and the Beveridge Plan," in *Yale Review*, XXXIII (1944), pp. 642–57, and Eveline M. Burns, "The Beveridge Report," in *American Economic Review*, XXXIII (1943), pp. 512–33. The entire report has been published by the Macmillan Company under the title *Social Insurance and Allied Services* (1942).

preparation and under consideration in Congress. Almost immediately after its publication, the British government announced its acceptance of the Beveridge Plan "in principle, with minor reservations only," but not until 1944 did it fill in the details of what it was willing to do to carry out this program.

Heralded as "the American Beveridge Plan," and more voluminous but narrower in scope and far less influential, was the report of the National Resources Planning Board in *Social Security, Work and Relief Policies* and its shorter report, *Post-War Planning*, which President Roosevelt transmitted to Congress in March, 1943.[4] These reports presented a program for social security which, as stated by the author in another article, represented "the views of the Washington officialdom concerned with the administration of the relief and social security programs of 1940, in combination with the ideas of the 'planners' of the later New Deal period." Into the former report went the wide knowledge of social security of Mrs. Eveline M. Burns and Dr. William Haber and several years' work of a sizable staff of able assistants. Unlike the Beveridge Report, it attempted to correlate social security and full employment. But somehow it did not catch the public's imagination, never received Administration endorsement, and was not even embodied in any bill introduced in Congress.

Instead organized labor came forward some months later with the Wagner–Murray–Dingell Bill.[5] This was a measure proposing very extensive changes in and additions to existing social security legislation, differing at many points from the recommendations made in the reports of the National Resources Planning Board. Introduced as stated by Senator Wagner "simply as a basis for legislative study and consideration," it provoked a vast amount of discussion, although never accorded a hearing by any Congressional committee. On the one hand, it drew bitter fire from organized medicine, because it

[4] As the National Resources Planning Board has gone out of existence, these reports are now obtainable only from the Superintendent of Documents. Among many articles summarizing the recommendations in these reports, two by Mrs. Eveline M. Burns, who headed the research staff which prepared them, are outstanding: "Freedom from Want: the NRPB Report," in *Survey Midmonthly*, Vol. 79 (1943), pp. 106–8; and "Social Security and our Post-War Economy," in *Journal of Educational Sociology*, XVII (1943), pp. 132–42. The author discussed these reports and the Wagner–Murray–Dingell Bill in "American Post-War Social Security Proposals," *American Economic Review*, XXXIII (1943), pp. 825–38. The quotations in this paragraph are from this article.

[5] S. 1161, 78th Congress, 1st session.

proposed a national health and medical care program to be financed on an insurance basis, and from the state unemployment compensation administrators, because it included provisions for the federalization of unemployment insurance. On the other hand it was unitedly supported by organized labor and was endorsed also by many farmer, women's, and welfare organizations. It was often referred to as an Administration measure but never was endorsed by President Roosevelt, and the Social Security Board never went further than to express support of its objectives.

The third of the widely publicized postwar programs for social security which made their appearance within a few months of each other in the winter of 1942–43 was the Marsh Report in Canada.[6] This report has been called "a Beveridge Plan for Canada" and in many respects resembles its prototype. It was much more hastily prepared, however, and, despite much acclaim, never attained the status of a Government-endorsed program, resembling in this respect the National Resources Planning Board reports in the United States, rather than the Beveridge Plan in England.

《《《《《《《《〇》》》》》》》》

Recommendations of the International Labour Conference

In 1944, several new noteworthy comprehensive programs for postwar social security made their appearance. Some progress also was made in some countries towards translating these and the earlier postwar social security programs into legislation. In the main, however, postwar social security is still in the planning stage but with every prospect of much new legislation soon.

Of the new postwar social security programs, note will first be taken of that adopted by the International Labour Organisation at its Philadelphia Conference, April 20–May 12, 1944.[7] This program

[6] *Report on Social Security for Canada,* prepared by Leonard C. Marsh for the Advisory Committee on Reconstruction (Ottawa, 1943).

[7] The International Labour Office (Montreal, Canada) prior to the Philadelphia Conference published studies and draft proposals prepared by its staff on each of the six items on the Agenda of the Conference. Of these, the following relate to social security and medical care: *Social Security Principles and Problems:* Part I, *Principles;*

is embodied in Recommendations and Resolutions on Income Security, Medical Care, and Employment Organization which set forth principles to guide member nations in social security planning. Preceding the conference, extended reports on these three subjects were prepared by the staff of the International Labour Office. These included draft Recommendations and Resolutions, which furnished the basis for the discussions at the conference and also for the proposals finally adopted—but only after long debate and with some significant changes. The draft recommendations presented in the report on the organization of employment in the transition from war to peace, which dealt not only with this subject but also with the advance planning of public works and public employment services, were adopted unanimously and without material modifications. This was true also of the "Recommendation Concerning Income Security and Medical Care for Persons Discharged from the Armed Forces and Assimilated Services and from War Employment" and of the "Resolution of International Administrative Coöperation to Promote Social Security." On the other hand, it was not until the last day of the conference that the recommendations on income security and medical care were adopted. Earlier, the British delegation aroused the ire of the Workers' delegate from the United States by its opposition to any action on these subjects—an attitude that seems to have stemmed from the fact that the British Government had by that time committed itself to the Beveridge Plan "in principle" but had not yet come forward with any detailed program for giving it effect. In the end, the income-security recommendation was divided into a brief statement of "Guiding Principles," supplemented by more detailed "Suggestions for Application." In the final vote, the

---

Part II, *Problems Arising Out of the War; Recommendations to the United Nations for Present and Post-War Social Policy.*

A complete record of the proceedings of the Philadelphia Conference, including the text of all recommendations adopted, has been published by the International Labour Office under the title *Record of Proceedings of the 26th Session of the International Labour Conference (Philadelphia, 1944).* The Recommendations adopted have also been published as a Document of the United States House of Representatives: *Recommendations Adopted by the International Labour Conference* (78th Congress, 2nd session, House Document No. 671, 1944).

Among articles dealing with the recommendations of this conference on social security and medical care, the article by Wilbur J. Cohen and Jessica H. Barr, "The 1944 International Labour Conference," in *Social Security Bulletin,* Vol. 7, No. 6, June, 1944, pp. 11–16, 32, is outstanding.

British delegates voted unanimously for the recommendation, while the American delegation was split, with the Employer delegate opposed. The "Recommendation Concerning Medical Care" underwent less change from the draft prepared by the staff of the International Labour Office, but also was adopted only with some negative votes and with other delegates abstaining from voting. The United States delegation was split three ways: the Workers' delegate voting for it, the Employers' delegate against it, and the two Government delegates abstaining from voting.

Although the International Labour Organisation at its annual Conferences between 1925 and 1937 adopted many conventions and recommendations on social security problems, never until the Philadelphia Conference did it promulgate an all-inclusive social security program. This program was built upon its prior pronouncements, plus the 1942–43 governmental social security proposals previously noted: the Beveridge Plan, the Marsh Report, the National Resources Planning Board Report, and the Wagner-Murray-Dingell Bill. It covers all risks and all workers, whether employed or self-employed, and is coördinated to avoid all gaps and overlaps. Along with this all-inclusive social security program, the Philadelphia Conference, for the first time in the history of the International Labour Organisation, recommended a comprehensive, national medical care program.

《《《《《《《《《〇》》》》》》》》

These recommendations concerning medical care represent the first official declaration by the International Labour Conference on the subject. They are distinctly more radical than those concerning income security. In the latter recommendation new ground is broken only in the presentation of a unified and all-inclusive national program, in lieu of the prior piecemeal approach. Medical care previously has been dealt with only as one of the benefits to be provided under compulsory health insurance. Now, medical care is dealt with apart from health insurance and other forms of social insurance, except that the social insurance machinery may be utilized in the administration and financing of the medical care services. What is recommended is not a compulsory health insurance plan, but a comprehensive program for all-inclusive national health service—a program for socialized medicine, rather than social insurance.

Government Proposals and Other Developments in Great Britain

Attracting wider notice and of greater importance, at least immediately, than the recommendations of the International Labour Conference are the government proposals in Great Britain dealing with full employment, a national health service, and social security—all of them in 1944.

Of these, the proposals relating to full employment lie largely outside of the scope of this article. Note needs to be taken of the fact, however, that in England, as in the United States, "full employment" more and more in recent years has come to be regarded as the key to economic security and national well-being. In England, however, unlike the United States, "full employment" is never thought of as rendering unnecessary the strengthening of "social security." In England, also, the subject has now passed beyond the stage of mere discussion and free-lance proposals to an official recognition by the Government of its responsibility for full employment.

This was made in a White Paper [8] which was presented to the House of Commons in May, 1944, as a "declaration of His Majesty's Government accepting as one of the primary aims and responsibilities the maintenance of a high and stable level of employment after the war." In this declaration it is set forth that the Government hereafter will be concerned not only with "measures to minimize the effect of unemployment" but with "active measures to promote and maintain economic health." "Unemployment was and is a social disease, which must be eradicated from our social life." While "the social services must continue to play their part, the first consideration must be to remove the cause." [9] The concrete proposals to this end in the White Paper relate mainly to the reconversion period, but include the general outlines of a policy which it is hoped will result in maintaining a high and stable level of employment when peace is restored.

The program outlined places main reliance upon private enter-

[8] Great Britain, H. M. Stationery Office, *Employment Policy*. Cmd. 6527 (1944). American edition by Macmillan Company (New York, 1944).

[9] The quotations are from the speech of Sir Ernest Bevin, in moving the government's motion in the House of Commons, Parliamentary Debates, June 21, 1944, p. 212.

prise and investment, but makes the Government responsible for maintaining the desired level of total (private and public) expenditures, stable wages and prices, and labor mobility between occupations and communities. Concrete suggestions toward the accomplishment of this purpose include automatic variations in the contribution rates in the social-insurance scheme, fluctuating with the level of employment.

This last suggestion illustrates the fact that the entire program is still vague with regard to the precise measures to be taken to insure full employment at all times. The much more concrete proposals of the Government in relation to social insurance presented three months later completely ignore this recommendation in the Employment Policy report, contemplating instead fixed rates which do not change with the level of employment. But there is nothing vague in the declaration that the maintenance of full employment is a responsibility of the government; and therein lies the significance of this report.

The social insurance proposals represent the next logical step in the fulfillment of the Government's acceptance, in February, 1943, of the Beveridge Plan "in principle." In the White Paper on Social Insurance,[10] the Government sets forth precisely what it proposes to do on all the matters covered in the Beveridge Report. In the main, it accepts the Beveridge recommendations, but with a fairly large number of modifications.

Like the Beveridge Plan, the Government's program calls for a unified and all-inclusive social insurance system, administered by the national government, through its Ministry of Social Insurance. It is designed to provide "cradle-to-grave" social security, embracing the entire population and affording protection in all major contingencies of life. For this purpose, the population is divided into six classes, with differing contribution and benefit status, but all of

---

[10] Great Britain, Ministry of Social Insurance, *Social Insurance:* Part I, *Social Insurance;* Part II, *Workmen's Compensation—Proposals for an Industrial Injury Scheme.* Cmd. 6550 and 6551 (1944). Good summaries of this White Paper appear in the *International Labour Review,* November, 1944, pp. 668–76, and December, 1944, pp. 788–90, the *Monthly Labor Review,* December, 1944, pp. 1183–89, and the *Social Security Bulletin,* November, 1944, pp. 27–35. Good discussions of the White Paper and related developments in England are Mary E. Murphy, "Britain's Plans for Social Reconstruction," *Social Service Review,* XIX (March, 1945), pp. 75–86, and Joan S. Clarke, "The British Government and the Beveridge Report," *Social Service Review,* XIX (June, 1945), pp. 171–84.

them and at all times within the scheme and assured protection
against extreme want and dependency. These six classes are the employed, the self-employed, housewives, adults whose incomes come
from other than earnings, children, and people over working age.
Only the first, second, and fourth of these classes are contributors—
each at a differing scale, but in all cases making a single contribution of a fixed amount, collected weekly through a stamp system.
The benefits provided are those appropriate to the situation of the
particular class to which an individual belongs. There are allowances in case of sickness, industrial injury, invalidity, maternity, and
unemployment, plus retirement pensions, death grants, widows'
benefits, orphans' benefits, and children's allowances. These benefits
have no relation to prior earnings, but vary with the number of
dependents. Judged by American standards, the weekly benefits are
low, whether expressed in absolute amounts or as a percentage of
average earnings. They are, however, of much longer duration. The
costs are divided between the insured, their employers, and the
Government, with the latter bearing the largest share.

Basically, the Government's program, like the Beveridge Plan,
represents only a unification and rounding out of social insurance
as it has developed in England. There are, however, some important
innovations and changes. Both contribution and benefit rates are increased. Workmen's compensation, which heretofore has been outside the social insurance scheme, is brought within its orbit, as an
industrial injury benefit. The friendly societies, around which the
existing health insurance system has been built, are deprived of all
independence and assigned only a very subordinate role in administration. A system of family allowances is instituted, which provides
for grants for the support of all children, regardless of the family's
financial position. Death benefits are introduced, which are likely
to reduce seriously the sales of industrial insurance.

The principal difference between the Government's program and
the Beveridge Plan is that the Government rejects the Beveridge
proposal that social insurance benefits should at all times be large
enough to provide an adequate minimum for subsistence. Beveridge
recommended that benefits should be varied with changes in the cost
of living and that all assistance (relief) payments should be abandoned. He contemplated unemployment and sickness insurance of
unlimited duration and proposed larger children's allowances. The

Government's program provides for fixed benefits, contemplates the continuance of assistance payments where the social insurance benefits are inadequate, and limits the duration of both unemployment and sickness benefits.

The third Government program, that for a national health service, also grows out of the Beveridge Report. Sir William discussed this subject only briefly, but sketched a national health service as a postwar essential, along with an improved social insurance system and a governmental full-employment policy. The Government accepted this recommendation "in principle" in February, 1943, but not until a year later did it present a White Paper outlining in some detail what it had in mind.[11]

The scope and purpose of this program were stated by the Prime Minister, Winston Churchill, when this White Paper was presented to Parliament:

> Our policy is to create a national health service in order to insure that everybody in the country, irrespective of means, age, sex or occupation, shall have equal opportunities to benefit from the best and most up-to-date medical and allied services available. The plan that we have put forward is a very large-scale plan, and in ordinary times of peace would rivet and dominate the attention of the whole country; but even during this war it deserves the close study and thought of all who can spare themselves from other duties for that purpose. We welcome constructive criticism; we claim the loyal and active aid of the whole medical profession.

The plan outlined in this White Paper goes far beyond compulsory health insurance, which has been in operation in Great Britain since 1911. It is a plan for making medical care a governmental responsibility, but utilizing all existing personnel and facilities. Ambitiously, it contemplates a complete health service for the entire population, both preventive and curative, although initially some types of service—for instance, dental service—will not be provided because there is insufficient qualified personnel. But from the outset there is to be available to everybody a general medical service to be supplied through individually selected family doctors, complete hospital and consultant services, and many types of clinical services. The

---

[11] Great Britain, Ministry of Health, *A National Health Service*. Cmd. 6502 (1944). An American reprint under the same title has been published by the Macmillan Company (New York). A good summary of the White Paper appears in *International Labour Review*, XLIX (1944), pp. 473–81.

service is to be free to all, in the sense that no charges will be made except possibly for appliances, with 30 per cent of the finances coming from social insurance funds and the balance from the national and local treasuries. Medical care will not be completely socialized and the individual will still be free to choose his doctor and he will not have to utilize the public provisions for medical care. On their part, the doctors may choose their patients and are left free to pursue their professional methods without outside interference. But the entire scheme will be under governmental control and is in every sense a public medical service, akin to public education.

The three great White Papers of 1944 would seem to merit a place alongside the national social insurance program of Lloyd George of 1911 as among the most ambitious plans for the advancement of the well-being of the masses ever presented by any government. The social insurance and medical care proposals call for an increase in expenditures for these purposes in the first year from £441,000,000 to £650,000,000, with most of the increase falling upon the Exchequer. These expenditures will increase to £831,000,000 in thirty years, not allowing for inevitable further extension and liberalization.[12] These programs were on the whole well received by nearly all elements in the British population. Sir Ronald Davison, who ranks second only to Sir William Beveridge as an authority on social insurance, expressed the general view: "It may be less good than some of us hoped, but is definitely better than we feared." In the recent British election, all parties promised prompt action on the subjects dealt with in the White Papers. Whether socialization of the heavy industries, the coal mines, the public utilities, transport, and the Bank of England is necessary to insure full employment was the major issue in the campaign. Social insurance and medical care figured in the election only in a minor way, the Labour Party confining its criticisms of the Government's program to details, principally advocating more liberal benefits. Only the friendly societies and the insurance companies have openly expressed unqualified opposition to the social insurance proposals.

[12] It is worthy of note that in England, unlike the United States, all proposals for the liberalization of social security legislation are accompanied by careful estimates of the costs, not only in the first years but for a generation to come. Every such proposal also includes a definite program regarding where the money is to come from. In Great Britain, hand-to-mouth financing with complete disregard of accruing liabilities, euphoniously termed "pay-as-you-go," has never enjoyed any popularity.

Besides the Government White Papers, several private publications of the last two years dealing with the same projects have attracted wide attention. Sir William Beveridge's *Full Employment in a Free Society* [13] actually has been discussed much more than the Government's White Paper. It contemplates more planning than does the government program, but believes that this can be reconciled with free enterprise. Beveridge's proposals have been widely acclaimed, particularly in this country, but apparently did not satisfy the constituency which Sir William represented in Parliament, as it replaced him by a Laborite, committed to socialism, in the recent general election.

In the medical care field, the Government's White Paper brought forth a report by the Council of the British Medical Association [14] in May, 1944, in which it approved the objectives of the plan for a national health service, but opposed putting it into effect in wartime. It further objected to the degree of control vested in local authorities, particularly to the creation of the proposed joint public health authorities and to their right to employ doctors on a salary basis. It insisted that all problems of administration and the terms and conditions of the employment of doctors should be settled through negotiations with the Medical Association before the scheme is put into effect. But it did not condemn outright the Government's program, and it pledged the coöperation of the profession to make the plan workable. In December, 1944, these recommendations were approved by the Representative Body of the British Medical Association.

In the social security field, at least, one notable private study made its appearance during the last year. This is Gertrude Williams' *The Price of Social Security*,[15] which is concerned with the problem that social security, especially unemployment insurance, is likely to weaken the incentive to find other employment and thereby interferes with occupational mobility, which is essential to the smooth functioning of the present-day industrial system. Miss Williams not only ably presents this problem but outlines a program for its solu-

---

[13] Published in London by Allen & Unwin, Ltd., and in New York by W. W. Norton & Company. See also Sir William's article, "The Government's Employment Policy," *Economic Journal*, LIV (1944), pp. 161–74.

[14] Summarized in the *Social Security Bulletin*, VII (1944), pp. 11–15 and in the *International Labour Review*, LI (1945), pp. 386–92.

[15] Oxford University Press, 1944.

tion. This includes making it obligatory for the recipients of un-employment insurance benefits to undergo training for other work if they cannot readily find employment in their old occupations; also extensive vocational guidance, aptitude testing, and better informa-tion about employment opportunities, all as functions of an im-proved employment placement service.

As the Government and private programs reviewed clearly indi-cate, full employment and improved social security and medical care are considered by nearly everybody in England to be essentials for the postwar period. All three, however, are still mainly in the discussion stage. No bill to carry out the proposals for a national health service has been introduced in Parliament. About the only thing accom-plished toward carrying out of the Government's program for full employment has been the recent passage of the Distribution of In-dustry Act. In the social security field greater progress has been made. In November, 1944, a Ministry of National Insurance, of Cabinet rank, was created, in which all governmental activities in the social security field were concentrated, but the principal immediate duty of which was stated to be to perfect the legislation outlined in the Government's White Paper. Since then a Family Allowance Act has been introduced and advanced to second reading in Parliament. Beyond this, the Churchill Government did not get far in carrying out its program before it was turned out of office in the July elec-tion. Its slowness in acting apparently was one of the causes for its overwhelming rejection by the electorate. The victorious Labour Party sees the solution of the postwar domestic problems primarily in socialism. As its support comes so largely from the working peo-ple, however, it can be relied upon to act promptly on the improve-ment of social security and medical care. Quite probably it will pro-vide larger benefits than the Churchill government promised, but there is every reason to expect it to adhere to the general pattern outlined in the Beveridge Report on Social Insurance and Allied Services of December, 1942.

Progress in Other Foreign Countries

Only brief note can be taken of the progress toward im-proved social security and better medical care in countries other than Great Britain and the United States.

Of these, developments in Canada are of greatest interest in this country. At the beginning of the period dealt with in this article, there appeared to be good reason to expect early action on the Government's proposals for compulsory health insurance, grants-in-aid to the Provinces for health services for the entire population, and the establishment of a family allowance system. The Family Allowances Act was passed in August, 1944, and has been a subject of vitriolic debate ever since.[16] Creation of a Department of National Health and Welfare in July, 1944, was less controversial and represented a distinct step forward. No legislation on health insurance and health services, however, has to date been enacted by the Dominion Government. A seventh draft of a Dominion Health Insurance Act was presented by the Advisory Committee on Health Insurance early in 1944. This bill provides for health insurance and medical services for the entire population to be administered by the Provinces. The total cost is estimated at $250,000,000 per year (exclusive of administration, the cost of which is to be borne by the Provinces), of which $100,000,000 is to come from the Dominion Treasury, another $100,000,000 from contributions collected from all adults in Canada or met by the Provinces for people too poor to pay their own contributions, and $50,000,000 from a special income tax levy. The popular reception of this measure has been very favorable. The Canadian Medical Association endorsed its main provisions, although objecting to some details. But up to this writing, no effort has been made to secure passage of the measure in Parliament. The explanation seems to lie, in part, in the fact that the coöperation of the Provinces is essential. This is tied up with the problem of the allocation of revenues between the Provincial and Dominion governments, which is, perhaps, the major domestic question in Canada today.

Failure of the Government to press for decisive action, perhaps, may also reflect the necessity it was under of getting a new mandate from the people in the general election of this year. Whether its victory by a slim margin has made it more feasible to go ahead with its projected program remains to be seen. In the meantime, Saskatchewan has enacted a Health Services Act, providing for full medical and hospital care at public expense for old-age pensioners, dependent children and their mothers, and other recipients of public

[16] See Charlotte Whitton, "The Family Allowance Controversy in Canada," *Social Service Review* (December, 1944), pp. 413–32.

aid; Alberta has enacted a law for free maternity care for all mothers; in Manitoba, the Premier has outlined a health insurance and medical care act in line with the proposed Dominion legislation; and in Ontario there has been introduced a Municipal Health Services Bill that would permit municipalities to provide medical and hospital services for their inhabitants, supported by taxes, on the plan which has been in operation in rural areas of Saskatchewan for nearly a quarter-century.[17]

In other parts of the British Empire the story is quite similar. The years 1944 and 1945 witnessed the filing of reports by two separate commissions in South Africa outlining, respectively, a comprehensive social insurance program and a health service plan for the entire population. A report has also been made on a social security system in India. In Australia there has been continued discussion of earlier reports recommending a national health service, with the physicians to be employed on a salary basis. In none of these countries, however, have these proposals progressed beyond the discussion stage.[18]

Far different is the story of developments in Latin-American countries. To quote from Dr. Arthur J. Altmeyer's excellent summary in "The Progress of Social Security in the Americas in 1944": [19]

New general systems or large-scale new programmes were either enacted or made operative in Argentina, Ecuador, Mexico, Paraguay, and Venezuela. Large-scale plans not yet adopted but published in their current form for the first time in 1944 appeared in Bolivia, Brazil, Canada, and Cuba.... In practically all the nations, including those mentioned, there was a steady development of social insurance. This was marked in some cases by extension of coverage to new groups, as in Uruguay, and in others, such as Peru, by geographical expansion towards the goal of nation-wide application.

Brief mention also should be made of the efforts which the liberated countries of Europe are making not only to restore their

[17] On the recent developments in Canada in relation to health insurance and public health services see "Postwar Medicine in the British Commonwealth," *Medical Care,* IV (1944), pp. 144–59; *International Labour Review,* LI (1945), pp. 649–52; Canadian Medical Association, *Principles Relating to Health Insurance* (1944).

[18] For a general discussion of developments within the British Empire in relation to medical care, see "Postwar Medicine in the British Commonwealth," *Medical Care,* IV (1944), pp. 149–59. On the reports in South Africa consult *International Labour Review,* XLIX (1944), pp. 684–86 and LI (1945), pp. 655–56; *Social Security Bulletin* (May, 1945), p. 22. On developments in India consult A. N. Agarwala, *Social Insurance Planning in India* (1944), and B. P. Adarkar, *Report on Health Insurance for Industrial Workers* (1944).

[19] *International Labour Review,* LI (1945), pp. 699–721.

prewar social insurance institutions but to improve upon them. In France, this has involved an increase in the contribution rates for sickness insurance and old-age pensions (shared equally between employers and employees) from 8 to 12 per cent to restore the social insurance funds to a sound financial basis, which the Vichy Government impaired by pursuing a hand-to-mouth financing policy.[20] In Belgium the framework of a general social insurance scheme of much broader scope than existed before the war was established within four months after liberation.[21]

Proposals in the United States

There were no new programs in 1944 for the revision of the existing social security and medical care systems of this country comparable in scope and importance to the report of the National Resources Planning Board or the Wagner–Murray–Dingell Bill, both of which made their appearance in 1943. There were several reports dealing with these problems which merit mention, but these were more in the nature of comments on the 1943 proposals than new programs.

The most comprehensive of these was the *Joint Statement on Social Security by Agriculture, Business, and Labor* [22] prepared by the three committees named of the National Planning Association, which included in their membership representatives of leading farm organizations and the two major labor federations, Beardsley Ruml and several other prominent business leaders, and a few college professors, of whom John D. Black and Theodore W. Schultz are the best known. Of the 59 members all but two signed the report, but with additional dissents by some of the members on particular recommendations. This statement called for a considerable extension and liberalization of social security and increased social service expenditures. It declared that "the major goal of the postwar economy should be enough jobs and lasting jobs at fair rates of pay and reasonable hours of work," and that "a social security program is not a substitute for a program of full employment, although by maintaining a maximum of purchasing power it is an important element

[20] *International Labour Review*, LI (1945), pp. 722–40.
[21] *International Labour Review*, LI (1945), pp. 524–27.
[22] Planning Pamphlet No. 33 (1944).

in such a program." All unemployment, however, cannot be prevented, and want and distress do not arise solely from unemployment. Social security provisions, hence, are a vital need, and the
present laws do not afford adequate protection and, moreover, do
not provide for democratic participation in administration by interested citizens. To this end, a large number of changes in the existing laws are suggested. These are very similar to those proposed
in the Wagner–Murray–Dingell Bill and the entire report may be
regarded as an endorsement of that bill, although there are minor
differences. Among these are triparty financing of all forms of social insurance (other than workmen's compensation, which is not
discussed), the establishment of advisory committees at every level
of administration, and wider participation by labor and management in the determination of the policies of the public employment
offices. The report also outlines some problems for further study:
minimum old-age pensions for the entire population, improved social security provisions for children, social security for agriculture,
and inducements to the maintenance of maximum employment.[23]

Another 1944 report dealing comprehensively with proposals for
the improvement of the existing social security legislation is that of
the Committee on Social Security of the Chamber of Commerce of
the United States.[24] This Committee has functioned for some years
and is headed by Marion B. Folsom of the Eastman Kodak Company,
the outstanding authority on social insurance in the ranks of business, who has been a member of every advisory group that has had
anything to do with the development of the Social Security Act since
its inception. In its report, this committee presented a 21-point program outlining the position of the Chamber of Commerce on all
major proposals for changes in the existing legislation on social security. This program was submitted to a referendum vote of the
constituent local chambers of commerce and all recommendations
were approved by large majorities.[25] The recommendations included
a considerable number that are in line at least with the general di-

---

[23] The report condemns experience rating as it now operates, Beardsley Ruml dissenting, but recommends further study of possible incentives in unemployment insurance to the maintenance of full employment.

[24] *Referendum No. 84 on the Report of the Committee on Social Security in the
United States* (1944).

[25] An exception is the extension of the coverage of the old-age and survivors' insurance system to domestic servants, on which the vote was very close.

rection of the proposals in the Wagner–Murray–Dingell Bill, among them extension of the coverage of the old-age insurance and unemployment insurance systems, increase in the unemployment insurance benefits, the establishment of total disability benefits, credits to veterans in old-age insurance and unemployment insurance systems for their period of military service, and readjustment allowances to veterans supplemental to unemployment insurance. As against the proposals in the Wagner–Murray–Dingell Bill, however, the Chamber opposes the federalization of unemployment insurance and extension of the control of the national government over unemployment insurance, while it supports the return of the public employment offices to the states, and experience rating in unemployment insurance. In relation to health insurance and medical care, the Chamber's position is that employers voluntarily should afford protection to their employees against nonindustrial disabilities and sickness, but that if, after a reasonable period of time, substantial gaps in coverage remain, compulsory legislation on the state and local level is warranted.

A third noteworthy report published in 1944 was that of the Health Program Conference . . . *Principles of a Nation-Wide Health Program*.[26] This report represents the views of a group of physicians, administrators, and economists, brought together by Dr. Michael M. Davis, Director of the Committee on Research in Medical Economics. All the conferees were known supporters of national legislation for a comprehensive national health program. They fell, however, into two groups, approaching this subject from quite different points of view—the one concerned with the medical aspects and the improvement of the medical care afforded the people of the United States; the other, with the economic aspects and the methods of payment for the cost of medical care. The conference served the purpose of thoroughly acquainting each group with the views of the other and led to the joint statement of principles which was published. This does not even refer to the Wagner–Murray–Dingell Bill and is far more specific than are the medical care provisions of this measure. It presents not a legislative program but a statement of objectives and methods which, it is hoped, will serve as a guide to legislators and administrators in the development of a nationwide health program.

[26] Published by the Committee on Research in Medical Economics, New York.

In actual legislation for the improvement of social security, however, accomplishments in 1944 were meager. The only real progress
made lay in the enactment of the Servicemen's Readjustment Act.[27]

《《《《《《《《〈O〉》》》》》》》》

In the seven months of 1945 which have elapsed at the
present writing, greatly increased interest in the improvement of
the existing provisions for social security and medical care has been
manifested both in and out of Congress. These months have witnessed the introduction of a large number of bills in Congress of
far-reaching effect, several of which have been widely discussed. To
date, no hearings have been held on any of them, but prospects for
action appear much better than a year ago.

Of these bills, the two most comprehensive are the Full Employment Bill and the revised Wagner–Murray–Dingell Bill.[28] The first
of these is not properly to be regarded as a social security measure,
but merits some consideration in this article. Its support in Congress
seems to come from the same members who are favorably inclined
toward the Wagner–Murray–Dingell Bill. Some of its supporters
among intellectuals, however, discuss this measure as if it rendered
unnecessary any consideration of social security legislation.

The Full Employment Bill was first presented just before the close
of the 78th Congress and came from the Subcommittee on War
Contracts of the Senate Military Affairs Committee, of which Subcommittee Senator Murray of Montana is the Chairman. This bill
boldly declares that every American able and willing to work has a
right to a job and that it is the responsibility of the national government to see that he has a job. The bill contemplates that jobs are to
be provided as far as possible through private enterprise. When the
prospects are that private enterprise, plus normal governmental employment, will not be sufficient, it is proposed that the national government shall make additional investments and expenditures to fill
the gap, giving preference to such expenditures as will have the
most stimulating effects upon private enterprise. Popularly, the bill
has been discussed as a measure to provide 60,000,000 jobs. Actually,
it makes no mention of the specific number of jobs to be provided

[27] Public Law 346, popularly referred to as the "GI Bill of Rights."
[28] Respectively, S. 380 and S. 1050, 79th Congress, 1st Session.

for, but calls for a national production and employment budget to be presented by the President to Congress in which a definite plan to insure full and continuing employment in the ensuing year is to be outlined. This bill represents the program of the economic planners for the solution of the major postwar domestic problem of the country, but in addition has very strong support from organized labor. The announcement has been made that hearings on the bill are to begin in the near future.

The Wagner–Murray–Dingell Bill now before Congress is a revision of the bill of the same title in the 78th Congress. This bill was not introduced until June 3, 1945. There have been many reports that President Truman will endorse this bill, but up to August 1 he had not done so. It has the open support, however, of the Social Security Board, which in its Ninth Annual Report, presented to Congress in January, recommended practically every provision included in the Wagner–Murray–Dingell Bill. It also is supported by the American Federation of Labor, the Congress of Industrial Organizations, and the Railroad Brotherhoods. An active campaign is now getting under way to get local labor unions and their members to bring pressure upon their members of Congress for passage of this measure. To date, only the American Medical Association has publicly attacked the bill, but the opposition of the state unemployment compensation administrators and of state officials generally is well known. The major business organizations have not expressed their attitude, but they were hostile to the earlier Wagner–Murray–Dingell Bill in the 78th Congress.

The major change made in this bill from the earlier measure lies in a reduction in the tax (contribution) rate. This rate is 4 per cent each from employers and employees, compared with 6 per cent previously proposed. At the same time, the present bill provides more liberal benefits. How this can be done has not been made clear, as no one to date has presented estimates on the finances of the program. Appropriations from the Treasury are authorized to supplement the contributions of employers and employees and evidently are counted upon to meet deficits.

Like the earlier measure, the current Wagner–Murray–Dingell Bill contemplates a single integrated national social insurance system embracing unemployment insurance, health insurance, temporary disability insurance, and retirement, survivors' and extended disability insurance. It proposes that the present federal-state system of unemployment insurance be replaced by a uniform national system, providing benefits, both in cases of unemployment and temporary disability, of from $5 to $30 per week, varying with earnings and the number of dependents, and extending for 26 weeks. Along with this goes the continuance of wartime nationalization of the public employment offices. Old-age and survivors' insurance is extended to include also permanent disability, the minimum benefit is increased from $10 to $20 per month, and the retirement age for women is reduced to 60 from 65. Coverage is extended to include all employees except governmental employees (with a provision under which state and local employees may voluntarily be included). A complete innovation is insurance against medical care and hospitalization costs. The bill also makes provisions for social insurance protection for discharged servicemen and women, by allowing credit for all time spent in the service on the basis of an assumed wage of $160 per month.

In addition to these social insurance provisions, the Wagner–Murray–Dingell Bill expands the federal aids for social security purposes. One innovation is federal aid toward general public assistance (relief); another, grants and loans for a ten-year program for construction and expansion of hospitals, health centers, and related facilities. Large increases are proposed in the federal aids to the states for public health services and for maternal and child health and welfare services. All federal aids for social security purposes are to be given on a variable grants basis, under which no state will receive less aid than now, but the poorer states will get additional grants up to 75 per cent of their expenditures for these purposes.

《《《《《《《《《〈〇〉》》》》》》》》》

Note needs also to be taken of the Interim Report of the Subcommittee (of the Committee on Education and Labor) on Wartime Health and Education, commonly referred to as the "Pepper Report," which was filed in the Senate just before the close of the 78th Congress.[29] In this report, the deficiencies in the present pro-

---

[29] U.S. Senate Committee on Education and Labor, Subcommittee on Wartime Health and Education, 78th Congress, 2nd session, Subcommittee Report No. 3 (1944).

visions for medical care are discussed, with particular reference to the rejections in the administration of selective service. As a first measure toward correction, it is recommended that federal aid be authorized for the construction of hospitals and health centers, in accordance with integrated state plans approved by the United States Public Health Service. This recommendation is carried out in one of the titles of the Wagner–Murray–Dingell Bill and also is the basis of a separate measure introduced by Senator Pepper and other members of his committee. Emanating from the same group is another very recent bill authorizing an appropriation of $100,000,000 per year for free maternity care, including pre- and post-natal care for mothers and infants.

《《《《《《《《〈〉》》》》》》》》

Of proposals coming from what might be called "Anti-Administration" sources, note will be taken only of the program presented by the American Medical Association as a substitute for the medical care and health insurance provisions of the Wagner–Murray–Dingell Bill, and the social welfare program of Senator Robert A. Taft, released through the Republican National Committee early in August, 1945.

The first of these is not a legislative proposal but a 14-point program "for extending to all people in all communities the best possible medical care." [30] Only one of the 14 points calls for legislation —federal aid for local public health services "where definite need is demonstrated." Instead, the AMA advocates voluntary hospitalization and medical care insurance under the auspices of the medical societies, along with better living conditions through improved housing, nutrition, and sanitation. This has been the AMA's answer to all proposals for compulsory health insurance and legislation for improved medical care ever since 1935, when it reversed its earlier stand in opposition even to voluntary forms of health insurance. The 14-point program, however, has been publicized as if it represented a new forward-looking program which will accomplish all of the objectives of the Wagner–Murray–Dingell Bill, without any of the dangers of "socialized medicine."

[30] Presented in the *Journal of the American Medical Association*, July, 1945.

Senator Taft's social welfare program [31] is significant primarily because it indicates the position of the "opposition" to the Wagner–Murray–Dingell Bill. It goes along with at least the objectives of that bill in favoring "the extension of the old-age pension system and unemployment compensation to all groups not now covered, improvements in the present system of contributory insurance ... (and) federal aid for a comprehensive public and private health program, to build hospitals, extend public health service, supply medical aid to low income groups, and medical inspection and physical education in the schools." It expresses uncompromising opposition to the federalization of unemployment insurance, "socialized medicine," and "any over-all compulsory insurance plan."

Finally, note must be taken of developments in the states. Except for old-age and survivors' insurance, social security in the United States is today primarily a matter of state legislation and administration, and it is in the states that most of the actual legislative progress of recent years has been made.

Few state legislatures met in 1944, but nearly all of them were in session in the winter of 1945. Immediately prior to the 1945 sessions, the Social Security Board wrote to all the governors urging upon them the importance of immediate action to improve the state unemployment compensation laws in anticipation of the probable increase in unemployment in the reconversion period. This was the first time the Social Security Board had taken such action since it promulgated the model bills upon which most of the existing laws were based. The Council of State Governments also promulgated specific recommendations for improvements in the state laws, differing considerably from those made by the Social Security Board.[32] Bills to increase benefits and otherwise to liberalize the state unemployment insurance laws were subsequently introduced in nearly all legislatures. Complete information on the fate of these bills is not available, but it is certain that substantial increases in benefits were made in many states, although most states did not go so far as the Social Security Board recommended.

Bills for compulsory health insurance or for the extension of free

[31] Statement published in the newspapers, August 5, 1945.
[32] The Council of State Governments, *Unemployment Compensation in the Post-War Period* (1944).

public medical care to people who receive public assistance in any form also were introduced in many legislatures in 1945. All bills for compulsory health insurance were defeated, but a number of states enacted laws providing for free medical care for old-age pensioners and other recipients of public aids. The measure dealing with health problems which attracted the widest attention was the compulsory health insurance bill sponsored by Governor Warren in California. Governor Warren made this bill the principal item in his legislative program and made many appeals on the radio for its enactment. It was nevertheless defeated, as was a bill for compulsory hospitalization insurance which was presented after the defeat of the Governor's broader proposal.

Present Status and Future Prospects

At this writing, world prospects for early great progress in relation to social security and medical care appear excellent. In the conquered nations of continental Europe the social security institutions have been destroyed, one of the consequences of the fatal blight of Nazi rule. The Allied occupation authorities have indicated that they desire the restoration of these institutions, but this will be a slow process. In the liberated countries, restoration of the social insurance institutions has made great strides, and in some of them steps have been taken looking toward improvements in the prewar patterns. In the Latin-American countries, there is every reason to believe that the very great progress made during the war years will continue, if it is not accelerated. But it is in the English-speaking countries that the greatest progress is to be expected in the next year or two.

Prospects for the early enactment of comprehensive revisions of social security legislation appear excellent in Great Britain, Canada, and South Africa, but less so in the United States. In this country the situation is by no means hopeless, but there are several factors which make it unlikely that there will be action before the next session of the Congress, which begins in January. There have been no hearings in either House on the Wagner–Murray–Dingell Bill, and none are scheduled. Even the Administration bill for federal supplementary unemployment insurance during the reconversion years has been shelved in the House Ways and Means Committee, after having been amended in the Senate to such an extent that President Truman has publicly stated that he was "let down."

At this moment, there is greater interest in full employment than in social security, alike in the United States, Great Britain, and Canada. The term comes close to expressing the major economic objective of the present day. Allied success in the war has made full employment more than the mere expression of a hope. There is a growing belief that it can be attained in peacetime no less than in war. With the end of the war, there is increasing concern lest this opportunity slip out of grasp. The combination of these factors has created a situation where every leader must concern himself with the subject. There is no agreement anywhere, however, regarding means and methods. Particularly is this true in the United States, where opinion ranges from a conviction that full employment depends upon the government getting out of business and relaxing its controls to a view that there is hope only in a completely planned economy. Yet in this country, as abroad, majority opinion clearly demands that the government must do something to insure full employment. So it seems certain that in the months immediately ahead there will be increased discussion of what the government ought to do to insure full employment, with a likelihood that some legislation will be enacted. What this will be, however, is very uncertain.

Outside the United States, there is no conflict between full employment and social security. Even in this country, few informed people believe that full employment will eliminate the need for social security legislation. The support for legislation like that proposed in the pending Full Employment Bill is practically identical with that for the Wagner–Murray–Dingell Bill. The latter measure, however, faces a stronger and better organized opposition. This centers in the American Medical Association and the state unemployment compensation administrators, who have on their side catchwords and slogans with a stronger popular appeal than any which the supporters of the proposed legislation have been able to muster. Taking account only of the immediate situation, it would seem that Congress is unlikely to enact legislation for either compulsory health insurance or the federalization of unemployment, or to revoke the promise to return the public employment offices to the states. It is still doubtful whether Congress will enact legislation for supplementary unemployment insurance in the transition period.

The present situation, however, is very dynamic. Changes in conditions may change the prospects for social security legislation overnight. For instance, should the end of the war bring with it widespread and continued unemployment, the prospects for the federalization of unemployment insurance or, at least, for federal supplementary unemployment insurance for war workers and federal employees during the reconversion period, will be greatly improved. What England or Canada do will also have some repercussions in this country, although these will be less extensive than those likely to result from basic changes in conditions within the United States. With the end of the war, however, some new social security legislation seems certain of enactment by Congress. Assuredly this country will not fail to give ex-servicemen the same rights in the national old-age insurance system which they would have had if they had been in private employment instead of in service with the colors. There also is little controversy over many other provisions of the Wagner–Murray–Dingell Bill. Congress has to act upon so many matters that once it tackles a problem it usually passes comprehensive legislation on the subject. When Congress will again tackle social security in this manner is uncertain, but the next session would seem to be a good guess.

Basic Considerations

in Medical Care and

Health Insurance

Excerpt from *Health
Insurance in America,* addresses at the Second
National Conference on
Social Security, sponsored by
the Chamber of Commerce of
the United States (1945),
pages 4–16

WHAT SHOULD BE DONE about this matter of medical care and
health insurance which promises to loom larger in the years immediately following the war? It has been suggested to me that I should
raise questions rather than to pontificate upon the solutions. I am
happy to adopt this suggestion, because I do not claim to know all
the answers. While I am on record as believing in compulsory health
insurance and have, on a number of occasions, expressed the view
that the situation requires a constructive program and not merely
criticism of proposals presented in Congress and elsewhere, I hope
that I am not totally unmindful that at many points there is a choice
of alternatives, about which there will, naturally, be differences of
opinion.

The first major question, about which there are wide differences
of opinion, concerns the extent to which insurance principles should
be utilized in making provisions of the costs of illness, which . . . include both the loss of wages incident to sickness and the cost of adequate medical care. That insurance principles can be utilized to meet
both these risks is not open to doubt. There is now private insurance
both on an individual and a group basis in this country against both

of these risks. Outside this country, health insurance is widely prevalent as a form of social insurance. It is the oldest form of social insurance and the most widely prevalent. It existed before the war in literally every European country and, as has been noted, is now in operation in nearly all the Latin-American nations. While the amount of sickness varies greatly among individuals, its total incidence does not change so very much from year to year. It presents a definable risk and a calculable cost, with lesser probabilities of error than in many other forms of insurance.

Whether insurance should be utilized in providing protection against these risks involves more than whether it is technically possible. It also raises the question of alternatives. Of the theoretically possible alternatives, two—individual savings and private and public charity—must be ruled out as no longer a solution of the problem deemed adequate by the American people. Savings, if large enough, are the surest safeguard against dependency as a consequence of illness. I believe in individual savings as a most valuable safeguard against all personal economic hazards, but a hazard as varying and costly as is illness cannot be met solely through urging people to be thrifty nor even by providing full employment. Only through insurance can the costs be reduced to average costs, rather than the much greater costs which some individuals experience annually. Neither will Americans be satisfied with a solution which leaves people with small or average family incomes to reliance upon charity— whether public or private—when they are confronted with the heavy costs of serious illness.

The real alternatives to some form of health insurance, I believe to be further extension of public medical care and sick leave plans. The latter will afford protection only against the loss of wages in cases of sickness; although a smaller item than the costs of medical care, this is not unimportant. Whether it is desirable to give production workers sick leave on the same basis as has become common for office employees, you are better qualified to say than I. I hazard the guess that if some legislation for partial compensation for loss of wages resulting from sickness is not quite soon generally adopted in this country, demands from unions for sick leave plans will multiply and that the time is not far distant when employers will be required to give reasonable sick leave with pay, through legislative enactment or the fiat of some labor board.

Public medical care I also believe to be an alternative to health insurance. No health insurance plan will eliminate the need for provisions to give medical care to indigents at public expense. The person without income, or but little income, cannot contribute to insurance funds. This means that if he is included in a health insurance plan, his costs must either be met by the other contributors or from the public treasury. If excluded, the public must provide him public medical care in some form or other. But the situation is different as to many people who are above the dependency line. Most of these can pay the costs of at least most of the medical care they need, if they can meet these costs on a budget basis, such as is afforded through insurance. If they do not pay these costs on such a basis, they are likely to make no provisions for possible illness and are swamped if unfortunate enough to be confronted with serious illness in their families. Many of the medically indigent can pay their costs on an insurance basis, but must have public medical care if not covered by some form of health insurance. It is not without significance that a large group among the people interested in more adequate medical care for all Americans, particularly among liberal-minded physicians, have come to the conclusion that public medical care, rather than health insurance, is the solution. And this further is to be said, that while the doctors as a group are very jittery about "socialized medicine," they have fought extension of public medical care much less unyieldingly than health insurance.

Once the basic question whether we want health insurance or not is answered in the affirmative (as was the answer given by the members of the Chamber of Commerce of the United States) many other questions emerge. The first of these is voluntary versus compulsory insurance. I will not go into this issue except to ask the question, whether it is likely that voluntary health insurance will become sufficiently widespread to stave off the demand for compulsory insurance? The most popular form of voluntary insurance in this field, hospital insurance, thus far covers only 12 per cent of the American population; the medical care plans of the medical associations, considerably less than 1 per cent; and all medical care plans only 2½ per cent of all our people. The spread of voluntary types of health insurance, moreover, may well have the effect of making the American public more receptive to compulsory legislation.

Next, there arises the question of the relation of cash benefits as partial compensation for loss of wages due to sickness and medical care services during periods of illness. Other than in France, health insurance has combined both these benefits. Initially, however, the services in kind were incidental and the core of health insurance lay in the benefits in cash to compensate for wage loss. In all countries there has been a tendency for the medical care and preventive services to become more important, although, in the great majority of the countries with compulsory health insurance systems, more is still being spent for cash benefits than for medical services. In the thinking on postwar health organization, however, cash benefits have everywhere become secondary to preventive and curative medical care services. In the British plans now under discussion, while both cash benefits and medical care services are to be provided and both are, in part, to be financed from contributions, the cash benefits are regarded and administered as a part of social insurance while the medical care services are the core of the national health programs.

In the United States the early proposals for compulsory health insurance all contemplated a combination of cash benefits and services in kind. This is still the concept of health insurance held by most of the people who approach the subject from the economic side of the medical care problem, as I have done. But this is not the approach of the liberal-minded members of the profession. Their interest and that of many others lies in the improvement of the medical care actually provided all Americans. To them, health insurance is only one part of a much larger national health program. Because they could not make headway with compulsory health insurance, combining benefits in cash and services in kind in traditional European fashion, many of the old-time advocates of health insurance have now come to the conclusion that the best hope for progress lies in separating cash benefits from medical care services. This is what was done in the pioneer Rhode Island cash sickness benefit law. I leave to you whether this is a sound development. But it must never be lost sight of that there are two aspects of the problem and that both are important: the aspect of partially making good the loss of income due to illness, and that of making adequate medical care available to all Americans and other than on a charity basis.

Problems of coverage also loom large in any consideration of health insurance. Health insurance, developing as a part of social insurance, was first applied only to the insured workers. In most countries, but not to date in England, the benefits have since been extended to include the dependents of the workers. More recently they have been extended in some countries to other groups in the population: old-age pensioners, public assistance recipients, the dependents of men called to the colors and the self-employed. The thinking of the post-war planners interested in a comprehensive national health program is definitely for inclusion within the medical care plan of the entire population. But cash benefits are still always thought of as partial compensation for loss of income and, hence, must be limited to the employed part of the population.

In this country, there has been more discussion of the contingencies in which medical care services are to be provided than of the part of the population to be included within the insurance scheme. The medical associations have taken the position that if there is to be any health insurance the benefits should be restricted to catastrophic or long-continuing illness. The people whose greatest interest is in the improvement of the standards of public health reject this view. I do not have time to further discuss this issue, but note that while a plan [dealing] with catastrophic illness only may conceivably prove a fairly adequate solution of the purely economic aspects of the problem, it will not serve the preventive objectives which are at least equally important in the national public health programs now under discussion the world over.

Looming large also are problems of administration. Here the basic question to be decided is that of the respective roles of the national and state governments. It is agreed that the actual administration of both health insurance and medical care services must occur on the local level, but this does not preclude a national system or what we have come to call in this country a federal-state system. If we are to have a truly nationwide postwar public health program, some participation by the national government would seem to be inevitable, but there are many possibilities as to the precise role of the respective levels of government we have in this country. It is inevitable, however, that if the national government supplies a large part of financing, it will also claim a large share in the control.

Then there are the many problems involving the relations of the medical practitioners to the governmental plan. There is no controversy over the free choice of the doctor by the insured or the choice of patients by the doctors. In this country there will be no compulsion in these respects. Neither is any one disposed toward interference with any of the technical aspects of the performance of medical services. But there are major questions relating to the degree of control which the medical profession is to have over the general administration of the health insurance and medical care plans and regarding the method by which practitioners are to be compensated for their services. Clearly, the profession should have a direct voice and part in administration, but it must also recognize that the patients have an interest in health, no less than the doctors. It seems to me clear also that in this country we will not have completely socialized medicine, but rather some modification of our present mixed system combining both private practice and public medical care.

Quite similar is the problem of the relation of any governmental plan to the existing insurance and other preservice payment plans. On this problem, it must be noted that most of the advocates of a national public health program would prefer to develop such a program without having to take the existing plans into consideration. Many of the outstanding weaknesses in compulsory health insurance as it has functioned in England to date are directly traceable to the fact that the governmental system incorporated a great variety of preëxisting voluntary systems, functioning through the friendly societies. Considering the problem realistically, however, it seems clear that any national public health program must take account of the existing voluntary plans and assign them a part in this program. What this should be opens a broad vista of possibilities.

This leaves the vital matter of financing. I am not one of those who believes that we can afford in the consideration of desirable social progress to pay no attention to the costs. I do not share the position many businessmen have taken in the controversy over the financing of old-age and survivors' insurance and tax freezing that current costs only need to be considered and that we do not even need a statement of the liabilities we are incurring which have to be met in the future. Health and medical care services, unlike old-age insurance, do not involve a factor of inevitable, rapidly increasing disbursements with the lapse of the years. Yet I deem it essential that we have careful estimates of costs and a clear idea of where the money is to come from. I also believe that no benefits should be promised that cannot be surely financed. You may differ from me in these views, as many of you have in relation to old-age and survivors' insurance, and I recognize that time may prove you right, although I expect the contrary. But even if you agree with me, the question remains of the distribution of the inevitable costs. With the large demands there will be upon the public treasury for many purposes, I do not believe it to be desirable to attempt to finance a national program of health insurance and medical care services exclusively from public funds. I believe triparty financing—from public funds and contributions of the beneficiaries and also of the employers—is indicated. One of the reasons I believe in insurance is that I deem direct contributions by the beneficiaries to be essential. I further believe employer contributions to be necessary, but would keep them as low as possible. The exact distribution is a matter on which any program that can gain majority support will be acceptable to me.

In concluding, I fear that I have been more positive than I intended. In so freely expressing my views I have not sought to convert you, but rather to challenge your thinking and to provoke discussion of the important problem with which we are dealing. It is, indeed, one of the major problems of the immediate postwar period and will demand the best thought of informed people in all groups in our population, and a desire on their part to find a solution suitable to our institutions and present-day thought.

Trends in Payment
for Medical Care

American Management
Association, *What's Ahead
in Employee Health and
Pension Planning,* Personnel
Series No. 126 (1949),
pages 25–33

L ET ME SAY at the outset that I shall deal with trends in payment for medical care only from a public point of view. Likewise, I shall deal only with what might be called the economic side of medical care—costs and methods of payment—not with the medical aspects. I am not a medical practitioner, but an economist. I am neither an employer nor a union member, nor have I ever been an adviser for compensation to either contending party in labor controversies. Throughout all my adult life, I have been a public employee or official and a student of industrial relations and social security problems. I can deal only with aspects which are within my competence and experience. These are the economic aspects of medical care, viewed from a general public point of view.

On its economic side, medicine in the United States appears at this time to be in transition. New methods of payment for medical care have been developed in the last fifteen years and their importance is rapidly increasing. More extensive changes are in prospect.

A little more than fifteen years ago when the Committee on the Costs of Medical Care published its numerous reports and studies, medical care was paid for predominantly on an individual, post-service, fee basis. Even then, one-sixth of the combined costs of all kinds of medical care were paid for from general tax funds. Several millions of Americans had individual accident and health insurance policies giving them stipulated cash benefits in cases of illness. There was a sizable volume of industrial medicine and there were a few voluntary plans for payment of medical care on a budgeted group basis. The American Medical Association strongly opposed all forms of group payment, whether voluntary or compulsory. Some eminent medical men favored experimentation with voluntary medical care insurance, while a few were on record for compulsory health insurance. Outside of medical circles, compulsory health insurance had much greater support. It seemed to be well within the range of possibility that many states might enact compulsory health insurance laws within a few years, under the stimulus of federal aid or compulsion.

That nongovernmental health insurance as a method of payment for medical care would attain great proportions seemed very unlikely.

As matters have turned out, the situation of fifteen years ago not only has been materially changed but has developed quite differently from the expected. The individual, post-service fee method of payments remains dominant, but there has occurred a very great growth in voluntary forms of health insurance, particularly in the last few years. In January, 1948, 30,000,000 Americans and Canadians were covered by Blue Cross hospital insurance policies and another 5,700,-000 had hospital insurance with commercial insurance companies. [Approximately] 7,500,000 Americans had medical care insurance under some type of group plan and around 4,000,000 others under individual insurance policies. Commercial insurance companies which until about ten years ago wrote only individual health and accident insurance, now aggressively promote all types of health insurance, both group and individual. An estimated 25,000,000 Americans had some type of health insurance through insurance companies, 17,000,-000 under individual policies. In the figures cited there is considerable duplication, but it would appear that around 50,000,000 Americans today have some protection through voluntary insurance providing cash benefits or services in cases of illness. A large percentage are industrial workers and their dependents. The protection provided, however, is generally only for specific aspects of the total costs of illness, with numerous restrictive limitations.

The American Medical Association has reversed its earlier stand on voluntary health insurance, although continuing its uncompromising opposition to all forms of compulsory insurance. As early as 1935, it approved voluntary medical care insurance if conducted by county or state medical societies. A little later it sanctioned Blue Cross hospital insurance. Since the close of the war, it has given its approval to substantially all forms of voluntary health insurance.

Another significant development in the methods of payment for medical care has been the rapid growth in recent years of joint labor-management health and welfare funds. Such funds were almost unknown fifteen years ago and as recently as the end of 1945 included only 600,000 workers. In July, 1948, they covered 3,000,000 workers and some important new plans have come into operation since. The largest number of the workers covered by such health and welfare plans are in the needle trades, with the coal miners and textile workers following in order, and some illustrations in many other industries and in all parts of the country. These health and welfare funds generally provide benefits in cash for time lost through sickness, and/or the costs of hospitalization, and, less commonly, surgical expenses, all subject to maximum limitations as to duration and amount. Quite often sickness benefits are combined in a package plan with life insurance and retirement benefits, and generally contracts are made with commercial insurance companies and Blue Cross organizations for the actual payment of the benefits. A few plans, principally in the needle trades, provide medical services in kind through union health centers. Most plans are contributory, but with quite a few illustrations already of health and welfare funds financed entirely by the employer.

Another major trend has been toward an increase in the absolute and proportionate shares of public financing in the mixed system of private and public medical care which we have in this country. The one-sixth of all medical care costs paid from taxes in 1929 has become close to a one-fourth share. In every session in recent years, Congress has increased the appropriations for public health and medical care purposes. Socialized medicine, in the sense of medical care provided at the taxpayer's expense, has been growing apace in this country.

Compulsory health insurance, on the other hand, has made but little headway. Recommended by the Committee to Coördinate Health and Welfare Activities and the National Health Conference in 1938, compulsory health insurance has been before Congress ever since. Such legislation has been endorsed by all major labor organizations and by many farm and women's organizations. Every indication is that it has much greater support than formerly among the general public; opinion polls, in fact, indicate support by a majority of all Americans. Despite assumed but never expressed support from President Roosevelt and unequivocal endorsement on numerous occasions by President Truman, compulsory health insurance has never even gotten to a vote in either house of the Congress. Health insurance proposals likewise have made but little headway in the state legislatures. While proposed repeatedly in the most industrial states, it is only in California that compulsory health insurance came even close to passage. A dozen years ago a California interim legislative committee endorsed compulsory health insurance and the state medical association gave it its blessing in principle, although proposing a different bill. But nothing came of all this; and Governor Warren's more recent espousal of the cause has resulted only in the enactment of the disability compensation act of 1946.

Disability or cash sickness compensation now exists not only in California, but also in Rhode Island (where it originated) and New Jersey and under the railroad unemployment insurance act. The emergence of this new type of social insurance reflects a recent change in the very meaning of compulsory health insurance. Until the last decade, compulsory health insurance, as it existed throughout Europe and as proposed in this country, provided two distinct types of benefits within the same program: partial compensation in cash for wage loss due to illness and medical care services in kind for insured workers and their dependents. Now the compensation in cash for wage loss has become completely separated from the medical care services and only the latter are included within the term health insurance as used in legislative proposals. Interestingly, the same thing happened in England when that country in the National Health Services Act, which became effective July 1, 1948, substituted for its prior system of compulsory health insurance a system of state medicine.

While compulsory health insurance has gotten nowhere, legislatively, it is certainly not dead. Its present strength is indicated by the fact that the American Medical Association has levied a special assessment of $25 on all its members to fight the proposal in Congress.

The proposal now before Congress is part of a Ten Year National Health Program, which was presented to the President last summer by Federal Security Administrator Oscar Ewing and endorsed by the President, both in his campaign and in his message to Congress last month. In legislative form it is now before the Congress in bills introduced by Senator Murray and five other Senators and by Representatives Dingell and Celler. How far these bills will get is uncertain. There are good prospects for a favorable report on at least part of the Administration's health insurance bill in the Senate. But I do not expect Congress at this session to enact a contributory health insurance law. Much more likely is a further extension of public medical care—something like the Taft bill in the 80th Congress, which proposed federal aid to the states, in the amount of $200,000,-000 per year, for medical care at public expense to the medically indigent. Whatever may happen this session, compulsory health insurance will continue to be an issue before Congress and it probably has a better chance for passage next year than this.

Passing from Congress to the state legislatures, I need say very little to give you the present picture, as Mr. Conohoe has dealt in detail with the current developments in disability legislation. To the picture he has given you I will add only that the Executive Council of the American Federation of Labor within the last two weeks has taken the position that disability insurance should be provided by the national government rather than by the states. In taking this position, it issued a statement that disability insurance laws which exempt employers who insure with private insurance carriers benefit far more the insurance companies than the workers who become ill. State federations of labor are urging state legislation, but the AFL, as well as the CIO, are looking to Congress for action, both on health and disability insurance. The position taken by the labor federations may well be used as an argument in many states to defeat proposals for disability insurance, although it can also be cited as a reason for prompt state action.

Defeat or stalling of legislation for disability and health insurance will not get rid of these demands for keeps, but will give further impetus to labor's demands for health and welfare funds to be established through collective bargaining and to be financed largely by the employers. The CIO in its publication, *Economic Outlook,* for December, labels its program a "Two-Way Drive for Social Security." On the one hand, it seeks a unified, enlarged, and improved social security system through congressional legislation. On the other, it hopes to win through collective bargaining "employer-financed plans which provide protection against the economic hazards of old age, premature death, sickness, and unemployment." It looks upon these programs as supplementary and states: "By keeping up the drive on both fronts we are more apt to get action." The American Federation of Labor officially is only demanding an all-inclusive national social security system, including both disability and health insurance. Many AFL unions, however, are also seeking social security through collective bargaining. John L. Lewis and his United Mine Workers are showing little or no interest in social security through legislation. They are planning retirement and health protection for all their members and their dependents through industry payments won in collective bargaining, pretty much independently of any government action.

The success Lewis has had with his program appears to be a major factor in the present demands by other unions. The 20 cents per ton of coal mined paid into the Welfare and Retirement Fund (which began as 5 cents in 1946, became 10 cents in 1947, and the present 20 cents in 1948) amounts to more than 10 per cent of the cost of coal at the mines. Out of this fund retirement pensions of $100 per month are paid to miners who have been members of the union for 20 years and who have attained 62 years of age. Significantly, these payments are additional to similar payment from any other source, including benefits under the Social Security Act. Out of the Welfare and Retirement Fund considerable payments also are made for health purposes. These are expended for the costs of treatment of miners suffering from illnesses or accidents requiring special and expensive treatment, for general medical, surgical, and hospital care of miners who are receiving so-called "distress payments" for disability, for such care to the survivors of deceased miners, and finally for medical research on coal miners' diseases. Under his contract with the operators, Lewis at any time can take over the contributory plans for industrial medical care which have long existed in many coal-mining communities. He has not done so to date, but has announced that it is the union's intention that the Welfare and Retirement Fund ultimately will provide complete health care to all of the United Mine Workers and their dependents. This would require a further large increase in the royalty payments and such an increase may well be made in the negotiations for new contracts which are due to begin next month.

No other union is developing its social security program without interest in or regard for existing or proposed governmental programs. But many unions have made or are about to make demands for social security and medical care benefits supplementary to those provided under governmental programs. Many unions are no longer satisfied with benefits provided unilaterally by employers through group insurance policies with commercial insurance companies. They demand a voice both in the determination of the benefits and in their administration.

The demands which the large unions will make in the negotiations of the next months have not been fully formulated, but can be anticipated from advance announcements. The Automobile Workers and the Steel Workers, as well as other unions, will ask for liberal and bargained retirement, death, disability, hospitalization, surgical, and medical care benefits. It will also be demanded, at least of the CIO unions, that these benefits shall be administered by a board of trustees ... either bipartisan or triparty in composition, which will contract with the insurance companies rather than the employers. And the unions are talking about having the employers pay the entire costs, without any contributions by the employees.

Something of what may be expected in negotiation is, perhaps, foreshadowed by the plan now in operation in the Kaiser-Fraser plant in Detroit, which the Social Security Department of the UAW–CIO calls its "pilot plan" and which covers 15,000 workers and 40,000 of their dependents. Under the contract between the Company and the Union, a social security fund is created which is controlled by a joint board of trustees. This board has contracted with insurance companies and Blue Cross and Blue Shield organizations for the benefits to workers and their dependents. These benefits are paid for by a 5 cents per hour payment of the employer, without any contribution by the employees. The benefits are a lump sum death benefit of $500 plus payments of $100 per month for 15 months thereafter; a cash disability benefit for nonoccupational illness, beginning on the first day of hospitalization or the eighth day in non-hospitalized cases, of $30 per week, continuing for a maximum of 26 weeks; Blue Cross hospitalization benefits, unlimited in amount and duration and including most hospital extras; and Blue Shield surgical benefits. It is to be noted that the 5 cents per hour employer contribution under this plan does not cover retirement benefits. These are a distinct Union demand, also to be financed exclusively by the employer. And there are some indications that in the demands the Union will present to other companies, it will seek payments from the employers not of 5 cents per hour, but of 5 per cent of payrolls for health and death benefits.

As is well known, there is today much rivalry among unions in demands made upon employers. What one major union asks, the others can be expected to top or at least equal.

Demands are one thing and what is really expected quite something else. Last year social security demands made by major CIO unions were pretty generally dropped when the employers made counter-offers of large wage increases.

But it does not follow that this will occur again. The recent downward trend in the cost of living and some increase in unemployment argue against wage increases, particularly in industries that are now ahead of the procession. No doubt, wage increases will be demanded along with social security and medical benefits, but this time it is quite likely the latter which the unions will press most vigorously.

It is also to be expected that quite soon it will be finally settled that employers must bargain over retirement, health, and welfare plans when the unions that represent a majority of their employees so demand. The United States Supreme Court has not decided the appeal in the Inland Steel Case. It would come as a great surprise, however, if in that case, which is expected to be decided in the near future, the Court did not uphold the NLRB and the lower courts.

The entire situation is one which presents great difficulties to employers. One of these is the fact that the costs of social security benefits such as will prove reasonably satisfactory to the employees are large. Unless the employers' contributions are limited to a fixed amount or percentage of payroll, the costs of pledged benefits, moreover, are quite likely to prove greater than estimated. The employer, whether he acts unilaterally or under an agreement with the union, becomes a guarantor of the promised benefits, morally and practically, if not legally. Hence, if benefits are promised, it is very important that most careful actuarial cost estimates precede all promises. A trustee plan of administration, such as is provided for in the

Taft-Hartley Act, may somewhat lessen the responsibility of employers, but they clearly remain partners in the enterprise and, as such, should know definitely what are their liabilities.

Health and welfare plans at their best are unlikely to provide truly adequate protection to workers against the economic consequences of illness. Even when benefits to employees are unlimited, there is still the problem of their dependents. Serious illness of any member of his family is apt to cost the wage-earner as much as his own illness, except for the wage loss. The costs of medical care of all kinds exceed the total wage loss due to illness at least in the ratio of three to two and probably closer to two to one. Further, under all plans (except that about which John L. Lewis has been talking, but has not put into effect) the worker's protection ceases with retirement or unemployment. As people get older, sickness becomes a more serious problem. So it is after workers are retired that their medical care costs are greatest.

Also ever to be borne in mind is industry's responsibility to the community. Industry's obligations cannot fully be discharged by taking care of its employees while they remain in its service. As the largest producer of income and the largest taxpayer, it will be called upon to foot a large part of the costs of insecurity throughout the community. A system that provides security for employed industrial workers but not for the farmers, the farm laborers, the officeworkers, the domestics, the retail and service industries, and the small businessmen, will not long be deemed satisfactory. Health and welfare plans, whether established on an industry or a company basis, will not end the demand for governmental systems of health and disability insurance. They may well operate to increase the support for compulsory health insurance among the people who do not share in the benefits of the plans established unilaterally by employers or through collective bargaining. As an alternative loom great extensions of medical care provided at the taxpayers' expense, with the largest part of the costs falling upon industry.

Sickness is one of the most serious of personal hazards. Except in periods of great unemployment, it is the most important single cause of poverty and dependency. It is also the most frequent cause of absenteeism and a large factor in producing a feeling of insecurity which is harmful to maximum production and to social stability. Industry is not solely or principally responsible for sickness among its employees. But sickness has some relation to employment as is obvious from the fact that the worker spends a third of his day in the plant. Moreover, we are rapidly coming to the concept that adequate medical care is a social necessity, if not the right, of every American. Industry cannot escape a large share of responsibility for making this concept a reality.

As I see it, all these considerations are strong arguments for an all-inclusive contributory health insurance system. This can only be established by law and must be compulsory. It is my belief that such a system in the long run will be both less expensive and much fairer to industry than the situation which is developing in the absence of a contributory, compulsory insurance system.

I hold this view because I staunchly believe in a contributory social security system. Employee contributions are the best possible safeguard against unreasonable costs and lax administration. I am convinced that unless we get a minimum, reasonably adequate protection against all hazards of life leading to poverty and dependency quite soon (although I favor attaining this objective in gradual steps), the contributory principle will be lost.

We may have delayed too long already in modifying our old-age and survivor's insurance system to make it all inclusive and its benefits adequate at least for subsistence. Today there is more support than ever before in Congress for universal flat rate pensions for all older people. This program has the support of many of the most conservative members of Congress; for instance, Senator Brewster championed such a "baby Townsend" plan in a radio talk earlier this month. Unless grapevine reports are incorrect, the Hoover Commission in its recommendations on social security administration, which is to be presented very soon, will also endorse flat rate pensions for all old people. What that will cost, right from the outset, is indicated by the fact that less than 40 per cent of all people over 65 years of age now receive either old-age insurance or old-age assistance. Its ultimate costs can be imagined from our record with veterans' pensions, which also are noncontributory and paid from general taxes and regardless of need.

Within the past week, the Rankin bill has been recommended for passage and all reports agree that it is likely to be passed at least by the House, despite administration opposition. This bill provides for pensions of $90 per month to all veterans on attaining age 65, which would cost $6 billion in the very first year. In contemplating this prospect, it needs to be remembered that there are far more nonveterans than there are veterans in our population. But unless we get an adequate old-age insurance system very soon, you can expect that we will soon have a system of flat rate pensions for all older people, which is paid regardless of need and is financed from general taxes.

With reference to a better and less burdensome distribution of the costs of medical care, as I see it, we have not reached the same stage as we have in relations to retirement protection. But the time when we can establish a contributory system of health security is likely to run out ere long.

Many will see the developments I have discussed very differently. Their views may turn out more correct than mine. I suggest only that the problem I have dealt with is one which deserves intelligent and open-minded consideration from management and labor alike. In such consideration it is essential that weight be given not only to immediate costs and advantages, but to probable long-time developments and results.

The Future

of Social Security

in the Health Field

Excerpt from an address in
the Series on Industrial
Relations Patterns for
1957, at Michigan State
University, January 25, 1957.
Published in *U.S. Industrial
Relations: The Next Twenty
Years,* by Clark Kerr and
others, East Lansing, Michi-
gan: Michigan State
University Press, 1958,
pages 137–165

W *Workmen's Compensation*

ORKMEN'S COMPENSATION is our oldest form of social insurance. It is the social insurance program for the man or woman who
suffers an industrial injury or an occupational disease. Workmen's
compensation is in effect in every state in the Union and is established
and administered by the states. There is no federal legislation on
workmen's compensation, except for federal employees, the District
of Columbia, and offshore workers.

Workmen's compensation, undoubtedly, has been of great value
to a good many workers who have been injured, and to their dependents. But it, too, is a system which, on the average, pays only
about one-third as much as a man who is not the victim of an industrial accident or occupational disease makes when he is employed.
Workmen's compensation works least well for the workers who suffer
the most serious injuries; improvement is badly needed. Fairer benefits are long overdue and, surely, coverage should be extended.

Workmen's compensation has been a popular program, but at this
stage a good many working people are saying that they would be
better off if we returned to the old employer's liability system. And
there is beginning to be considerable demand for the federalization

of workmen's compensation. This is a demand which, fortunately, I think, is not yet dominant in labor ranks; but, unless we improve workmen's compensation, we will have, I predict, a very strong demand for fundamental changes in the system. This year the prospects for improvements in workmen's compensation seem good. Such improvements have been recommended by the President and in all messages of the governors I have seen. Let us hope that long-overdue improvements will, indeed, be forthcoming.[1]

Cash Sickness Compensation (Disability Insurance)

The latest of the social insurance programs in this country is cash sickness compensation or disability insurance, as it is often called. This is not "disability" or "invalidity" insurance in the European meaning of these terms, since it provides no protection against the larger of the two principal sources of loss resulting from nonoccupational illness, the costs of medical care.[2] It provides protection only against the smaller of the sickness costs, the loss of earnings resulting from illness.

The workers generally in four states—Rhode Island, California, New Jersey, and New York—and the railroad industry under a federal law (less than a third of all industrial workers) enjoy the protection of compulsory cash sickness compensation laws. These laws provide benefits on the same basis as unemployment insurance (workmen's compensation in New York). Most of them allow employers to contract out of the law. It can be said, with some element of truth, that they have proved more of a boon to the insurance companies than to the mass of the workers. But on balance, these laws represent a forward step in social security protection, with the most serious deficiency being that the great majority of the states lack such laws altogether.

A considerable number of employers have established cash sickness compensation programs unilaterally or under collective bargain-

---

[1] As in unemployment insurance, the improvements actually made in 1957 were disappointing. Most of the state legislatures changed their workmen's compensation laws in some respects and most of the changes were improvements. The increases in benefits did not, in most states, keep pace with the increases in the cost of living and still less with rising wage levels. Coverage was extended in only a few states.

[2] In California the cash sickness compensation law provides protection against part of the cost of hospital care.

ing agreements with unions. The claim is often made that there is no need for compulsory legislation in this field because so many employers voluntarily are paying cash sickness compensation, either under insured plans or in the form of paid sick leave. But it must be noted that progress in this respect has been very slow for at least a half-dozen years. The last of the compulsory laws was enacted in 1949, and the rate of growth of voluntary programs for partial compensation of income loss due to sickness has greatly declined, although some progress is still being made. The present situation is summarized in the January [1957] issue of the *Social Security Bulletin,* the organ of the Social Security Administration, as follows:

Insurance and various other forms of protection against income loss resulting from sickness experienced rapid growth during the years immediately after World War II. In the last three years, however, the growth has only barely kept up with the increase in per capita income and expansion of the labor force. There has been little overall increase in income loss protection in cases of sickness since 1952.

American industry and, probably, a majority of all Americans have had a decided preference for voluntary rather than compulsory action "where it will do the trick." We have depended mainly upon voluntary programs for protection against the great hazard of income loss resulting from illness. That voluntary action in this field has proved disappointing must now be acknowledged. Insurance protection against this great risk covers less than one-eighth of the total loss of earnings resulting from illness—and most of this protection is in the states with compulsory laws. Voluntary methods are now distinctly on trial. It is my view that unless better results appear soon, the American people will demand governmental action.

Protection against Medical Care Costs

A much greater risk, from a dollar and cents viewpoint, than that of income loss due to illness, are the costs of medical, hospital, and related care. Of the total present costs of illness, loss of earnings represents two-fifths and the health care bill represents three-fifths. Health care costs in the United States now total $15 billion per year, and are increasing at a rate of about 1 per cent a month. About 70 per cent of those costs are met from private funds, 30 per cent from tax funds. Of the costs met from private funds, about 20 per cent is paid through insurance, all of it on a voluntary basis.

For ten or fifteen years we have been saying, "Let voluntary insurance do the job." Voluntary health insurance has made progress, but its progress has slowed up in the last few years and doubts are developing about our voluntary methods. Nearly two-fifths, or 40 per cent, of the American people still do not have any hospital insurance, and one-half have no medical or surgical care insurance. Only a minute percentage have insurance against the costs of dental care, drugs and medicines, and the many miscellaneous items in health costs. Even these percentages overstate the protection afforded through voluntary health insurance, as most of the insured have coverage for only part of the costs. More than 60 per cent of all Americans today have some hospital insurance, but only 40 per cent of the total hospital bills of the country are paid through insurance. Of the medical and surgical care costs, less than 20 per cent are paid by insurance; of the other types of medical care costs, almost nothing comes from insurance. Sickness is for many Americans the most serious personal hazard they confront. In times of deep depressions, unemployment is the most serious hazard, but in normal times more Americans sink to the poverty level and become dependent by reason of sickness than for any other cause.

This year [1957] President Eisenhower has again recommended that we strengthen our voluntary health insurance systems. In 1954 the President's recommendation resulted in an Administration bill for a national reinsurance plan for the voluntary health insurance carriers. This bill was strongly opposed by the commercial insurance companies and by the American Medical Association, and was defeated by a few votes in the House of Representatives. Whether the President's recommendations will get even that far this year, I doubt.[3]

It seems clear that voluntary health insurance must be extended and improved if it is to continue to be our major reliance for protection against the rapidly increasing health care costs. If we continue to rely upon voluntary insurance, it must reach the people

[3] No attention whatsoever was paid in the First Session of the 85th Congress to the President's recommendation to strengthen voluntary health insurance. No bill to carry out this recommendation was introduced and no hearings were conducted on the subject.

who need insurance most—the older people, who have the most
sickness, the poorer people, who cannot afford to pay premiums, and
the rural people, who are seldom covered. The very groups that
have much more than the normal amount of sickness are the ones
that do not have health insurance on a voluntary basis.

The president of the American Medical Association, in a recent
address, acknowledged that the present situation is unsatisfactory
and said that the state and local governments should pay the health
insurance premiums of those who cannot afford to pay such premiums—at least 20 per cent and probably more of the entire population. This address reflects a current trend which merits more attention than it has received. We have made no progress toward
compulsory health insurance in this country. We are today the only
major nation, with the exception of Canada, India, and China, which
does not have compulsory health insurance; and Canada is now in
the process of adopting such a program. In contrast, we have completely rejected compulsory health insurance. But, almost unnoticed,
we also have greatly increased the public element in the mixed
system of paying for medical care that we have.

We are wont to talk about having private medical care in the
United States. As has been noted, however, 30 per cent of the nation's medical care costs today are met by the taxpayers. This may
not be generally known, but is an ever-growing characteristic of
American medical care. To begin with, veterans have public medical
care for all service-connected disabilities and also for a large part
of their nonservice-connected sickness. Dependents of veterans also
enjoy much medical care at public expense, as, of course, do all dependents of servicemen. Medical care of all kinds, at the taxpayer's
expense, is also provided to indigents and to recipients of all forms
of public assistance. The great bulk of hospital construction costs
today comes from general taxes, as does the cost of treatment of the
most expensive diseases, such as mental disease and tuberculosis.
Three-fourths of all hospital beds in the country are in public institutions. The types of public medical care are ever increasing, and
never more rapidly than in recent years.

Medical care paid for from tax funds is "socialized medicine,"
if those scare words mean anything. "He who pays the piper calls
the tune," and increasingly, the public is paying the piper. Under
insurance, whether voluntary or compulsory, the costs are met, not

from general tax funds, but from contributions or premiums paid by employees and employers. Rejecting compulsory insurance, we get ever more public medical care. Fearful that compulsory health insurance will lead to "socialized medicine," we are actually getting more and more socialized medicine.

BIBLIOGRAPHY

INDEX

A Bibliography of the
Writings of Edwin E. Witte
on Social Security

NOTE: For references to additional writings pertaining to this subject see the Witte bibliographies on Wisconsin and on Labor. These bibliographies, as well as Witte correspondence covering almost fifty years, are to be found in the Library of the State Historical Society of Wisconsin. See also the catalog in Wisconsin Legislative Reference Library for additional clippings, letters, and so on.

In some instances the only copies available are those included in the Witte collection in the Wisconsin State Historical Society. These references have been marked by asterisks.

The bibliographical entries are listed chronologically by year and within the year.

1921

"Workmen's Compensation: Increased Compensation to Minors Illegally Employed under the Wisconsin Workmen's Compensation Statute," *Monthly Labor Review,* Vol. XII, No. 3 (March, 1921), pp. 179–80.

1922

"State Legislation upon Private Employment Agencies," by Grace M. Dill and Edwin E. Witte, *Monthly Labor Review,* Vol. XV, No. 4 (Oct., 1922), pp. 1–22.

1923

"Treble Compensation for Injured Children," *American Labor Legislation Review,* Vol. XIII, No. 2 (June, 1923), pp. 123–29.

1926

"Principal Provisions of the Huber Plan," in Allen B. Forsberg, ed.,
Unemployment Insurance. New York: H. W. Wilson Co., 1926. Pp.
124–27.
"How Wisconsin Purchases Health for Its Citizens," *Wisconsin Medical
Journal*, Vol. XXV, No. 1 (Jan., 1926), pp. 7–11.

1927

"Increased Compensation in Cases Involving Violations of Law," *American Labor Legislation Review*, Vol. XVII, No. 1 (March, 1927), pp.
70–72.

1928

*"Unemployment Insurance," an address delivered before the Milwaukee
County League of Women Voters Public School of Citizenship, Mil-
waukee, March 2, 1928.
"Legal Status of Issuance of Group Life Insurance Policies to Labor
Unions," *Monthly Labor Review*, Vol. 27, No. 5 (Nov., 1928), pp.
108–11.

1929

"The Theory of Workmen's Compensation," an address delivered at 23rd
Annual Meeting of American Legislators' Association, New Orleans,
December 28, 1929. Later published in *American Labor Legislation
Review*, Vol. XX, No. 4 (Dec., 1930), pp. 411–18.

1932

*"Labor's Interest in Social Security," outline of address.
*"British Unemployment Insurance and Its Lesson for Wisconsin," out-
line of talk.
"British Unemployment Insurance at the Crossroads," *American Labor
Legislation Review*, Vol. XXII, No. 1 (March, 1932), pp. 47–53.
*"The Prospects for Unemployment Insurance," guest editorial, *Chicago
Daily News*, Aug. 26, 1932.
*Correspondence with Arthur J. Altmeyer concerning revenues in con-
nection with the administration of workmen's compensation acts,
Dec. 1, 5, 1932.

1933

Review: Ruth M. Kellogg, *The United States Employment Service,* Chicago: University of Chicago Press, 1933, in *American Economic Review,* Vol. XXIII, No. 4 (Dec., 1933), pp. 743–45.

1934

*"What We Ought To Do about Unemployment," an address delivered at the New York State Conference of Social Work, Albany, New York, Oct., 1934.

"The Government and Unemployment," an address at the Joint Sessions of the American Association for Labor Legislation and the American Statistical Association, Chicago, Dec. 27, 1934. Later published in *American Labor Legislation Review,* Vol. XXV, No. 1 (March, 1935), pp. 5–12.

1934–1935: Articles in reports of the Committee on Economic Security (folder compiled by Witte in Wis. State Hist. Soc.)

"America's Old-Age Problems," 1935. In *The National Municipal Review,* Vol. XXIV, No. 7 (July, 1935), pp. 371–74 [slightly altered].

"An Analysis of the McGroarty Bill," 1935.

"The Economic Security Act," 1935. In *Book of States,* Council of State Government and the American Legislator's Association (1935), pp. 411–15 [slightly altered]. Also in *The Program for Economic Security,* by the President's Committee on Economic Security, Washington, D.C., Jan. 8, 1935, p. 14 [slightly altered].

"Estimated Costs of Old-Age Pensions to the States," 1935.

"Factual Data Relating to the Townsend Old-Age Revolving Pension Plan," 1935, prepared for members of the U.S. House Ways and Means Committee.

"Features of the Economic Security Program," 1935. Paper presented before the Pacific Southwest Academy, Los Angeles, California, in *The Annals of the American Academy of Political and Social Science,* Vol. 178 Supplement (March, 1935), pp. 88–94.

"Limitations and Value of Unemployment Insurance," 1935. In *Economic Forum,* Vol. 2, No. 4 (Winter, 1935), pp. 411–24, under title "Job Insurance: Its Limitations and Value."

"Major Issues in Unemployment Compensation," 1935. In *Social Service Review,* Vol. IX, No. 1 (March, 1935), pp. 1–23.

"Need for Additional Measures to Afford Economic Security to Individuals," 1934.

"Old-Age Pensions," 1935.

"Possible General Approaches to the Problem of Economic Security,"
 1935. [This article is missing from manuscript collection.]
"Possible Measures to Attain a Greater Degree of Economic Security,"
 1934.
"Postponement for a Year of the Beginning Date in Title IX," 1935.
"Preliminary Report of the Staff of the Committee on Economic Secu-
 rity," by Edwin E. Witte and Staff, 1934.
"Reasons Why the General Welfare Bills (H.R. 2, H.R. 11, and H.R.
 5620) Should Not Be Enacted into Law." Reprinted in *Hearings
 Relative to the Social Security Act Amendment of 1939 before the
 Committee on Ways and Means,* U.S. House of Representatives, 76th
 Congress, 1st session, Feb.–March, 1939, Vol. 2, pp. 1794–1800.
"Report of the Technical Board on the Major Alternative Plans for the
 Administration of Unemployment Compensation," 1935.
"Security for the Blind," statistics by Wilbur Cohen, 1935.
"Social Security Act and the Business Man," 1935. Synopsis of address
 delivered before the Minneapolis Civic and Commerce Association,
 April 18, 1935.
"Social Security Act and Sales Taxes," 1935.
"Suggestions for a Long-Time and an Immediate Program for Eco-
 nomic Security Submitted for Consideration to the Advisory Coun-
 cil," 1935.
"Theories with Regard to Unemployment Relief Now or Formerly Held
 in England," 1935.
"The Unemployed in the Social Security Program," 1935. In *Wharton
 Review of Finance and Commerce,* Vol. VIII, No. 6 (March, 1935),
 pp. 3–4, 16–17.
"Why the Social Security Board Should Be in the Labor Department,"
 1935.
"Why the Townsend Old-Age Revolving Pension Plan Is Impossible,"
 1935. In *Hearings before the Committee on Ways and Means,* U.S.
 House of Representatives, 74th Congress, 1st session, on H.R. 4120,
 a bill to alleviate the hazards of old age, Jan. 21–Feb. 12, 1935, pp.
 894–96.

                                    1935

"The Committee Digs In," the Administration's viewpoint with regard
 to its study of health insurance for the American public, *Medical
 Economics,* Vol. 12, No. 4 (Jan., 1935), pp. 21, 90 ff.
Introductory Statement and Testimony of E. E. Witte on the Economic
 Security Act, H.R. 4120, a bill to alleviate the hazards of old age,
 Jan. 21–Feb. 12, 1935, in *Hearings before the Committee on Ways
 and Means,* U.S. House of Representatives, 74th Congress, 1st ses-
 sion, pp. 2–9, 31–35, 56–79, 187–225, 237–53.

Statements and Testimony by E. E. Witte on the Economic Security Act, S. 1130, a bill to alleviate the hazards of old age, Jan. 22–Feb. 20, 1935, in *Hearings before the Committee on Finance,* U.S. Senate, 74th Congress, 1st session, pp. 31, 81, 187, 211.

*"Townsend Plan is Analyzed," *N.E.A. Service,* Feb. 17, 1935; also in *The Bangor Daily News,* Bangor, Maine, April 8, 1935.

"Planned Security for an Older Population," *New York Times,* Feb. 17, 21, 1935.

*"Some Reasons Why the Economic Security Bill Should Be Enacted into Law," an address delivered over station WMAL (NBC), Washington, D.C., March 28, 1935.

"Economic Insurance and the Life Insurance Business—Friends or Enemies," *Manager's Magazine,* Vol. X, No. 2 (March–April, 1935), pp. 2–3.

*"The Value of Social Security," synopsis of address before the Minneapolis Statistical Association, Minneapolis, April 19, 1935.

* "Wisconsin's Interest in the National Security Program," an address delivered over radio station WTMJ, Milwaukee, April 20, 1935.

"Balance of Power: Federal and State Governments' Share in the Suggested Unemployment Compensation Program," *State Government,* Vol. 8, No. 5 (May, 1935), pp. 111–12.

"Paying for Social Security," Lecture No. 2, You and Your Government, Series XI, *Taxation for Prosperity,* address over nationwide NBC network, June 25, 1935. Reprinted in *National Municipal League* (June, 1935), pp. 7–10.

"The Social Security Act," an address delivered before the Wisconsin State Bar Association at 57th Annual Convention at Green Lake, Wisconsin, June 27–29, 1935. *Proceedings of the Wisconsin State Bar Association,* pp. 22–36.

"The Federal Social Security Act and Changes in Its Laws Which Wisconsin Must Meet to Take Advantage of Its Provisions," *Wisconsin Assembly Journal,* July 18, 1935. Available in files of Assembly Journals in State Capitol, Madison.

*"Remarks on Social Security." Correspondence and stenographic transcript from meeting of American Mining Congress, October, 1935.

*"The Relation of Relief to Society," an address delivered over station WHA, Madison, *Wisconsin Emergency Relief Administration Series,* Nov. 1, 1935.

*"The Social Security Act," an address delivered before the Plains State Conference, Des Moines, Iowa, Nov. 16, 1935.

*"The National Security Act," summary of an address delivered before the annual meeting of the Wisconsin State Chamber of Commerce, Milwaukee, Nov. 19, 1935.

Review: I. M. Rubinow, *The Quest for Security,* New York: Henry Holt & Co., 1934, in *Journal of Political Economy,* Vol. 43, No. 6 (Dec., 1935), pp. 834–35.

"Social Insurance in Europe during the Depression," *American Labor Legislation Review,* Vol. XXV, No. 4 (Dec., 1935), pp. 158–64.

*"Constitutionality of the Wagner Workmen's Compensation Bill for Interstate Transportation Employees," discussion on paper by Robert F. Wagner at American Association of Labor Legislation meeting, New York, Dec., 1935.

Review: E. Wight Bakke, *Insurance or Dole? The Adjustment of Unemployment Insurance to Economic and Social Facts in Great Britain,* New Haven: Yale Univ. Press, 1935, in *Social Service Review,* Vol. IX, No. 4 (Dec., 1935), pp. 781–82.

*"What Is Wrong with the Townsend Plan," Dec. 11, 1935.

*"Can the United States Finance Social Security?" an address in the *Current American Scene Discussions* of the Wisconsin Union Forum Committee, Madison, Dec. 11, 1935.

"The National Social Security Program: A Study of the Development and the Aims of the Federal Government's Plan," an address before the Alumni Institute of the New York Alumni Club, New York, Dec. 27, 1935, in *The Wisconsin Alumni Magazine,* Vol. XXXVII, No. 4 (Jan., 1936), pp. 104–7.

*"Administration of Unemployment Insurance," introductory remarks at Joint Session of the American Association for Labor Legislation and the American Statistical Association, Dec. 28, 1935.

"Are Old Age Pensions Worth Their Cost?" an address before the Joint Session of the American Association for Labor Legislation and the American Statistical Association, New York, Dec. 28, 1935, in *American Labor Legislation Review,* Vol. XXVI, No. 1 (March, 1936), pp. 7–14.

1936

*"The Economic Basis of Unemployment Compensation," prepared for possible use in defending the Wisconsin Unemployment Insurance Law, 1936.

*"Economic Security in Old Age," 1936.

*"Economic Arguments in Support of the Constitutionality of Unemployment Compensation," 1936.

"An Historical Account of Unemployment Insurance in the Social Security Act," *Law and Contemporary Problems,* Symposium on Unemployment Compensation, Duke University, Durham, N.C., Vol. III, No. 1 (Jan., 1936), pp. 157–69.

*"The A.A.A. Decision and the Constitutionality of the Social Security Act," Jan. 20, 1936.

Three articles for the *Capital Times,* Madison, Wis.:

    "Charges Townsend Plan Is Deceptive upon Elderly People of U.S.," Jan. 23, 1936.

"Townsend Plan Is Sales Tax Plus Whose Burden Would Hit the Poor," Jan. 24, 1936.

"Hints Hand of Big Business Behind Drive for Townsend Plan," Jan. 26, 1936.

*"Consistency, Thou Art a Jewel," summary and criticism of Abraham Epstein's attack on the Federal Social Security Act, 1936.

Letter to *New York Times,* Jan. 26, 1936. [Articles by Mr. Epstein, clippings and correspondence pertaining to his stand against the act, are also included.]

"Pensions and the Social Security Act," in *News from the Wisconsin Conference of Social Work,* Vol. 3, No. 1 (Jan. 25, 1936), mimeo. 7 pp.

"Social Security Legislation," *Wisconsin Law Review,* Vol. 11, No. 2 (Feb., 1936), pp. 171–80.

"Why I Am Against the Townsend Plan," three articles in the *Watertown Daily News,* February 29, March 2, March 3, 1936.

*"Old Age Security," radio address over station WHA, Madison, in *Consumer's Search Light Series,* March 20, 1936.

"The Essentials of Unemployment Compensation," Symposium of Articles in *National Municipal Review,* Vol. XXV, No. 3 (March–April, 1936), pp. 157–63. Reprinted in *Social Security,* Joseph P. Harris, ed., National Municipal League, 1936, pp. 36–42.

*"Unemployment Compensation with Special Reference to Wisconsin," notes for paper presented at 3rd annual meeting of Mid-West Economics Association, Des Moines, April 10, 1936 [somewhat revised and expanded].

Review: Industrial Relations Counselors, Inc., *Administration of Public Employment Offices and Unemployment Insurance,* New York: 1935, in *Journal of the American Statistical Association,* Vol. 31, No. 194 (June, 1936), pp. 452–53.

The Development of the Social Security Act, prepared for the President's Committee on Economic Security, July, 1936. Published, Madison: University of Wisconsin Press, 1962.

Review: Abraham Epstein, *Insecurity: A Challenge to America,* New York: Random House, 1936, 3rd rev. ed., in *American Political Science Review,* Vol. 30, No. 4 (Aug., 1936), p. 793; in *Journal of Political Economy,* Vol. 44, No. 6 (Dec., 1936), pp. 845–47 [longer review].

"Unemployment Compensation in Wisconsin," Labor Information Bulletin, Vol. III, No. 8 (Aug., 1936), pp. 4–5; also in South Dakota State Federation of Labor, *Official State Year Book of Organized Labor* (1936), pp. 78–80.

*"The Record of the Progressives on Social Security as Compared with the Republican Promises," prepared for Governor Philip La Follette, Oct., 1936.

*"Reply of Senator Robert M. La Follette, Jr." to attack on the Social Security Act by Governor Landon, Oct. 6, 1936.

*"The Revision of Wisconsin Welfare Laws and Their Administration,"
    outline of address before the Winnebago County Bar Association,
    Oshkosh, Oct. 14, 1936.
*"Comments on the Dodger 'A Direct Tax on Wages'" [distributed by
    the Republican State Committee] prepared for the *Capital Times,*
    Madison, Nov. 2, 1936.
*"Old-Age Security," synopsis of address in the Lecture Series of the
    City Club of Milwaukee, Milwaukee, Nov. 13, 1936.
"Financing Social Security: Reserves Versus Current Taxation," sym-
    posium conducted by the Tax Policy League, Dec. 28–29, 1936,
    Chicago. Published as chapter XII in book, *How Shall Business Be
    Taxed,* pp. 154–67.
*"Unemployment Insurance and Relief," discussion at Joint Session of
    the American Economic Association and the American Association
    for Labor Legislation, Chicago, Dec. 28, 1936.
"In Defense of the Federal Old-Age Benefit Plan," an address before
    the 30th annual meeting, Joint Session of the American Statistical
    Association and the American Association for Labor Legislation,
    Chicago, Dec. 29, 1936, in *American Labor Legislation Review,* Vol.
    XXVII, No. 1 (March, 1937), pp. 27–33; and in *The Social Security
    Analyst,* Vol. I, No. 1 (Jan., 1937), pp. 7–8, 24–25.

                                1937

Preface to *Social Security in America,* published for the Committee on
    Economic Security by the Social Security Board, Washington, D.C.:
    Government Printing Office, 1937 [out of print].
*"Some Notes on Social Security," prepared for E. A. Ross, Feb., 1937.
"Old-Age Security in the Social Security Act," *Journal of Political Econ-
    omy,* Vol. 45, No. 1 (Feb., 1937), pp. 1–44.
"Social Security as a Major Purpose of Government," *Wisconsin State
    Employee* (March, 1937), pp. 5, 19. [Collection contains ms. longer
    than printed copy.]
*"Alternatives in Relation to Old-Age Security," summary of an address
    at meeting for the Discussion of Social Security, Stevens Point, Wis.,
    March 16, 1937.
*"Unemployment and Recovery," *The Yale Review,* Vol. XXVI, No. 3
    (March, 1937), pp. 475–90. [Ms. 21 pp. under title "Improving Our
    Labor Supply," slightly different.]
*"Social Security and the Teachers," summary of an address delivered
    before the Northeastern Wisconsin Teachers' Association, Appleton,
    Wisconsin, April 8, 1937.
"The Approaching Crises in Public Welfare in Wisconsin," an address
    delivered before the annual dinner of the Family Welfare Associa-

tion, Madison, April 15, 1937. Reprinted in *Wisconsin Public Welfare Review* (May 18, 1937), pp. 18–30.

Review: Harry A. Millis, *Sickness and Insurance,* Chicago: University of Chicago Press, 1937, in *American Political Science Review,* Vol. XXXI, No. 3 (June, 1937), pp. 575–76.

*"What's Ahead in Social Security," University of Washington Summer Radio Broadcasts address over station KVD, Seattle, July 28, 1937.

"The Social Security Act and Proposed Changes," an address at the Twelfth Annual Conference of the Association of Clinic Managers, Sheboygan, September 23–24, 1937, in *Proceedings,* pp. 32–37.

"America's Next Steps in Social Security," an address before the Joint Session of the American Association for Labor Legislation and American Statistical Association, 21st annual meeting, Atlantic City, N.J., Dec. 29, 1937, in *American Labor Legislation Review,* Vol. XXVII, No. 1 (March, 1938), pp. 5–6.

1938

Review: Twentieth Century Fund, *More Security for Old Age,* New York: Committee on Old-Age Insurance, Twentieth Century Fund, 1937, in *American Political Science Review,* Vol. XXXII, No. 1 (Feb., 1938), pp. 159–60; also in *The Social Service Review,* Vol. XII, No. 1 (March, 1938), pp. 34–40.

*"Thoughts Relating to the Old-Age Insurance Titles of the Social Security Act and Proposed Changes Therein," revision of statement presented to the Social Security Advisory Council at its meeting on Feb. 18–19, 1938.

Review: Peter T. Swanish, *Trade Disputes Disqualification Clause under the British Unemployment Insurance Acts,* Chicago: University of Chicago Press, 1938, in *American Political Science Review,* Vol. XXXII, No. 2 (April, 1938), pp. 386–87.

*"Social Security: A Wild Dream or a Practical Plan," prepared for the Wisconsin Alumni Institute, June 17, 1938.

*"Objectives in Social Security," an address at the University of Alabama, Tuscaloosa, Ala., June 17, 1938.

*"Health Insurance, the Problem of General Medical Care," remarks at the Health Conference, Washington, D.C., July 20, 1938.

*Memoranda to Arthur J. Altmeyer, Aug., 1938:
"Effective Penalty Against Manipulation of Social Security Grants by States."
"Outline of a Bill to Replace McKellar and Byrnes Bills on Merit Basis Standards for State Personnel Administering Assistance Grants."
Suggested New Federal Grant in Age Plan."

"Thoughts Regarding Amendments to the Social Security Act Which Appear Feasible in the Next Session of Congress."

*"What the Social Security Act Has Meant for Wisconsin," radio address over station WIBA, Madison, Wisconsin, Sept. 15, 1938.

*"What's Next in Social Security and Retirement Pensions," synopsis of an address delivered before the Business and Professional Women's Club of Milwaukee, Milwaukee, Oct. 18, 1938.

Review: W. S. Woytinsky, *Labor in the United States: Basic Statistics for Social Security*, Washington: Social Science Research Council, 1938, in *American Political Science Review*, Vol. XXXII, No. 6 (Dec., 1938), p. 1204.

1939

Statement and Testimony on H.R. 6635, an act to amend the Social Security Act. In *Hearings before the Committee on Finance*, U.S. Senate, 76th Congress, 1st session (June, 1939), Washington, D.C., pp. 244–54.

In *Hearings Relative to the Social Security Act Amendment of 1939 before the Committee on Ways and Means*, U.S. House of Representatives, 76th Congress, 1st session (Feb.–March, 1939), Washington, D.C., pp. 1753–1812.

*"Social Security in the United States," an address before the 12th National Conference on Social Security, American Association for Social Security, New York, April, 1939, in *Proceedings* of conference.

*"Discussion of the Stabilization of Earnings and Employment," an address before the Industrial Relations Conference, sponsored by the Social Science Research Council, Harvard University, Cambridge, April 22, 1939.

"Social Security Revision," communications in *The New York Times*, June 22 and July 2, 1939.

"Social Security—1940 Model," *American Labor Legislation Review*, Vol. XXIX, No. 3 (Sept., 1939), pp. 101–9.

*"Socialized Medicine and the National Health Program," an address at the Fourteenth Annual Conference of the Association of Clinic Managers, Eau Claire, Wis., Sept., 22, 1939.

*"The Issues Raised by the Social Security Act," an address in the University of Wisconsin Forum Series, Madison, Wis., Oct., 1939.

*"The Problem of Extending Old-Age Insurance Protection to a Larger Part of the American People," confidential memorandum for the Social Security Board, Dec., 1939.

Review: Robert T. Lansdale, Elizabeth Long, Agnes Leisy, and Byron T. Hipple, *The Administration of Old Age Assistance*, Chicago: Social Science Research Council, 1939, in *American Political Science Review*, Vol. XXXIII, No. 6 (Dec., 1939), pp. 1087–88.

*"Increase of Unemployment Insurance Benefits" and "Extension of

Coverage—The Vitally Necessary Next Step in Old-Age Insurance,"
remarks before Round Table on Economic Issues in Social Security
Policy at Joint Session of American Economic Association and American Association for Labor Legislation, Philadelphia, Pa., December
27, 1939, in *American Labor Legislation Review*, Vol. XXX, No. 3
(Sept., 1940), pp. 115–23 [revised to bring up to date to Sept. 15,
1940], under title of "The Approaching Crisis in Old-Age Security."
*"Health Security Progress" and "The Prospects for Health Security,"
remarks and address at the Joint Session of the American Association for Labor Legislation and the American Statistical Association,
Philadelphia, December 29, 1939. Later published in *American
Labor Legislation Review*, Vol. XXX, No. 1 (March, 1940) under
title of "Health Security Progress," pp. 5–7.

1940

Review: Margaret Grant, *Old-Age Security: Social and Financial Trends*,
Washington: Social Science Research Council, 1939, in *American
Economic Review*, Vol. XXX, No. 1 (March, 1940), pp. 207–9.
*"Health Security," an address at the convention of the Wisconsin
Dietetics Association, Madison, March 29, 1940.
*"President Roosevelt, The Social Security Act, and Wisconsin," *Demo-
cratic Digest for Wisconsin*, June–Nov., 1940.
"Whither Unemployment Compensation?" an address at the Regional
Institute on Employment Service and Unemployment Compensa-
tion Procedures at the University of Minnesota, April 10, 1940, in
Proceedings of the Institute of Economic Security, Center for Con-
tinuation Study, University of Minnesota, April, 1940, pp. 46–57;
and in *The Social Service Review*, Vol. XIV, No. 3 (Sept., 1940),
pp. 421–37 [somewhat condensed].
*"Health Security: Needs, Progress, and Prospects," an address at the
Iowa Conference for Social Welfare, Des Moines, Iowa, April 20,
1940.
*"Why Social Security—Does It Meet Our Problems?" synopsis of views
at the Town Hall Meeting of the Wisconsin Association of County
Pension Departments, Fond du Lac, Wis., June 13, 1940.
*"Next Step in Social Security," an address at the Wisconsin Conference
of Social Work, Milwaukee, Sept. 28, 1940.
*"What's Ahead in Employment Security," an address at the Employ-
ment Security Institute, Williams Bay, Wis., Oct. 9, 1940.

1941

"What's Ahead in Social Security," *Harvard Business Review*, Vol. XIX,
No. 3 (Spring, 1941), pp. 311–25.
"Is the Continued Drive for Universal Pensions a Social Menace?"

American Labor Legislation Review, Vol. XXXI, No. 1 (March, 1941), pp. 38–46.

Review: Raymond C. Atkinson, *The Federal Role in Unemployment Compensation*, Washington, D.C.: Social Science Research Council, 1941, in *Survey Midmonthly*, Vol. LXVII, No. 4 (April, 1941), pp. 131–32.

*"Experience Rating," an address at the Regional Institute on Employment Security, Minneapolis, May 13, 1941.

Review: E. Wight Bakke, *The Unemployed Worker*, New Haven: Yale University Press, 1941, in *Yale Review*, Vol. XXX, No. 4 (June, 1941), pp. 841–43.

"Employee Relations and Social Security," *Business Week*, Aug. 16, 1941, p. 64.

*Addresses at the New England Employment Security Institute, Amherst, Mass., Aug. 16, 1941: "Unemployment Compensation and the General Welfare" and "Current Problems of Unemployment Compensation."

Review: Elizabeth W. Gilboy, *Applicants for Work Relief: A Study of Massachusetts Families under the FERA and WPA*, Cambridge: Harvard University Press, 1940, in *Journal of Political Economy*, Vol. XLIX, No. 5 (Oct., 1941), pp. 777–79.

"Experience Rating and Other Forms of Incentive Taxation to Promote Employment," an address at the 34th Annual Conference on Taxation, National Tax Association, St. Paul, Minn., Oct. 13–16, 1941, in *Proceedings*, pp. 479–83.

*"The Operation of the Unemployment Insurance System," a stenographic transcript of address at special meeting of the Employment Service State Advisory Council, New York City, Dec. 29, 1941. Also statement by John B. Andrews [?].

Review: Eveline M. Burns, *British Unemployment Programs, 1920–1938*, Washington: Social Science Research Council, 1941, in *American Political Science Review*, Vol. XXXV, No. 6 (Dec., 1941), p. 1205; also in *Political Science Quarterly*, Vol. LVIII, No. 1 (March, 1943), pp. 118–19 [longer review].

1942

Foreword in J. S. Parker, *Social Security Reserves*. Washington: American Council on Public Affairs, 1942.

"Statement on the Report of Sir William Beveridge on Social Insurance and Allied Services," *Daily Cardinal*, Madison, Jan. 7, 1942.

Review: Seymour E. Harris, *Economics of Social Security*, New York: McGraw-Hill, 1941, in *American Economic Review*, Vol. XXXII, No. 1 (March, 1942), pp. 189–91.

" 'Federalization' of Unemployment Compensation?" *American Labor Legislation Review,* Vol. XXXII, No. 1 (March, 1942), pp. 41–48.

*"What Shall We Expect from Social Security?" an address at the Midwest Economics Association [?], April 17, 1942.

Review: Arnold Wilson and G. S. McKay, *Old-Age Pension, An Historical and Critical Survey,* London: Oxford University Press, 1941, in *Harvard Law Review,* Vol. LV, No. 8 (June, 1942), pp. 1413–16.

Review: Helen Fisher Holman, *Old Age in Sweden: A Program of Social Security,* Washington: Federal Security Agency, Social Security Board, 1940, in *Journal of Political Economy,* Vol. L, No. 4 (Aug., 1942), pp. 609–11.

"Befuddled Social Security Finances," *American Labor Legislation Review,* Vol. XXXII, No. 4, pp. 149–52.

1943

"Postwar Social Security," chapter XV in Seymour E. Harris, *Postwar Economic Problems,* New York: McGraw-Hill, 1943.

"American Post-War Social Security Proposals," *American Economic Review,* Vol. XXXII, No. 4 (Dec., 1943), pp. 825–38.

"Comments on Medical Care and Hospital Provisions of the Wagner-Murray-Dingell Bill," at Wayne County Medical Society, Detroit, Mich., Nov. 29, 1943.
In *Detroit Medical News,* Vol. XXXV, No. 16 (Dec. 13, 1943), pp. 6, 16–18.

1944

"What to Expect of Social Security," *American Economic Review,* Vol. XXXIV, No. 1, Part 2 (March, 1944), pp. 212–221.
In William Haber and Wilbur J. Cohen, *Readings in Social Security,* New York: Prentice-Hall, 1948. Pp. 58–67.
In Arthur D. Gayer, C. Lowell Harriss, and Milton H. Spencer, *Basic Economics, A Book of Readings,* New York: Prentice-Hall, 1951. Pp. 324–31. [These articles all slightly different.]

1945

Review: W. S. Woytinsky, *Earnings and Social Security in the United States,* New York: Social Science Research Council, 1943, in *Journal of Political Economy,* Vol. LIII, No. 3 (Sept., 1945), p. 284.

"Basic Considerations in Medical Care," an address at the Second National Conference on Social Security sponsored by the Chamber of Commerce of the United States. In *Health Insurance in America,* U.S. Chamber of Commerce, 1945, pp. 4–16.

In William Haber and Wilbur J. Cohen, *Readings in Social Security,* New York: Prentice-Hall, 1948, under title "Medical Care and Health Insurance," pp. 351–59.

In *Review of Economic Statistics,* Vol. XXVII, No. 4 (Nov., 1945), pp. 171–88, under title "1944–1945 Programs for Postwar Social Security and Medical Care."

*Reply to letters from *U.S. News* regarding "President Truman's Health Message," Nov. 30, 1945.

"Development of Unemployment Compensation," *Yale Law Journal* (Dec., 1945), pp. 21–52. Later published in William Haber and Wilbur J. Cohen, *Readings in Social Security,* New York: Prentice-Hall, 1948, pp. 160–72.

1946

"Steadying the Worker's Income," *Harvard Business Review,* Vol. 24, No. 3 (Spring, 1946), pp. 306–25.

*"Relationship Between Old-Age and Survivors' Insurance and Old-Age Assistance," an address at the Institute for County Welfare Directors [?], June 17, 1946.

"The Future of State Labor Legislation," an address at Convention of International Association of Governmental Labor Officials, Milwaukee, October 1, 1946. Reprinted by Division of Labor Standards, U.S. Department of Labor, Washington, D.C., March, 1947.

1947

"Social Security in a Stable Prosperity," synopsis of remarks at American Economic Association, Social Security Session, Jan. 24, 1947, in *American Economic Review,* Vol. XXXVII, No. 2, Part 2 (May, 1947), pp. 363–64.

*"Social Security and Wage Administration," an address before the Institute of Salary and Wage Administration, University of Wisconsin, Madison, Feb. 26, 1947.

*"Social Security Prospects," synopsis of observations at Pacific-Northwest Banking School, University of Washington, Seattle, Aug. 14, 1947.

Review: Lewis Meriam, *Relief and Social Security,* Washington: Brookings Institution, 1946, in *American Economic Review,* Vol. XXXVII, No. 4 (Sept., 1947), pp. 723–27.

*"Economic Aspects of the Problems of Health and Medical Care," an outline of lecture to Class on Medical and Health Problems, Department of Social Work, University of Wisconsin, Madison, Oct., 1947.

1948

"Social Security," chapter XXVI in Seymour E. Harris, ed., *Saving American Capitalism, A Liberal Economic Program,* New York: Alfred A. Knopf, 1948.
*Two talks to California Institute on Social Security and Health and Welfare Plans, Berkeley, Cal., Aug. 14, 1948: "Social Security" and "Health, Welfare and Pension Funds."

1949

Introduction in Domenico Gagliardo, *American Social Insurance,* New York: Harper & Bros., 1949 and 1955.
Review: George W. Bachman and Lewis Meriam, *The Issue of Compulsory Health Insurance,* Washington: Brookings Institutions, 1948, in *The Survey,* Vol. 85, No. 1 (Jan., 1949), pp. 51–52.
"A Panoramic View of Social Security," *Wisconsin Ideas in Education,* Vol. I, No. 1 (Feb., 1949), pp. 9–10, 26, 29.
*"Trends in Payment for Medical Care," an address delivered before the Midwest American Management Association, Chicago, Feb. 14, 1949, in American Management Association, *What's Ahead in Employee Health and Pension Planning,* Personnel Series No. 126 (1949), pp. 25–33.
*"The Development and Present Status of Social Security," a summary of an address in Lecture Series on Social Security, University of Wisconsin Extension Division, Milwaukee, March 20, 1949.
*"Social Security and the College Teacher," abstract of views expressed in panel discussion at Ohio College Association meeting, Columbus, Ohio, April 8, 1949.
*"Developments on the Economic Side of Medical Care," an address at the Wisconsin Public Welfare Association, Wausau, Wis., June 7, 1949.
*"Pending Social Security Legislation," outline of an address to Industrial Relations Section of the Los Angeles Town Hall, Los Angeles, Cal., July 6, 1949.
*"Whither Social Security?" synopsis of address in the UCLA Summer Lecture Series, University of California, Los Angeles, July 21, 1949. Abstract of same at Minnesota Economic Conference [?], Oct. 12, 1957.
"The Bug-a-Boo of the Welfare State," an address at the Town Hall of Los Angeles, Cal., July 25, 1949. Introduced by Senator Wayne Morse in *Congressional Record,* Oct. 19, 1949, pp. 15381–83.
*"Issues in Health and Welfare Planning," summary of views before the Stanford Business Conference, Stanford, Cal., July 27, 1949.

*"The Relationship of Private to Government Employee Security Programs," outline of an address at Wayne University, Symposium on Employee Security Program, Detroit, Oct. 13, 1949.

Introduction to *John B. Andrews Memorial Symposium on Labor Legislation,* Industrial Relations Center, University of Wisconsin, Madison, Nov. 4–5, 1949.

*"The Federal Old-Age and Survivors' Insurance System and Teachers' Insurance," outline of talk at Teachers' Union, Madison, Nov. 14, 1949.

*"Social Security: How Far Shall We Go?" introductory statement over radio-television broadcast of the Columbus, Ohio, Town Meeting, Nov. 25, 1949.

*"Labor and Social Security Legislation," lecture to Foreign Service Institute, Labor Economics and Politics Lecture-Seminar Series, Department of State, Washington, D.C., Dec. 12, 1949.

"Social and Economic Security in Old Age," excerpts from address, "Living Through the Older Years," Series of Lectures, Rockford, Ill., Dec., 1949. In *Iowa Register,* Des Moines, Dec. 14, 1949.

*"Compulsory Health Insurance," broadcast recording for labor-owned radio stations, New York City, Dec. 30, 1949.

1950

*"Labor Legislation and Social Security," in *Report of the Second Midwestern Conference on Teaching of Industrial Relations and Labor Economics,* University of Illinois, Monticello, at Allerton Park, pp. 16–18.

"Contributory versus Noncontributory Industrial Pension Plans," address at Conference at University of Minnesota, March 23–24, 1950. In *Employee Welfare and Benefit Plans,* Research and Technical Report 7, University of Minnesota, Industrial Relations Center, Dubuque: William C. Brown Co., 1950, pp. 20–22.

*Two talks at Management Short Course for the Managers and Directors of the Wisconsin Farmer Coöperatives, University of Wisconsin, Madison, March 28, 1950: "Employee Security" and "Industrial Pension, Health and Welfare Plans."

Review: Ralph Altman, *Availability for Work: A Study in Unemployment Compensation,* Cambridge: Harvard University Press, 1950, in *The Survey,* Vol. 86, No. 4 (April, 1950), pp. 214–15.

*"Social Security and Free Enterprise," an address at Kansas State Teachers' College, Pittsburgh, Kansas, April 13, 1950. [Available in John R. Commons' Library, University of Wisconsin.]

"Should Teachers Be Included under Federal Old-Age Insurance," *Wisconsin Journal of Education,* Vol. 82, No. 9 (May, 1950), pp. 6–7.

"How Much Improvement in Social Security," *The International Laundry Worker* (Aug., 1950), p. 7. [Also 2 pp. ms.]

"Problems of Aging," radio discussion by E. E. Witte and others on NBC broadcast, Chicago, Illinois, Aug. 13, 1950. In *The University of Chicago Round Table*, No. 646.

*"Social Security Act Amendments," Aug. 24, 1950.

*"Social Security and the Small Business Man," summary of an address to Nutrition School for Feed Men, University of Wisconsin, Madison, Aug. 28, 1950.

"Teaching of Social Security," remarks before the 4th Annual Conference on the Teaching of Labor Relations, New York State School of Industrial and Labor Relations, Cornell University, Ithaca, New York, September 7-9, 1950. In *Preliminary Digest of Conference Discussions*, Part 2, pp. 72-78.

*Review: Earl E. Muntz, *A Review of Unemployment Compensation*, in a letter to the Director, Research Council for Economic Security, Chicago, Sept. 25, 1950.

Review: Eveline M. Burns, *The American Social Security System*, Boston: Houghton Mifflin, 1949, in *Review of Economics and Statistics*, Vol. XXXII, No. 4 (Nov., 1950), pp. 357-58.

"Social Provisions for the Aged," *Aged and Society*, Industrial Relations Research Association (Dec., 1950), pp. 115-36.

"Social Security—1951," address to the Tenth Biennial General Assembly of States, Panel Session on Social Security, Chicago, Illinois, Dec. 7, 1950. Summary in *State Government*, Vol. XXIV, No. 1 (Jan., 1951), pp. 16-17.

Introduction at Panel on The Older Worker in Industry, 3rd Annual Meeting of the Industrial Relations Research Association, Chicago, Dec. 28-29, 1950.
In *The Older Worker in Industry: An IRRA Symposium* (1950), pp. 317-18.

Lectures on Social Security delivered at University of Puerto Rico, Rio Piedras, Labor Relations Institute, Nov., 1950, in *Five Lectures on Social Security* (Rio Piedras, P.R.: Labor Relations Institute, College of Social Science, University of Puerto Rico, 1951). I. "The Nature, Purposes, and History of Social Security"; II. "Social Assistance and Social Services"; III. "Old-Age and Survivors' Insurance"; IV. "Other Forms of Social Insurance"; V. "The Future of Social Security."

1951

*"Practical Factors to be Taken into Account in Connection with Pensions," an address at Conference on War-Time and Long-Range Issues in Collective Bargaining for Pensions, Feb. 16-18, 1951, Allerton Park, Illinois. In *Proceedings*, University of Illinois, Monticello, Illinois, pp. 24-31.

*"Economic Problems Associated with an Aging Population," outline of talk at National Conference on Aging [?], March 29, 1951.

"Social Security Needs and Opportunities," *State Government,* Vol. XXIV, No. 6 (June, 1951), pp. 150–53.

*"Government Attitude and Responsibility to an Aging Population," address at Centennial Conference on the Problem of an Aging Population, Northwestern University, Evanston, Ill., June 8, 1951.

*"Economic Security for the Aged: An Important Problem of Today, A Major Problem Tomorrow," lecture [?], July, 1951.

"What Is Needed for Economic Security in Old Age?" an address before the Second Gerontological Congress, St. Louis, Mo., Sept. 11, 1951. Brief abstract in *Public Health Reports,* Vol. 6, No. 2 (Feb., 1952), p. 141, under title, "Needs for Economic Security in Old Age."

1952

*"Security and Progress in the Welfare State," an address in the *Great Issues Series of Lectures,* Purdue University, Lafayette, Indiana, Jan. 10, 1952.

Review: Stephen K. Bailey, *Congress Makes A Law: The Story Behind the Employment Act of 1946,* New York: Columbia University Press, 1950, in *Wisconsin Magazine of History,* Vol. 35, No. 3 (Spring, 1952), pp. 222–23.

Review: Robert W. Thomas, *Workmen's Compensation in New Mexico,* Albuquerque: University of New Mexico, 1950, in *Journal of Business,* University of Chicago, Vol. XXV, No. 2 (April, 1952), p. 131.

*"Medical Economics," outline of talk to Junior Medical Students, University of Wisconsin, Madison, April 10, 1952.

*"Problems of Old Age," summary of an address at Annual Meeting of the Family Service Association, Madison, April 29, 1952.

*"Financing Old-Age and Survivors' Insurance," outline of talk [?], June, 1952.

*"The Prospects for Unemployment Insurance," outline of talk at Regional Unemployment Insurance Administrators' Conference, Madison, June 24, 1952.

*"Social Security—A Panoramic View," outline of two talks at the Family Financing Planning Workshop, University of Wisconsin, Madison, July 3–7, 1952.

*"Economic Security of the Aged," summary of address delivered at the Town Hall Meeting, Lansing, Michigan, Aug. 18, 1952, in *Town Hall,* Lansing, Aug. 25, 1952, pp. 2–4.

*"Age Trends in Our Population," outline of talk to Institute on Industrial Vision, University of Wisconsin Extension Division, Madison, Dec. 15, 1952.

1953

*"Issues and Prospects in Social Security," an address at Ohio State University, Columbus, Ohio, Feb. 16, 1953.
*"Medical Benefit Plans in Collective Bargaining," outline of observations at Industrial Relations Research Association meeting, Pittsburgh, April 24, 1953.
*"Social Security," an address at the Janesville Industrial Relations Center Institute, Janesville, Wis., May, 1953.
*"The Present Danger to Social Security," outline of views presented at the National Conference on Social Security, Washington, D.C., May 14, 1953.
*"Labor Economics," lectures to School for Workers' classes, University of Wisconsin, Madison, Aug. 17–19, 1953.
Review: Ida C. Merriam, *Social Security Financing*, Washington, D.C.: Federal Security Agency, Social Security Administration, 1952, Division of Research Statistics, Bureau Report No. 17, in *The Review of Economics and Statistics*, Vol. XXXV, No. 4 (Nov., 1953), pp. 356–57.
*"The American Approach to Social Security," outline of talk to French Team on Industrial Training, at Cornell University, Ithaca, N.Y., Nov. 10, 1953.
*"Background and Problems of Retirement Income for Employees," outline of talk at Human Relations in Administration Program [?], Nov. 19, 1953.
*"Issues in Social Security," outline of an address to the [American Political Science Association], Syracuse University, Syracuse, New York, Nov. 20, 1953.

1954

Introduction in Floyd Bond and others, *Our Needy Aged: A California Study of a National Problem,* New York: Henry Holt, 1954.
*"Social Security," lecture at a Convocation at the American University of Beirut, Lebanon, March 4, 1954; adaptation of addresses.
*"Health and Welfare Plans," outline of remarks at the Machinists' Union Institute on Health and Welfare Plans, University of Wisconsin, Summer School for Workers, Madison, July 8, 1954.
*"Maintaining Purchasing Power Through Social Security," talk to the Economics-in-Action Program, University of Wisconsin, Madison, July 29, 1954.
*"Health Security," outline of talk at University of California at Los Angeles, Oct. 1, 1954.
*"Old Age Security: The National Picture," adapted from address to

Conference on Social Security in a Free Society, Pomona College, Claremont, Cal., Oct. 2, 1954.

"The Balanced Program in Employment Security," lecture to the Center for Continuation Study, University of Minnesota, Minneapolis, Oct. 7–8, 1954. In *Proceedings.*

"The Development of Labor Legislation and Its Effect upon the Welfare of the American Workman," address at the Conference on Government and Public Affairs, University of Illinois and Twin City Federation of Labor, Urbana, Ill., Oct. 31, 1954.

In University of Illinois, Institute of Labor and Industrial Relations, *Lecture Series, No. 11,* Oct., 1954.

*"Honesty in the Administration of Health, Welfare, and Retirement Funds," letter in reply to Mr. Potofsky of the CIO Committee on Ethical Practices, Nov. 12, 1954.

1954–1955–1956

The following material in relation to a course in *Social Security* is available in mimeographed form in the John R. Commons Library, University of Wisconsin, Madison:

Agencies of the National Government Concerned with Social Security.

Basic Data on the Old Age Problem.

The Basic Terms in Social Security.

Data on the Financing of Old-Age and Survivors' Insurance.

Data on Health Security.

Financial Data Relating to American Social Security Programs.

General Public Assistance: History and Present Status.

Outline of course.

Postwar Social Security in Great Britain.

Private Economic Security Institutions Related to Social Security.

Private Social Security Institutions.

Recent Information on the Old-Age Security Programs of the United States.

Social Security Administration in Wisconsin.

Social Security for Special Groups in the Population.

Some Data on the Overall Need for Social Security.

Some Data on Workmen's Compensation in the United States.

Supplemental Unemployment Compensation.

1955

*"What's Ahead in Social Security" [?].

*"A Panoramic View of Social Security," lecture to Labor Problems Class, University of Wisconsin, Jan. 17, 1955.

*"Manpower Aspects of an Aging Population," address to Interstate Conference on Labor Statistics, Madison, July 6–8, 1955.

*"Some Unsolved Problems in the Economics of Welfare," lecture to Economics-in-Action Program, University of Wisconsin, Extension Division, Madison, July 28, 1955.

Abstract of address to Institute of Chartered Life Underwriters, University of Wisconsin, Madison, June 31, 1956.

"Twenty Years of Social Security," outline of talk to Wisconsin Chapter of the American Society for Public Administration [?].

Address at Twentieth Anniversary of the Social Security Act, U.S. Department of Health, Education, and Welfare, Washington, D.C., Aug. 15, 1955.

In *Social Security Bulletin,* Vol. 18, No. 10 (Oct., 1955), pp. 15–21.

In *Public Welfare,* Saluting 25 Years of Social Security, Vol. 18, No. 3 (July, 1960), pp. 138–47, 169–71, under title of "Birth and Early Days of Social Security in the United States."

*"Employing Older Workers," reply to letter of Les M. Drachar, in *New York Times,* Sept. 8, 1955.

"The Changing Role of Labor, Management, and Government," address at Wayne University, Detroit, Mich., Nov. 16, 1955.

In *Conference on the Quest for Security—1955 Version,* Institute of Industrial Relations, Wayne University, 1955.

Abstract of address to Institute of Chartered Life Underwriters, University of Wisconsin, Madison, July 31, 1956.

*"The Economic Position of the Professional Worker," address to American Nurses' Conference on Economic Security, University of Wisconsin, Extension Division, Madison, Dec. 6–8, 1955.

"Facts on Aging," outline of talk to Wisconsin Welfare Conference, Milwaukee, Dec. 12, 1955.

In *Wisconsin Welfare,* Vol. XV, No. 1 (Feb., 1956), pp. 14–17.

1956

*"Social Welfare Legislation of the 1930's," synopsis of address at Rosary College, Riverside, Ill., Feb. 16, 1956.

*"Economic Aspects of the Old-Age Problem," talk to Class in Social Aspects of the Old-Age Problem, University of Wisconsin, Madison, Feb. 21, 1956.

"Security and Economic Change," address at Eighth Annual Industrial Relations Conference, McGill University, Toronto, Canada, April 16, 1956.

In *Security in an Industrial Economy,* Industrial Relations Centre, Eighth Annual Conference, McGill University (April, 1956), pp. 57–71; comments, pp. 118–33 *passim.*

*Two addresses at Educational Institute of Wisconsin Chapter of the International Association of Personnel in Employment Security, Milwaukee, May 3–4, 1956: "Factors Affecting the Economic Development of the United States," and "How Economic Progress Is Related to Employment Security."

Review: John J. Corson and John W. McConnell, *Economic Needs of Older People*, New York: Twentieth Century Fund, 1956, in *Industrial and Labor Relations Review*, Vol. 10, No. 1 (Oct., 1956), pp. 142–44.

1957

"Organized Labor and Social Security," chapter 7 in Milton Derber and Edwin Young, eds., *Labor and the New Deal*. Madison: University of Wisconsin Press, 1957.

"The Future of Social Security," an address in the Series on Industrial Relations Patterns for 1957 at Michigan State University, East Lansing, Jan. 25, 1957.

In Clark Kerr and others, *U.S. Industrial Relations: The Next Twenty Years*. East Lansing: Michigan State University Press, 1958.

Review: Eveline M. Burns, *Social Security and Public Policy*, New York: McGraw-Hill, 1956, in *Journal of Political Economy*, Vol. LXV, No. 2 (April, 1957), pp. 180–81.

"Compulsory Health Insurance—Voluntary Plans," views in *Wisconsin Medical Journal* (May, 1957), p. 34.

"Private Pension, Health and Welfare Plans," letter to Senator John F. Kennedy in reply to inquiry, in *Hearings on Welfare and Pension Plan Legislation before the Subcommittee on Welfare and Pension Legislation*, U.S. Senate Committee on Labor and Public Welfare, 85th Congress, 1st session, May–June, 1957, pp. 679–80.

Review: Peter O. Steiner and Robert Dorfman, *The Economic Status of the Aged*, Berkeley: University of California Press, 1957, in *Industrial and Labor Relations Review*, Vol. 11, No. 1 (Oct., 1957), pp. 123–24.

*"Government Employees and Old-Age Security," address to Michigan Municipal Employees Retirement System Conference, Lansing, Mich., Oct. 10, 1957.

*"Historical Background of Employment Security," address at Institute for Employment and Security Personnel, Continuation Center, University of Minnesota, Minneapolis, Oct. 22–23, 1957.

In *Proceedings* of Annual Fall Institute of the Minnesota Chapter of the International Association of Personnel in Employment Security, pp. 1–14.

*"Social Security," outline of address to U.S. Chamber Managers' Seminar at Kellogg Center, East Lansing, Mich., Dec. 9, 1957.

1958

*"Recent and Prospective Developments in Social Security," outline of talk to Graduate Students in Social Work, Michigan State University, East Lansing, Jan. 17, 1958.

*"Current Social Security Proposals Affecting the Medical Profession," outline of talk to Legislative Committee of the Michigan State Medical Association, Lansing, Mich., Jan. 23, 1958.

*"Financing Social Security," outline of talk to Economics Department, Michigan State University, East Lansing, Feb. 26, 1958.

*"The Growing Role of Employment Security," an address to the Employment Security Workshop of the Michigan Chapter of the International Association of Personnel in Employment Security, Michigan State University, Labor and Industrial Relations Center, East Lansing, March 18, 1958, in *Proceedings*, pp. 9–14.
  In *Employment Security Review*, Vol. 25, No. 6 (June, 1958), pp. 24–27.

*"The Labor Scandals," outline of talk to Lansing Chapter of the Industrial Relations Research Association, Lansing, Mich., March 25, 1958.

*"Social Security—Current Developments," outline of talk to Hi-Fi Club, Lansing, Mich., March 28, 1958.

*"A Sketchy Outline of What Happened in Relation to Health Insurance in the Days of the Committee on Economic Security," letter to Odin W. Anderson, former student, April 14, 1958. Other correspondence on the same subject in 1959.

*"Public Policy on Economic Security," an address at Midwest Economic Association, Des Moines, Iowa, April 18, 1958.
  In *Speeches of Estey, Hays, Ise, and Witte,* Midwest Economic Association, April, 1958, pp. 1–9.
  Reprinted in *Business Topics,* Michigan State University, Vol. V, No. 6 (May, 1958), pp. 1–8.

*"Social Security after Twenty Years," outline of talk at Lansing Eccentrics Club, Lansing, Mich., June 4, 1958.

Review: Wilbur J. Cohen, *Retirement Policies under Social Security,* Berkeley: University of California Press, 1958, in *Journal of Insurance,* Vol. XXV, No. 1 (July, 1958), pp. 72–73.

"Solvency of Social Security," address at Michigan State University, East Lansing, Aug. 1958.
  In *Challenge,* New York University, Vol. VI, Nos. 11–12 (August–September, 1958), pp. 25–29, under title "Is the Social Security Fund Solvent?"

*Discussion of speeches of Wilbur Cohen on OASDI and Herman Somers on Workmen's Compensation at Social Security Conference, Michigan State University, East Lansing, Nov. 24, 1958.

"The Objectives of Social Security," address at meeting of the Catholic Economic Association, Chicago, Dec. 28, 1958.
In *Review of Social Economy*, Vol. XVII, No. 1 (March, 1959), pp. 23–33.

1959

*"Social Security in the United States," two 9-minute talks in Series Devoted to the United States, Université Radiophonique Internationale (International University of the Air), Sept., 1959.

Index